Proper Guardians

An Introduction and Guide to

John Stuart Mill's *On Liberty*

Stephen Loxton

For a period steeped in waves of political correctness, with varied assaults on the liberty of expression, John Stuart Mill's *On Liberty* (1859) remains a signal work, championing the vital worth of personal and political liberty. Mill promotes the liberty of thought and expression, affirming 'the inward domain of consciousness, demanding liberty of conscience in the most comprehensive sense, liberty of thought and feeling, absolute freedom of opinion and sentiment on all subjects, practical or speculative, scientific, moral or theological' (*OL* I: 12). Against the claims of those who think that all should respect and defend whatever views they self-affirm, Mill defends the 'liberty of expressing and publishing opinions'. He thinks that although this 'may seem to fall under a different principle, since it belongs to that part of the conduct of the individual which concerns other people', such liberty of expression is actually 'almost of as much importance as the liberty of thought itself and resting in great part on the same reasons, is practically inseparable from it'. Liberty also 'requires liberty of tastes and pursuits, of framing the plan of our life to suit our own character, of doing as we like, subject to such consequences as may follow, without impediment from our fellow creatures, so long as what we do does not harm them, even though they should think our conduct foolish, perverse, or wrong'. Mill also defends the liberty of association, for the 'liberty of each individual follows the liberty, within the same limits of combination among individuals; freedom to unite for any purpose not involving harm to others; the persons combining being supposed to be of full age and not forced or deceived'.

Many questions are raised by Mill's defence of liberty, but he senses that human worth, individual and social, prospers when each person accepts that they are 'the proper guardian' (I: 13) of their 'own health, whether bodily *or* mental and spiritual'. The crucial idea for Mill is that humanity gains in a reciprocal life, 'by suffering each other to live as seems good to themselves', rather 'than by compelling each to live as seems good to the rest'. Thus, as individuals possessing self-regarding and other-respecting liberty, we defend and develop an authentic and civilized society.

Proper Guardians

An Introduction and Guide
to
John Stuart Mill's *On Liberty*

Stephen Loxton

Published by New Generation Publishing in 2022

First Edition

ISBN
        Paperback   978-1-80369-521-1
        Hardback   978-1-80369-522-8

www.newgeneration-publishing.com

New Generation Publishing

For Abigail Mumbi.

'Individuals are the proper guardians of their own interests, and… government owes nothing to them but to save them from being interfered with by other people'. (CW III 803).

Also by Stephen Loxton

Plato and Aristotle (2013). Wells, Pushme Press.*
Conscience (2014). Wells, Pushme Press.*

Words and Deeds: An Introduction to the Thought of Ludwig Wittgenstein (2020). London, New Generation Publishing.

Nietzsche and The Old Flame: An Introduction to Nietzsche and On the Genealogy of Morals (2021) London, New Generation Press.

Dialogic Life: an Introduction and Guide to Charles Taylor's The Ethics of Authenticity (2022) London, New Generation Press.

*Updated and revised second editions of the books published by Pushme Press are being prepared for re-publication with NGP.

Forthcoming: *Religious Language: A Philosophy of Religion Guidebook for GCE A-Level Religious Studies.* (Second Edition) London: NPG

Cover photo: John Stuart Mill (www.shutterstock.com).

From *On Liberty*:

'The only freedom which deserves the name is that of pursuing our own good in our own way, so long as we do not attempt to deprive others of theirs, or impede their efforts to obtain it. Each is the proper guardian of his own health, whether bodily *or* mental and spiritual. Mankind are greater gainers by suffering each other to live as seems good to themselves than by compelling each to live as seems good to the rest' (I: 13).

'There is the greatest difference between presuming an opinion to be true because, with every opportunity for contesting it, it has not been refuted, and assuming its truth for the purpose of not permitting its refutation. Complete liberty of contradicting and disproving our opinion is the very condition which justifies us in assuming its truth for purposes of action; and on no other terms can a being with human faculties have any rational assurance of being right' (II: 6).

'As it is useful that while mankind are imperfect there should be different opinions, so it is that there should be experiments of living; that free scope should be given to varieties of character, short of injury to others; that the worth of different modes of life should be proved practically, when anyone thinks fit to try them. It is desirable, in short, that in things which do not primarily concern others, individuality should assert itself. Where not the person's own character but the traditions or customs of other people are the rule of conduct, there is wanting one of the principal ingredients of human happiness, and quite the chief ingredient of individual and social progress' (III: 1).

'Human beings owe to each other help to distinguish the better from the worse, and encouragement to choose the former and avoid the latter. They should forever be stimulating each other to increased exercise of their higher faculties and increased direction of their feelings and aims towards wise instead of foolish, elevating instead of degrading, objects and contemplations' (IV: 4).

'A government cannot have too much of the kind of activity which does not impede, but aids and stimulates, individual exertion and development. The mischief begins when, instead of calling forth the activity and powers of individuals and bodies, it substitutes its own activity for theirs; when, instead of informing, advising, and upon occasion, denouncing, it makes them work in fetters, or bids them stand aside and does their work for them. The worth of a State, in the long run, is the worth of the individuals composing it; and a State which postpones the interest of *their* mental expansion and elevation to a little more of administrative skill, or of that semblance of it which practice gives in the details of business; a State which dwarfs its men, in order that they may be more docile instruments in its hands even for beneficial purposes – will find that with small men no great thing can really be accomplished; and that the perfection of machinery to which it has sacrificed everything will in the end avail it nothing, for want of the vital power which, in order that the machine might work more smoothly, it has preferred to banish' (V: 23).

Illustrations in the Text[1]

---

[1] The photograph on p. 59 was taken by the author. The other illustrations are courtesy of www.shutterstock.com.

Contents

Introduction

This book is offered as a guide to John Stuart Mill (1806-1873) – hereafter Mill – and his text of 1859, *On Liberty*. It is intended as an introduction and aid for those coming to study or teach Mill and his famed defence of liberty in the context of such examination courses as the International Baccalaureate, or perhaps within an undergraduate course. It might also appeal to anyone interested in the pressing contemporary issues of liberty in the modern world, such as those of whether there should be free debate over trans rights and gender self-assignation, the pros as well as the cons of colonialism, or even the importance of scope for free debate within academia or in society in general over the significance and worth of works of art, moral preferences, and options for ways of living.[1]

The origins of the book lie in the 1980s when my teaching career in the UK embraced a new course in Philosophy A-level.[2] The course was assessed via two three-hour written papers, one on themes in philosophy and the other on set texts. Amongst the themes we studied were political philosophy and ethics, and one of the texts was *On Liberty*. There proved to be a helpful synergy between these areas of study, probably enhanced because another book chosen for study was *The German Ideology* by Marx and Engels. I taught this course for seventeen years, and Mill's text remained one of those offered. Some years and another school later, my work entailed teaching the International Baccalaureate (IB) Philosophy course. Again, there were themes on ethics and political philosophy, and *On Liberty* was one of the texts available for fruitful study.

Given that *On Liberty* is written in the style and manner typical of high Victorian prose, as composed by one who was, at the time of his death, seen as 'the philosopher-laureate of England'[3], it was a surprisingly popular choice for both A-level and IB students. The text provoked strong debate, with students finding Mill an engaging, relevant and persuasive thinker to study, critique and apply, to very good effect in terms of scores in the final set texts paper.

The process of teaching set texts successfully for public examinations was always highly interactive. To ensure that the text as a narrative was read and understood, it would have been something of a non-starter to give the students summaries of the ideas and a list of key quotations to discuss based on their own reading of the text. Instead, the better method was to get the students to discuss the issues that Mill was dealing with, often with reference to relevant topics in the news, and then to read the text with them, with them sharing the task, getting into the pattern and flow of the arguments, and pausing to review the questions arising. So long as the students could multitask to make notes as we went along, both on the text and from the discussions, they built up a solid resource of ideas about Mill, his case for liberty and the issues this provoked. Writing essays regularly, many under timed conditions, gave the opportunity to check and correct understanding, a handy preparation for revising with more timed essays leading to the final examinations.

---

[1] These and related issues are reviewed in Chapters 13 to 15 below.
[2] This was the course first devised and offered in 1983 by AEB – the Associated Examining Board, later subsumed into AQA.
[3] Himmelfarb (1962) 'Introduction' p. xxxi.

When planning to teach *On Liberty*, it was clear that there was no shortage of impressive high-quality academic studies that gave the text a thorough interrogation. It was equally clear that many of these books would not be within the students' budget, compass, or schedule. Accordingly, while I bought various texts for school and department libraries, I also wrote my notes and ideas into a commentary on the book for use as a study and revision guide for the students to use once we had finished reviewing the text. In subsequent years the study guide was revised and updated in light of the regular feedback received from the students, so in terms of its genealogy, this somewhat more elaborate book is derived from the study guide first written in 1987-88 and used last in a developed form the last time I took an I.B. class through the full course in 2017-19.[1]

The plan of this book is as follows:

After these prefatory remarks and the Prologue, Part I, 'Introductions', opens with a review of Mill's life (Chapters 1-3); we then look at the important issue of how Mill developed utilitarianism (Chapter 4): Chapter 5 explores how *On Liberty* came to be written.

Part II (Chapters 6-11) provides a guide and commentary to the text of *On Liberty*. Chapter 6 looks at the issue of liberty and philosophical necessity (or free will and determinism) that Mill skims over in *On Liberty* but attends to in some detail in other writings; Chapters 7-11 successively cover the five chapters that make up *On Liberty*.

In Part III, '*On Liberty* in Review', Chapter 12 picks up and assesses some of the key issues considered earlier, reflecting on some of the arguments that can be made for and against Mill's ideas in *On Liberty*. The next three chapters (13-15) review some of the core ideas Mill is dealing with in *On Liberty* by focusing on recent trends in the law in relation to liberty and looking at aspects of the contemporary debate on freedom of thought and expression.[2] These chapters reflect the practical teaching experience, whereby relating the issues in a set text to a review of a contemporary area of debate would indubitably lead to a relevant discussion as the text was reviewed and revised. The issues discussed help us consider the weight and worth of some fundamental concerns about the shape and scope of liberty. They also suggest the abiding worth and relevance of Mill's thinking on these matters, which is reviewed in the final chapter.

---

[1] As with other books that I have written based on the same process of teaching set texts for philosophy both with A level and the I.B., a lot of ideas herein are derived from the generations of students who confronted Mill and his ideas against the backdrop of their busy lives as sixth-form students. Here see my books on Nietzsche and the *Genealogy of Morals* and Taylor and *The Ethics of Authenticity*: Loxton (2021) and (2022).

[2] As will be seen later, the case studies are taken from matters in public debate, mostly from 2017 to 2021-22. Doubtless some of these matters will run and run.

A Note on Mill's Writings.

On Liberty was published in 1859 and has since gone through many editions, plenty of which are now available. Apart from the chapter titles, *On Liberty* is presented without an analytical contents page, sub-headings, or an index. Because of this, and as so many editions are available, to ease referencing, a convention has grown to give quotations by chapter and paragraph number – so I:1 for Chapter I, paragraph 1, and so on. Mill did not himself write numbered paragraphs in *On Liberty*; however, in the custom of his age, he writes substantial and distinct paragraphs, so it is not difficult to enumerate them.[1] In Part II of this book, the commentary is also written around sub-headings chosen to highlight the sequence of issues Mill discusses. Quotations from *On Liberty* and *Utilitarianism* will be referenced by chapter and paragraph number. In *On Liberty*, Mill's 'one very simple principle', for example, is I: 9. As a rule, quotations from *On Liberty* are registered with just the chapter and paragraph numbers, but for some references, *OL* is used as an abbreviation for *On Liberty*. Similarly, *Util* is the abbreviation for *Utilitarianism*, *Auto* for the *Autobiography*, *Logic* for *A System of Logic*, and *Principles* for *Principles of Political Economy*.[2] The *Logic* is a work of great length, divided into six books, each made up of a series of chapters, divided into numbered sections, with Mill using Roman and Arabic numbering. References are, therefore, by Book, Chapter and Section number – VI: XII: 4 means Book 6, Chapter 12, Section 4.

Mill's *Collected Works* were produced in 33 volumes under the general editorship of Professor John M. Robson and published by Toronto University Press between 1963 and 1991; the books are also published by Routledge, and eight volumes of the *Collected Works* have been published by the Liberty Fund. The *Collected Works* with original publication dates are as set out below:

I: *Autobiography and Literary Essays* (1981)
II, III: *Principles of Political Economy* (1965)
IV, V: *Essays on Economics and Society* (1967)
VI: *Essays on England, Ireland and the Empire* (1982)
VII, VIII: *A System of Logic: Ratiocinative and Inductive* (1973)
IX: *An Examination of Sir William Hamilton's Philosophy* (1979)
X: *Essays on Ethics, Religion and Society* (1969)
XI: *Essays in Philosophy and the Classics* (1978)
XII, XIII: *Earlier Letters* (1963)
XIV, XV, XVI, XVII: *Later Letters* (1972)
XVIII, XIX: *Essays on Politics and Society* (1977)
XX: *Essays on French History and Historians* (1985)
XXI: *Essays on Equality, Law and Education* (1984)
XXII, XXIII, XXIV, XXV: *Newspaper Writings* (1986)
XXVI, XXVII: *Journals and Debating Speeches* (1988)

---

[1] Paragraphs in *On Liberty* can be numbered by chapter as follows: I. 'Introductory': 1-16; II. 'Of the Liberty of Thought and Discussion': 1-44; III. 'Of Individuality, as One of the Aspects of Well-Being': 1-19; IV. 'Of the Limits to the Authority of Society over the Individual': 1-21; V. 'Applications': 1-23.
[2] Some other works cited will be similarly abbreviated.

XXVIII, XXIX: *Public and Parliamentary Speeches* (1988)
XXX: *Writing on India* (1990)
XXXI: *Miscellaneous Writings* (1989)
XXXII: *Additional Letters* (2016)
XXXIII: *Indexes* (1991)[1]

The following volumes (with, in some cases, more recent publication dates than those listed above) were invaluable in preparing this book:

Mill, J. S. (1963) *The Earlier Letters of John Stuart Mill 1812-1848*. (Edited by F. E. Mineka) *Collected Works of John Stuart Mill* Vols XII-XIII. Toronto: University of Toronto Press.

Mill, J. S. (1972) *The Later Letters of John Stuart Mill 1849-1873*. (Edited by F. E. Mineka and D.N Lindley) *Collected Works of John Stuart Mill* Vols XIV-XVII. Toronto: University of Toronto Press.

Mill, J. S. (2016) *Additional Letters of John Stuart Mill* (Edited by M. Filipiuk, M. Laine and J. M. Robson) *Collected Works of John Stuart Mill* Vol XXXII. Abingdon: Routledge/Taylor Francis.

Mill, J. S. (2009) *Principles of Political Philosophy with Some of Their Applications to Social Philosophy*. (Edited by J. M. Robson). *Collected Works of John Stuart Mill* Vol II & III. Abingdon: Routledge/Taylor Francis.

Mill, J.S. (2006) *Essays on Economics and Society*. (Introduction by Lord Robbins and Textual Introduction by J. M. Robson) *Collected Works of John Stuart Mill* Vols IV & V. Indiana: Liberty Fund.

Mill, J. S. (2009) *An Examination of Sir William Hamilton's Philosophy*. (Edited by J. M. Robson) *Collected Works of John Stuart Mill* Vol IX. Abingdon: Routledge/Taylor Francis.

Mill, J. S. (2014) *Essays on Ethics, Religion and Society*. (Edited by J. M. Robson) *Collected Works of John Stuart Mill* Vol X. Abingdon: Routledge/Taylor Francis.

Mill, J. S. (2016) *Public and Parliamentary Speeches* (Edited by J. R. Robinson and B. L. Kinzer) *Collected Works of John Stuart Mill* Vols XXVIII-XXIX. Abingdon: Routledge/Taylor Francis.

Quotations from the volumes of the *Collected Works* will be referenced by the abbreviation CW and then the volume and page number(s).

Mill's works are also available in a range of relatively affordable editions, and those used in this book or recommended for further reading are as set out below.[2]

Mill, J. S. (1987) *On Liberty*. (Edited and Introduced by G. Himmelfarb). Harmondsworth: Penguin Classics. This edition is used for quotations from *On Liberty*.

Mill, J. S. (2015) *On Liberty, Utilitarianism and Other Essays*. (Edited by M. Philp and F. Rosen). Oxford: Oxford World Classics. This edition is used for references to *Utilitarianism*. However, it is a valuable collection for readers and

---

[1] Mill's works online can be found at: https///oll.libertyfund.org/title/robson-collected-works-of-john-stuart-mill-in-33-vols.
[2] Apart from the works of Mill listed in here, other works consulted are listed in the bibliography below. Websites, articles from the media and other sources are referenced in the footnotes.

students, also including *On Liberty*, *The Subjection of Women* and *Considerations on Representative Government*.

Mill, J. S. (2018) *Autobiography*. (Edited, with an Introduction and Notes by M. Philp). Oxford: Oxford World's Classics. This is a very helpful edition as in the Appendix, the passages from the earlier draft of the *Autobiography* are reproduced.

Mill, J. S. (1988) *The Subjection of Women*. (Edited with an Introduction by Susan. M. Okin). Indianapolis: Cambridge, Hackett.

Mill, J. S. (1998) *Principles of Political Economy and Chapter of Socialism*. (edited with Introduction and Notes by J. Riley). Oxford: Oxford World Classics). This is a much-abridged version of the *Principles*, with a focus on the later books of the work, and it adds the 'Chapters on Socialism' that Mill was working on at the time of his death. These chapters were drafts for a study on socialism Mill was planning at the time of his death.

Mill, J. S. (1998) *Three Essays on Religion*. New York: Prometheus Books.

Mill, J. S. (1961) *The Early Draft of John Stuart Mill's Autobiography*. (ed. J. Stillinger). Urbana, Ill: University of Illinois Press. As noted, the distinctive parts that were left out of the final version of the Autobiography are reproduced in the edition cited above.

Mill, J. S. (1967) *A System of Logic*. (8th Edition) London, Longmans.

Mill's Style and Vocabulary

Modern readers of *On Liberty* may or may not have been keen followers of the original *Star Trek* TV series. Within which the crew of the spaceship Enterprise regularly came upon some mysterious alien species - at which point Captain Kirk would ask of the ship's doctor: 'What is it, Bones?' The doctor's invariable reply was, 'It's life, but not as we know it'. Much the same dialogue comes into play when *On Liberty* is being read – it is written in English, but not quite as we, in modernity, may be accustomed to using it.

As mentioned, Mill often writes paragraphs a page or more in length: II: 37, or V: 11, for example. Accordingly, colons and semi-colons are employed more than we might find in today's written discourse. Sometimes we find long sentences with several clauses as Mill builds to a climactic peroration. Alternatively, we find shorter, punchier sentences, still working up to a point that delivers a telling blow (See III: 19, IV: 21 and V: 23). Something Mill does that can lead the reader astray is that he commonly elaborates ideas that he is actually opposed to as fluently as if he believed in them with the utmost sincerity. As a rule, this is signposted by qualified openings to the paragraphs, which alerts us to the possibility that Mill may be about to lead us to a view that will be found wanting – although, again, sometimes this is not the whole story. Examples of the things in mind here can be seen in the first chapter at I: 3, I: 4, I: 5 and I: 6.

Modern readers might sometimes be brought up short by Mill's use of vocabulary, which is apposite for his time, but less so for ours. Terms like 'tribe' and 'caste' are used for what we might term 'groups' (see I: 2). Mill references these terms when referring to religious groups, often in order to point up the perils of attitudes of dogmatic certainty, something he fears to be increasingly prevalent in other social contexts: in a similar way, he uses the term 'sect' for a group with a body of opinion or an outlook (see I: 7), but sometimes sees such outlooks as providing a guide to life might be termed a 'creed'(see IV: 12).[1] Mill uses these terms, with their religious connotations, to allude to moral and political views which become doctrinaire and to emphasise something he thinks vital – the contrary view, that a person would not live by ideas that had not been thoroughly examined as to their cogency and worth. He wrote that on its own, an opinion 'suggests hardly anything to the uninformed mind; it may become a watchword, but can never be a moving & influencing and living principle within him'.[2] Mill means that if ideas are to be of practical value for life, they must be examined, analysed, and tested through experience. Mill often uses the term 'mischief', and he deploys it with varying levels of intensity; however, he is never referring to the antics of children or kittens. Sometimes it refers to arguments or actions causing others to be upset (see II: 44); alternatively, it is used to refer to how a person may do themselves harm (see IV: 10 or V: 5), as saying that so and so has 'done themselves a mischief' or that some errant policy had brought about a 'mischief', again, meaning harm of some kind.

Mill often uses terms that have fallen somewhat out of common use. A usage that he employs widely in his writing that might seem odd is 'approbation' for the approval or praise that one may give or receive and, in contrast, 'disapprobation' for disapproval.[3] Modern editions of Mill usually update his distinctive spelling, reflecting the conventions of his educative upbringing in the early nineteenth century.

If we venture into Mill's letters or the *Autobiography*, we find, for example, 'shew(s)' for show(s), 'stile' for style, 'chuse' for choose, 'inclose' for 'enclose', 'mistification' for 'mystification', 'burthen' for burden, and 'develope' for 'develop'.[4]

As might have been noticed, Mill often uses the term 'opinion' (or 'opinions'). As a rule, he means one of three things: as mentioned earlier, an opinion can be held provisionally, without much reflection, and so it has limited worth until there has been the relevant testing of the opinion through experience and reflection; often, he refers to people or individuals having 'opinions', and he means in such cases something akin to a legal opinion – a view reached through reflection on experience and evidence see I: 6; I: 16; II: 1; II: 4; II: 7; II: 10; V: 2. In contrast, at some points, Mill refers to the general 'opinion' expressed by the majority – sometimes as a 'tyranny', and here he means something that is altogether less worthy, as he thinks it will be a mediocre view, a trend, a limited and limiting outlook all the better to challenge or ignore – see I: 8; III: 13; III: 15.

On a more technical point of academic convention, in political philosophy, the terms 'freedom' and 'liberty' are sometimes used interchangeably in relation to the matters of freedom – or liberty – of thought, speech, discussion, worship, and association.[5] We will notice Mill habitually moves between these terms too. It is

---

[1] See also *Auto* p. 92.
[2] CW XII p. 42.
[3] See *OL* p. 58 – Mill's dedication to Harriet – and IV: 21.
[4] For this last example, see *Auto* p. 143. J. M. Robson notes that in later years, Mill's editing of his texts when new editions were needed involved a lot of work on regularising spellings in the light of greater conventionalism. See J. M. Robson, 'Textual Introduction' to CW II p. lxxvf.
[5] Berlin is a notable scholar keen on the interchangeability of the terms – see Berlin (2017) p. 169.

perhaps tempting to follow the trend and use the more everyday term 'freedom' to cover all these variables, but there is a value in maintaining a distinction between the two. The issue of personal freedom has a subjective aspect, for it has to do with the quintessential matter of what it is to be distinctly human. It has been written that freedom in this sense is 'a fundamental presupposition of all meaningful human action'.[1] In contrast, issues of liberty have to do with the dynamic of wider interpersonal and political life, whereby individuality may or may not be constrained by some external body or force. A person is at liberty when those constraints are removed, and various entitlements are conferred on individuals subject to their responsible activity within ongoing life. Issues of contention over liberty turn out to be over the legitimacy of constraints on the individual. It makes sense to use the term liberty to denote the generic field for the range of concerns that arise over the various modes of liberties of thought, discussion, of the press and publication, and of action and association – and for the individual freedoms that are set within them. Keeping a sense of this distinction helps us understand and analyse what Mill is after in *On Liberty*.

Finally, Mill commonly uses terms such as 'concerns', 'interests' and 'harm' to refer to what occupies or worries humans. He is not often given to defining these terms, so we need to look carefully at his meaning in use and context to check and draw out the sense of what he intends.

---

[1] Capaldi (2012) p. 249.

Prologue

On Liberty was published in February 1859. The following December, we can imagine many copies found themselves gift-wrapped for Christmas. Mill's book would have had some stiff competition as a present or as a stocking-filler, as 1859 turned out to be a bumper year for book lovers. For those keen on big ideas, Charles Darwin's *Origin of Species* had appeared, as had Samuel Smiles' *Self Help*. Although few people were aware of it, and it was not widely available, Karl Marx also wrote *A Contribution to the Critique of Political Economy*. In the more literary genre of the novel, 1859 bought some notable works: Charles Dickens told *A Tale of Two Cities*; Wilkie Collins unleashed *The Woman in White*, and George Eliot revealed all about *Adam Bede*: for those enjoying poetic writing, Alfred Tennyson published *Idylls of the King*.

In this, a '.com-free' reading age, the discussion of innovative ideas and how to progress understanding was taking on a broader and deeper significance. Newspapers, journals, and reviews were widely read, and ideas were presented and criticised, not just in the universities but through the lending libraries and in the clubs, pubs, coffee shops, public libraries, homes and the many reading rooms and Literary and Philosophical Societies spread about the land.[1] Mill was a great reader, but he was also a prolific writer of letters, reviews, pamphlets, and books, such that, as we have noted, his collected works run to thirty-three thick volumes.

1859 was also a year of two significant deaths amongst those of broadly liberal disposition, both of whom Mill knew personally. Alexis de Tocqueville, the French writer whose work *Democracy in America* influenced Mill, and Thomas Babington Macaulay, Baron Macaulay, the liberal historian, writer and politician – with whom Mill often disagreed.[2] Macaulay did manage to read *On Liberty* before he died, and we will come to what he thought of it later. Mill's book was thus, in one sense adding to the canon of liberal and progressive thought, and like Darwin's book, *On Liberty* has had an ongoing influence on intellectual and cultural life, becoming one of the masterworks in the tradition of political philosophy and a more or less non-negotiable focus for study within any undergraduate course that touches on political thought, often featuring as a set text.[3]

A reason for all of this was noted by Gertrude Himmelfarb, who edited the book for Penguin Classics in an edition first issued in 1974. She writes that for 'an age which prides itself on its liberation from all absolutes, which has succeeded in

---

[1] In 1859 there were nine universities in Britain. There were three in England – Oxford (established in 1096), Cambridge (1209) and London (1836). There were four universities in Scotland: St Andrews (1410), Glasgow (1451), Aberdeen (1495 and Edinburgh (1582). In Ireland there were two: Trinity College Dublin (1592), now a part of the University of Dublin, and Queen's University, Belfast (1845). Public libraries came into being after the Public Libraries Act (1850): see
https://www.politics.co.uk/reference/public-libraries/
[2] See Berlin (2017) p. 219. De Tocqueville's *Democracy in America* was published in two volumes in 1835 and 1840. Mill corresponded with de Tocqueville (1805-1859) first in 1835, having read and reviewed the first volume of *Democracy in America*. See CW XII p. 265. Himmelfarb (1962) contains the reviews of de Tocqueville – pp. 187-287. Macaulay's most famous work was his five-volume *History of England* (1849-1861). Mill blows hot and cold in his writings on Macaulay (1800-1859), who he knew from the 1820s: see for example, CW XIV p. 332f.
[3] As in the International Baccalaureate Philosophy course.

making the very word "absolute" sound archaic, there is one concept that has very nearly the status of an absolute. That is the idea of liberty'.[1]

Himmelfarb was right in both respects. She was right to characterise liberty as 'very nearly… an absolute' because, as Mill presents it, liberty, even of thought and discussion, is to be restricted when the expression of views 'are such as to constitute their expression a positive instigation to some mischievous act' (III: 1). Mill refers to our actions being limited by our being prevented from doing 'harm to others' (I: 9), and this limitation is consequently known as the harm principle.[2] Mill also places liberty under utility – 'the ultimate appeal on all ethical questions' (I: 11).

Himmelfarb was also right about the age she had in mind, the post-war, mid-to-late twentieth century. In developed societies, this was a period of increasing plurality, relativism, equality and subjectivism, with secular patterns of life assuming greater significance and traditional values and ideals all being subordinated to the imperatives of personal choice and individual taste, all equally safeguarded by the growing canopy of law, especially laws defending rights.[3] However, in that age, an ideal that seemed almost inviolate was liberty, meaning freedom of thought, discussion and association.

Another factor in Mill's ongoing influence is the afterglow of his status in his own times. Mill's influence and reputation were immense for the times in which he lived: his thinking and writing on liberty and other issues imprinted themselves on the wider intellectual consciousness.[4] His reputation has ebbed and flowed since then. At a point in the early-mid twentieth century, F.A. Hayek observed that Mill's seemed a thinker 'of the recent past'[5] whose ideas 'ceased to be interesting because they have become commonplace'. A feature of this carries on in that it is certainly common for people in modernity to affirm the importance of liberty but to be vague on the reasons that underpin the liberties developed and defended by Mill.[6] It is as if the case of liberty has fallen into the realm of what Mill terms 'dead dogma' (II: 21) – something asserted but not rightly apprehended and understood as a 'living truth'. In contrast, there are issues in current debate with clear implications for the quality and range of liberty and wider concerns for the present age and beyond over climate change and pandemics. In reassessing the way to live for the best, Mill's ideas in *On Liberty* remain vital to how we might, through the liberties of thought and discussion, examine and review our sense of endeavour to live and yet develop our individuality responsively and responsibly.

---

[1] *OL* 'Editor's Introduction' p. 7. Gertrude Himmelfarb (1922-2019) was a distinguished historian of ideas and of culture, and a notable scholar of the ideas and values of the Victorian age and the nineteenth century in general. She was professor of history at City University, New York. Her ideas in Mill are notable for the emphasis given to Harriet Taylor's influence on Mill's life and work especially during the time of their marriage, the time of the composition of *On Liberty*. On this, see Himmelfarb (1974), especially pp. 239-275.

[2] See *OL* I: 9 and III:1, for example, and Chapters 7 & 9 below.

[3] For a review of this see Taylor (2003).

[4] On this see *OL* 'Editor's Introduction', pp. 9-10.

[5] F. A. Hayek, 'Introduction' CW XII/XIII p. xv. Subsequently, Mill's reputation has been recharged by the writings of, for example, Ryan, Rees and Gray. See Ryan (1974) and (1987), Rees (1985) and Gray (1983).

[6] We see something of this in the contemporary debates considered in Chapters 13-15 below.

Part I: Introductions

1. Mill's Background and Early Life

John Stuart Mill - The Life of 'an isolated thinker'[1]

On March 16th 1865, John Stuart Mill was doing something to which he devoted much time. He was at his home at 113 Blackheath Park, in South East London. At the time in question, he might have been reading, drafting an article or a chapter of a book, or checking the proofs of a work already in the process of publication. However, what he was doing was writing a letter, one in which he declined to take an active part in what he referred to as 'the projected Reform Conference'.[2]

The proposal was for a conference to build on a series of meetings that had brought together those keen to promote radical political and parliamentary reform. Mill explains that while he is strongly in favour of reform, he cannot support this particular campaign because he does not feel able 'to join in any movement for what is called manhood suffrage'.[3] Mill is emphatic in wanting to extend the entitlement to vote, but he wants to promote the principle of 'adult suffrage' to include in the reforms a move to give voting entitlements to women as well as men. He emphasises that 'no reason, either of right or of expediency, can be found to justify giving the suffrage to men exclusively of women'. He dislikes how the proposals for the conference use the term 'manhood suffrage' instead of 'universal suffrage'. This substitution has been done 'for the express purpose of showing that women are not included' and so 'to adopt it is to give a direct assent to their exclusion'. Mill withholds his support and says later in the letter that he can 'do better as an isolated thinker, forming and expressing my opinions independently, than by associating myself with any collective movement, which in my case, would almost always imply putting some of my opinions in abeyance'.

Mill's self-projection of himself as an isolated and independent thinker plays well as an image of a philosophical reformer working over and above the vicissitudes of everyday life. But Mill is being slightly disingenuous: while he was true to his principles to reject a reductive campaign for reform, in his life, he was, in fact, a highly interactive thinker, with constant exchanges with friends, associates and opponents in debating groups and through correspondence, as well as through a writing career notable for the degree to which the ideas of adversaries were examined, explored, and criticised. In general, Mill presents as a highly responsive thinker and writer, engaging with his critics and revising his ideas in the light of the valid criticism he could find.[4] Thinking in isolation was but a part of a life that was socially active and interactive, and in thinking in isolation, Mill was scrupulous in thinking and then writing for a public, an audience and a future, with an ongoing assurance that whatever he wrote would provide him with a response that would, as a rule, be factored into the next phase of his thinking and writing.

---

[1] CW XVI p. 1014.

[2] CW XVI p. 1012.

[3] CW XVI p. 1013.

[4] This is shown extensively by Mill in his extensive correspondence and highlighted by Reeves' considerations of Mill's open-mindedness: Reeves (2007) pp. 108-9, 198, 212 and 273-4; . See also Mill (1988) p. 64, where he is critical of the 'mere thinker'. As we will see later, Mill makes something of an exception to his usual methods of revision when it comes to *On Liberty*.

Our concern is to examine, explore and review one of Mill's works, *On Liberty*. To set the scene for this, the life of our not-so 'solitary thinker' needs to be unpacked, not least because Mill's career took shape and had many real and lasting achievements long before he came to the composition and publication of *On Liberty*. In any case, the circumstances of Mill's life are of interest in understanding the point and purpose of this work. As is widely known from the *Autobiography* Mill prepared for publication after his death, his life had a most unusual start as the eldest son of the writer and radical thinker James Mill.[1]

James Mill and an Experimental Education

James Milne, later Mill, hailed from Scotland. His parents, James and Isabel Milne, were of modest means, but Isabel, in particular, had considerable ambitions for her son, which included changing the family name from the Scottish 'Milne' to the more English sounding 'Mill' and schooling young James very emphatically in a manner that anticipates the education Mill was to receive. James' academic potential came to the attention of Lady Jane Stuart, wife of Sir John Stuart MP. Mill tells us he was 'one of the Barons of the Exchequer in Scotland'.[2]

The Stuarts had a philanthropic fund to support gifted students through school and university, and on the strength of this, James Mill went to Montrose Academy and then to Edinburgh University. His studies proceeded well, with a particular focus on the classics. After graduation and following his family's and patrons' aspirations, James Mill trained to become a Presbyterian preacher. He completed the studies, but along the way, he found that intellectually, he did not have the vocation for the role of a preacher. Mill wrote later that his father had 'satisfied himself that he could not believe the doctrines of this or any other Church'.[3]

James Mill turned to teaching and spent a good deal of time studying history, philosophy and economics. These latter interests grew, and in 1802, he came to London and began an initially precarious career as a journalist and critic.[4] He soon met and married Harriet Burrow, whose mother gave the couple a house in Pentonville as a wedding gift.[5] In 1806, they celebrated the birth of their eldest son, named in honour of James Mill's patron. James Mill also began writing *The History of British India*, which eventually found publication in 1818.[6]

Meanwhile, from 1808, James Mill widened the circle of his acquaintances when he met the stockbroker, economist and radical David Ricardo and the

---

[1] See *Auto* pp. 5ff for plentiful detail. James Mill (1773-1836).
[2] *Auto* p. 5. Sir John Stuart MP (1732-1821).
[3] *Auto* p. 6.
[4] The move to London may have been related to disappointments in love: James Mill had tutored and then fallen in love with Wilhelmina, the eldest daughter of Sir John Stuart. Due to the proprieties of the day, James Mill was not considered a credible suitor for the daughter of a baronet. This experience of societal inequality is a factor in James Mill's subsequent radicalism and concern for wider equality. See Capaldi (2012) p. 2.
[5] See Reeves (2007) p. 11. The house was at 12, Rodney Terrace, Pentonville, London. Mill's mother – another Harriet – features little in his *Autobiography* and she seems to have played a much less significant role in his personal life than his father or, later Harriet Taylor. On this see Himmelfarb (1974) pp. 187-193 and Capaldi (2012) pp. 2-6.
[6] See *Auto* p. 17

philosopher and legalist Jeremy Bentham.[1] From this time, Bentham became a committed supporter of James Mill, giving him and his growing family financial help by providing places to live on subsidised terms.[2] Over this phase of his life, Mill got to know both Bentham and Ricardo, and both took a positive interest in his intellectual development.[3]

In the *Autobiography*, Mill provides an account of his upbringing at the hands of his father. There is another slightly different account in what is published as *The Early Draft of John Stuart Mill's Autobiography*.[4] In the earlier draft, first written during the 1850s when Mill was married and to a degree alienated from his wider family, he is notably both more critical of the pressures of his early education and the severity of his father. In the version Mill revised in the last phase of his life, he softens the picture, but by any measures of education, the experience and the achievements were exceptional and challenging.

From Mill's accounts, we sense that James Mill had an active, robust and combative mind and that he set clear but exacting standards for his son.[5] Not only was Mill to be home-educated, but he was also insulated from outside contact and not permitted to associate with boys of his own age. James Mill was, it is suggested, influenced by Rousseau's book *Emile* and the doctrine of human development being receptive to influence.[6] This was very much a case of nurture, rather than nature, being seen as of key influence on the individual's development. However, it is axiomatic in a biographical understanding of Mill that he was fortunate in possessing a precocious and distinctive intellect. Under his father's scheme of education, he was inducted into classical thought, learning Greek from the age of three, and by the age of eight, he had proceeded in mathematics and science and had read most of the relevant works on the literature and history of England. Through the years between twelve and fourteen, Mill became so well-versed in classical and scholastic philosophy that his education was as complete as any who might have graduated from university ten years his senior.

To some, Mill's educative programme appears severe; to others, James Mill's encouragement of his son to engage in critical discussion from an early age seems enlightened.[7] It is clear that Mill rather conspicuously missed the range of experiences he might have enjoyed had he gone to one of the Public Schools and then to university. Given the inconsistencies of nineteenth-century schools, Mill

---

[1] See *Auto* p. 19 and CW XII pp. 8-9 n. 4. David Ricardo (1772-1821); Jeremy Bentham (1748-1832).

[2] From 1814 Bentham's improved financial state enabled him to provide the Mill family with a house at 1, Queens Square in Westminster. This was the family home until 1830. See Capaldi (2012) p. 17. James Mill's friend Francis Place (1771-1854), also gave some financial support. Place was notable social reformer and activist influential in the work to repeal the Combination Laws, which was achieved in 1824. The Combination Laws made such organisations as trade unions illegal. See Capaldi (2012) p. 20.

[3] See *Auto* pp. 33-35.

[4] Mill (1961). Mill's *Autobiography* is, in the published version, a very deliberately written work, which Mill uses as an explanation and *apologia* for the pattern of his life and thought.

[5] See *Auto* pp. 7-20. James Mill seems to have seen the education of his eldest son as something of an experiment, based on the empiricist assumption that the human mind was a *tabula rasa* at birth: see Reeves (2007) p. 12ff. James Mill tried to encourage Mill's physical and athletic development, but in this he quickly realised that there was no great hope of improvement. See Capaldi (2012) p. 10.

[6] See Capaldi (2012) p. 21. J-J Rousseau (1712-1778) – *Emile* was published in 1762.

[7] On this see Reeves (2007) pp. 12-23. See also Capaldi (2012) p. 24.

might not have missed out too much academically, but socially and culturally, a broader education would have been helpful for Mill's wider development and thought. This point was stressed by Ricardo, who spent some time discussing political economy with the young Mill in 1818-1819. Corresponding with James Mill, Ricardo said that Mill needed the benefit of 'that collision which is obtained only in society, and by which a knowledge of the world and its manners is best acquired'.[1] Ricardo's point also covers another possibility, that wider associations might have given Mill a capacity for greater use of wit, humour and irony than ever seems to be the case in his later life and work.[2]

As it turned out, up to the time that Mill worked with Ricardo, he was more or less fully under the routines of study set by James Mill. Once the young John Mill was past the elementary phase of education, his daily programme of study included writing summaries of what he or his father was reading as research for a project of his own[3]. Mill would then go on a walk with his father to discuss what he had written and hear what his father thought of its content and form. In effect, James Mill arranged things to combine exercise with reasoning.[4] He also thought that in so educating his son, he was ensuring a worthy successor to Bentham and himself.[5]

The process of this tutorial education leads Mill to three significant insights. One is a tribute to the focus his father put on clarity and precision in the use of language. Mill thinks there is 'nothing, in modern education' that 'tends so much, when properly used, to form exact thinkers'.[6] The second point comes through the reading and discussion of Platonic dialogues. Mill quickly appreciates that Plato's genius lies in his provocation of discussion, not in the presentation of final solutions. In light of this, he says the following:

'I have felt ever since that the title of Platonist belongs by far better right to those who have been nourished in, and have endeavoured to practise Plato's mode of investigation, than to those who are distinguished only by the adoption of certain dogmatical conclusions, drawn mostly from the least intelligible of his works, and which the character of his mind and writings makes it uncertain whether he himself regarded as anything more than poetic fancies, or philosophic conjectures'.[7]

Finally, while Mill never leaves us in doubt that his father was a demanding tutor, he is clear that what was imposed was never 'an education of cram'.[8] Instead, the objective was always 'to make the understanding not only go along with every step

---

[1] Ricardo as cited in CW XII p. 9 n. 5. There would have been a problem in Mill attending Oxford or Cambridge, as his upbringing was outside the contours of Anglicanism, and at this time, least nominal allegiance to the established Church was an requirement for admission to the universities in England.
[2] Mill's letters reveal the seriousness of his interests and his commitment to develop better ways of thinking and living. But he exhibits little by way of humour or irony in his reflections on the human condition.
[3] Mill was called John at home. The 'J. S. Mill' identity came later, probably to distinguish Mill from his father when both were publishing articles and reviews.
[4] See *Auto* p. 8.
[5] James Mill says as much in letter of 1811 to Jeremy Bentham – as quoted in Capaldi (2012) p. 19-20.
[6] *Auto* p. 15. Ironically, some Mill's critics think that in his philosophical writing as in *On Liberty*, he is notably remiss in his linguist precision. We shall see how this emerges later.
[7] *Auto* p. 16.
[8] *Auto* p. 21.

of the teaching, but if possible, precede it. Anything which could be found out by thinking, I was never told, until I had exhausted my efforts to find it out for myself'.[1]

One other influence from James Mill's educative programme may be noted. James Mill had rejected the orthodoxies of sectarian forms of Christianity and all other forms of theism. A consequence was a similar scepticism towards other certitudes – certain atheism was no more plausible.[2] Mill retains this agnostic view in ways that come to expression in *On Liberty* with the view that humans are 'fallible' beings so incapable of absolute certainty.[3] What is considered more reasonable was a view akin to the classical dualist view of Manichaeanism, the idea of reality exhibiting a pattern of conflict between the principles of good and evil. Without evidencing any disapproval, Mill thinks his father saw this as a more plausible hypothesis consistent with the real experiences of morality.[4]

With Jeremy Bentham, James Mill collaborated in presenting the utilitarian philosophy, and with Ricardo, he aided in promoting the *laissez-faire* free-trade economic theory that had been promoted in Adam Smith's *The Wealth of Nations* (1776).[5] A further step was taken when, with James Mill's encouragement, Ricardo wrote and published his *Principles of Political Economy and Taxation* (1817). The ideas in this radical free-trade school of thought were gaining momentum, and James Mill applied the method of getting his son to read and make summaries by using Ricardo's *Principles* as the prescribed text.[6] The notes Mill produced then served to aid James Mill in writing a more introductory study, *Elements of Political Economy*, published in 1821.

While this collaborative work was being written, James Mill took an important step: despite the criticisms that he had made of the British approach to India in his *History*, in 1819, he accepted an appointment as an official at India House, the headquarters of the British East India Company, which managed the administration of India on behalf of Britain. James Mill rose to become Head of the Examiner's office in 1830, but from the start, the job gave him greater financial security and independence, enabling him to free himself and his family from Bentham's patronage.[7]

While working for the East India Company, James Mill continued his other life of radical activism and economic writing, developing his influence and reputation. In 1821, he was amongst a group that founded a new discussion group, The Political Economy Club: Ricardo, the economist Thomas Tooke, and Thomas Malthus were other founding members.[8] Of these, Malthus was, at the time, highly influential and

---

[1] Mill makes a point akin to this in a letter to Thomas Carlyle in October, 1832: 'I was not *crammed*; my own thinking faculties were called into strong though partial play; & by their means I have been enabled to *remake* all my opinions'. CW XII p. 128. Mill was countering Carlyle's view that the young have breadth of thought and wide imagination that in general, in adult life narrows to negativity.
[2] See Capaldi (2012) p. 22.
[3] See *OL* II: 8-9. See also *Auto* pp. 25-27.
[4] See *Auto* pp. 25-26. Mill's developed views on this are found in in his *Three Essays on Religion*. See Mill (1998).
[5] Adam Smith (1723-1790). Philosopher and economist. Smith, with the later contributions of Ricardo and James Mill, does much to stimulate the discipline of political economy.
[6] See *Auto* p. 19 and Mill CW XII pp. 8-9.
[7] James Mill moved his family to a house in Kensington Park and this became Mill's home for many years ahead.
[8] The Political Economy Club continues to this day: details of its activities can be found at: hetwebsite.net/het/schc

prominent. His *An Essay on the Principles of Population* (1798) made an abiding impact. The main argument on population suggests that unchecked population growth would invariably outstrip economic growth and wealth, leading to a general decline into poverty. Linked to this, the philosophical radicals developed a strong interest in promoting voluntary population control.[1]

With this expanding circle of influential friends, James Mill was one of those who engaged in discussions through the 1820s that led to the founding of University College London in 1826, a move that aided moves to the more formal establishment of London University by Royal Charter in 1836.[2] His writings in the area of politics influenced the 1832 Reform Act. Through his endeavours, he supported the ideas of population control and land tax and suggested a labour theory of value that was to have significance later in the century in the presentations of Karl Marx.

In 1829 James Mill published *Analysis of the Phenomena of the Human Mind*, a study in psychology grounded on the principles of associationism, and throughout the latter stages of his career, he continued to write for a variety of radical journals. General themes in his work include a stress on the role of reasoning and analysis, a commitment to an empirical and experimental approach, and in ethics, economics and political thought, the adoption of the utilitarian 'Greatest Happiness Principle', the notion of the greatest happiness to the greatest number as the criterion for judging the worth of the outcome of an action.[3] This principle was linked to support for increased democracy and *laissez-faire* policies in economics, and James Mill and his friends were active in promoting reforming views of politics and economics, opposing political constraints on economics, industry and trade and promoting the virtues of the free market to the end of releasing market forces to boost achievement and prosperity. All-round, James Mill and his friends are engaged in activities and arguments expressive of the mood and energy of Britain as the first industrial economy.[4]

It is greatly to James Mill's credit that he encouraged his son to form views and to be able to defend and justify them in a clear and ordered fashion. Through this came in quick order the capacities upon which rests what Capaldi sees as Mill's particular genius: he had a rare ability 'to identify and restate issues and arguments with exemplary clarity, simplicity, and rhetorical force'.[5] He could also 'synthesize all of the major intellectual and cultural factors of his time into a coherent narrative'. These qualities were to come to expression as Mill's intellectual career progressed. However, for the Mill of 1820, in his fifteenth year, the prevailing mindset of his

---

[1] Thomas Malthus (1766-1834); Malthus was a Fellow of Jesus College, Cambridge, and became Cambridge's first Professor of History and Political Economy in 1805. Thomas Tooke (1774-1858). Tooke's son, William Eyton Tooke (1808-1830) was a good friend of Mill's. Mill was much affected by Eyton Tooke's death by suicide. See CW XII p. 44-45 and CW XXXII p. 9. Mill joined the Political Economy Club as a very young man, and attended meetings throughout his life, the last in December, 1872 – see Mill CW XVII pp. 1929-1930. W.E. Gladstone (1809-1898) was a member in later years, joining when he was Chancellor of the Exchequer (1863).
[2] This initially involved bringing University College and Kings College into association as constituent colleges of the University of London. Kings College was founded in 1829.
[3] See *Util* II:9.
[4] The historically interesting aspect of this period so often overlooked is that government intervention or initiative played almost no direct role at all in the industrial revolution, and only came into play through the various hikes in taxation associated with the period of the Napoleonic wars. On this see Mathias (2015).
[5] Capaldi (2012) p. 25.

life and education led him to adopt utilitarian views consistent with Jeremy Bentham and his father.[1]

A plan then arose for Mill to go to France to spend some time with Sir Samuel Bentham, the brother of Jeremy Bentham. Mill was now fourteen, and he tells us that before he went, he was walking through Hyde Park with his father, who explained that he would find, as he went on in life, that he had knowledge and understanding that others of his own age would not have.[2] James Mill explained that this was not because of Mill's exceptional ability but due 'to the very unusual advantage' that had befallen him, namely, to have had a father who could so educate him. Even in the *Autobiography*, Mill is not inclined to dispute his father's explanation.

Soon afterwards, Mill was off to France, duly spending the best part of 1820-21 with Sir Samuel Bentham and his family.[3] This opportunity boosted Mill's enjoyment of travel and particularly of walking in the countryside to study and collect plants. The botanical interest Mill cultivated became a hobby he retained for the rest of his life. He greatly improved his command of French and also studied more advanced science and mathematics. He also read more into the patterns of thought that prevailed within European culture. According to the *Autobiography*, he particularly appreciated 'the free and genial atmosphere of Continental life'[4] and this enthusiasm for continental life contrasts with what he, reflecting themes unpacked later in *On Liberty*, regards in retrospect as 'the low moral tone of what, in England, is called society'.[5]

In his comments on the state of affairs in England, Mill elaborates some of the worrying trends he sees, mentioning how 'conduct' is overly 'directed towards low and petty objects; the absence of high feelings which manifests itself by sneering deprecation of all demonstrations of them, and by general abstinence… from professing any high principles of action at all, except in those preordained cases in which such profession is put on as a part of the costume and formalities of the occasion'.[6]

In more modern times, we can be sure that Mill would strongly favour the EU and be an eloquent opponent of Brexit. In effect, Mill was developing a critical capacity that served him well as time progressed. He was critically alert to the trends and dispositions in his own country, and as he studied and read more into continental thought, his criticism deepened and took on a more definite character.[7] We shall look at this in more detail in a later chapter, but the gist of the matter is that Mill

---

[1] See *Auto* pp. 39-40.

[2] See *Auto* pp. 22-23.

[3] See *Auto* pp. 34-35. Brigadier General Sir Samuel Bentham (1757-1831) was a naval architect by profession. While working on a job in Russia, Catherine the Great of Russia awarded his military title after he had aided in the defence of a Russian port against a Turkish attack. See Reeves (2007) p. 30. When Mill visited, he had retired to an estate in the south of France. See CW XII p. 6 n. 1 and *Auto* pp 34-37.

[4] *Auto* p. 35. Mill became fluent in French and later conducted extensive correspondence with his French friends in their native language.

[5] Mill's letters sustain this higher appreciation for continental life and thought than for the situation in England. See for example CW XIV p. 95, p. 277 – 'The nuisance of England is the English'; and CW XV p. 553 and p. 646.

[6] *Auto* p. 36.

[7] This is major theme developed in Capaldi's biography of Mill: see Capaldi (2012) pp. 31f.

had been schooled in a version of the empirical approach to philosophy that was well-regarded in Britain, with Hobbes, Locke, Berkely and Hume as notable precursors.[1] This gave consistent support to inductive methods of enquiry and to an analytic approach. Mill always retained an active allegiance to and use of this approach. But in contrast, continental thought had a wider interest in the human condition, embracing the cultural movement of romanticism and building a more positive view of the creativity of each individual. Mill's ongoing concern turns out to be 'the task of synthesizing these two great traditions of thought'.[2]

Mill's time in France had another intellectually significant moment. While staying in Paris, he briefly saw the philosopher Saint-Simon.[3] Mill was not at this stage wholly aware of the fine detail of the ideas of Saint-Simon and his followers, but the interests he developed in Continental thought later led him to read into the Saint-Simonian school of thought, which emphasises what is presented as a civilized and civilizing form of socialism.

Mill returned to England in the summer of 1821, and some discussion arose over what he might do next. A visit to Cambridge University with a new friend, Charles Austin, raised the possibility of attending as a student in the coming years.[4] Mill enjoyed the visit, which included a debate at the Cambridge Union, and he says that in the company of Austin and his friends, he felt for the first time that he was 'a man among men'.[5]

Charles Austin was the younger brother of John Austin, an eminent lawyer and an acquaintance of James Mill through the widening circle of utilitarian philosophical radicals. Ideas of studying at Cambridge were put aside; Mill's secular upbringing, and his lack of membership of the Church of England, meant that he could not attend Cambridge or Oxford. Instead, over the winter of 1821-22, Mill extended his repertoire of learning through a study of law with John Austin – James Mill thought the law might make a good profession for his son.[6] Mill enjoyed his legal studies, but the plan did not lead to his entering the Bar examinations. Instead, in 1823, at the age of 17, he followed his father into India House as a clerk in the Examiner's Office.[7] He undertook a commitment to administrative work that would last for thirty-five years.

.

---

[1] Thomas Hobbes (1588-1679); John Locke (1632-1704); George Berkely (1685-1753); David Hume (1711-1776).
[2] Capaldi (2012) p. 31.
[3] See *Auto* p. 37. Claude-Henri de Rouvroy, comte de Saint-Simon (1760-1825): philosopher, economist and writer – advocate of a form of socialism.
[4] See Reeves (2007) p. 40. Charles Austin (1799-1874) – a lawyer.
[5] *Auto* p. 46. Mill was fifteen at this point.
[6] See *Auto* pp. 38-39 and Reeves (2007) p. 41. John Austin (1790-1859) – a lawyer and academic. Later, from 1828, Mill attended many of Austin's lectures on Law at the University of London. See CW XII p. 51. Austin's wife Sarah was a highly educated and widely read individual and she became a friend and supporter of Mill through the 1820s. See Capaldi (2012) pp. 35-36.
[7] See *Auto* pp. 48-49.

Mill at Work

Given Mill's subsequent career as a public intellectual and writer, it might appear odd that he went to work in what might seem a rather hum-drum administrative role. For a radical thinker in the making, it also seems strange that Mill would work within what would seem to be the business of empire. This last point needs qualification. Since 1813, so before either Mill worked for the company, it had lost its monopoly on trade with India, and in 1833, the company ceased commercial activity altogether and concentrated on administrative and political matters.[1]

In any case, Mill thought his administrative work was beneficial to his other endeavours. He says in the *Autobiography* that full-time writing for publication was not the best way to produce works of real value, for such a life is one of 'literary drudgery'.[2] In contrast, the office job work provided respite 'from the other mental occupations' occurring simultaneously. Work gave him a routine, an income, and a degree of independence. Only after absences, such as Mill took from time to time for his health, was the work at India House less congenial. Returning from a trip to Italy in 1837, Mill found a 'quite oppressive weight of business'[3] on his desk, and work for a period became 'a through mechanical drudge'.

Mill did well in his work at India House. From early on, he moved from routine administration to drafting political dispatches on a range of subjects and, in effect, starting on the business of work that would occupy him until retirement in 1858. A key point about the job was that being a fast and efficient worker, Mill could usually complete his day's tasks by the early afternoon; this meant he had time to think, develop ideas, and begin to write.[4] Mill also points out that the administrative work allowed him to engage in 'learning by personal observation the necessary conditions of the practical conduct of public affairs'.[5] He adds points expressing, albeit positively, the kind of imagery that evokes much that will be familiar to anyone who has worked in the culture of bureaucratic management:

'The occupation accustomed me to see and hear the difficulties of every course, and the means of obviating them, stated and discussed deliberately, with a view to execution; it gave me opportunities of perceiving when public measures, and other political facts, did not produce the effects that had been expected of them, and from what causes; above all it was valuable to me by making me, in this portion of my activity, merely one wheel in a machine, the whole of which had to work together'.

Mill understood that working in the collaborative office culture meant that the ideas being developed had to be presented to others who would have to agree that what was being proposed 'was fit to be done'. Mill registers that, in a sense, his working routines had a collegiate structure, and the process of negotiation to points of agreement gave a model of how to build and sustain progress. This fed back into

---

[1] See Capaldi (2012) p. 37. See also pp. 241-245 for a considered view of Mill's work at India House and his liberal view of colonialism,
[2] *Auto* p. 49.
[3] CW XII p. 322.
[4] Mill explains this in some detail in his *Autobiography* – see *Auto* pp. 48-51.
[5] *Auto* p. 50.

Mill's interests in moral, social and political matters, generating a methodology that lasted for the rest of his life.

As Mill says later, in a letter in 1852, the ongoing project he was concerned with as 'the great end of social improvement' within and for society, is to work to cultivate a 'state of society combining the greatest personal freedom with that just distribution of the fruits of labour which the present laws of property do not even profess to aim at'.[1] He has a similar remark in the *Autobiography*, saying that the ongoing issue for social reform is 'how to unite the greatest individual liberty of action, with a common ownership of the raw material of the globe, and an equal participation of all the benefits of combined labour'.[2] Here he expresses a possible fusion of liberal and socialistic aspirations, something subsequent experience suggests being a more complex political ambition than Mill thought.

Through the 1820s, he met many who became good friends, associates or protagonists over the coming years, including Macaulay, J. A. Roebuck, and George Grote.[3] Mill's interests were developed through mixing with other radical thinkers and engaging in debating and discussion groups. At the time, parliamentary politics was in a turbulent state. There was no clear system of party politics, so much as broad groups of loosely connected Tories – or Conservatives – and Whigs – who became the Liberals. Mill and his radical friends were on the edge of the liberal wing.

At this time, Mill began a journalistic career of his own, building on the contacts that his father had and treating a similar range of subjects in the areas of social ethics, politics and philosophy.[4] He first published articles in 1822, and in 1822-23, he took the lead within a group of some of his friends, founding a discussion group, The Utilitarian Society, to give some focus for reviewing radical ideas for political and social reform.[5] Interestingly, the topics he wrote about in his earliest published letters and pieces were on the importance of freedom of speech, feminism, and France and what could be learnt from the French.[6]

Thinking back to this time, Mill suggests that in giving the society a name including 'Utilitarian', he more or less introduced the term into wider usage.[7] This is not unrelated to the fact that at this time, he was reading with improved discernment the work of Jeremy Bentham, and he says it gave him 'what might truly be called an object in life; to be a reformer of the world':

---

[1] CW XIV p. 87.
[2] *Auto* p. 130-131.
[3] See *Auto* p. 46-48. J. A. Roebuck (1801-1879): lawyer, politician and writer: a strong supporter of Bentham's legal and moral views, and a close friend of Mill's in the 1820s. he met Mill via his relative, the writer and poet Thomas Love Peacock (1785-1866), who was also working in the East India Company. India House had something of a reputation for employing writers – the essayist and poet Charles Lamb (1775-1844) worked as a clerk at India House from 1792-1825. See Capaldi (2012) p. 42-43. Roebuck and Mill drifted apart later, probably due to the tensions caused by Mill's relationship with Harriet Taylor. George Grote (1794-1871), a politician, writer, historian and classicist – see CW XII p. 14.
[4] See *Auto* p. 52.
[5] In 1822 Mill published articles in the *Traveller* newspaper – see Capaldi (2012) p. 52.
[6] See Reeves (2007) p. 52.
[7] *Auto* p. 47. Mill's point is that previously, references were invariably to utility.

'My conception of my own happiness was entirely identified with this object... as a serious and permanent personal satisfaction to rest upon, my whole reliance was placed on this'.[1]

He also thinks that it was through this period and participation in the debating societies that he experienced his 'own real inauguration as an original and independent thinker'[2]:

'I acquired, or very much strengthened, a mental habit to which I attribute all that I have ever done, or ever shall do, in speculation: that of never accepting half-solutions of difficulties to complete; never abandoning a puzzle, but again and again returning to it until it was cleared up; never allowing obscure corners of a subject to remain unexplored because they dd not appear important; never thinking that I perfectly understood any part of a subject until I understood the whole'.

One of the aspirations he and his friends shared was for what was termed 'philosophic radicalism.'[3] Following the lead from James Mill, they imagined developing a new radical movement for political reform, as mentioned, allied to but more ambitious for change than the Whig or liberal political establishment. In the *Autobiography*, Mill portrays the historical and political elements of this period: it was an age of 'rapidly rising Liberalism'[4], the 'fears and animosities' of the years of war with France were receding, and so 'people had once more a place in their hearts for home politics' such that 'the tide began to be set towards reform'. Mill thinks that in the period from 1820 onwards, 'political economy' was starting to make a mark in public affairs, and that various political and economic reforms were unfolding, exhibiting an 'air of strong conviction' and an 'equally strong faith' in their radical 'creed'. The main elements of this system of radical commitment included arguments to end restrictive protectionism to promote free trade and open competition, to improve the pace of reform to enable a liberalisation of society, to reform parliament to the end of making for a wider and, it was assumed, more effective representative democracy. All these aspirations were cloaked with the principles of utilitarian thinking, with ideals of equality under the greatest happiness maxim.

Mill also tasted the risks and perils of social campaigning for liberal and enlightened causes. In the opening episode of his biography of Mill, Richard Reeves relates that in 1823, while walking to work one day, Mill came upon the wrapped and abandoned body of a baby that had been strangled at birth.[5] Alert to this as a symptom of desperation over unwanted pregnancies and mindful of the deeper problems of overpopulation as advanced by Malthus, Mill and a friend arranged to distribute leaflets in the area, explaining and illustrating some methods of contraception.[6] Unfortunately, copies of the leaflets came to the attention of the police, who decided the material on how to use the contraceptives constituted

---

[1] *Auto* p. 77.
[2] *Auto* p. 71.
[3] *Auto* p. 61.
[4] *Auto* p. 58-59.
[5] See Reeves (2007) pp. 1-2.
[6] The leaflet, entitled, 'To Married Working People' was written by Francis Place. See Capaldi (2012) p. 41.

obscenity, so Mill and his friend were arrested and presented at Bow Street Magistrates' Court. Mill spoke well in his own defence, but he spent two nights in custody. However, Mill retained a concern for the social issues of parenthood, poverty and overpopulation. In the same year (1823), the seventeen-year-old Mill had articles published in the *Morning Chronicle*, a paper sympathetic to the case of radicalism and reform.[1]

In 1824, with the main impetus and cash coming, Mill says, from Bentham, a new journal – the *Westminster Review*[2] – was established to provide a platform for the growing wave of radical liberal and utilitarian thinking and to compete as a public arena for debate with other established journals that represented more conventional political and philosophical outlooks.[3] Mill became a frequent contributor to the journal. In one early article on 'War Expenditure', he makes a remark that foreshadows the emphasis on individuality that percolates through *On Liberty*: writing on the economic principles of supply and demand, he offers the following:

'The demand of a country is made up of the demands of every individual in the country. The supply of a country is the aggregate of the supply of every individual. If, therefore, it can be proved, that every person's demand exactly equals his supply, it will be established that the demand of the whole country, and its supply, exactly balance each other'.[4]

Mill was active in the ongoing discussion around the edges of the debating societies and the community of writers preparing articles to publish in the Westminster Review. The circle of friends developed at this time drew considerable incentive, he says, from the involvement of James Mill, whose energetic personality and radical ideas 'gave the distinguishing characteristic to the Benthamite or utilitarian propagandism of that time'.[5]

From 1825 to 1827, Mill took on another task. Working in his own time, he acted as editor on the disparate mounds of paper that Bentham had drafted but not organised, but which became the volumes of his *Rationale of Judicial Evidence* (1827) through Mill's hard work.[6] Bentham was a productive drafter of ideas and had made three attempts over the years to write this particular text. However, he was less organised in preparing his works for publication, so Mill had a somewhat arduous task of sifting, sorting and structuring the work.[7] One positive aspect of the experience on the personal front was that Mill became acquainted with Edwin (later Sir Edwin) Chadwick, thereafter a life-long friend and correspondent.[8] Chadwick, a student of law, was working as a secretary to Bentham. He later served with

---

[1] See *Auto* p. 53 and Capaldi (2012) p. 45.
[2] See *Auto* p. 54.
[3] Mill mentions 'the Edinburgh and the Quarterly' – *Auto* p. 54f. He means the broadly liberal *Edinburgh Review or Critical Journal* (established in 1802) and more conservative *The Quarterly Review* (1809).
[4] CW IV p. 16. This piece appeared in the *Westminster Review* in July, 1824.
[5] *Auto* p. 60.
[6] See *Auto* pp. 66ff.
[7] When the volumes were published Bentham wanted Mill to be listed on the title page as editor, something Mill did not want. See CW XII pp. 18-19. Mill did, however, sign the preface to the work – as John S. Mill – see CW XII p. 19..
[8] Edwin Chadwick (1800-1890) – lawyer and reformer.

distinction in areas of social reform, notably dealing with sanitation and reforms to the Poor Law.

Mill's work with Bentham through these years was something of a high water mark in their association. From 1828 onwards, relationships became more distant due to factors going back to 1823-24, the period when Bentham was looking to set up the *Westminster Review*. Bentham's plan was for the journal to be edited by James Mill, but as Mill explains, this was not something his father felt he could do, consistent with his duties at India House.[1] Bentham eventually appointed another of his followers, John Bowering, to the post.[2] The problem with this, Mill says, is that James Mill was sure that Bowering was not the right person for the job of editing a radical journal and that it would not work well. This proved to be the case.[3] Although the journal made a good start, it gradually fell into problems stemming from how Bowering ran it. By 1828 Mill gave up writing for the *Westminster Review*. This happened because the journal was losing money, and Mill and his father discussed remedial measures with Bowering, who was still editor. Unbeknownst to the Mills, Bowering was looking for funding from others and having found it, he assumed the Mills would continue to write for publication in the *Westminster Review*. Mill explains that the 'concealment' practised by Bowering made that impossible, which ended his association with 'the original Westminster'.[4]

Despite this, all-round, as Mill lived and worked on various fronts through the mid to late 1820s, he seemed to be busy, well-connected and with a very bright future. He was engaged in purposeful tasks, and his activities within the circle of philosophical radicals promised positive reforms. It would seem that nothing could possibly go wrong.

---

[1] See *Auto* p.54f.

[2] John – later Sir John – Bowering (1792 – 1872): linguist, writer, merchant and diplomat, he supported radical and liberal causes and in the 1850s he was appointed Governor of Hong Kong. He edited and published Bentham's works – 1838-1843 - albeit in a version that was far from complete. See https://www.britannica.com/biography/John-Bowring

[3] See *Auto* p. 57f and p. 75f.

[4] *Auto* p. 75. In 1843, Mill wrote in defence of his father's reputation after the publication of a review of Bowering's *Memoir* of Bentham in which comments Mill thought wholly misleading about James Mill were reproduced. That Mill had a very low opinion of Bowering is evident from the letters. See Mill CW XIII pp. 598-599 and pp. 600-601.

2. Mill's Crisis

Contrary to outward appearances, during the hyperactive period of the late 1820s, Mill later reveals that he suffered a crisis, a kind of nervous breakdown.[1] Apparently, this started in 1826 and is something of a feature of his life for the next few years. As Mill describes it, it is clear that he did not fall into an overt depressive mood and manner and that equally, his engagement with various activities may be seen as therapeutic, and at the time, the process seems to have been something of which his family and friends were completely unaware. It may be that this was the first of what was to be several bouts of introspective depression, given the mood and tone we find in some of his letters.[2] However much his earlier life had been guided by his father, Mill, again, writing years later, is adamant that his father was 'the last person'[3] to look to for help. Mill says that given his father's efforts educate him, the outcome was the very last thing his father would expect, and Mill saw no value in 'giving him the pain of thinking that his plans had failed'.[4] These remarks suggest that Mill's crisis had a psychological as well as an intellectual aspect.

The Limits of Utilitarian Reasoning

In the case in question, Mill says he felt 'in a dull state of nerves'[5], that he was 'unsusceptible to enjoyment or pleasurable excitement' and in 'one of those moods when what is pleasure at other times, becomes insipid or indifferent'. Rising to what, for Mill, is a witticism, he says he imagines that his experience is like what a convert to Methodism feels when they have their first 'conviction of sin'.

The cause of the immediate crisis of diminished mood with attended low spirits appears to have been the tension between the rather austere and rational ethos that Mill had taken from his education and a more liberal, expansive and artistic manner to which he now inclined. Mill says in the *Autobiography* that, to some degree, his early life and interests had made him into something akin to 'a mere reasoning machine'.[6] The background to this included the associationism to which James Mill had so strong a commitment. In his psychology, Mill explains, James Mill's 'fundamental doctrine was the formation of all human character by circumstances, through the universal Principle of Association, and the consequent unlimited possibility of improving the moral and intellectual condition of mankind by education'.[7] By these means, the human individual acquires 'mental and moral feelings and qualities'.[8] These, 'whether of a good or of a bad kind, were the results of association':

---

[1] See *Auto* pp. 77-104 and also Himmelfarb: *OL* 'Editor's Introduction' pp. 12-16.
[2] See for example, CW XII p. 149.
[3] *Auto* p. 78.
[4] *Auto* p. 79.
[5] *Auto* p. 77.
[6] *Auto* p. 64.
[7] *Auto* p. 63. James Mill was a follower of the physician and philosopher David Hartley (1705-1757) the originator of associationism as tradition of thought in philosophy and psychology. His main work (of 1749) was *Observations on Man, His Frame, His Duty, and His Expectations*.
[8] *Auto* p. 79.

'That we love one thing and hate another, take pleasure in one sort of action or contemplation, and pain in another sort, through the clinging of pleasurable or painful idea to those things, from the effects of education or of experience'.

Thinking back, Mill considers that 'this doctrine appeared inexpungable'. However, a benefit assumed to flow from it was that it linked to the fusion of education and experience that led to the view that by reasoning and through debates and the publication of articles, it would be possible 'to alter people's opinions; to make them believe according to evidence, and to know what was their real interest, which when they once knew, they would, we thought, by the instrument of opinion, enforce a regard to it upon one another'.[1]

We can note that here, Mill gives evidence of his variable view of 'opinion', assuming a constructive role for social opinion – a view he refines in the future when writing *On Liberty*, where social opinions are sometimes considered tyrannical and sometimes seen again as positive, with an instructional mode of operation for informed opinion, not so very different from the early aspirations of philosophical radicalism.

The deeper problem that Mill sensed in and through his period of crisis was that he found himself in a state of tension over how to correlate his ideas on what mattered with how to live with qualitative assurance. The utilitarian approach to which he was committed had the background assumption, harking back to the outlook of Hobbes, that human individuals were fundamentally selfish. Yet, according to utilitarianism, humans were also able to act to bring about 'the greatest happiness to the greatest number'.[2] This form of action presupposed a capacity for humans to choose to act selflessly. The problem is that the causal elements of circumstance and association seem to result in an outlook where individual action is governed by determinism. The issue then in play is that without an element of freedom of the will, a crucial factor in ethical decision-making is absent. Linked to this, utilitarianism was conceived as consistent with the methods and ethos of natural science: it was inductive and objective and gave rise to clear prescriptions for decisions over action. Again, this implied a deterministic perspective whereby every event is the predictable outcome of a prior cause or series of causes. If this was true, then once more, a person was not free to choose how to act ethically.

Mill expresses the problem as something of an abiding feature of his 'dejection' in terms of 'the doctrine of what is called Philosophical Necessity'.[3] This implied that the individual was 'scientifically proved to be the helpless slave of antecedent circumstances', that the 'character and that of all others had been formed... by agencies beyond our control'.[4]

The upshot of these tensions was that Mill was confronted by the intellectual problem of finding a rationale for the liberties of thought, decision and action in the face of philosophical necessity, and to build this rationale, he also had to confront

---

[1] *Auto* p. 65.
[2] Mill often uses this common descriptor for the principle of utility, or the greatest happiness principle, in many of his writings, but notably in *Utilitarianism*. See *Util* I: 4; II: 2; V: 36.
[3] *Auto* pp. 96-97. We will deal with this doctrine – Mill's term for determinism – later: see Chapter 6 below.
[4] *Auto* p. 97.

how it seemed that his upbringing led him to be a reasoning, calculative individual, attuned to the causes of utility, with a consciousness of 'the formation of the character by circumstances': this seemed to render down the notion and experience of what it was to be an individual to that a being devoid of the authentic dynamics of feeling.

Mill seems to have found himself staring into a dark and unfathomable tunnel. Yet he saw a distant glimmer of light insofar as he realised that his frustration with, as he saw it, a limiting and limited perspective was a sign of his capacity to overcome it. Mill says that from his state of inner turmoil, a turning point came when he was reading Marmontel's *Mémoires d'un père*.[1] The key passage concerns the death of the author's father, detailing the misery this brought, as well as the saving realisation that after this sad loss, all responsibility for the family falls on the son. Mill was 'moved to tears' by the passage.[2] That he could experience emotion and a new depth of feeling gave him the positive thought that he could find new avenues of experience to enrich and strengthen his life:

'I was no longer helpless: I was not a stock or stone. I had still, it seemed, some of the material out of which all worth of character, and all capacity for happiness, are made'.[3]

Some writers on Mill, seeing that he lives in a pre-Freudian age, enjoy pointing out how he does not make the connection between Marmontel's and his own situation, where liberation from the father's influence might be a helpful thing.[4] This may be so, but it is not always helpful or wise to impose points of later interpretation on a writer from the past of which he or she could have no idea. The main point within Mill's emergent self-understanding is that he is in the grip of new thought; the realisation that the mechanical calculus of happiness employed by Bentham and James Mill to the end of determining the 'greatest happiness of the greatest number' had not so conditioned him with the equalising idea that 'everyone counts as one, but no one counts as more than one' that he was incapable in making personal responses exhibiting his own individuality, and so developing a greater 'worth of character' and a capacity for a richer 'happiness'. Mill saw that the utilitarian framework was not a sufficiently rich rationale for the point and purpose of his life as the individual J. S. Mill.[5]

Mill suggests that his emerging sense involved realising that he had adopted 'a theory of life very unlike that upon which I had before acted… I never, indeed, wavered in the conviction that happiness is the test of all rules of conduct, and the end of life. But I know that that this end was only to be attained by not making it the direct end'.[6]

There are two important elements in this observation. The first is that Mill expresses a resolution over a theory of life and the mode of action he adopted. In

---

[1] See *Auto* p. 81: J. F. Marmontel (1723-1799) – a French philosopher whose *Memoire* was published posthumously in 1804.
[2] *Auto* p. 81.
[3] *Auto* p. 82.
[4] On this see Himmelfarb (1974) pp. 5-6.
[5] These one-line phrases on utilitarianism are widely quoted, but Mill articulates them in *Utilitarianism*. See *Util* I:4; II:2; V:36.
[6] *Auto* p. 82. See also CW XII p. 36 as discussed in Chapter 4 below.

contrast to his state in the time of more acute crisis, he has a reconciled understanding that meets a prime objective – a life orientated to examined and consistent beliefs: for Mill, a general principle throughout his life is that a person is not rightly sorted if thoughts about how to live are not organised to be consistent with the practice of life. Secondly, we have a sense of how Mill is adapting the notion of happiness as the ideal embedded in utilitarianism: happiness is now not 'the direct end' of action. Mill notably elaborates this in his *System of Logic*, and we will look at this modified utility in a later chapter.[1]

The position Mill comes to affirm includes the realisation that 'both in theory and practice'[2] his educative experience had neglected 'the cultivation of feeling' – meaning, in particular, aesthetic appreciation, which led to what, from his later perspective, seemed to be 'an undervaluing of poetry and of Imagination generally as an element of human nature'.

If we stand back from this, the change in Mill's outlook can be traced in summary: the earlier tradition of reformers, including Jeremy Bentham, believed that human motivation was predominantly one of self-interest; indeed, this was considered something common to all human individuals. Accordingly, the principle of utility aimed to ameliorate this by promoting actions that bring about the greatest happiness or pleasure for the greatest number. Mill says that in this tradition, there was a full recognition of 'the superior excellence of unselfish benevolence', but also the view that 'the regeneration of mankind' would come from 'the effect of educated intellect, enlightening the selfish feelings'. In contrast, as Mill's thinking developed, he realised that this view of the human condition was given to a 'narrower' view of life than was viable.[3] He probably reflected a good deal on this before writing a passage on the proto-existential dilemma he faced. Given the 'frame of mind'[4] he was in, he writes that he asked himself the following question:

'Suppose that all your objects in life were realised; that all the changes in institutions and opinions which you were looking forward to, could be completely effected at this very instant: would this be a great joy and happiness to you?'[5]

Mill thinks the answer he would give would be 'No!' The outcome was a sense of 'the whole foundation' of his life collapsing:

'All my happiness was to have been found in the continued pursuit of this end. The end had ceased to charm, and how could there ever again be any interest in the means? I seemed to have nothing left to live for'.[6]

Mill's self-analysis of his troubles places much of the cause on the systematic programme he had followed through his upbringing that put emphasis on the

---

[1] See Chapter 4 below. Mill's modified notion utility is best termed 'indirect' utility: see Grey (1983) p. 12f.
[2] *Auto* p. 65.
[3] *Auto* p. 123.
[4] *Auto* p. 77.
[5] *Auto* p. 77-78.
[6] *Auto* p. 78.

reasoned examination of problems. He thought 'the habit of analysis has a tendency to wear away the feelings'.[1]

Mill's fear, in part, was that his early life and educative training had made him of one disposition, with a programmed orientation to reasoning and analysis: then, the breakthrough into being a person open to an appreciation of art, poetry and culture led to the realisation that to be a person in the round, one's feelings were an important aspect needing as much cultivation as the reasoning and reflective aspects of thought and character. Indeed, the feelings could be seen as providing the 'natural complement and correctives' to the 'analysing spirit'. Crucially, that it was possible to make this adjustment also showed that the human condition was not wholly shaped or determined by circumstance and prior action.

Mill wrote about this many years later, and the impression he conveys is that he came through the crisis on the strength of realising that critical rational thinking, which emphasizes finding evidence and so developing reasons and justifications for all views, had to be balanced by the more diverse cultivation of feelings for the poetic and artistic domains. He makes a point of elaborating an explanation of his reading of poetry and its influence on his outlook.[2] He read Pope's *Essay on Man* and remarks that 'though every opinion in it was contrary'[3] to his own, the work was a powerful stimulus to his 'imagination'. He also tried Byron, but he found little benefit, as Byron's turn of mind 'was too like my own'.[4] He then read into the works of Wordsworth, in effect a poet of an older generation, but whose writings from 1797 to around 1815 had made a significant impact through the evocation of a depth of thought and feeling through the contemplation of nature and of people of everyday life in their struggles to live

Mill appreciated the setting of much of Wordsworth's poetry, in the beautiful but challenging landscape of the Lake District, but even more, how the work evoked 'states of feeling, and of thought coloured by feeling, under the influence of beauty'.[5] Mill considered that from Wordsworth, he learnt to 'feel that there was real, permanent happiness in tranquil contemplation'.[6] He also thought that this personal experience was not at the expense of but rather, with 'a greatly increased interest in, the common feelings and common destiny of human beings'.[7]

Mill's developing appreciation for the importance of cultural and aesthetic experiences within and for individual and cultural life owes much to this poetic influence, and fuelled by these richer insights, Mill recharged his enthusiasm for the life of radical reform.[8]

---

[1] *Auto* p.79

[2] Mill, in common with readers of poetry down the ages, came to see that the poet can convey more in a stanza than a philosopher or novelist can express in several hundred pages.

[3] *Auto* p. 66. Alexander Pope (1688-1744). Poet and writer. The *Essay on Man* was written 1733-1734. See Pope (2008) pp. 270-309.

[4] *Auto* p. 84. George Gordon, Lord Byron (1788-1824). Poet, writer and activist.

[5] *Auto* p. 85. In 1831, Mill visited the Lake District and spent four days in conversation with Wordsworth – William Wordsworth (1770-1850), poet. See Reeve (2007) p. 74.

[6] *Auto* p. 86.

[7] On this see also Bate (2021) pp. 447-451.

[8] See Chapter 4 below for a more detailed look at how Mill revised utilitarianism in and through this recovery from crisis.

A Pattern of Recovery

As Mill worked through his crisis towards a new equilibrium, he became more open to an increased range of human capacities and interests, so exhibiting an altogether more experimental and less sectarian disposition. He worked on developing modes 'of self-cultivation'.[1] He learnt to read German, working with Sarah Austin[2] and organised regular study and discussion groups to cultivate a greater depth of insight and understanding. This process, coupled with the editing of Bentham's work that overlapped with this phase of his life and his own work to prepare for the debates to which he contributed, all 'gave a great start to my powers of composition'.[3] Mill also notes that the experience of public speaking led to 'important effects' on his 'development'.[4]

At this stage of his life, Mill was putting a good deal of time into the debating groups, and the incentive to work in this medium was increased when a long series of competitive debates were set up between the philosophic radicals and the Cooperative Society.[5]

The Cooperative Society was committed to reform but was orientated to a particular form of socialism. The inspiration came from the work and ideas of the entrepreneur and social reformer Robert Owen.[6] Mill association with the Owenites, and with other organisations later, led to him gaining, within his own times, the unusual accolade of being considered both a liberal and a socialist. A reason for this is that what these terms meant in the early-mid nineteenth century is distinct from the meanings that came to general understanding later. The mode of socialism that Mill understood as coming through the debates would confront the radical wing of liberalism with the Owenite alternative in terms of a commitment to one of the more prominent strands of socialism and social determinism – the view that the individual is ever a product of the society that nurtures them.[7] Mill did not consider himself a natural speaker, but participation in these debates from 1825 until 1830 gave him the incentive to work hard on writing his speeches, and he thought that this 'greatly increased' his 'power of effective writing'.[8] He says this involved 'acquiring not only an ear for smoothness and rhythm, but a practical sense for telling sentences,

---

[1] *Auto* p. 69.
[2] See Capaldi (2012) p. 87. As mentioned earlier, Sarah Austin was married to Charles Austin.
[3] *Auto* p. 68.
[4] *Auto* p. 71.
[5] The Cooperative Society is not to be confused with the later cooperative movement coming from the Rochdale Society of Equitable Pioneers of 1844. By stages, and through a move to Manchester in 1863, this movement became the Cooperative Wholesale Society by 1872, and the Cooperative Group of today. See https://www.coop.co.uk/
[6] Robert Owen (1771-1858).
[7] Robert Owen's ideas are linked to his business interests, which prospered early so that in 1799, he and his partners bought New Lanark, a village and four textile mills, on the river Clyde about twenty-four miles from Glasgow. Owen had strong humane and philanthropic interests and New Lanark rapidly became a noted centre for effective production but also for a humane lifestyle for the people who worked there. Owen's later life involved a range of cooperative communal projects, some in the USA. Not much success came from these ventures, but Owen sustained positive initiatives for effective education. He wrote and published and campaigned for his ideas and values and his outlook gave rise to the 'Owenite' movement that Mill encountered.
[8] *Auto* p. 74.

and an immediate criterion of their telling property, by their effect on a mixed audience'.

The debates with the Owenites exposed Mill to thinkers who were social determinists, taking the view that society was the constructive force for humanity.[1] Mill was not inclined to support this, however much he shared with the Owenites a concern for reform. He says that as he worked through the crisis, the 'influences of European, that is to say, Continental thought' had a positive influence, indicating that he appreciated the ideas of those who, in 'the nineteenth century', were reacting against 'the eighteenth'.[2] Mill means that he enjoys how writers and thinkers in the Romantic period were offering a contrast with and development from the emphasis on reason in the period of the Enlightenment; they did this by elevating the roles of imagination, creativity and feeling. They contributed a richer view of human life, within which individuals possessed creative capacities for self-development in ways expressive of their individual character and worth.[3]

'Practical Eclecticism' and Encountering Coleridge

Through the period of his recovery and in contrast to his prior commitment to a precise and clinical form of utilitarianism, Mill's development embraced a strengthened sense of the incompatibility of overlaying theoretical solutions to the divergent varieties found within life. A notion that expresses his emerging view is 'practical eclecticism'.[4] What Mill means by this is that in working up to better ideas of what was truest and best for life, the way to proceed was to operate free of any pre-ordained doctrine and to examine the range of ideas and principles on offer openly and critically; the aims would be to find positive thoughts to garner, study and adapt for application within life while being ready to reject or attack those that seemed inadequate. Through the critical process of sifting the wheat from the chaff and so keeping a wider frame of possible views in mind, a richer variety of options would come to bear. The process maximised the chances of making positive progress over what happened in the alternative method of taking a prior commitment to one school of thought and using it as the criterion for assessing all other views. Using biblical terminology, Mill distances himself from the 'zealots' who affirm ideas, even good ones, without regard for alternatives or improvements. Mill thought it was artificial to try to convert people to a different view, even to a better one, by presenting an edifice of ideals and values. Instead, there had to be a process to encourage the active cultivation of discussion between individuals, so

---

[1] The views Mill developed in these issues are reviewed in Chapter 6.

[2] *Auto* pp. 92-93. On this, Mill also sees his father as 'the last of the eighteenth century' (*Auto* p. 116), which is, in part, a polite way of indicating that as the nineteenth century proceeds, James Mill has had his day.

[3] Mill builds on these themes in the third chapter of *On Liberty* – see Chapter 9 below. The romantic notion of self-development – '*Bildung*' in German - is seen by Capaldi to be a significant theme for Mill. See Capaldi (2012) especially pp. 86-132 and p. 253.

[4] CW XII p. 42.

building up their capacity for the moral and intellectual examination of the evidence for the best ways to live.[1]

With his new, more enriched outlook, Mill wanted to build up perspectives on life, truth, and how to live individually and collectively from whatever is presented, examine the cases that can be made and weigh the points in favour and those against from all sides.[2] This method of 'practical eclecticism' is a forerunner of the conflict theory of acquiring better truths found in *On Liberty*.[3] Mill is keen to tie together the need to refine ideas about how best to live with respect to testing how ideas play out in life.[4]

During the period of the debates with the Owenites, there was a new initiative in 1826 to establish what became The London Debating Society.[5] Mill was involved with this, and as may be appreciated, the work and discussions gave a context for developing his ideas towards a richer notion of the possibilities for becoming an individual. Central to this is an influence that starts in 1828 when Mill records that he came into contact with those he termed 'the Coleridgians'.[6] This sounds as if he encountered a veritable band of devotees of the poet and thinker Samuel Taylor Coleridge.[7] In fact, Mill means just two men particularly influenced by Coleridge's writing whom he met when they came from Cambridge to join the London Society: these were John Sterling – soon to become a close friend of Mill's – and Frederick Denison Maurice. Maurice went on to an eminent career in theology with Professorships at Kings College London and at Cambridge.[8] Sterling, a writer, was instrumental in Mill going to meet Coleridge, whose ideas gave more fuel to the development of Mill's eclectically alert mind.

Since 1816, Coleridge had resided in Highgate and by 1828 had settled into a routine of life and study, sometimes giving public lectures and holding meetings on Thursday evenings to discuss ideas with his friends and followers.[9] Mill went to one such meeting with Sterling and, after that, attended more in 1829-30, and these meetings and conversations, together with his reading of Coleridge, formed a very positive view of the thought emanating from him. Coleridge's influence tied in with that of Wordsworth and other continental writers in the romantic movement, giving Mill further grounds for a positive view of the human capacity for an integrated and

---

[1] This view has implications for Mill's thoughts about education, as we see when looking at the last chapter of *OL*. See Chapter 11 below.
[2] See CW XII pp. 42, 46 and 49.
[3] See *OL* II: 6-9: 34-35; 42.
[4] See CW XII p. 97.
[5] See *Auto* pp. 72-74.
[6] *Auto* p. 74.
[7] Samuel Taylor Coleridge (1772-1834): poet, critic, philosopher and thinker – he was a major influence in the Romantic movement, and on Mill.
[8] F. D. Maurice (1808-1872) became one of the major figures in nineteenth century Anglican thought. He was a founding figure in the Christian Socialist movement, a Professor at Kings College, London (1840-1853) and at Cambridge (1866-1872). His many writings have influenced Christian thought on social matters to the present. John Sterling (1806-1844), a writer and critic, became one of Mill's closest friends until his early death in 1844 – see Mill CW XIII pp. 634-655.
[9] See Capaldi (2012) p. 97. See also Holmes (1999) pp. 426ff. Early in life, Coleridge was treated for rheumatic illness with laudanum, the medical tincture derived from opium. Unwittingly, Coleridge was thus draw into a life-long addiction at a time when the risks and perils of addiction were not properly understood – thus the addict was seen, and saw themselves, as a person of moral weakness, not as an addict in the modern sense. See Holmes (2005) p. 37. Towards the end of his life, not least through his own self-analysis, Coleridge found more sympathetic medical help. See Holmes (1999) pp. 426ff.

creative form of intellectual and moral self-development.[1] Mill went on to write a long essay, largely in praise of Coleridge, published in 1840.[2]

Samuel Taylor Coleridge as portrayed in 1834 by Washington Allston.[3]

Coleridge had a range of ideas that would appeal to Mill; he had moved in his thinking from an early commitment to associationism to an anti-reductive outlook embracing the importance of encouraging the creative and expressive side of the individual. Like all romantic thinkers, Coleridge saw a dynamic relationship between the human and the wider natural world – albeit from a more orthodox Christian perspective than Mill. For example, Coleridge thought that ideas on promoting a national scheme for education were inadequate if they simply looked at improving the standards of literacy. Instead, the need was '*educing* the faculties, and forming the habits'[4] of the person as a whole. Coleridge thought that a 'liberal Education' was one 'which *draws* forth and trains up the germ of free-agency in the individual'.[5] More widely, he saw life as moving through a 'progressive transition'[6], and so the ideas that come from a rightly-ordered education and from

---

[1] For a testimony Mill provides on how Coleridge's work influenced his 'thoughts and character', see CW XII p. 221.
[2] See CW X pp. 117-163.
[3] Washington Allston (1779-1843).
[4] From *The Lay Sermons*, as quoted by Holmes (2005) p. 441. To 'educe' is bring out or develop the inherent potential in someone.
[5] From the *Collected Letters* of Coleridge, quoted in Holmes (1999) p. 551.
[6] From the *Collected Letters* of Coleridge, quoted in Holmes (1999) p. 483.

critical discussion could become 'a living movement in the progress of human philosophy'.[1] Another of Coleridge's ideas of weight for the political, cultural and intellectual life is what he termed 'the clerisy of the nation'.[2] Although Coleridge looked for reforms in terms of greater equality within society, he also thought that in and for the improvement, guidance and well-being of people, it was vital for the expertise of specialists – the so-called 'clerisy – in all disciplines – in 'all the so-called liberal arts and sciences' – to have a sanctioned role, analogous to priests in earlier times, so that in every part of the country there would be 'resident guide, guardian, and instructor' to aid in the process of advancing the 'knowledge', and the 'civilization' of 'the community'.[3] Capaldi suggests that the idea of 'clerisy' gives a notion of an 'intellectual elite, with which Mill aways identified and within which he always sought a leadership role'. This is a plausible diagnostic, despite the claims Mill makes that he is not an elitist.[4]

These lines of thought anticipate themes and perspectives we will find Mill developing in *On Liberty*. In the *Autobiography*, Mill says that the Coleridgian influences contributed much 'that helped to build up' his 'new fabric of thought'.[5] In his essay on Coleridge, Mill saw the poet-philosopher as presenting his variant of the doctrines of the 'great Germans'[6] of the later part of the eighteenth century, and as 'the type and main source of that doctrine', he was 'the creator rather of the shape in which it has appeared among us, than of the doctrine itself'. Mill also thought that Coleridge's philosophy was yet to be fully embraced: people were either very much for or very much against it. However, this leads Mill to state one of his definitional views on what makes a 'true thinker'[7]:

'A true thinker can only be justly estimated when his thoughts have worked their way into minds formed in a different school; have been wrought and moulded into consistency with all other true and relevant thoughts; when the noisy conflicts of half-truths, angrily denying one another, has subsided, and ideas which seemed mutually incompatible, have been found only to require mutual limitation'.

Mill – writing this in 1840 – thought that the 'spirit of philosophy in England' was still too 'rootedly sectarian' for ease of true thinkers, but we may say that he was working on trying to resolve that matter. Mill, working in eclectic style, drew encouragement from Coleridge, who was, as 'a moral and religious philosopher'[8], possessed of both 'earnestness' and a 'catholic and unsectarian... spirit'. All-round, Mill takes Coleridge as significant for the way he presents the human condition as a richly variegated phenomenon, capable of positive and creative development, as

---

[1] From Coleridge's *Philosophical Lectures*, quoted in Holmes (1999) p. 491.
[2] From Coleridge's *On the Constitution of Church and State*, quoted in CW X p. 147. See also Coleridge (2008) pp. 692-696.
[3] CW X p. 147. Arguably, Coleridge's ideas of an intellectual body to guide, educate and inspire, goes back to his days as a pupil at Christ's Hospital School (1782-1791), where the best scholars, the Grecians, had that role. Coleridge duly became the senior Grecian of his year. See Holmes (2005) pp. 23-38.
[4] Capaldi (2012) p. 120. We shall see later that that Mill tends to resist any charge that he is elitist. See Chapter 5 below.
[5] *Auto* p. 88.
[6] CW X p. 121.
[7] CW X p. 122. Here see *OL* II: 20 and 23 where Mill elaborates this view of 'true' thinkers.
[8] CW X p. 158.

through fusing the expertise and confidence of critical thinking from the Enlightenment[1] with the empowering sense of creativity that comes through Romanticism. In contrast to the risk of the negative reductionism that could arise with overly critical approaches, the romantic imperatives entailed a wider and deeper appreciation of the creative individual in historical and cultural settings that were capable of interpretation.

Mill was keeping these lines of thought in mind, but on more personal matters, writing to Sterling in 1829, he refers to what he later terms his crisis with an allusion to 'the very various states of mind, some of them very painful ones, through which I have passed during the last three years'.[2] Writing again, two years later, Mill confides in the shape of his ambitions. The project for work going forward will be 'to work out *principles*: which are of use for all times, though to be applied cautiously & circumspectly to any: principles of morals, government, law, education, above all self-education. I am here much more in my element. The only thing that I believe that I am really fit for, is the investigation of abstract truth, & the more abstract the better'.[3] Given that Mill's focus in the coming years was on a work eventually called *A System of Logic*, he was in one sense true to this new style of operation: and he sustains this with other investigations that come later – into the *Principles of Political Economy* and the principles of utility and liberty. That Mill was concerned with the development of principles has a further significance: as he develops these ideas, he cultivates a sophisticated but not overly abstracted view wherein the principles – of utility and liberty, for example – offer criteria and limits for a richer variety of activities and interests to permit the processes of living, or, as is expressed in *On Liberty*, to encourage 'individuality to assert itself' (III:1).

Ironically, in his letter to Sterling, Mill also developed a line of thought that contrasts with the affirmations of liberty and individualism on which *On Liberty* trades: he notes that there is a form of poetic conservatism associated with Wordsworth and Coleridge, entailing 'a reverence for *government* in the abstract'.[4]

On this view, it is thought 'good for man to be ruled; to submit both his body & mind to the guidance of a higher intelligence and virtue'. This view is said by Mill to be 'the direct antithesis of liberalism, which is for making every man his own guide or sovereign master', and here Mill writes of a powerful aspect of his liberty principle as reaffirmed later in *On Liberty* – that 'over himself, over his own body and mind, the individual is sovereign'. (I: 9).

It is due to points like this that this section is linked to Mill's self-diagnosed 'practical eclecticism'. The component of governance identified with the poetic line of guidance is something Mill transfers, in later thinking, into the ethos of guidance in *On Liberty*. By the time *On Liberty* is ready to be published, Mill's thinking has

---

[1] The spirit of the Enlightenment is captured by Kant who, in an essay answering the question, 'What is Enlightenment?', wrote that 'Enlightenment is man's emergence from his self-imposed immaturity. Immaturity is the inability to use one's own understanding without guidance from another. This immaturity is self-imposed when it cause lies not in lack of understanding but in lack of resolve and courage to use it without guidance from another. Spere Aude! "Have courage to use your own understanding!" – that is the motto of the enlightenment'. Kant (1983) p. 41.

[2] CW XII p. 29. See also *Auto* p. 96.

[3] CW XII p. 78.

[4] CW XII p. 84. On Mill's acquaintances with both poets see Reeves (2007) p. 74 and p. 107.

distilled further ways in which the core principles of utility and liberty, and indeed, society, can be applied to moral, social and political spheres of life. The key issue becomes how exactly these principles cohere to enable other activities and interests to be pursued – and we will return to consider this matter later.

John Sterling also features in the *Autobiography*, where he is cited as someone who had initially found Mill to be 'a "made" or manufactured man', with 'a certain impress of opinion stamped' on him which he could 'only reproduce'.[1] This impression changed when they debated the merits of Byron and Wordsworth – where Mill was defending Wordsworth – and this revealed that depth of insight and feeling that Sterling recognised as signalling a distinctive individual talent.

Mill gives singular praise to Sterling, saying that there was no other man to whom he was 'more attached' and that 'he was the most lovable of men'. Mill's last letter to Sterling, written just before his death in 1844, is poignant in its expression of their mutual regard and affinity.[2]

Recalibrating the French Connection

Mill's reading in 1828-29 gave further attention to Saint-Simonian thinking and the thought of the French positivist philosopher and sociologist Auguste Comte.[3] Over the coming years, Comte became another regular correspondent, with Mill's initial enthusiasm for Comte's ideas gradually being eroded as the later works the French thinker produced suggested to Mill too dominant a role for society over individuality.[4] Adding to the activity, Mill encountered another individual who was to become a friend and long-term correspondent. At a meeting of the London Debating Society in May 1828, he met a former pupil of Comte's, Gustave d'Eichthal.[5] At this stage, Mill was impressed with how the Saint-Simonians appeared to have ideas and an analysis of the human condition and to be able to use these to influence social change and improvement. Writing to d'Eichthal the next year, Mill reflected on the contrast he thought there was between the pace and scale of reform in France and Britain:

'You are far ahead of us in France. You have only to teach men what is right, & they will do it: they are uninformed, but they are not prejudiced, & are desirous & eager to learn. Here, the grand difficulty is to make them desire to learn. They have such an opinion of their own wisdom that they do not think they *can* learn; & they have too little regard for other people to care much whether they learn or no, in things which only interest the nation in general, or mankind at large. Our middle class moreover have but one object in life, to ape their superiors; for whom they have an open-mouthed & besotted admiration, attaching itself to the bad more than to the good points, being those they can most easily comprehend & imitate'.[6]

---

[1] *Auto* p. 89.
[2] CW XIII pp. 634-635.
[3] *Auto* pp. 93-96. A. Comte (1798-1857). Comte was briefly associated with the Saint-Simonians.
[4] Of great value to modern students of Mill is the translation of the Mill-Comte correspondence – conducted in French – into an English translation. See Haac (2018). The two philosophers exchanged eighty-nine letters between 1841 and 1847.
[5] Gustave d'Eichthal (1804-1886). See CW XII p. 26 n. 1. See also Mill (2016a) p. 76.
[6] CW XII p. 32.

There is some generalising here, but Mill's concern with the power of the mood of opinion in society, especially in British society, stays with him, and the comments prefigure the critique of social opinion presented years later in *On Liberty*. In the same letter, Mill also comments on how he thinks there is a good chance for ideas to make an impact and create a movement for change – but as regards the situation on the home front, he wonders where these ideas will come from – 'there are no men of talents among us. Our writers & orators are, almost to a man, *des gens mediocres*'.[1] This concern about mediocrity and the pessimism about the culture of thought in Britain are also themes that anticipate what Mill says in *On Liberty*.

Amid these matters, Mill was further exercised into rethinking more elemental aspects of his outlook when, in 1830, Macaulay published a critique of James Mill's *Essay on Government*.[2] The main objection was against the abstracted and ahistorical view of government that James Mill presented. Macaulay, the emerging historian, looked for a view of notions of government that were set within historical situations. Mill did not want to endorse Macaulay's critique of his fathers' doctrines, but on reflection, he appreciated that James Mill's theory was amiss. To an extent, Mill thought that his father overstressed the importance for good government of an 'identity of interest between the governing body and the community at large'.[3] Nor could this identity be assumed to be fixed through the process of an election. These points mean that Mill sensed that the utilitarian view was not, in all respects, on the right lines, something that, in his time of crisis, he was thinking about a lot. Mill explains how his thinking on logic, arising from his engagement with some of the other discussion groups, helped him see a more fruitful way of classifying what we might call political science.[4] He was able to see how political science might be classified as 'a deductive science', but not in a manner akin to geometry, with a focus on axioms and deduction, but more like 'natural philosophy', or what we would now term natural science.[5] Here the focus would be on hypotheses and induction, and Mill evolved the view that all matters to do with 'political institutions' are 'relative, not absolute' in relation to the stage of 'human progress'.[6] Human progress, and the condition of political society would also, he thought, be conditioned and shaped by 'the strongest power in society'.

Mill's thinking on viewing politics and history was influenced by his ongoing reading into the Saint-Simonian school of thought. More practical experience came into play, as Mill was again in Paris in August 1830, in the wake of the revolutionary uprising at the end of July. He met some people engaged in this and wrote several letters to his father relating his thoughts and experiences.[7] He is enthusiastic about the changes being made against the policies of repression enacted by the previous regime. Mill's thoughts were positive as he considered that the collective will of a well-informed and articulate population had overcome a somewhat despotic regime

---

[1] CW XII p. 33.
[2] See Reeves (2007) p. 75. James Mill's 'Essay' was an article written for *The Encyclopaedia Britannica* in 1820. Macaulay's assault on James Mill came in articles published in the *Edinburgh Review* in March, June and October 1829.
[3] *Auto* p. p. 91.
[4] See *Auto* pp. 91-92. Political science was at this time in a quite embryonic state.
[5] *Auto* p. 92.
[6] *Auto* p. 93.
[7] See CW XII pp. 54-67.

of Charles X. He thought that the power and value of the Saint-Simonian thought was a force in all this, and this time was the peak of his enthusiasm for this tradition. However, as the new regime in France steadily lost favour, protests grew, as did divisions between the protesters and the philosophical Saint-Simonians.

In light of this, Mill's positive thoughts about the Saint-Simonians and Comte reached a zenith of enthusiasm before beginning to fade. In his various letters, we see how Mill's thinking changes. With regard to the Saint-Simonian tradition, the positives identified include the way that they sought to promote the '*Pouvoir Spirituel*'[1] – the spiritual power – of the age. They also exposed how institutions could inhibit and damage human progress.[2] Further, Mill likes their view that the pattern of activity in human development oscillates between two predominant strands, the 'critical' and the 'organical'.[3] The idea here was that periods of social development came through a stage of criticism, and then there was a phase of integrated consolidation. In a moment of enthusiasm, Mill thought that the Saint-Simonian ideas on 'social organisation' were 'likely to be the final and permanent condition of the human race'.[4] He appreciated the strand in their thinking where there was the vision of the end of the historical process in a situation where 'the body of the people' were in deference to 'the activity of the instructed'.[5] This was because the Saint-Simonians, and indeed Comte, thought that the moral, social and political sciences were analogous to the physical sciences. Just as most people depend on the expertise of natural scientists, so they should depend on the evidence and findings of the moral, social and political sciences. Mill – with Coleridge's notion of a 'clerisy' lurking in the background – was attracted to the idea of there being scope for moral, social and political thought to be put into such a condition, thinking that such a body of expertise could minimise, if not eliminate, erroneous social ideals. Here Mill is not quite at the state he reaches in *On Liberty*, where he is much more in favour of an elemental collision of truths with apparent errors, this in the setting of a more explicitly fallibilistic notion of the human capacity for truth.[6]

Mill's reservations about the Saint-Simonians grew as he began to see that they were locked into the view that a school of thought can recharge the spiritual force of a nation; while Mill's early enthusiasm for philosophic radicalism inclined him to support this aspiration, his developing view was that change was going to come by variations of open and free discussion and by the ideals and values in question being put practically and experimentally into practice – discussion between individuals was the way to foster progress, rather than simply a clash of ideologies.[7] He cites as key to the process 'the instruments of private communication, the pulpit and the press'.[8] It is through such free areas of debate as are here entailed, and through practical life, rather than through theoretical systems, that real personal and social development takes place. Mill is cultivating regard for the communicative power of liberal discussion as an instrument for reform: he values this and has a

---

[1] CW XII p. 40.
[2] See CW XII p. 41.
[3] CW XII p. 42.
[4] CW XII p. 88.
[5] CW XII p. 40.
[6] See *OL* II: 6-10, and Chapter 8 below.
[7] This is a major theme of *OL* III – see also Chapter 9 below.
[8] CW XII p. 41.

deeper suspicion of theoretical solutions to the practical problems of life. This suspicion lies behind Mill's criticism of Comte's thought, made in a letter to d'Eichthal of 1829, saying that although he was 'an exceedingly clear and methodical writer... one is apt to mistake the perfect coherence and logical consistency of his system, for truth'.[1] In the *Autobiography,* Mill comments on Comte's emphasis on the notion of a religion of 'Humanity'[2] as the guide and basis for all social values. But so emphatic is this that Comte loses sight of 'the value of Liberty and Individuality'.

The Widening Circle

Amongst the flux of activity in this period came a meeting of greater long-term significance for Mill. In 1830 he met John and Harriet Taylor. This came through the agency of another friend from the debating circle, the Unitarian preacher, publisher, writer and critic William Johnson Fox.[3] The Taylors were in Fox's congregation, and like Mill and Fox, they had radical leanings and were keen on reform; meeting Mill must have seemed a good move. Fox encouraged the Taylors to host a dinner and invite Mill, amongst others.[4] All went well, with Mill and Mrs Taylor swiftly building a positive rapport. In short order, Mill's friendship with Harriet Taylor was to prove both contentious and esteemed.[5] Harriet and Mill fell deeply in love. All the imagined difficulties arose. They conducted an affair for some twenty years, eventually marrying in 1851, some two years after the death of John Taylor. The marriage lasted for seven years before Harriet's death at Avignon in 1858. Mill bought a house near the churchyard where Harriet was buried, and thereafter he spent a substantial part of each year there. His stepdaughter, Helen Taylor, remained living with him until the end of his life.[6]

In 1830-31, Mill's more varied social life apart, he also read some of the articles of the critic and historian Thomas Carlyle. Carlyle was another of the thinkers of the age that, in due course, Mill was to correspond with and meet.[7] The initial contact came through letters after Mill started to write a series of articles on the theme of 'The Spirit of the Age'.[8] He comments that he was trying to portray the period as one where the older ideas were becoming obsolete, and new ones that were viable had yet to form, so it was an age of transition and uncertainty. Mill

---

[1] CW XII p. 35. Comte was associated with the Saint-Simonians for a while, in the late 1820s, but as Mill notes, he soon moved away from them. See *Auto* pp. 94-95. Mill's anti-ideological stance also inoculates him against Marx and the Marxists.

[2] *Auto* p. 120.

[3] W. J. Fox (1786-1864).

[4] See Reeves (2007) pp. 80ff.

[5] John Taylor (1796-1849) and Harriet Taylor (1807-1858). In Chapter 5 below more is said on the relationship between Mill and Harriet Taylor.

[6] After Mill's death, Helen Taylor became his literary executor, and she saw into publication a number of his writings, including the *Autobiography* and the *Three Essays on Religion*. See Reeves (2007) p. 482f and CW X pp. 369-489.

[7] *Auto* p. 93. Mill first met Carlyle (1795-1881) in September, 1831: see CW XII p. 73 n. 2, and p. 85. Carlyle had, in 1824, also attended Coleridge's meetings in Highgate. See Holmes (1999) p. 543f.

[8] *Auto* p. 99. Mill did not retain a high opinion of this unfinished series of articles, and they were not reprinted in his collections of essays – *Dissertations and Discussion* (4 volumes 1859-1875). They are found in Himmelfarb (1962) pp. 5-50.

reflects that the public did not seem keen to think about this message, but Carlyle, who was at that time residing in Scotland, told Mill that he thought, '… here is a new mystic'. No other critic or commentator has ever found Mill in the least bit mystical as a writer or thinker; that Carlyle thought this tells us a lot more about his outlook and disposition than it tells us anything about Mill.

The bronze of Thomas Carlyle by Edgar Boehm (1882) in Chelsea, London.[1]

Mill and Carlyle eventually met.[2] Later, Carlyle wrote the following description – Mill was a 'rather tall, elegant youth, with a small, clear Roman-nosed face, two earnestly-smiling eyes; modest, yet remarkably gifted with precision of utterance, enthusiastic, yet lucid, calm; not a great, yet a distinctly gifted and amiable youth'.[3] It was to Carlyle that Mill explained a significant reason for his dissatisfaction with the radicals with whom he had allied himself in the preceding years. The problem was, he said, that they gave 'abundant experience of the incapacity to… cooperate'.[4] By default, the philosophical radicals were strongly independently minded, and so they found allegiances to common campaigns hard to sustain. We may reflect that the trend for divergence in this movement was not so different from the Saint-Simonians or other ideologically committed groups.

Mill and Carlyle survived a potential calamity in their friendship in March 1835. Carlyle had given Mill the only manuscript of the first volume of his upcoming book, *The French Revolution*, which Mill had taken home to read. Unfortunately, due to a misunderstanding on the domestic front, the manuscript had been swept up with some waste paper and used to light fires to warm the house.[5] A horrified and distraught Mill went to Carlyle's house to explain, but Carlyle was calmness

[1] Edgar Boehm (1834-1891).
[2] See CW XII p. 85 n. 25.
[3] Hayek (2020) p. 27.
[4] CW XII p. 216.
[5] See CW XII p. 252 n. 2.

personified and simply resolved to write it better next time. Mill was at a loss at what to do and was determined to compensate Carlyle for the delay his error would entail in getting the book ready for publication. He wanted Carlyle to accept £200: Carlyle refused, and Mill had to work hard to persuade him to take £100.[1]

Mill says in the *Autobiography* that he found that 'the wonderful power' that Carlyle put into his writings 'made a deep impression'.[2] Throughout their close association, there is a sense that Carlyle was looking to him as a disciple of his particular outlook and style, while Mill, in an opposite sense, was sure that he was not. It was clear, to Mill, at least, that their outlooks and methods approached the human condition from distinct angles. Mill reverses the attribute given to him by Carlyle, writing that he sees Carlyle as more of a 'mystic', a 'man of intuition' and 'a poet'. In contrast, Mill felt his approach was more grounded in the methods of inductive enquiry – so Carlyle had the vision to see things that Mill could only 'hobble after and prove'. In time, Mill and Carlyle drifted apart, and contact became minimal after Carlyle published some extreme racist views in several articles. Mill's defence of liberal individualism and his hatred of enslavement meant that he had no time for Carlyle's view, which, Mill thought, would only be damaging to the anti-slavery movements in Britain and America.[3]

Mill had another significant meeting, leading to a fruitful longer-term association, when he first encountered the French writer Alexis de Tocqueville. De Tocqueville was in London, and they met in May 1835.[4] The two formed an enthusiastic mutual appreciation society. As we noted earlier, Mill was very impressed with de Tocqueville's critique of democracy as expressed in *Democracy in America* and having read Mill's reviews, de Tocqueville thought that Mill was his most insightful critic. We will find Mill's use and development of de Tocqueville's critique of democracy deployed in *On Liberty*, with Mill, like de Tocqueville, seeing as problematic the habits of mind and life that democracy cultivates, rather than democracy as such as a political system.[5]

---

[1] See CW XII p. 257 n. 2.
[2] *Auto* p. 100.
[3] Here see *Auto* p. 101, and also Capaldi (2012) pp. 225-226 and Reeves p. 220ff.
[4] See Reeves (2007) p. 113 and Brogan (2006) p. 303.
[5] For Mill's correspondence with de Tocqueville from 1835 to 1842 see CW XII/XIII pp. 271-273; pp. 283-284; pp. 287-289; pp. 300-301; pp. 304-305; pp. 305-306; pp. 308-310; pp. 316-317; pp. 433-435 and pp. 535-537.

3. Mill's 'Continued Mental Progress'[1]

The *Logic* and the *Principles*

During the remaining period of his life, Mill emerged as a leading public intellectual, and, as Nicolas Capaldi puts it, as 'the greatest of the English Romantics'.[2] This was achieved against the backdrop of his ongoing commitment to his administrative job. Work at India House continued, with Mill advancing his career, becoming an Assistant Examiner in 1828, involved in the business of arranging and managing the civil service style examinations taken by the officials working in the East India Company. In 1836 Mill was given another promotion and was put in charge of the relations between the East India Company and the various Indian states. During this period, he worked under Tomas Love Peacock, giving the organisation's leadership a distinctly literary character.[3] In 1856, Mill succeeded in his father's role as Chief of the Examinations Office. Mill was the second-highest official at the Company, a position akin to that of a modern Secretary of State.[4]

Most of his office time over the two years 1856-1858 was spent writing a rationale for the East India Company's work in the face of moves from parliament to close down the company and manage matters from within the systems of government. Mill's defence was a model of reasoning, but the company was closed, and Mill retired from his day job.[5] Through this lengthy period, Mill continued to work for many of the reforms arising from philosophic radicalism. One campaign Mill worked on concerned the independently-minding peer, the Earl of Durham – John George Lambton (1792-1842). Mill and the radicals wanted Durham to take the lead in forming a political party. This came to nought, as Durham was appointed to be High Commissioner and Governor-General in British North America – meaning Canada. Durham's suggestions for reform to give Canada independence as a dominion were unpopular with the Tories, and he was duly recalled. He was given a positive reception in London by the liberal fraternity and then joined the Whigs – which disappointed Mill and the radicals.[6]

Alongside his administrative duties, Mill also evolved his reputation as a writer and thinker. From his early activities, writing articles and taking part in debating societies in the circles of the young radicals, he progressed to become the editor and, for a time, owner of *The London and Westminster Review*.[7] He began to write more detailed and considered essays for publication, and in the 1840's he produced the first editions of his two most extensive works: *A System of Logic* (1843) – and *Principles of Political Economy* (1848). These books achieved remarkable status

---

[1] See *Auto* p. 125. The life that Mill shared with Harriet Taylor up to the time of their marriage, what happened thereafter, and its impact on Mill's work, particularly *On Liberty*, is examined in Chapter 5. Here we consider other aspects of Mill's ongoing life.
[2] Capaldi (2012) p. 365. See also p. 186 & p. 192.
[3] See Capaldi (2012) p. 123.
[4] See Ryan (1974) p. 1.
[5] See *Auto* pp. 135-136.
[6] See CW XII pp. 258 & 355 n. 14 See also Capaldi (2012) pp128-130.
[7] In effect this was a development of *The Westminster Review*. Mill edited the journal from 1834 owned it from 1837. See Capaldi (2012) p. 128.

within Mill's lifetime and gave him a platform of high renown. Both are important texts in their own right, and both contain significant groundwork for what is later expressed in *On Liberty*.

We discover from Mill's *Letters* that he worked on the *Logic* for many years. He started thinking about it after discussions in a study group in 1829-30.[1] He then worked on it intermittently, finishing it late in 1841 and publishing it in 1843.[2]

The *Logic* was the antithesis of the articles and reviews that Mill had been writing. They were fluent, often topical and provocative, and appealing to a wide readership. Most were the sort of thing a person could sit and read in one sitting. In contrast, the *Logic* is a massive and formal treatise grounded in the empirical tradition and defending the role of inductive reasoning as a component of logic and giving the method for developing the natural, human and social sciences. Mill put immense time and care into the work and nurtured it repeatedly through eight editions to the end of his life. He remarked that the book dealt with its subject in a way that differed from the main school of thought but that it 'is the concern of a higher power than mine: my concern is to bring *out* of me what is *in* me', even if those who considered it should find the bread it metaphorically offered to be so much 'sawdust' as opposed to anything 'wholesome'.[3] Mill means he was, to a considerable extent, in the grip of a passion to write a consistent view of a complex subject but in a style that sustained the vision that he possessed and that, in a sense, possessed him.

Developing what was in him, Mill explained in his correspondence that logic dealt with the 'Methods of Philosophic Investigation'.[4] Logic was the 'art', not 'of knowing things, but of knowing whether you know them or not'.[5] In the text, he notes that 'the proper subject... of Logic is Proof'.[6] Being able to have a method of proof is, Mill appreciated, a precondition for defending the truth claims we make. However, the sort of proof that Mill was most interested in was not the purely logical proof revered in classical and rational logic: he was more impressed by the contingent truths that came from proofs of experimental science, and it was this less conventional mode of thinking he applied in the *Logic*. Accordingly, he describes the work as 'a text-book' of the 'doctrine... which derives all knowledge from experience, and all moral and intellectual qualities principally from the direction given to the associations'.[7]

Mill sets out his stall, making clear that the *Logic* was written to oppose the view 'that truths external to the mind may be known by intuition or consciousness, independently of observation and experience'. This meant that Mill opposed the rationalist and critical rationalist traditions in logical and metaphysical thought, as was prevalent in much of Continental philosophy. Mill thinks that such views,

---

[1] See *Auto* pp. 91-92; pp. 103-104; pp.117-118; pp. 125-127.
[2] See also CW XII and XIII for progress reports on the long period of writing, revision and attempting to get published the *Logic*, as referenced in various letters; for example: p. 79; p. 163; p. 345; p. 347; p. 388; p.406; p. 412; p. 448; p. 449; p. 455; p. 471; p. 474; p. 478; p. 481; p. 485; pp. 493-494; p, 496; pp. 497-498; pp. 505-506; pp. 514-515; p. 520; p. 523; pp. 527-528; p. 541; p. 564; p. 569 – and it was published in February 1843. See also CW XXXII pp. 64-65.
[3] CW XIII p. 474.
[4] CW XIII p. 496.
[5] CW XII p. 347.
[6] *Logic* II: I: 1.
[7] *Auto* p. 127.

which in general sought to operate from purely theoretical assumptions, give 'great intellectual support' to 'false doctrines and bad institutions'.

It is worth showing how Mill approached one of the most fundamental elements in philosophical thought, the syllogism, which is usually related as a purely deductive mode of thought – although Mill likes to call this intellectual process 'ratiocination'.[1] Mill thinks that when truth claims take a propositional form, 'some logicians' express syllogisms in 'three *figures*'. This style of thought is set in a tradition initiated by Aristotle, who developed the principle of '*syllogistic*' reasoning.[2] This is a classical type of formal logical reasoning.

The following example – which Mill, as we will see, uses differently – clarifies the basic idea: *All humans are mortal: Socrates is human: Therefore, Socrates is mortal*. Here we have the three elements, or 'figures', as Mill calls them. The syllogism has two factual premises. The first factual premise is 'All humans are mortal': this is the major factual premise because, in this case, it makes a generic claim about 'all humans'. 'Socrates is human' is the minor factual premise; it makes a specific claim that a given individual is human. From these, the conclusion 'Socrates is mortal' follows as a clear and valid deduction. The conclusion is reasoned, and the conclusion is necessarily true. Put into the kind of notation Aristotle initiated and Mill also uses, the syllogism can be expressed as $A = B$. $C = A$. Therefore, $C = B$. What we set out here, to the traditional rational logician, are logical relations of entailment, something quite distinct from mapping inductive generalisations to point out patterns of contingent association. However, it is at this point that Mill offers his alternative and, he thinks, correct version.

The suggestion is that in the usual treatments of the syllogism, two errors have been made. One is the assumption that the purely intellectual truths produced are sufficient to discover and prove 'the larger half of the truths, whether of science or of daily life, which we believe'.[3] Given his broadly empirical outlook, Mill is not disposed to register agreement with this option. The other line is that there is 'uselessness and frivolity' with syllogistic reasoning in that operationally, it always begs the question, or more technically, commits the error of 'the *petitio principii*'.

Mill thinks this is an instructive error. Syllogisms are supposed to exemplify the deductive process, but it can be shown that they beg the question because the major premise already contains the answer reached in the conclusion. For example, when we state that 'All humans are mortal', this sounds like a verbal definition, but Mill's idea is that it is a generalisation from a range of particular experiences, and in fact, the reasoning through to the conclusion is inductive.[4]

Mill supposes that if we have always found that humans are mortal, our experience gives consistent evidence of human finitude. It follows that we might claim that 'All humans are mortal'. This claim stands as a strong empirical hypothesis that all humans, including Socrates, will also be mortal. Here we can say that the proposition ('All humans are mortal') is synthetic and probabilistic, not analytic and certain. If we defend the view that intellectual principles alone are needed to justify the deductive character of this reasoning, we are, Mill thinks,

---

[1] See *Logic* II: II: 1.
[2] See Aristotle (1989) A4 27 - A22 16, pp. 4-36.
[3] *Logic* II: III: 1.
[4] See *Logic* II: II: 3.

operating with a redundant 'system of metaphysics'.[1] If, however, we see that even syllogistic reasoning is inductive, we can make much better progress.

Mill thought that mathematics was explicable in the same inductive manner. Numbers did not have purely intellectual or rational significance: they arose from the experiences we had of collectable resemblances of association.[2] Mill's view is that from early in our experience, we encounter, amongst many other things, instances of two and then two more spoons of porridge – and so four spoons, cases (if we are lucky) of two and then two more and so four strawberries and so four. If we buy two pens and two pencils, we see that we have four items, and so on. Mill's idea is that the accumulated rule, '2+2 = 4', summarises this and is a handy guide for predictive work on future like cases. Mill is sure that the elemental truths of mathematics are sustained by the experiential success of mathematics for many cases. In contrast, we do not have experiences sufficient to warrant the generalised claims that *all cases* of '2+2 =' cannot not be 4.

Mill's thinking is that what we cast as logical truths are expressions of the strongest trends that are found in experience, and so essentially, all knowledge is inductive.[3] As Ryan points out, Mill's work within the tradition going back to Aristotle was, a generation later, swept away by the new and revolutionary lines of thought in mathematical and philosophical logic. Mill's thinking on these topics did not have a long shelf life, but on the other hand, the endeavour to ground mathematics and logic in experience and through inductive reasoning shows 'how far Mill was prepared to go in his attacks on intuitionism, and how far reaching his empiricism was'.[4]

The *Logic* moved on to consider the implications of the inductive method for the social sciences, cultivating an introduction to the social science of Ethology, the study of the development of human character. In the final sections of the text, Mill cultivated themes of great significance for his ongoing thought, the notion of the 'Art of Life', and the revised 'indirect' form of utility linked to ideas on human development which tie in with the defence of the liberties, to which we will return in later chapters.[5]

In contrast with the *Logic's* lengthy gestation, the *Principles of Political Economy* was written and published more quickly over the years 1845-47.[6] Mill had already written a set of five *Essays on Some Unsettled Questions of Political Economy* in 1830-31.[7] These were revised and published in 1844, by which time Mill was moving on his thinking on economics to consider, as the full title of the work suggests, to consider 'their applications to social philosophy'. Accordingly, the *Principles* elaborated a more systematic review of the subject, with Mill giving his version of the economic approaches that others (including James Mill) had already espoused, retaining a commitment to the free-market theme in Adam Smith and Ricardo, whereby the freedom of trade is seen as the means to defend and

---

[1] *Logic* II: II: 2.
[2] See *Logic* II: VI: 2.
[3] See Ryan (1987) pp. 75-85.
[4] Ryan (1987) p. 75. We shall see later how Mill applies his inductivism to the concept of necessity. See Chapter 6 below.
[5] See *Logic* VI: I-XII.
[6] See *Auto* pp. 132-133.
[7] See *Auto* p. 103. The Essays are reproduced in CW: IV pp. 229-339.

develop real economic values. Mill also developed more of a focus on social matters, with a move, giving attention to some forms of socialism and also affirming the importance of liberty for human well-being.

To illustrate this, the most obvious broad point is that the *Principles'* economic stance anticipates some themes in *On Liberty*: the defence of free trade presupposes the liberty of thought, discussion and action. For example, Mill thinks that economic development and the aspiration for a more equitable distribution of wealth will involve a commitment to an empowered view of human individuality. The aspiration to improve production within an economy 'depends more on the qualities of the human agents, than on the circumstances in which they work'.[1] It is consistent with this to argue that positive developments with be relative to the system of social organisation that is most 'consistent with the greatest amount of human liberty and spontaneity'.[2] Mill then eases into a point of abiding weight in his thought, that the view that 'after the means of subsistence are assured, the next in strength to personal wants of human beings is liberty'. Socialist and communist systems for governance give promise of social organisation with 'restraints', although these systems offer to give 'freedom in comparison with the present condition of the majority of the human race'.[3] However, in the long run, Mill thinks that the issue to focus on is how any approach to social organisation that gives attention to improving equality will lead to liberty being diminished, which would deprive humanity 'of one of the most elevated characteristics of human nature'.

We do not need a crystal ball to anticipate how Mill will lean: he writes with heartfelt concern about what is popularly termed the 'labouring classes'.[4] He dislikes this generalised term, not for semantic reasons, but because he considers that it is blindingly obvious that to labour is to work, and so, as a rule, no one is 'exempt from bearing their share of the necessary labour of human life'. Accordingly, Mill cannot 'recognise as either just or salutary, a state of society in which there is any "class" which is not labouring'. With regard to those who are particularly engaged with manual work, the classic tension for their organisation is whether they should operate under 'the theory of dependence'[5] or according to the theory 'of self-dependence'.

To live under a condition of dependence is to live as in traditional and historical circumstances. Analogous to military life, where 'the commander and officers of an army' take responsibility for the rest of the soldiers, the 'higher classes' in society take responsibility for the management and life of the rest, who, accordingly, 'should not be required or encouraged to think for themselves, or give to their own reflections or forecast an influential voice in the determination of their destiny'. This implies a life of 'passive and active obedience', of 'tutelage' – so again, by analogy, they are treated as perpetual 'children'. Mill, the radical-at-heart, has no truck with the theory of dependence; he sees it as long outmoded and restrictive, demanding to the individuals concerned and so to the wider condition of society. As his earlier comments suggest, he wants to promote individuality and for

---

[1] CW II p. 103.
[2] CW II p. 208.
[3] CW II p. 209. The socialism and communism that Mill has in mind is arises from his encounters with Owenism and from the French thinkers he had studied in the 1820s and early 1830s.
[4] CW III p. 758.
[5] CW III p. 759.

individuals to think for themselves, giving 'influential voice' to their own 'reflections and forecasts'. In a phrase harking back to Aristotle, Mill affirms that the 'well-being and well-doing of all labouring people'[1] – so in effect, all who work – rests 'on their own qualities', and the lesson for Mill's and our own modernity is that 'the well-being of a people must exist by means of the justice and self-government of... the individual citizens', and here, 'the prospect of the future depends on the degree to which they can be made rational beings'. Mill's notion of individuality included the view that positive development would be enhanced if there was an 'opening of industrial occupations freely to both sexes'.[2] The argument against dependency implies that women should not be socially, politically, morally or economically dependent upon men:

'Justice requires... that Law and custom should not enforce dependence... by ordaining that a woman, who does not happen to have a provision by inheritance, shall have scarcely any means open to her of gaining a livelihood, except as a wife and mother. Let women who prefer that occupation, adopt it, but that there should be no option, no other *carrière* possible for the great majority, except in the humbler departments of life, is a flagrant social injustice'.[3]

With regard to the scope envisaged for government, Mill is greatly on the side of an anti-bureaucratic promotion of small government as good government ticket. In a handy phrase, he affirms that 'individuals are the proper guardians of their own interests, and... government owes nothing to them but to save them from being interfered with by other people'.[4] The only limit here is to those incapable 'of acting in their own behalf' – and Mill thinks here of infants and those possessed of 'lunacy' or 'imbecility'.

The *Principles'* defence of individual 'spontaneity', of liberty, and of individuals as 'the proper guardians' of their interests recur, often more or less word for word, in *On Liberty*.[5] In this later work, Mill also sustains a strong defence of a division between the self and other-regarding spheres of individual life.[6] This is a matter emphatically rehearsed in the *Principles*. Mill's point is that whatever view we have of how we might ground 'the social union'[7], there is 'a circle around every individual human being, which no government, be it that of one, of a few, or of the many, ought to be permitted to overstep: there is a part of the life of every person who has come to years of discretion, within which the individuality of that person ought to reign uncontrolled either by any other individual or by the public collectively'.

With no overt challenge to human sociality, Mill elaborates the defence of individual liberty as follows:

---

[1] CW III p. 763.
[2] CW III p. 765.
[3] Mill here rehearses arguments he uses in many other contexts, as in *On Liberty*, in parliament in the 1860s and in *The Subjection of Women* (1869).
[4] CW III p. 803.
[5] See *OL* I: 11 (individual spontaneity) and I: 13 (individuals as proper guardians). On liberty, see, for example, *OL* I: 1 and I: 9.
[6] See, for example, *OL* I: 9 and IV: 2.
[7] CW III p. 938.

'There is, or ought to be, some space in human existence thus entrenched around, and sacred from authoritative intrusion, no one who professes the smallest regard to human freedom of dignity will call into question: the point to be determined is, where the limit should be placed; how large a province of human life this reserved territory should include. I apprehend that it ought to include all that part which concerns the life, whether inward or outward, of the individual, and does not affect the interests of others, or affects them only through the moral influence of example. With respect to the domain of the inward consciousness, the thoughts and feelings, and as much of external conduct as is personal only, involving no consequences, none at least of a painful or injurious kind, to other people; I hold that it is allowable in all, and in all the more thoughtful and cultivated often a duty, to assert and promulgate, with all the force they are capable of, their opinion of what is good or bad, admirable or contemptible, but not to compel others to conform to that opinion; whether the force used is that of extra-legal coercion, or exerts itself by means of the law'.[1]

The *Logic* and the *Principles* firmly established Mill as a leading intellectual figure, and from this time, the response, 'Read Mill' became a regular tactic in academic, intellectual and political circles when a problem arose in the wide areas of ethics, politics and philosophy that these writings covered.[2]

As well as these major writings, Mill continued to produce articles and reviews on social and ethical issues, developing a distinctive fusion of political liberalism set within a steadily enriched utilitarian structure. Mill gradually added the self-development of individuality as a mode of life that is set under utility as the criterion, with reference to liberty as the principle to set limits for individual, and thereby social development – as we shall see later when we come to the relevant section of *On Liberty*, with its defence of the liberty of the individual against the constraints of social opinion.[3]

Ongoing Philosophical Work and a Parliamentary Career

A remarkable feature of Mill's life is his ability to maintain a colossal workload. For example, if we take the period from October 1846 to January 1847, Mill was attending to matters in his day job; he was working on the *Principles*, he was also writing for the *Morning Chronicle* and producing forty-three leading articles for them over this period.[4] He was juggling life in Kensington with the family, writing long and engaged letters to a range of correspondents, and when possible, he was seeing Harriet. Mill was working and multitasking on an industrial scale.

During the 1850s, Mill worked up a good deal of material that came to publication later, including the work for which he is now best known. In 1859, Mill published *On Liberty* (1859), and later in the same year, a collection of essays, *Dissertations and Discussions* (in two volumes).[5] An essay on *Considerations on*

---

[1] Here, what Mill terms 'extra-legal coercion' becomes the tyranny of majority opinion or of custom in *On Liberty*.
[2] Himmelfarb notes that Leslie Stephen made this remark – see *OL* 'Editor's Introduction' p. 10. See also Capaldi (2012) p. 186 and 192.
[3] There is a long tradition of critical debate in Mill scholarship over the extent to which he is, or is not, successful in combining utility and liberty. For a helpful review of this see Gray & Smith (1991) p. 1ff. We explore this matter in the next chapter as well as in the review of the text of *On Liberty*.
[4] See CW XIII p. 705 n. 2.
[5] Mill later produced two more volumes in this series, the last coming out posthumously in 1875.

Representative Government (1861) discussed aspects of the parliamentary system with ideas for reform, and the ideas here were elaborated in many subsequent letters and debates. After publishing a series of articles in 1861 that introduced Utilitarianism, Mill worked the material into the book, *Utilitarianism* (1863). In the mid-1860s, Mill arranged with his publisher to produce cheaper editions of his works.[1] These more affordable editions sold well, expanding Mill's readership considerably.[2]

Throughout his active life of writing and campaigning, Mill had a strong interest in improving the role of parliament and for reforms that would make it a more effective deliberative assembly and legislature. He had some front-line experience of parliamentary affairs when in 1852, he was called as an expert witness to appear before the Select Committee on Income and Property Tax: in 1857, he was called before the Select Committee on the Bank Acts and then, in 1861 he was again called to appear before the Select Committee on Income and Property Tax.[3] His responses in these long and intense sessions are a model of cogent, informed expertise, with Mill's concern to reform matters towards greater justice and equality emerging as a consistent theme. One example illustrates his outlook: on the question of what proportion of a person's income should be untaxed, Mill thought along lines that remain persuasive, that it was 'right to exempt from income tax, and from all taxes as far as you can, the amount of income required for the necessaries of life'.[4]

From 1863, amidst his other endeavours, Mill turned his mind to philosophical criticism and wrote two studies of other philosophers: *Auguste Comte and Positivism* and *An Examination of Sir William Hamilton's Philosophy* – both published in 1865.

The book on Comte drew on Mill's longer-term thoughts about Comte and was a fusion of two substantial articles published in the *Westminster and Foreign Quarterly Review* in the April and July editions of 1865. The first article became the first part of the book, dealing with Comte's early thought; his 'later speculations'[5] were the focus of the second article and part two of the book. Needless to say, the estimate of Comte's thought we noted earlier received more extensive treatment. The early Comte is praised for elaborating a rationale for the social sciences; the later Comte is criticised for the illiberalism of his over-systematic view of the ideal social order.

Mill's book on Hamilton has become the least read of Mill's writings, not least because the thought of Sir William Hamilton is no longer of particular interest to readers at either a popular or scholarly level.[6] Hamilton, the Professor of Logic and

---

[1] *Auto* p. 156. This came about as his original publisher (John Parker: 1791-1870) had sold his business to Longmans. See also Mill XVI p. 1035 and pp. 1040-1041. The cheap edition of *OL* cost 1s 4d (around £4 in 2021 values) and when this and some of Mill's other works came out in this format, the sales far exceeded the publisher's expectations.

[2] The edition of the *Logic* used in preparing this book is of this type: a single-volume compact hardback with very small print, the text is printed in double columns over 622 pages: so it would be 1244 pages in normal printed pages.

[3] See CW V pp. 463-498 (1852); pp.499-547 (1857); pp. 549-598 (1861). The committee examining Mill in 1861 included the Chancellor of the Exchequer, W. E. Gladstone.

[4] CW V p. 473.

[5] CW X p. 328. *Auguste Comte and Positivism* is pp.261-368 of this Volume of Mill' Collected Works.

[6] See Ryan (1974) pp. 218-19. Sir William Hamilton (1788-1856) – Scottish philosopher. He was Professor of Logic and Metaphysics at Edinburgh University, 1836-1856.

Metaphysics at Edinburgh, was a widely respected scholar, well-grounded in the common-sense school of thought deriving from Thomas Reid.[1] He had also read into the German Idealists and was familiar with Kant's critical rationalism. His writings were extensive but mainly through the medium of articles published in the *Edinburgh Review* and through published lectures. Hamilton represented an approach in philosophy and especially to logic that Mill opposed in *A System of Logic*. Mill saw him as exemplifying too great a reliance on intuition to explain human knowledge, and in critiquing Hamilton's philosophical enterprise, he redeployed and refined insights long defended in the *Logic*.

Accordingly, the human capacity for reasoned investigation and analysis was not fully explicable as a purely intuitional or theoretical process. Mill intensified the objections to deductive and purely rational approaches, which he saw flowing in a modern tradition from the mathematically informed work of Descartes, leading to a form of 'mathematical cultivation'[2] to 'reign unbalanced and supreme'. The problem is that this gives an 'abuse of Deduction', as in the mathematician's habit of working to an 'ideal of Science in deriving all knowledge from a small number of axiomatic premises, accepted as self-evident, and taken for immediate intuitions of pure reason'.

Mill's habit, within a wider tradition of empiricism, is to emphasise with pejorative implications rational thought as having an indefensible reliance on intuition. Instead, reasoning in and through the inductive process is the preferred option to ground the natural and social sciences within an understanding of the cultural, historical and moral aspects of human experience. Mill, as ever, works with the wider project to, as Ryan notes, 'incorporate the insights of Coleridge into an enlarged utilitarian morality and theory of government'.[3] Against the idea of logic possessing a self-contained system of consistency, Mill argues for a 'more comprehensive Logic'[4] that considers how human reasoning arises through engagement with a wider range of phenomena than the conceptual domain beloved by the formal logicians. What the formal 'logic of mere consistency cannot do, the logic of the ascertainment of truth, the philosophy of evidence in its larger acceptation, can': the 'philosophy of evidence' – Mill's shorthand for reasoning from and through the inductive processes – has the following benefit:

'It can explain the function of the Ratiocinative process as an instrument of the human intellect in the discovery of truth, and can place it in its true correlation with the other instruments. It is therefore alone competent to furnish a philosophical theory of reasoning'.

Parliamentary matters came back into Mill's life in a more emphatic way in 1865, when, after years of resisting such invitations, he was persuaded to accept the offer to stand as a parliamentary candidate for the Westminster constituency.[5] Accepting such an invitation was difficult for Mill: he was resolute in not wanting to stand for

---

[1] Thomas Reid (1710-1796). Professor of Philosophy at Aberdeen and later of Moral Philosophy at Glasgow. His writings include *An Inquiry into the Human Mind, on the Principles of Common Sense* (1764).
[2] CW IX p. 485.
[3] Ryan (1987) p. x
[4] CW IX p. 371.
[5] See *Auto* pp. 156ff.

a political party – although his main sympathies were always more with the Liberals, who were, in turn, eager for him to stand. Preparing for the election, Mill promised his potential constituents that he would not take into parliament their views and concerns: he was adamant that he would not work in parliament for 'local interests'[1] but on the issues that were of concern to him and on the basis of which he was, perhaps, a worthy candidate. His thought was that the political arena was corrupted by people promising to do things they would never be willing or able to do just to be elected.[2] He aimed to use the opportunity to advance the causes represented in his writing, including electoral reform and promoting greater equality between women and men; he says that this made clear that he would be arguing for women to be represented in parliament 'on the same terms as men'.[3] He wanted to argue for land reform and vigorously campaign for his usual causes.

Despite these stipulations, Mill was prevailed upon to attend election meetings and to give some speeches. In one of the meetings at which he gave an address in explanation of his willingness to stand, he said that the 'advanced Liberalism' he represented suggested that the most important aim was not to increase the dependence of people upon the government but to aim for 'more freedom, more equality, and more responsibility of each person for himself'.[4] Liberty as a responsibility for each individual was, of course, a core idea in *On Liberty*. Redeploying the *Principles*' notion of 'proper' guardians, Mill says in the later work that:

'Each is the proper guardian of his own health, whether bodily *or* mental and spiritual. Mankind are greater gainers by suffering each other to live as seems good to themselves than by compelling each to live as seems good to the rest' (I: 13).

To his surprise, in the election of 1865, Mill won the seat and entered parliament.[5] He was duly active in arguing for various reforms, including working on his favoured theme by bringing a petition before parliament to extend the voting to include women, as he had said when seeking election.[6] Mill hoped the measures he supported would be included in the 1867 Reform Act. In this, he was disappointed, but he considered that the debates in which he defended women's entitlement to equality helped strengthen the case for reforms in the near future. Mill sometimes linked this to his consistent opposition to slavery, as evidenced in his remarks in support of the cause of the Union in the American Civil War.[7] Outside of parliament, Mill was also elected as Rector of the University of St Andrews, serving in that role from 1865 to 1868.

During his time in parliament, one matter well illustrates Mill's capacity to take on issues of controversy, and it also sheds some light on a later issue of philosophical criticism. In 1866, it became clear that E. J. Eyre, the Governor of

---

[1] *Auto* p. 158.
[2] Mill writes more on this theme in his *Considerations on Representative Government* – see *Util* pp. 272-273. He was much influenced in his ideas for electoral reform by the ideas of Thomas Hare (1806-1891), a proponent of a view of proportional representation.
[3] *Auto* p. 158.
[4] CW XXVIII p. 23.
[5] See *Auto* pp. 156-172.
[6] This was in June, 1866. See CW XVI p. 1164.
[7] See for example, CW XXIX pp 379-380 and CW XXXII p. 141.

Jamaica, had been severe to the point of brutality in suppressing an uprising.[1] Troubles on the Island led to Eyre imposing martial law, and in reimposing law and order, and on his commands, some 439 Jamaicans were killed, and a popular local politician, George Gordon, was executed on very dubious grounds. Mill served on the Jamaica Committee, and although the British Government set up a Royal Commission to investigate Eyre, and although he was relieved of his post for issues of mismanagement, Mill was not alone in thinking that this was enough. Mill was voted in as Chairman of the Jamaica Committee, replacing a colleague who saw no way that Eyre could be successfully prosecuted. Mill and the rest of the Committee felt that Eyre needed to be brought to justice on criminal charges.

The case became major news and split opinion down the middle. Mill, in his capacity as Chairman of the Jamacia Committee, raised the case in parliament but made little progress.[2] Conservative opinion rallied around Eyre, who had a considerable and largely successful career in exploration and governance behind him. A defence fund was set up to support him, including Carlyle, amongst other eminent figures.

The case centred on whether martial law – in operations during the disturbances – trumped the operations of the regular civil and criminal law. Mill's arguments were about the extent to which the law, the criminal law, in particular, applied equitably to all. He thought it did and wrote that he had 'never in the whole course' of his life 'felt more clear as to the course indicated by the principles' that he had 'always endeavoured to promulgate'.[3] He thought to leave such matters unquestioned would put 'the ties of civil society'[4] at risk and that 'the real or supposed crimes of men in authority should be subject to judicial examination, is the most important guarantee of English liberty'.[5]

On behalf of the Committee, the lawyer J. F. Stephen, a utilitarian and a member of the Political Economy Club, argued before the magistrates of Shropshire (where Eyre lived on his return from Jamaica) that Eyre should be committed for trial. This proceeding and other legal measures did not work, and Stephen duly advised the Committee that no further legal action could be taken. Mill was not satisfied and relieved Stephen of his duties. He found another lawyer for the Committee, but Stephen's legal advice was correct, and although matters dragged on into 1868, the case against Eyre collapsed.[6]

Mill received much criticism for his commitment to the Eyre case. It is probable that the unpopularity he suffered for his campaign upset many of his voters, although there were other issues he had supported that were also lacking kerb appeal.

---

[1] See *Auto* pp. 165ff and Reeves (2007) p. 376-382. E. J. Eyre (1815-1901). Eyre had a distinguished career as an explorer in Australia, and had been awarded the Gold Medal of the Royal Geographical Society in 1847. He had published journals and other accounts of his explorations. See https://adb.anu.edu.au/biography/eyre-edward-john-2032
[2] Mill's speeches on the disturbance in Jamacia as given in the House of Commons can be read in CW XXVIII pp 90, 93ff and 123.
[3] Mill CW XVI p. 1410.
[4] Mill CW XVI p. 1411.
[5] Mill CW XVI p. 1412.
[6] In 1869, Mill wrote in a letter that J. F. Stephen was 'always brutal' in manner and not someone who was always consistent in what he said or did – see CW XVII p. 1600.

Another focus for Mill in his parliamentary career that comes into this category was working to promote a system of proportional representation that he came across and which he thought would greatly help minorities to gain appropriate representation.[1] In discussing parliamentary and other reforms, Mill often spoke on this issue in the House of Commons.[2]

In the election of 1868, Mill was neither surprised nor disappointed when he lost his seat.[3] A greater longer-term threat was to emerge from J. F. Stephen, who had gone to India to do more legal work, but on the long journey home, he wrote some articles later published as the book *Liberty, Equality, Fraternity* (1873), mounting a full-scale assault on Mill's teachings in *On Liberty*.[4]

Final Years

Once out of parliament, Mill turned his mind to working on revisions to his *Logic* and *Principles* and engaged in much support through letter-writing for the ongoing reforms he supported. A particular focus remained on working for reforms to improve the position of women. As we have seen, he had written about this in the *Principles* and had campaigned about it for years in his journalism as well as while in parliament: once free of his political duties, Mill thought that the case for reform was building, so he decided to publish the essay, *The Subjection of Women* (1869).

As we noted, Mill wrote the essay in 1861, developing some of the ideas from *On Liberty* to focus on the political and legal entitlements of women. Mill asserted that the principle of the 'freedom of individual choice is now known to be the only thing which procures the adoption of the best processes, and thrown each operation into the hands of those who are best qualified for it'.[5] This knowledge would be grounded in anyone well-versed in the principles of liberty found in *On Liberty*, and it follows – Mill as consistent as ever on this point – that if we thought the principles of individualism and liberty right, then:

'... we ought to act as we believed it, and not to ordain that to be born a girl instead of a boy, any more than to be born black instead of white, or a commoner instead of a nobleman shall decide a person's position through all life – shall interdict people from all the more elevated social positions, and from all, except a few, respectable occupations'.

In this clear defence of personhood as a core unifying concept for humanity, as well as for the correlated equality of opportunity for all, Mill was consistent with his

---

[1] *Auto* p. 160 and pp. 169f: see also *Util* pp. 269-279.
[2] See for example, CW XXVIII pp.239-242.
[3] See *Auto* pp. 173f. Mill was defeated by a Mr. W. H Smith, son of the founder of a certain bookseller and newsagent. Mill had defeated Smith in 1865: in 1868 it transpired that Smith had spent an inordinate amount on his campaign to win the Westminster seat. See Reeves (2007) pp. 407-408.
[4] J. F. Stephen's book came out right at the end of Mill's life, building on earlier reviews he made written. Although Stephen was critical of the ideas of *On Liberty* in particular, he paid tribute to Mill's endeavours and contributions in such works as the *Logic* and the *Principles of Political Economy*. He also wrote an obituary in the *Pall Mall Gazette*, in which he said that with the death of Mill, 'one of the tenderest and most passionate hearts that ever set to work an intellect of iron was laid to rest' (CW XV pp. 787-788 n. 13). We consider Stephen's critique of Mill later in this study. See Chapter 12 below.
[5] Mill (1988) p. 18.

earlier writing as well as his campaigning in parliament. Perhaps due to the positive radicalism of these ideas, *The Subjection of Women* did not make the hoped-for impression in the following years. It was not until the twentieth century that the text began to make an impact as an increasingly pertinent study in the case for equality and the development of feminist thought.

Through the years 1867 to 1869, Mill's literary endeavours took on an element of paternal regard, as he collaborated with his friend Alexander Bain and others to update, revise and publish a new edition of his father's book of almost forty years before, the *Analysis of the Phenomena of the Human Mind*.[1]

Mill's correspondence in this period remains as full as ever and contains one startling alteration of view: throughout his life, Mill held French thought and Continental thought in general in high regard. In *Hamilton*, Mill evidenced his ongoing awareness of recent trends in French intellectual life.[2] But as we have seen, he was also critical of the emphasis on intuitionism, and writing (in 1869) to the political economist John Elliott Cairnes, Mill ventures the more critical view:

'French philosophic writers seem to me decidedly inferior in closeness and precision of thought to the best English, and more in the habit of paying themselves with phrases and abstractions'.[3]

Mill's correspondence also extended in some ways that offer surprising links to Nietzsche and his correspondents. In February 1870, Mill wrote[4] to the Danish scholar Georges Brandes, who had arranged a Danish translation of *The Subjection of Women*. Mill and Brandes met later that year. In the 1880s, Brandes was more or less the first academic in Europe to read and understand Nietzsche, characterising his work as a form of 'aristocratic radicalism'.[5] Brandes' promotion of Nietzsche was a great support to Nietzsche, whose capacity to write and publish was countered by the fact that, in his active lifetime, almost nobody read him. Mill also corresponded with the French cultural historian Hippolyte Tain – with whom Nietzsche was to correspond in 1886.[6] Mill's interest in developing his ideas through new contacts continued with his thoughts resonating through letters and discussion as well as though his wirings. As ever, Mill enjoyed walks in the country, collecting new botanical specimens to cultivate at home. He was busy, engaged, and

---

[1] Bain (1810-1877), a logician and psychologist, became a longstanding friend and correspondent. Bain wrote *The Senses and the Intellect* (1855) and *The Emotions and the Will* (1859) and reviewed issues Mill had examined in the *Logic*. The two exchanged many letters criticising each other's work, but in a spirit of great mutual respect. Bain later wrote a study of Mill – *John Stuart Mill* (London, 1882). James Mill's book was duly published: *Analysis of the Phenomena of the Human Mind, with notes illustrative and critical by Alexander Bain, Andrew Findlater and George Grote*, edited, with additional notes by John Stuart Mill (London 1869). See also CW XXXII p. 205.
[2] CW IX p. 250.
[3] CW XVII p. 1664. John Elliott Cairnes (1823-1875) – political economist and professor of political economy at Trinity College, Dublin and later at University College, London. Cairnes and Mill have a long-running correspondence on a hight intellectual plane. For more of the Mill's criticisms of French intellectuals see CW IX p. 485.
[4] See CW XVII p. 1699ff. See also pp.1874f for another letter from 1872. Georges Brandes (1842-1927). Friedrich Nietzsche (1844-1900).
[5] See Loxton (2021) p. 17 and p. 111.
[6] See CW XVII pp. 1751ff. See also Loxton (2021) p. 111. Hippolyte Tain (1828-1893).

in mostly good health over the next few years, spending at least half of each year in Avignon.

Mill and Helen Taylor went on a regular trip to Avignon in April 1873, intending to spend time studying and relaxing. On Saturday, May 3rd, Mill took a long walk looking to extend his botanical collection. On his return, he developed a chill that soon developed complications and a fever. His condition quickly worsened. The doctor was called to attend and found that Mill had developed the bacterial infection, erysipelas, which proved resistant to any treatments. Mill weakened, and his life ebbed.

J. S. Mill died on Wednesday, May 7th 1873.[1] Apparently, his last words to Helen Taylor were: 'You know that I have done my work'.[2] During his lifetime, Mill's work ensured that his reputation exceeded those of his father and Jeremy Bentham. He was regarded as the 'Saint of Rationalism' by the Liberal politician and Prime Minister, W. E. Gladstone.[3] As a consequence of his prolific writing and his capacity to address the problems of the day, his views had wide influence, making him the leading public intellectual of his age, full of vigour and interest, open to change and innovation, fuelled by a reforming passion and informed by a critical mind.

Mill's general approach to philosophy reflects the critical and radical tradition of British empiricism and the Enlightenment into which he melds a significant influence from Romanticism. Mill was thirty-one when the Victorian age took flight. He lived in a period where the development of an industrial economy was operating on a worldwide scale. On the home front, the nation was transformed by the expansion of the railway system, and on the social front, activism and philanthropic pressure were moving forward a range of reforms. The population grew rapidly, and a prevailing ethos was of nature, so life being subject to manipulation, change and development through human endeavour and the use of reason. Not least, this progress and development came through various modes of applied understanding. Through such efforts and the power of reason, humanity was able individually and collectively to triumph over the constraints of the natural world, just as through moral and artistic achievement, humanity was able to conquer instinct.

In relation to this, Mill's outlook and his writing were consistently in support of liberalism and reforms, with liberal individualism becoming a stronger theme as his life progressed. Mill saw the natural and humane sciences as operating with parallel, experimental methods of discovery. In the earlier phase of his life, he was committed to the utilitarian doctrine that right or good actions are those which result in 'the greatest happiness to the greatest number'. Mill steadily modified utilitarianism over the years before he published *Utilitarianism* in 1863, but despite this development, utility, in some form, remains the last word on ethical matters for him.[4]

---

[1] In more recent times penicillin or some other similar antibiotic would have been the favoured treatment to cure erysipelas. See https://dermnetnz.org/topics/erysipelas
[2] CW XVII p. 1952 n. 1.
[3] See Reeves (2007) p. 2. Mill was not, of course, a rationalist in the philosophical sense: he was a rationalist in the more popular sense meant by Gladstone, one who sought reasons and justification for the views one espoused.
[4] See *OL* I:11 and Chapters 4 and 7 below.

Mill is also, not least in *On Liberty*, emphatic in promoting individuality and liberty for individual thought and action as the basic presupposition for development in and for a just and progressive society. The question of how liberty and utility are to be defended in relation and proportion to each other remains an engaging one for Mill's readers.

The bronze statue of John Stuart Mill in Victoria Embankment Gardens – the Temple Section – as photographed in August 2021 by the author. The statue was designed and cast by Thomas Woolner RA in 1878.[1]

[1] T. Woolner (1825-1892). For more information on Woolner see the Royal Academy website - www.royalacademy.org.uk › name › thomas-woolner-ra

4. Utility in Transition

Looking over the trajectory of Mill's life and thought, we noted that after an early commitment to Benthamite utilitarianism, Mill emerged from his crisis, having already initiated some modifications to his understanding of utilitarianism as an ethical, social and political theory. Since this and subsequent modifications have significance for the later production of *On Liberty*, it is important to track what Mill did to revise and develop utility so that, as he came to think, it worked in conjunction and not in conflict with liberty. A common objection to Mill's project in *On Liberty* is that the principle of liberty is bound to conflict with utility. An examination of what Mill at least thought he was doing will aid us in either debunking or seeing the weight of this objection.

To make sense of what is at stake, we start by looking at the ideas Mill had in mind when he adopted the utilitarian mode of thought and action and what he says later as he moves on through his life. To illustrate some points, we will refer to *On Liberty*, mindful of the fact that the detail of the text will be explored in the next part of this study.

Mill's Evangelical Utility

In the *Autobiography*, Mill has an eloquent account of coming into an appreciation of utilitarian thinking. He writes with evangelical zeal about the transformative experience of conversion to the full appreciation of the merits of utility. He understands that his education had been within the outlook of Bentham's notion of 'the greatest happiness'.[1] While Mill appreciates that he has imbibed this outlook in general, it was from 1820, as he began reading Bentham's works, that the power of utilitarian thinking 'burst upon me with all the force of novelty'. What Mill likes at this point is that Bentham shows how so many aspects of thought and morality are based on feelings and sentiments.[2] Such notions as 'natural rights'[3], 'right reason', 'the moral sense' and 'the law of nature', are commonly presented as if they have some intrinsic value, but Bentham's presentation shows that they are aspects of sentiment, and so sentiment set up 'as its own reason'.[4] The empirically-based utility of Bentham sweeps aside the concept-rich ideas of traditional schemes of thought and replaces them with a calculative method for classifying 'the morality of actions' around the maxims of the greatest happiness.

Mill is struck with the realisation that he is encountering 'a new era in thought'. In effect, it was a style of thought emphasising practical matters and problem-solving rather than intellectual contemplation. With the precise and interrogative disposition he possessed, Mill thought that the utilitarian approach had a scientific

---

[1] *Auto* p. 39.
[2] See the editor's note, *Auto* p. 198: Mill was reading a French translation of Bentham's work, *Traités de législation* (Paris, 1802), later republished in English as *An Introduction to the Principles of Morals and Legislation*.
[3] See *Auto* p. 39 and Mill's 1833 essay 'Remarks on Bentham's Philosophy' in CW X p. 5.
[4] *Auto* p. 39.

character and that the capacity to classify moral actions was close to the methods of classification found, for example, in Botany.[1]

The clarity and the humanistic, secular tenor of utilitarianism appealed to Mill – and many others since. Utilitarianism presents as an ethical scheme to sort out moral dilemmas, but equally as a social and economic method for decision-making, operable as an instrument for social improvement. It offers a clear method of determining the best means to the desired outcomes, shaping and defending responsible moral decision-making free from metaphysical clutter or over-reliance on personal or subjective whims.

Once Mill had finished this reading of Bentham, he felt that 'the principle of utility' was, as he puts it:

'... the keystone which held together the detached and fragmentary component parts of my knowledge and beliefs. It gave unity to my conception of things. I now had opinions; a creed, a doctrine, a philosophy; in one of the best senses of the word, a religion; the inculcation and diffusion of which could be made the principal outward purpose of a life'.[2]

The enthusiasm of Mill's commitment fuels confidence in the creed of utility to underpin his thinking, writing, debating and work on into the 1820s, with the criterion for the worth of an action being given by the calculation of the extent to which a proposed action could be seen as delivering the greatest happiness to the greatest number, subject to the principle that the interests of individuals were considered to be equal. Mill sees this as a credible and compelling explanation for personal, social, political and economic life, efficacious for the general enhancement of the human condition and worthy of endeavour as a form of religious commitment 'in one of the best senses' possible.

As we have seen, Mill's life was one of intense activity: work at India House, articles for papers and journals and the organisation of and participation in debates. This wide range of activities later grew into the reading and research that led to him writing books. Working with this range of intensity is a life-long endeavour for Mill, and anyone reading the collection of his *Letters* will be struck by how Mill's life exemplifies the description of the human condition in *On Liberty*, of being 'progressive' (I:11).

The crucial matter is that as Mill's life unfolds, his thinking about the operational status of utilitarianism alters and evolves, as is evident from how he shifts the orientation of his utilitarian creed, as we can now show.

---

[1] See *Auto* p. 40. Botanical study was one of Mill's abiding pastimes. See for example, CW XII p. 50, pp. 67-69; and CW XIV pp. 41-42; CW XV pp. 566-67, pp. 621-22 and pp. 704-05; CW XVII pp. 1826-27.
[2] *Auto* p. 40.

Mill's Development of Utility

A clear turning point in Mill's attitude to utility is evident in his comments in a letter of 1829. He says it is right to affirm that it is the duty and purpose of governments to operate 'for man's good: and the highest and most important of these purposes is the improvement of man himself as a moral and intelligent being'.[1] In an early version of his larger view of utility, Mill remarks that 'the united forces of society' cannot be 'directed towards one single end'. This comment, recalling the one made in the *Autobiography*, is tied to how humans 'do not come into the world to fulfil one single end, and there is no single end which if fulfilled even in the most complete manner would make them happy'.

Here we see Mill, some thirty years before publishing *On Liberty*, qualifying the role that society can play in enhancing life: he embraces a sense of human variety, diversity and individuality as something that can only be defended consistently with the revised and developed notion of utility which is emerging and within which far greater regard can be given to individuality. All of this is in stark contrast to the trend to uniformity and the appeal to the generalised greatest number seen in the earlier Benthamite mode of thought. By rejecting the idea of 'one single end' for the realisation of happiness, Mill has a theme that has a considerable impact on the longer-term development of his thought. Linked to this is the sense that creative individuality is a very distinct and important factor in the project of cultivating a civilized society.

Mill's re-engineering of utility, as suggested in his correspondence, is elaborated in phases over the next few years. In another letter from 1830, Mill touches on the theme of truth and the human quest to pursue better insights and understanding.[2] He says that the best way of 'eradicating error' is to find and put into tension 'the opposite truth'. The contrast between this and the 'moral or intellectual state of mind' that gives rise to error allows the existing and novel truths to develop. Mill is worried about the habit some have of promoting the use of the '*esprit critique*' – a critical spirit – to attack the views they oppose because this method inhibits the more effective process of looking for truth 'in the midst of error'. This notion of how to progress understanding, with the sense that we acquire better and more refined truths from examining alternative perspectives rather than looking to use some absolute truth, is highly consistent with the fallibilistic sense of truth that we have in *On Liberty*[3], and we also have an anticipation of the theme of truth colliding with error.[4]

Mill's consistency in affirming these ideas can be seen from points in a letter to Carlyle reviewing the affinity and common ground between them in their work; he says that they share a task of speaking 'a certain portion of special Truth'.[5] He means to suggest they are each offering distinct perspectives on the truths from experience, insight and reflection on life, and explains that if a person 'does the best he can', working with 'a sincere mind', and gains all the 'insight into a thing' that

---

[1] CW XII p. 36 . Mill is writing to Gustave d'Eichthal. See the comment akin to this in Auto p. 82, and cited in Chapter 2 above.
[2] CW XII pp. 45-46. Mill again writes to d'Eichthal.
[3] See *OL* II: 41.
[4] See *OL* II: 42.
[5] CW XII p. 111.

is possible, then what can be truthfully presented is 'itself a truth'. Mill moves towards a form of reasoned perspectivism – a person can truly present what they have truthfully developed as an idea or insight – they can 'speak their truth' as some might say today. Mill generally assumes that this is not a self-justifying process or one that is wholly subjective but rather one linked to a form of dialogic assessment that provides a means to review proposed truths.

One such means now open to all who can read them is provided by Mill's letters, which contain much interactive discussion over all manner of points and insights. Mill is notable for asking for and responding to corrective insights and better truths from his correspondents. What he says to Carlyle is illustrated by some remarks making an analogy with painting.[1] Assuming a pre-expressionist mode of painting, Mill suggests that the artist paints things as he sees them, and similarly, the thinker can present the results of what he has experienced, reflected on, and considered, and so present a way of seeing and a mode of thought about some aspect of life. The implication is that Mill sees reality and then writes about it differently from Carlyle – a sign of Mill's pluralism.

In a letter to Sterling, Mill, in a low moment, relates how he has given up any aspiration to be any 'happier' than he is in life.[2] This is a far from complex encoding of a withdrawal from orthodox utilitarianism, where the greatest happiness principle holds sway. Instead, Mill favours something closer to the classical notion of *eudaimonia*: 'well-being' – a notion we will be considering later as it comes into play explicitly in *On Liberty*.[3] What Mill indicates here is strengthened in comments to Carlyle in another letter, where he comments on the 'old narrow school of Utilitarians', which he refers to very much in the past tense as something that has faded away. He says that he was one of 'the narrowest of them all'[4] – this in consequence of his upbringing – which is, in effect, a criticism of the narrowness of the educative outlook in which he was schooled by his father.

Writing again to Carlyle, Mill suggests that 'a great change' might be detected in his character.[5] He explains:

'... a change, not from any kind of *in*sincerity, but *to* a far greater sincerity than belonged to me before. This change has been progressive, and had barely begun to take place when you were in London two years ago. I was then, and had been for some years, in an intermediate state – a state of reaction from logical-utilitarian narrowness of the very narrowest kind, out of which after much unhappiness and inward struggling I had emerged, and taken temporary relief in its extreme opposite'.[6]

Here we have a hint of the struggles of the years of crisis, and a repetition of the critique of the narrow form of utility, again placed in the past tense. The 'opposite' Mill has in mind is the poetic romanticism he had been overwhelmed by in the late 1820s: this is contrasted with the 'logical utilitarian narrowness' of his earlier state, which he says had been a position 'of intense philosophic intolerance' grounded in

---

[1] See CW XII p. 111.
[2] CW XII p. 100.
[3] See *OL* II: 32 and Chapters 8 and 9 below.
[4] CW XII p. 128.
[5] CW XII p. 204.
[6] CW XII p. 205.

'the onesidedness of the understanding', from which, he thinks, only limited aspects of the truths in question could be seen. Mill thinks that in this earlier phase, even his utilitarian friends saw him as one who exaggerated 'the doctrines of utilitarianism'. Moreover, he thinks 'one-sidedness' was 'almost the one great evil in human affairs' – one that 'had been the bane of my own teachers' – here he is, without naming them, criticising the approach of Jeremy Bentham and James Mill.[1] With clinical precision, Mill analyses his younger self: 'a schoolboy fresh from logic-school' who had never 'conversed with a reality'.[2]

In his new operational mode, Mill uses spatial imagery to explain how his condition changed. Previously, he had generalised from what he now appreciated was only 'one of the innumerable aspects of Reality': then, with the new approach, he went '*all round* every object... so as to have the best chance of seeing all sides'. Mill explains that he does not doubt that his life involves a determination to respect those who have clear and strongly held views: 'most opposite opinions' could be seen to some 'good & truth in the positive part'. In addition, Mill admits to Carlyle that he is, and is in all probability remaining 'a utilitarian'.[3] However, he affirms that he is 'not one of the people called utilitarians'. He means that he is no longer one of the customary utilitarians in the style of Jeremy Bentham and James Mill, but one moving on towards a view grounded in a modified version of utility and, crucially, a richer notion of human nature.

By the time Mill wrote to Carlyle on his rather contingent association with utilitarianism, he had written the first of two articles on Bentham, the 'Remarks on Bentham's Philosophy (1833), which was built upon in the much more substantial essay – 'Bentham' – that he wrote and published in 1838.[4]

In these writings, the first of which came the year after Bentham's death, Mill gives Bentham's philosophy a highly critical review. He notes how Bentham assumes that 'happiness'[5] – as ever the core value in utilitarianism – is defined in terms of 'pleasure and exemption from pain'. This alone is said to have the status of being 'desirable in itself'. Anything else in the scheme is 'solely as means to that end'. The wider aim of the 'greatest possible happiness' becomes 'the only fit purpose for human thought and action, and consequently, all morality and government'. These are bold, clear aspirations, but Mill thinks some difficulties must be addressed and resolved. He suggests that the principle of 'the greatest-happiness'[6] cannot rest 'solely' on 'the probable *consequences*' of acts aiming for the end of the greatest happiness. In a phrase that anticipates the view he will use later, he suggests that what is needed is 'a more enlarged understanding' of the 'greatest-happiness principle'.

---

[1] CW XII p. 206.
[2] CW XII p. 205.
[3] CW XII p. 207.
[4] Both pieces are in Mill CW X: 'Remarks on Bentham's Philosophy' is pp. 3-18 and 'Bentham' is pp. 75-115. The 'Remarks on Bentham' was originally a piece written for E. L. Bulmer's *England and the English* (1833), where it appeared anonymously as an appendix. Mill alludes to the piece in two of his letters; see CW XII p. 152 and p.236. 'Bentham' was first published in the *London and Westminster Review* in August 1838. Both essays have been widely anthologised.
[5] CW X p. 5.
[6] CW X p. 7.

The problem Mill sees is that Bentham assumes that the 'principle of Utility'[1] can be linked seamlessly to the 'principle of specific consequences'. In other words, utilitarianism is committed to a consequentialist approach. As Bentham presents it, utilitarianism is a self-evidently clear method for ethical decision-making. With the commitment to consequentialism, ethical solutions are presented as if they are 'fully justified; and any disapprobation or aversion entertained towards the individual by reason of it, is set down from that time forward as a prejudice or superstition'. The difficulty Mill sees with this is the problem that, for the individual at the point of deliberation over an ethical matter, future consequences cannot be in evidence: desired consequences can be envisaged and estimated, but at the point of action, how far this or that course of action can render happiness and avoid displeasure can only be estimated. Thus, while utility has apparent ease of operation and is understandably popular, it operates misleadingly in that such action as may be estimated as 'necessarily or probably productive of unhappiness', cannot be safely assumed to be 'fully justified' to produce happiness. It is neither a 'prejudice' nor a 'superstition' to point this out. Mill thinks it is more accurate to the human situation to see the considerations of possible or probable consequences as a part of what ethical deliberation entails in the process of reflection that thoughtful individuals undertake in deciding on the best courses of action.[2]

Mill thinks a core issue is that Bentham has a method that lacks a proper consideration of 'the state and character of mind' within the individual making and so originating the ethical act in question. Mill's point is that the neglect of the cause gives rise to a problem with registering the consequence. Giving attention to the 'entire moral being of the agent' is the suggested correction, and with the more complex view of the individual in mind, Mill suggests that humans agents in moral scenarios are 'swayed by a balance of motives, or, if you will, of interests'.[3] By 'interests', Mill wants to include the range of components an individual can have in mind as contributing to what can be conceived as 'the *means*' to 'an *end*'.[4] Mill thinks that the individual's motives will be 'innumerable', not least because 'there is nothing whatever which may not become an object of desire or dislike by association'. Accordingly, Bentham's reduction of all motives to self-interest or sympathy as related to 'the greatest-happiness principle' limits the truer state and range of being human.

In developing his critique, Mill references Bentham's work of 1824, the *Book of Fallacies*, and exposes his former mentor's commitment to the 'predominance of the selfish principle in human nature'.[5] Mill's revised view of these matters is that the view of human nature here assumed is 'perverting'[6] the 'whole moral nature' of those who employ it and is decidedly 'inconsistent with all rational hope for good for the human species'. As with the earlier reference to Mill's rationalism noted in

---

[1] CW X p. 8.
[2] CW X p. 12.
[3] CW X p. 12.
[4] CW X p. 13.
[5] For example, that 'there exists not, *nor ever can exist*, that human being in whose instance any public interest he can have will not, in so far as depends upon himself, have been sacrificed to his own personal interest'. CW X p. 14 – Mill is quoting from Bentham's *Book of Fallacies* (London 1824) p. 363.
[6] CW X p. 15.

66

respect of Gladstone's comment, 'rational hope' in Mill's usage here does not mean a resort to rationalism in the style of Continental philosophy: Mill simply means he hopes for a better-reasoned justification for the coherence of a person's actions with their beliefs.

In the later and much more ornate treatment of Bentham in the essay of 1838, to which the essay of 1840 on Coleridge was a companion piece, Mill praises Bentham as 'the father of English innovation'[1], acknowledging the importance of introducing utilitarian thinking and reforms to the law: Bentham is thus 'a great *subversive*, or, in the language of continental philosophers, the great *critical* thinker of his age and country'. But this greatness is leavened by the qualification that the greatness of Bentham comes less from his own writings than 'through the minds and pens which those writings fed'. Here we feel that the minds and pens of James and J. S. Mill are uppermost in mind. Thus Bentham was 'not a great philosopher, but he was a great reformer in philosophy'[2] – his contribution was to introduce something 'greatly needed': this is not the specific 'doctrines' he propounded, so much as 'his mode of arriving at them' – the 'habits and modes of investigation which are essential to the ideas of science'. Here Mill means to emphasise the analytical and inductive methods by means of which Bentham was 'treating wholes by separating them into their parts, abstractions by resolving them into Things'. All-round, Bentham can be considered 'among the great intellectual benefactors of mankind'.[3]

These points of positive assessment are but decorative comments around and amongst more emphatic criticism of the limitations that can be found in Bentham's thought, with the limitations being akin to those identified in Mill's earlier 'Remarks'. Thus Bentham is said to make a presentation that retains too overt a habit of 'surveying a complex object (though every so carefully) in only one of its aspects'.[4] This leads to the perspective we saw Mill identifying in some of his letters, to do with Bentham's partial insights: now he is said to have, at best, 'half of the truth'[5] and to be 'one-sided'[6] with his solutions.

A reason for this partiality is that Mill thinks Bentham 'failed in deriving light from other minds'[7] – there is little evidence that he had an 'accurate knowledge' of other 'schools of thought' and plenty to suggest that he thought that 'they could teach him nothing worth knowing'. Thus, unless an approach in moral philosophy was based on 'a recognition of utility as the moral standard', it was considered speculative and to fall into 'vague generalities'.[8] What Bentham needed – and what, of course, Mill himself does – is to 'study the opinions of mankind in all ages and nations'.[9] Instead, Bentham tries to develop his philosophy 'wholly out of the materials furnished by his own mind', and worse, his own mind suffered the fault of 'incompleteness… as a representative of universal human nature'. The particular shortfall in Bentham's mentality was his 'deficiency of Imagination', which meant

---

[1] CW X p. 79.
[2] CW X p. 83.
[3] CW X p. 115.
[4] CW X p. 89.
[5] CW X p. 94.
[6] CW X p. 108.
[7] CW X p. 90.
[8] Again Mill alludes to Bentham's *Book of Fallacies*.
[9] CW X p. 91.

he was incapable of understanding and entering into the thought and feelings of others.[1] Here Mill does not weigh the years of financial support and friendship Bentham had given to the Mill family: the focus is on the style and implications of Bentham's intellectual work.

A specific problem that Mill is keen to press is that these matters all centre on the limitations that arise from Bentham's reductive view of the human condition. His view is limited by being 'wholly empirical'[2], and the 'empiricism' is 'of one who has had little experience'. Bentham cannot recognise that human beings are 'capable of pursuing spiritual perfection as an end'.[3] Mill is not thinking of matters when he refers to 'spiritual perfection': he has explicitly in mind how a person can seek the virtues of 'the conformity of his own character to his standard of excellence, without hope of good or fear of evil from other sources than his own inward consciousness'. Matters of '*honour* and personal dignity' and the 'love of *beauty*'[4] are amongst the other aretaic values Mill suggests that are important but neglected by Bentham.[5]

Mill considers Bentham to have in mind an inadequate concept of what it is to be human, and the signal problem for Bentham is that he fails to see that mature reflection on morality requires not just a reasoned method but also an understanding and programme for human 'self-education'.[6] The human capacity for self-development is vital to Mill, and the potential for personal development and progression is the 'coequal' and enlarging aspect Bentham missed; in contrast, Mill's richer notion of 'utility, or happiness'[7] is emerging in a manner consistent with what is later alluded to in *On Liberty* as 'utility in its largest senses, grounded on the permanent interests of man as a progressive being'.[8] What Mill, in the 1838 essay, says as a contribution to this larger view, is that the criterion of happiness used in utilitarianism is:

'... much too complex and indefinite an end to be sought except through the medium of various secondary ends concerning which there may be, and often is, agreement among persons who differ in their ultimate standard; and about which there does in fact prevail a much greater unanimity among thinking persons, that might be supposed from their diametrical divergence on the great questions of moral metaphysics'.[9]

Mill's emergent view also included something he reviewed in his correspondence with Carlyle, namely, a recognition of 'the infinite notion of Duty' as amongst the aspects of life and thought that contribute to the whole life of the person.[10] Mill is on a philosophical tightrope here: he is not quite invoking the whole package of the Kantian critical-rational metaphysic of duty. He just thinks that amongst the

---

[1] Mill details this aspect of his critique – see CW X pp. 91-92.
[2] CW X p. 92.
[3] CW X p. 95.
[4] CW X p. 96.
[5] Aretaic values stem from Aristotle's virtue theory, whereby *aretē* – excellence' of character was cultivated through 'the activity of the soul in accordance with virtue'. Aristotle (2004) I: 1098a. On Mill's interest in the virtues see Semmel (1984).
[6] CW X p. 98.
[7] CW X p. 110.
[8] *OL* I: 11.
[9] CW X p. 110.
[10] See CW XII p. 207.

characteristics that are central to the character of the person is the sense of obligation that arises in and through relationships and in the performance of other responsibilities in life. Mill is, in all likelihood, alert to the point that if a person has an obligation, when and how to discharge it is something that requires the reason and sense that is cultivated by what, in *On Liberty*, is developed through the defence of the liberty of thought and discussion and the development of individuality. However, in his ongoing thinking, Kantian notions have a more positive impact.[1] Mill adds that the 'alpha and omega' of his emergent utilitarianism is 'the good' of humanity, which is seen as 'the *ultimate* end'. And this end can only be realised 'by each taking for his exclusive aim the development of what is best in *himself*'.[2] Here Mill is anticipating the sense of the creative individual as the core component of the greater whole of society, again generating his stronger sense, as in *On Liberty*, of the worth and value of individuality as 'one of the elements of well-being'.[3]

With reference to utility being related as 'the *ultimate* end' in connection with 'the good' of humanity, Mill is developing a perspective on utility as an overarching value for his ethical theory and also expressing a developmental view. As regards the role of the greatest happiness principle at the centre of classical utilitarianism, Mill modulates the role that happiness played in the still broadly utilitarian perspective to which he adhered: happiness was 'the test of all rules of conduct, and the end of life'.[4] But here we come again to the crucial tweak to orthodox utilitarianism: Mill says that happiness was an end 'only to be obtained by not making it a direct end'. This formulation in the *Autobiography* is anticipated by a phrase we encountered in the essay on Bentham, where Mill says that 'the medium of various secondary ends'[5] is required to righty achieve happiness. What we see emerging is that as happiness was not 'a direct end', it becomes the indirect end that can be realised by and through a much wider range of interests supportive of the growth of character. As John Gray explains, in more recent times, this tweaked view Mill develops can fairly be termed '*indirect utilitarianism*'.[6]

What Mill favours, through his now unstated 'practical eclecticism', is a more plural, 'many-sided' outlook on human life, garnered and refined from reading and encounters with, amongst others, Carlyle, Coleridge and Goethe.[7] Happiness is now to be considered as the outcome of the other activities and interests that might, for particular individuals, be the product of the interests and activities of their life. Still linked to the utilitarian scheme for determining actions, what this modified 'indirect' utility entails comes to expression through Mill's new thought that people are only happy if they have 'their minds fixed on something on some object other than their own happiness'.[8] This personal happiness might come from 'the happiness of others', a sense of 'the improvement of mankind', or 'even on some art or pursuit'. The point was that these objects were considered as ends, and then,

---

[1] We will see later that Mill does draw some themes from Kantian ethics.

[2] CW XII pp. 207-208.

[3] See *OL* Chapter III and Chapter 9 below.

[4] *Auto* p. 82.

[5] CW X p. 110.

[6] Gray (1983) p. 12. Gray's point is that this is a more appropriate tag than, for example, those of 'rule' or 'act' utility. A contrasting view can be found in Ten (1991) pp. 212-220.

[7] See *Auto* p. 93. J. W. von Goethe (1749-1832) – a leading writer and intellectual of the Romantic period: one of the great writers in German.

[8] *Auto* p. 82.

but only then, they bring about the higher end of personal happiness. Mill's idea is that happiness, or well-being as it becomes in *On Liberty*[1], derives in and through the other activities and pursuits that we find important and worthwhile. Mill's development of utility takes him away from the blanket focus of utilitarianism, whether as a personal and hedonistic or more general pursuit for happiness or pleasure. This is evident as he reflects on the problem that in life, if 'you ask yourself whether you are happy... you cease to be so':

'The only chance is to treat, not happiness, but some end external to it, as the purpose of life. Let your self-consciousness, your self-scrutiny, your self-interrogation, exhaust themselves on that; and if otherwise fortunately circumscribed you will inhale happiness with the air you breathe, without dwelling on it or thinking about it, without either forestalling it in imagination, or putting it to flight by fatal questioning'.[2]

Mill has a fair point here. Some people derive positive fulfilment and boost their well-being through cooking, others through gardening, others through managing a cricket team, and so on. Any of these and many other modes of activity can promote an individual's sense of well-being and realise the pleasure and contentment of happiness. But if these people got up in the morning and were told, 'Be happy!', they would find happiness as such to be much more elusive. Mill is pleased with this theory and writes that it gives the 'the basis' of his 'philosophy of life'. Since this is written in the *Autobiography*, in the final version drafted before his death, we can take Mill as indicating that this is a perspective on life that applies to the period of composing *On Liberty*.

Mill's most powerful insights about his changed outlook come in the phrase he uses to express what he came to see as one of 'the prime necessities of human well-being'.[3] This is 'the internal cultivation of the individual':

'I ceased to attach almost exclusive importance to the ordering of outward circumstances, and the training of the human being for speculation and for action. I had now learnt by experience that the passive susceptibilities needed to be cultivated as well as the active capacities, and required to be nourished and enriched as well as guided'.

Mill affirms that this perspective embraces the previous commitment to 'intellectual culture' and the 'power and practice of analysis'. But he also appreciated that the 'cultivation of feelings' gave a corrective and ensured a 'due balance among the faculties'. All this forms the enriched view of what it is to be human that Mill forged from his utilitarian foundation and the subsequent superstructure of insights from Romanticism.

---

[1] See for example *OL* II: 32. As mentioned earlier, well-being as Mill expresses it is strikingly close to what Aristotle terms *eudaimonia*, often translated loosely as 'happiness' – but eudaimonia means the sense of well-being associated with the contentment of fulfilment. See Aristotle (2004b) – where 'eudaimonia' (I. 4) is linked to 'rational activity in accordance with virtue' (I. 7).
[2] *Auto* p. 82.
[3] *Auto* p. 83.

Utility, *The System of Logic* and 'The Art of Life'

Some of the most important ideas on how Mill adapts utility and moves the theory to another level, as expressed in both *Utilitarianism* and the *Autobiography,* have their origin in the final sections of *A System of Logic*, where the ideas reflect Mill's reaction to the concerns he had about how utilitarianism had been popularised and oversimplified.[1] It makes good sense to look at some of these ideas in concert, not least to demonstrate the consistency of Mill's thinking through time.

We start with a point in *Utilitarianism*, where Mill references links between desire, the will and the development of character, and expresses the empiricist view that the moral development of a person comes through experience, as 'the moral feelings are not innate, but acquired'.[2] The idea here is that initially, humans start operating through instinct and feeling to maximise the pleasures of comfort and avoid the miseries of distress. In time, the simplicity of the pleasure/pain divide is replaced by the more sophisticated sense that, in real life, 'desiring a thing and find pleasure, aversion to it, and thinking of it as painful, are phenomena entirely inseparable, or rather two parts of the same phenomenon; in strictness of language, two different modes of the same psychological fact'.[3]

The development here is analogous to the move from Bentham's utility to Mill's enriched version, as evidenced in Mill's writings on Bentham. Ideas from the *Logic* become relevant in several ways. To begin with, in this work, we have a neat elaboration of an important distinction between desire, as in the desire for pleasure, and 'the will'.[4] Crucial to Mill's project is 'the importance of what humans can do to shape the character of one another'.[5] This is an idea promoted by defenders of the 'free-will' doctrine, the classical view of which Mill is not keen on, as we will see later.[6] Nevertheless, the idea of the freedom of the will offers an important strand to Mill's thought, the notion of 'the power of the mind to co-operate in the formation of its own 'character'. This gives individuals the autonomy of a 'spirit of self-culture'[7] and what can be termed 'a power of self-formation'.[8]

With reference to the relationship between pleasure and pain as the residual objects of desire, Mill thinks that the more persuasive view is one with a developmental character. Through self-cultivation, by 'practised self-consciousness and self-observation'[9], individuals acquire the ability to act in conformity with the will, by which Mill means 'a purpose'.[10] It is through the purposefully informed

---

[1] *Logic* VI: XII: 7. As mentioned earlier, Mill revised this work through the eight editions it went through between 1843 and 1872: the ideas remined before his mind throughout and were not simply a part of his personal archaeology.

[2] *Util* III: 8.

[3] *Util* IV: 9.

[4] *Logic* VI: II: 4. See also *Util* IV: 10.

[5] *Logic* VI: II: 3.

[6] See Chapter 6 below.

[7] *Logic* VI: II: 3.

[8] *Logic* VI: II: 4.

[9] *Util* IV: 9.

[10] *Logic* VI: II: 4. See also the last of the *Essays on Some Unsettled Questions of Political Economy* – CW IV pp. 316-321- where Mill writes in a similar manner. The *Essays* were first published in 1844 but were first written in the early 1830s.

will, rather than bare desires, that mature human action is motivated. In *Utilitarianism,* this is taken up and expressed as follows:

'The will is a different thing from desire; that a person of confirmed virtue, or any other person whose purposes are fixed, carries out his purposes without any thought to the pleasure he has in contemplating them, or expects to derive from their fulfilment; and persists in acting on them, even though these pleasures are much diminished, by changes in his character or decay of his passive sensibilities, or are outweighed by the pains which the pursuit of the purposes may bring upon him'.[1]

Mill reviews how, given the will is distinct from desire, acts of the will become a form of 'habitual purpose', such that 'instead of willing the thing because we desire it, we often desire it only because we will it'. Habitual action along the lines set by a prior motivational act of the will is, Mill thinks, a common phenomenon, sometimes enacted consciously and sometimes unconsciously. But in the case of 'the person of confirmed virtue', this is either way, a 'fulfilment' of 'the general intention'. Here, the reference to virtue again reveals the neo-Classical aspect of Mill's ethical framework: the individual who, through self-correction and collaborative character development, has made a qualitative progression will evidence this through seeking and exemplifying virtue. How this fits with the utilitarian element is something we find with another look at what Mill says in the *Logic*.

In the *Logic*, Mill has another instance of the 'indirect' style of utilitarianism: he rejects the notion that 'the promotion of happiness should be itself the end of all actions, or even of all rules of action'.[2] Happiness could serve as 'the justification, and ought to be the controller, of all ends'. However, these ends come through the development of the 'many virtues' and 'virtuous modes of action' within which 'happiness is... sacrificed' with 'more pain being produced than pleasure'. What is proposed as an ideal mode for human life again, with the references to virtue, suggests a range of meritorious and beneficent qualities that cohere with and through an individual life as means to the end of generating a deeper quality of happiness. Mill sees this as a positive:

'Because it can be shown that on the whole more happiness will exist in the world if feelings are cultivated which will make people, in certain cases, regardless of happiness'.

Mill has a similar remark in *Utilitarianism* where he is summarising the case for establishing the principle of utility:

'... happiness is a good... each person's happiness is a good to that person, and the general happiness, therefore, a good to the aggregate of all persons'.[3]

As a letter from 1867 shows, this last formulation could be construed as meaning the aggregation of general happiness, such that 'every human being's happiness is a good to every other human being'.[4] Mill denies this was his meaning: it suggests

---

[1] *Util* IV: 10.
[2] *Logic* VI: XII: 7.
[3] *Util* IV: 3.
[4] CW XVI p. 1414.

a worrying level of consensus about the mode of happiness that will suit everyone. What Mill means is the more general point: the utilitarian ideal of people achieving whatever, for them as individuals, gives happiness as a good that would promote an increase in the general well-being of society. As Mill puts it, 'since A's happiness is a good, B's is a good, C's is a good, &c, the sum of these goods must be a good'. This makes sense so long as all of these modes of happiness operate within the parameters of what Mill terms in *On Liberty* 'the region of human liberty' (I: 12). As Mill has it in the *Logic*, the processes of cultivation that 'will make people'[1] have a teleological character, with connotations of developmental growth.[2]

Mill continues:

'The cultivation of an ideal of nobleness of will and conduct should be to individual human beings an end, to which the specific pursuit of either their own happiness or of that of others (except so far as included in that idea) should, in any case of conflict, give way. But I hold that the very question, what constitutes this elevation of character, is itself to be decided by a reference to happiness as the standard. The character itself should be, to the individual, a paramount end, simply because the existence of this ideal nobleness of character, or of a near approach to it, in abundance, would go further than all things else towards making human life happy, both in the comparatively humble sense of pleasure and freedom from pain, and in the higher meaning of rendering life, not what it now is almost universally, puerile and insignificant, but such as human beings with highly developed faculties can care to have'.[3]

With these remarks, we see how Mill trades off the simplicity of calculative utility, as related to the specific worth of actions registered against the greatest happiness principle, for a much richer and inclusive theory, where a range of values are included under the 'ideal of nobleness of will and conduct'. In effect, Mill has in the *Logic* an early version of the mode of utilitarian thought used in his *Utilitarianism*, where, as we have seen, 'lower' and 'higher' utilitarian notions of pleasure are distinguished, with the greater worth being placed on the cultivation of the higher and more individualised pleasures.[4]

Significantly, the ideas expressed in the *Logic* are also akin to the pattern of thought we have in *On Liberty*, where again, the worth of individual character is a major theme. The contrast between what Mill is developing is much greater with the legislative utilitarianism of James Mill and Jeremy Bentham. In the modified view, the process that can 'make people' through the development of human 'character' is the 'paramount end', and that end is found with 'happiness as the standard'.

As he moves on in his life and work, Mill develops rather than replicates the earlier utilitarian approach. Again, he sees that the earlier modes of utility imply a simplistic and reductionist view of human nature and society. Mill consistently argues the imperative value of individuals cultivating their interests and capacities,

---

[1] *Logic* VI: XII: 7.
[2] Mill builds on this idea of teleological development in the *Logic* as well as later in *On Liberty* – see *OL* III: 4.
[3] *Logic* VI: XII: 7.
[4] See *Util* II: 5-7.

and in *On Liberty*, he affirms this as 'the privilege and proper condition of a human being arrived at in the maturity of his faculties, to use and interpret experience in his own way' (III: 3). Mill sees this developmental experience as encompassing the appreciative feelings, the poetic and imaginative faculties, and the moral and rational aspects of being human. Rather than happiness being the end of all good actions, Mill favours the pursuit of well-being through a range of other ends pursued for their own sake, giving an enhanced idea of happiness as the overall criterion.

With this, it is clear that there is much sense in the view that of all the tags that are possible, 'indirect utilitarianism' best fits Mill's revised perspective, with 'happiness' as 'the test of all rules of conduct, and the end of life'.[1] As we saw, in this formulation, happiness is not 'the direct end'. The 'indirect' diagnosis fits extremely well with the way Mill expresses his thoughts, and a way of explaining this is to leap into modernity and the computer age. We might say that Mill begins to see utility as an operating system, and other values and principles – like liberty – are akin to programs that run on the system. The aim, consequential and teleological in shape, is for the satisfaction of the programs running well for the good of the user. Transposed to human life, what Mill means is that happiness is not the axiomatic value to find in all acts and deeds but the cumulative outcome of actions and purposes that flow through the lives and endeavours of progressive individuals, making human life richer, more distinctive, and better.

We find from Mill's *Letters*, the *Logic* and from the *Autobiography* that he moves on from his initial Benthamite phase of utilitarianism in the vital respect of defending a principle that embraces and defends the complexity and plurality of interests that are consistent with individual life. Insofar as Mill in *On Liberty* develops the case for the defence of liberty of thought, discussion and action against the threatening trends of social interference and constraint, he explicitly states this in relation to the 'civil' and 'social' modes of life (I: 1). His concern with liberty is on the nature of the relationship between individuals and the greater whole of society. He continues to oppose the reductionism and uniformity of the earlier mode of utility. He does this in the interests of the larger ethical sense of utility, consistent with the *Logic*'s rather neo-classical aim of cultivating 'nobleness of character, or… a near approach to it'.[2]

Accordingly, Mill thinks that he has retained utilitarian credentials and gained the operational advantage of principles to serve as the basis and criterion for the view that the rest of *On Liberty* seeks to present. He is then in the rare position of being able to have his cake and eat it: he can claim to be a defender of liberty and diversity and complexity (against reductionism), yet he does so by means of the principle of liberty, which is under the auspices of an enriched indirect concept of utility orientated to the ethical end that can 'make' people.[3]

Mill elaborates these themes in the *Logic*, in the context of sketching a theory of what he calls 'the Art of Life'.[4] The remarks on the Art of Life come through Mill's reflection on a range of other points, such as the issue of the character of and the contrasts between the natural sciences and the social and moral sciences. He

---

[1] *Auto* p. 82.
[2] *Logic* VI: XII: 7.
[3] See *Logic* VI: XII: 6 and 7.
[4] *Logic* VI: XII: 6.

signifies a crucial difference in that the natural sciences operate in what he terms 'the indicative' mode of expression.[1] Accordingly, the sciences describe and point up the data of the natural world as revealed through their characteristic methods and techniques. In contrast, the social and moral sciences express much of what they are concerned with in 'the imperative mood'. The subject matter of anything in the imperative mood, where 'rules or precepts' are dealt with, rather than 'assertions concerning matters of fact, is art; and ethics or morality is properly a portion of the art corresponding to sciences of human nature and society'.

The disciplines in this 'imperative' mode of thought have a method of 'Art, or Practice', which leads to a key point, that by 'Art', Mill does not mean poetry and such art-forms; the 'Art of Life' is not a mantra for an aesthetic morality, a transfusion of the good into the beautiful. Instead, by 'Art', he means the cultivation of the process of making things – of developing potentialities from actuality, as in the manner of looking to 'make people' we noted earlier.

Mill suggests the working relationship between the 'rules of art' and the 'doctrines of science':

'The art proposes to itself an end to be attained, defines the end, and hands it over to the science. The science receives it, considers it as a phenomenon or an effect to be studied, and having investigated its causes and conditions, sends it back to art with a theorem of the combination of circumstances by which it could be produced. Art then examines these combinations of circumstances, and according as any of them are or are not in human power, pronounces the end attainable or not'.[2]

These remarks are from the *Logic*, not the *Autobiography*, but what Mill describes is very much in his own style of making a synthesis and employing the natural and human sciences to render more intelligible and effective methods for progressing the better options for the individual and wider human condition. He elaborates some illustrations, touching on the role of Judges in administering law and legislators in making it, 'German tacticians' bested by Napoleon, and physicians who are 'the slave of... formulas' as opposed to those who are not, to show that he is dealing with a process where the ideal method is one where theory and practice interrelate.

When a thinker of considerable breadth such as Mill operates with this comprehensive and multi-disciplinary method, it might seem clear how the theoretical and practical or applied aspects of life and thought interact. Mill's idea of collaborative interaction between theory and practice is appealing, but he is perhaps over-optimistic about how this can be a smooth and regularised process. A wider point, consistent with Mill's thinking, is that in more recent times, it is much more the case that narrow, specialised and non-communicative forms of study are far less effective than those that are inter or multi-disciplinary, but that getting such processes working can take quite a lot of time and effort.

If we take an example from debates and processes in what we now call 'bioethics', in the 1970s, parents, healthcare specialists, doctors and many others within the practice or art of life were dealing with a range of issues to do with conception, genetic anomalies, and the opportunities for gaining insight through further research. Medical researchers in the domain of medical science were

---

[1] *Logic* VI: XII: 1.
[2] *Logic* VI: XII: 2.

developing proposals for embryo research, assuming the use of spare embryos donated from IVF procedures. A host of moral and religious issues arose over the use and abuse of embryos that, on some views of human life, constitute human life. No legislation existed under which embryo research could proceed, so in 1982, the UK Government established a Committee of Inquiry to investigate and advise. The committee membership was highly multidisciplinary, with medical, legal, ethical and religious specialists, and evidence was taken from representatives of various interest groups. The Committee's report – the 'Warnock Report', named after its Chairman, Dame Mary Warnock, reported in 1984.[1] The recommendations of the Committee led to the Human Fertilisation and Embryology Act 1990, which embodied the Committee's finding that up to fourteen days, research on donated embryos would be lawful. Without going into the details, the process of interrelating theory and practice and infusing the process with imperative ethical reasoning and indicative scientific data was procedurally complex. Theory and practice were engaged in collaborative review, and in time, a form of legislation was developed that has proved durable. This was not quite an operation as per Mill's scheme in the *Logic*, but it embodies the broad ethos that we make better progress with a collegiate relation between the disciplines of study and the business of practising the Art of Life.

Mill has more moments of affinity with Aristotle when he says that 'the definition of the end itself belongs exclusively to Art, and forms its particular province'.[2] Mill, like Aristotle, uses the examples of medicine and building, where the abiding point, as in the case of a building, is that all the materials for and even the design of the building and the expertise to construct it are eventually subordinate to the aim, point or purpose of the building – the making of a home, say – and that is what may be considered its 'end'.[3] The emphasis on the 'end' has a teleological ring to it, and Mill is emphatic that the teleological thinking he employs is not to be confused with the attempts in classical and medieval thought to utilise teleological explanation to explain 'the phenomenon of the universe'.[4] The benefit of Mill's more particularised notion of teleology is that it enables the assessment of specific processes so that what happens can be supported to its rightful end and aided and corrected if things go astray.

The ethical dimension comes to the fore in Mill's explanation when he says that whereas the natural sciences deal with what is the case, ethical thinking deals with that which 'should be'. This is a variant of the 'indicative – imperative' distinction Mill notes, and with these points, we come to Mill's version of the distinction in ethics between 'is' and 'ought'. This is clear from his sense that there is a generic difference between propositions expressing '*ought* or *should be*' in contrast with '*is* or *will be*'.[5] In contrast to some narrower lines of thought in empiricism, Mill does

---

[1] Dame Mary Warnock (1924-2019), philosopher and educationalist, was then Mistress of Girton College, Cambridge. The Warnock Report pdf is available from
https:///www.hfea.gov.uk/media/2608/warnock-report-of-the-committee-of-inquiry-into-human-fertilisation-and-embryology-1984.pdf
[2] *Logic* VI: XII: 6.
[3] Aristotle's thinking about ends and building can be found in *Metaphysics* – Aristotle (2004a): Delta 2: pp. 114-115. See also the version in the *Physics* – Aristotle (2008) II: 3.
[4] See *Logic* VI: XII: 6 n.
[5] *Logic* VI: XII: 6.

not think that the language of obligation is empty of meaning and purely emotive.[1] Mill puts weight on the fact, as he defines it, that the language of obligation 'excites in the speaker's mind the feeling of approbation'.[2] This feeling is not enough, however. Mill thinks that, in addition, the individual must be able 'to justify his approbation'. Feelings and reasons go hand in glove in Mill's sense of how morality forms a part of the activity of the Art of Life.

Mill duly outlines the 'body of doctrine which is properly the Art of Life, in its three departments, Morality, Prudence or Policy and Aesthetics; the Right, the Expedient and the Beautiful, in human conduct and works'. Mill thinks that anyone operating as a 'scientific observer or reasoner' cannot be a direct mentor for the practice of life. The scientific approach advises on the relation of causes to certain effects, means to specific ends, and actions to particular consequences. The idea Mill has is that science can link with what is embraced under the specification for the Art of Life to provide insight into the 'laws of nature' and the Art of Life dealing with 'the general principles of what has been called Teleology, or the Doctrine of Ends'. Mill maintains his holistic view that just as there is a concern for the 'first principles of Knowledge' – the province of science – there is also one for 'the first principles of Conduct'.[3]

Mill now comes to one of the larger problems for the business of reasoning about values: if we want to say that 'so and is good', we operate with some sense of whatever it that something must have in virtue of which it is 'good'. Mill is alert to the issues here, as he considers the variables of 'goodness or badness'; he thinks that 'there can be but one' standard of value – 'for if there were several ultimate principles of conduct', some particular form of conduct might be endorsed by some and rejected by others. Mill then sounds as if he is becoming metaphysical, as he suggests the need for the umpiring capacity of 'some more general principle'. He is, as Gray explains, more correctly operating axiologically.[4] He is looking for a core or residual theory of value to underpin 'all other rules of conduct' and so achieve consistency. Mill is advancing a case against a trend in ethical theory with which he has no truck whatever, and this is anything that could be placed under the singular umbrella of moral intuition. He thinks there are some who think that no ultimate principle of moral value is needed as individual moral sense will guide us on what values to use, in what order and for what circumstances. Rather like Jane Austen, Mill wants to fuse sense with sensibility.[5] The moral sense and wider sensibilities allow the moral aspects of life and the prudential and aesthetic dimensions to develop a perspective on 'some general principle, or standard' for life that will, if 'rightly chosen', work for the whole of life.

Mill does not think the *Logic* is the work to elaborate a view about 'the foundations of morality'. This suggests to the hopeful and motivated reader that Mill's canon of works will contain such a study – but the sad news is that although Mill worked for another thirty years after finishing the first edition of the *Logic*, he never wrote a treatise on the foundations of morality.

---

[1] See for example Ayer (1970) especially Chapter 6.
[2] *Logic* VI: XII: 6.
[3] *Logic* VI: XII. 7.
[4] See Gray (1983) pp. 19-29.
[5] See Austen (2019).

As we saw earlier, what Mill comes to is an affirmation of happiness as that which gives 'the test' to moral rules and theories of the practice of life. This is not happiness as the specific 'end of all actions', but 'the happiness of mankind' being the test of 'all rules of practice', building to the ideal of 'the elevation of character': here, happiness operates as the standard of reference in the indirect manner identified above.

In *Utilitarianism*, Mill sets out a view that Anthony Quinton observes to contain 'several heretical deviations from Benthamite orthodoxy'.[1] The point on heresies is, as we have seen in this chapter, that Mill's deviations began in 1829, a long time before he published *Utilitarianism*, within which he defines the core ideas as follows, conjoining happiness and pleasure:

'Actions are right in proportion as they tend to promote happiness, wrong as they tend to promote the reverse of happiness. By happiness is intended pleasure, and the absence of pain. By unhappiness, pain and the privation of pleasure'.[2]

By 'actions' here, Mill does not elaborate on the scale he has in mind, whether to personal or more general actions. That is due to his view that utility has the unique capacity of rendering solutions to both personal and wider social, political and economic issues. What Mill says does not sound like an especially modified take on classical utility, but explaining his view, Mill develops what we mentioned earlier, a qualitative distinction between 'higher' and 'lower' pleasures.[3] This distinction reflects the deeper sense of humans as beings with 'higher faculties'[4] who require a qualitative increase to achieve happiness. Mill is keen to elaborate on this point to counter the criticism that the reliance on the maxims of pleasure and pain gives a crude estimate of the values through which to estimate human life. As a 'theory of life'[5], utility can be seen as 'utterly mean and grovelling; as a doctrine worthy only of swine'. In explaining a deeper, qualitative sense of values can be justified, Mill thinks several explanations can be given: it might be 'pride', the 'love of power' or the 'love of excitement': but Mill thinks it has much more to do with 'the love of liberty and personal independence', but it also all it signals something else:

'A sense of dignity, which all human beings possess in one form or another, and in some, though by no means in exact, proportion to their higher faculties, and which is so essential a part of the happiness of those in whom it is strong, that nothing which conflicts with it could, otherwise than momentarily, an object of desire to them'.

The suggestion is that we should not confuse human happiness as a experiential state with the 'content': the individual with the capacity for qualitative increases will appreciate and 'learn to bear' the imperfections of the world. Self-understanding and the reflective capacity to know 'all sides of a question' fuels the progression – hence - and returning to the reference associated with the critics of

[1] Quinton (1989) p. 38. Here Quinton probably draws on Mill's self-diagnosis of heresy from Bentham's utility – see *Auto* p. 130.
[2] *Util* II: 2.
[3] See *Util* II: 4-7.
[4] *Util* II: 5.
[5] *Util* II: 2

utility – it qualitatively 'better to be a human being dissatisfied than a pig satisfied; better to be Socrates dissatisfied than a fool satisfied'.

With the theme of higher and lower pleasures, Mill looks to delineate the distinct ways of thought and action of which humans are capable, where fulfilling our basic needs – our 'animal appetites'[1] involves the lower pleasures and developing our character and individuality the higher. The sciences – natural and humane – as well as the arts, as in the senses of the Art of Life, are for Mill, layered means he expresses for determining what will be of happiness or, again, as in *On Liberty*, the well-being of humanity.[2]

It is because of this openness to self-correcting development and to the sense of human individuality being central to well-being that Mill says in *On Liberty* that utility remains 'the ultimate appeal on all ethical questions; but it must be utility in the largest sense, grounded on the permanent interests of man as a progressive being' (I:11). Here, the notion of humanity being seen as permanently 'progressive' is also the most authentic way of explaining Mill's particular transition of utilitarian thought, from the unitised equality of Bentham's utility to a view altogether more operationally valid and coherent as an ethic fit for use.

Utility, Moore's Critique and Other Problems

Mill's relationship with utility is akin to that of the devotee who initially has a transformational experience of commitment and then, over time, a period of revisionary reform leading to a sectarian divide before moving on to his own new vision of a redemptive solution. A consistent feature of Mill's writing on utility and many other matters is the sense that whatever else a person considers, there has to be a correlation between what we think and what we do, and Mill understands that this is grounded in the assessment that we make of what it is to be human. A main reason for his dissatisfaction with the utilitarian style of Bentham was the realisation that it operated too rigidly and with an overly quantitative assessment of the human condition, with a narrow view of human motivation and interest. Mill sought a revision to accommodate the richer and more complex view of the authentic human condition, with reference to qualitative considerations.

Utilitarianism has subsequently moved into the spectrum of normative ethical theories found by any who take an excursion into modern moral philosophy, where it is presented as a theory ready for use, as a method for making ethical decisions when moral dilemmas present us with a challenge, or for planning a longer-term decision-making process. As such, utilitarianism is profiled as an ethical approach working with a method of calculative prediction of the likely results of potential preferences relative to the balance of pleasure and pain or happiness and unhappiness. The utilitarian concern is thus a form of consequentialism as it seeks to determine the worth of an act in terms of its likely outcome, relative to its effect in terms of pleasure or pain on those involved with or affected by the act. This approach is held to provide a measurable and objective basis for ethical action. The implication is that individual liberty might be placed as relative to the general

---

[1] *Util* II: 4.
[2] See again *OL* Chapters II & III and Chapters 8 & 9 below.

happiness of the greatest number, for no area of private life could be said by the utilitarian to be free from interference in the name of the greatest happiness of the greatest number.

For all that can be said in its favour, utilitarianism, in general, faces a range of difficulties, one of which is that it assumes but actually avoids possessing any tangible moral norms. This is obvious when we reflect on the connotations of the phenomena of 'pleasure' and 'happiness'. A long list of the activities and experiences that can give pleasure or bring happiness could be made without the slightest reference to anything that touches on virtue or moral goodness. A key diagnostic for the problem is expressed by G. E. Moore as the 'naturalistic fallacy'[1] In *Principia Ethica* (1903), Moore orientated his review around the question 'what is good?'[2] His thought was that most developed moral theories fail to answer this question since they attempt to base moral claims on theological, metaphysical, scientific, or humanitarian theories. Such views may rest on speculation or more secure factual or experimental premises, but on Moore's view, such premises cannot serve as legitimate grounds for asserting a moral view.

Moore is against what could be termed moral realism, the view that there are eternal values grounded in a transcendental domain, but he is equally opposed to what he sees as 'naturalism', the view that the good can be known and proved as a part of the world of general experience – including the worlds of pleasure, happiness and utility. The error consistently committed is, he thinks, the 'naturalistic fallacy'.[3] This fallacy happens when we define moral terms like 'good' in non-moral terms, in terms of something arising from the descriptive theory in question that is said to manifest the good. The key example for us is how happiness, as in the utilitarian approach, defines the good as that which produces the 'greatest happiness to the greatest number'. The fallacy occurs as we identify 'happiness' as 'good'. Moore's point, which he always considered starkly obvious, is that in our discourse, we cannot replace 'good' with 'happy' or 'goodness' with 'happiness', for we simply do not think that 'good' and 'happy' are synonyms. If, for example, I follow utility, and I say 'It is good to make people happy' since happiness is the good, all I have said is 'It is happy to make people happy', which is clearly nonsense. But if we think utility works, as utilitarians do, we commit the 'naturalistic fallacy'. This point can be recast as the open question argument: if pleasure or happiness *were* good, it would make no sense to ask on a specific occasion whether this or that pleasure or happiness was good. But that is precisely what we do: we ask in given circumstances whether this or that pleasure or happiness is good.

To take an engaging example, a group of students might feel very happy (and good) if they were put on a drip sending champagne into their bloodstreams as they sat down to take their final examinations. They might not feel so happy (or good) when they get the results. The obvious point is that happiness may be good, or it may be bad – it is, in reality, an open question, and to assume the identity of happiness and good is to commit the naturalistic fallacy afresh.

---

[1] G. E. Moore (1873-1958). A major British philosopher of the twentieth century. A fellow of Trinity College, Cambridge, Moore was a lecturer in philosophy from 1911 and Professor of Philosophy (1925-1939). Moore was a long serving editor of the journal *Mind* and, through his association with the Bloomsbury group, an influence on the moral and cultural life of the twentieth century.
[2] Moore (1965) p.3.
[3] See Moore (1965) pp. 10ff.

Moore's concerns suggest the uncomfortable thought that utilitarianism offers less a moral theory and more a method for calculating what the majority desire, using the measures of pleasure or happiness.[1] The deeper problem is that as pleasure and happiness as preferences are sensate states that can be experienced in non-moral and a-moral, as well as in moral contexts, the regular forms of utility literally lack moral weight, appearing to function simply as justifications for wants. As so many seem to consider that their wants are for them their goods, utilitarian thinking appears to be in popular use, as in personal and public life, where estimates of what will be in the interests of the most, the majority, the public or national interest, is invariably a common appeal, whether it is over what a family might do on a Saturday, or what a government proposes to do to alleviate shortages in the health service.

As we explained, Mill's book *Utilitarianism* was published first as a series of articles in 1861 and in book form in 1863, but in terms of compositional history, Mill drafted much of the material used in the book in 1854, when he also made the first draft of *On Liberty*.[2] Reading both works with this in mind, it is as if Mill sought in *On Liberty* to set out the case for the societal areas of life where the liberty of thought, discussion and action would allow for the range of endeavours that serve as various means for achieving the overarching end of utility.

In *Utilitarianism*, Mill writes, in part, to provide an introduction and guide to utility, giving some reference to the tradition that he has been a part of but also indicating how he has moved on with that tradition. One thing he says is that utility has faced the reproach that it presents as 'cold and unsympathizing', putting the focus on the 'dry and hard consideration of the consequences of actions'.[3] As far as Mill, with his developed outlook on utility, is concerned, this impression is misconceived, but it is a valid point to make that if we try out life as utilitarians using the Benthamite scheme, we will notice that the calculative aspect appears clean, simple and useful. The greatest happiness for the greatest number for an individual or within a group or class can be invoked to calculate the best options for everyday life, the priorities for homework as opposed to social engagements and so on. However, we will also see that it is hard-headed and becomes much more complex in operation as soon as issues of care, compassion and interests in the well-being of others are factored in.

Mill's point is that if we consider utilitarian operation – in his modified, 'indirect' manner – the process should take into the assessment a review of 'the rightness or wrongness of an action' in relation to 'the qualities of the person who does it', or else the problem, which is not unique to utility, just means that the operation lacks any reference to 'any standard of morality at all'. Mill means that the 'rightness and wrongness of actions is not the sole focus for utilitarian

---

[1] See also Ryan (1987) p. 209.
[2] See Reeves (2007) p. 324.
[3] *Util* II: 19. Mill is perhaps mindful of the use in Bentham's utility of the so-called felicific calculus. As set out in by Bentham in his *Introduction to the Principles of Morals and Legislation* of 1789, this suggests that 'when determining what action is right in a given situation, we should consider the pleasures and pains resulting from it, in respect of their *intensity, duration, certainty, propinquity, fecundity* (the chance that a pleasure is followed by other ones, a pain by further pains), *purity* (the chance that pleasure is followed by pains and vice versa), and *extent* (the number of persons affected). We should next consider the alternative courses of action: ideally, this method will determine which act has the best tendency, and therefore is right'. Bentham (1961) Chapter 4.

assessment – there are also 'considerations relevant' to 'persons', and the issue of whether a person is 'good or... bad' is significant. Mill's ability to think in these terms comes from his prior views that put the ultimate end of happiness as the criterion of value to employ with reference to other values, virtues and qualities that embroider human life. He thinks in such a way that we can link the ideas in *Utilitarianism* to the notion so importantly affirmed in *On Liberty* of humans as 'progressive' beings (I: 11), and also as fallible and capable of self-improvement. He suggests that over time, individuals and humanity can refine and improve their understanding of what enhances human life and individual happiness and that it is, in part, the job of the philosophers to work on aiding this process. Alluding to the idea of the Art of Life, he accepts that 'the principle of utility, like the precepts of every practical art, admit of indefinite improvement, and, in a progressive state of human mind, their improvement is perpetually going on'.[1]

That Mill has lines of thought reflecting a level of harmony between his utility and his thinking on liberty is good news, but it is also a fair point to note that Mill's work in his explanation of utility is uneven, and that it falls into the sort of error later identified by that Moore. An example of this comes when Mill is considering how to justify the principle of utility, and in particular, the idea that 'happiness is desirable, and the only thing desirable, as an end: all other things being only desirable as means to that end'.[2] Mill then thinks that it follows that subjective proof gives the justification for happiness analogous to the proof that a person has seen or heard something: the idea is that only the person in question knows what he or she has seen or heard, so similarly, 'the sole evidence it is possible to produce that anything is desirable is that people actually do desire it'.[3] He adds that 'no reason can be given why the general happiness is desirable, except that each person, so far as he believes it to be attainable, desires his own happiness' and that 'each person's happiness is a good to that person, and the general happiness, therefore, a good to the aggregate of all persons'.

As we suggested, a problem for utilitarianism, as in Bentham's formulation, arises from the way that the positive of pleasure is the assumed good in contrast to the negativity of pain. There is a massive assumption in this insofar as the question of whether pleasure is invariably beneficial or good is glossed, leaving open the issue of whether there is tangible moral content to this form of utility or whether it is simply a functional justification for want. Mill's explanation in the passages we have just considered falls back into the same error.

It is regrettable that Mill rejects the wider use of reason and thinks that what any person affirms as desire and believes to be attainable, is desirable as a good because they desire it so that this desired object is then morally significant in a positive way in line with an ends orientated utility. A given person's desires might involve exploitation, corruption, deceit, or more tangible crimes against another person. The aggregate of what people desire is vulnerable to the same problem. Mill almost certainly assumes that desires and consequent actions are monitored by the harm to others principle he sets out in *On Liberty*[4], as related to the interests of developing

---

[1] *Util* II: 23.
[2] *Util* IV: 2.
[3] *Util* IV: 3
[4] See *OL* I: 9, for example.

human well-being, but in *Utilitarianism,* this is blurred; he denies that desire is linked to reason and, on the whole, has a very bad day at the office.

It is unfortunate that in *Utilitarianism*, Mill partially rows back on, or fails to deploy, the ideas in his earlier writing that reasoned on how 'the promotion of happiness should be itself the end of all actions, or even of all rules of action, and ought to be the controller of all ends, but is not itself the sole end'.[1] Mill's thinking here, in the *Logic*, makes the compelling point that 'there are many virtuous actions, and even virtuous modes of action', and, and in more recent parlance, Mill sees that often we have to accept that there is no gain without pain, to the end that we cultivate the means to 'make people'.

Mill has some better reasoning when he links utility to justice, not least because he grounds a good deal of what he says on notions that, in social and political terms, serve the common good. He firstly links justice to the principle of desert, impartiality and the common need for security, using the same reciprocal argument as in *On Liberty* for the return individuals owe for the liberties and protection they enjoy.[2] Mill also makes some strong points when unpacking the dynamics of what human beings face in their existence when possessed by 'faculties more elevated than the animal appetites'.[3] Here Mill needs to be rightly understood. In such remarks, he knows that humans are animals and that they, too, have 'animal appetites' appertaining to what may be termed the bare necessities of life. Humans also have other capacities, which include 'the pleasures of the intellect, of the feelings and the imagination, and of the moral sentiments', which have, Mill says, 'a much higher value as pleasures than to those of mere sensation'. Here Mill strikes a subtle blow for his revised utility against the earlier style, pointing out that 'utilitarians' might have done better to explain that 'some kinds of pleasure are more desirable and more valuable than others', and that to focus on matters of 'quantity' without regard to 'quality' in the 'estimation of pleasures' was a mistake.

Mill writes more on the features and qualities of life when a person is possessed of 'the higher faculties' and, in so doing, shows that it is not a life of contemplative bliss. Living with the powers of intellect and imagination means that a person needs more than superficiality for happiness and is vulnerable to more disappointments and frustrations. Nevertheless, such a person will not want to 'sink into what he feels to be a lower grade of existence'.[4] However we explain it, and Mill suggests it might be to do with 'the love of liberty and personal independence', the capacity to operate with the higher faculties gives the experience of discovering imperfections in life and understanding – but these imperfections are a prompt and challenge to more exploration and discovery. It is in this that the thinking on utility and liberty cohere.[5]

---

[1] *Logic* VI: XII: 7.
[2] See *Util* V: 7; 10; 25 and *OL* IV: 3. We look at some of the idea here again later.
[3] *Util* II: 4.
[4] *Util* II. 5
[5] See Gray (1983) p. xi.

5. The Origins and Writing of *On Liberty*

J. S. Mill and Harriet Taylor

When considering Mill's life and work, we noted that in widening his social circle from the time of his mental crisis, he met Harriet Taylor.[1] Little in retrospect seems to have contributed more than this relationship to his self-development as a many-sided person, with a more alert internal self-cultivation of himself. As mentioned, Mill met her through his friend William Johnson Fox, who, in turn, knew John and Harriet Taylor as members of his Unitarian Congregation. Mill and Harriet rapidly developed a close and reciprocally important love, and this relationship was, for Mill, a central aspect of the transformative experience he underwent. In 1851, over twenty years after their first meeting, Mill and Harriet Taylor married.

It was in the year after Harriet's death in 1858 that Mill published *On Liberty*, and that the work had a special significance for them is evident from the dedication to Harriet that Mill writes at the start of the book:

> 'To *the beloved and deplored memory of her who*
> *was the inspirer, and in part the author, of all that*
> *is best in my writings – the friend and wife whose*
> *exalted sense of truth and right was my strongest*
> *incitement, and whose approbation was my chief*
> *reward – I dedicate this volume. Like all that I*
> *have written for many years, it belongs as much to*
> *her as to me; but the work as it stands has had, in*
> *a very insufficient degree, the inestimable advantage*
> *of her revision; some of the most important portions*
> *having been reserved for a more careful re-examination,*
> *which they are now never destined to receive.*
> *Where I but capable of interpreting to the world one*
> *half the great thoughts and noble feelings which are*
> *buried in her grave, I should be the medium of a*
> *greater benefit to it, than is ever likely to arise from*
> *anything that I can write, unprompted and unassisted*
> *by her all but unrivalled wisdom'.*[2]

This elaborate homage includes the claim that the book 'belongs as much to her as to me', giving rise to questions over Harriet's influence on and responsibility for *On Liberty*.

When Mill met Harriet Taylor in 1830, he was twenty-four, and she was a year younger. Her husband, John Taylor, was a successful pharmaceutical merchant. There were two children within the marriage at that time, and Mr and Mrs Taylor were both committed to radical reforms, so they had much in common with Mill. John Taylor was not, however, a lively, vibrant enthusiast: he was calm, measured and a wholly devoted and dutiful husband. Harriet was lively, quick-minded and

---

[1] See Chapter 2 above.
[2] *OL* p. 58.

85

articulate. She wrote articles praising reforms and arguing for female emancipation in the magazine the *Monthly Repository*. Little that she wrote through this period survives, but of her pieces, unpublished but retained amongst her papers and probably dating from 1832, is on the 'Sources of Conformity', where we find the following:

'Whether it would be Religious conformity, Moral conformity or Social conformity, no matter which the species, the spirit is the same: all kinds agree in this one point, of hostility to individual character, and individual character if it exists at all, can rarely declare itself openly while there is, on all topics of importance, a standard of conformity raised by the indolently minded many and guarded by... opinion which, though composed individually of the weakest twigs, yet makes up collectively a mass which is not to be resisted with impunity... What is called the opinion of Society is a phantom power, yet as is often the case with phantoms, of more force over the minds of the unthinking than all the flesh and blood arguments which can be brought to bear against it. It is a combination of the many weak, against the few strong; an association of the mentally listless to punish any manifestation of mental independence... Society abhors individual character. It asks the sacrifice of body, heart and mind'.[1]

The themes in Harriet's essay anticipate and overlap with parts of *On Liberty*. The virtue of individuality is asserted as superior to that of varying modes of conformity to society; the dangers of conformity and the need and benefit of individuality are themes that recur in *On Liberty*. *On Liberty* is a far longer and more nuanced work than the early essay by Harriet and also reflects the way that, from the 1830s, Mill's work became more alert to and engaged with the diversity of human nature and the plurality of ideas, values and interests that constituted a civilized society. This development was fuelled by the various projects Mill was engaged in, his ongoing reading and other intellectual contacts, but it was also inspired by the relationship and ongoing dialogue he had with Harriet.

From the start of their friendship, she found a stimulating companion in Mill, sharing a deep interest in radical and reforming ideas with him. He was quickly besotted with her. In the *Autobiography*, Mill claimed that their friendship did not become confidential or intimate until much later.[2] It was, he says, a friendship of 'thought, feeling, and writing'.[3] It is important to appreciate that Mill drafted the *Autobiography* with Harriet during their marriage. Some who have written about Mill's life with Harriet are inclined to the view that the relationship between the friends was intimate and confidential from an early stage.[4] Whether it was an intimate relationship in the sexual sense is not at all clear. We know that tensions swiftly arose in the Taylor household, and in 1831 Mill and John Taylor had to be reconciled.[5] In 1833, Mill and Harriet managed a holiday together in Paris, and Mill writes about this to Fox in terms which would resonate with any romantic spirit who has visited Paris with their true love:

---

[1] Quoted in Hayek (2020) pp. 264-269. The passages quoted here are from pp. 264-265 and p. 268.
[2] See *Auto* p. 105 and p. 129.
[3] *Auto* p. 135.
[4] See Himmelfarb (1974) pp. 209-212 and Reeves (2007) pp. 80-86.
[5] See Reeves (2007) p. 83.

'I could have filled a long letter to you with the occurrences and feelings and thoughts of any one day since I have been here – this fortnight seems an age in mere duration, and *is* an age in what it has done for us two. It has brought years of experience to us – good and happy experience most of it. We never could have been so near, so perfectly intimate, in any former circumstances – we never could have been together as we have been in innumerable smaller relations and concerns – we never should have spoken of all things, and in all frames of mind, with so much freedom and unreserve'.[1]

Over the next two decades, Harriet Taylor was, Mill says, his 'incomparable friend'.[2] She lived with her husband and spent time with Mill – sometimes going to the country and abroad with him, and it was clear to their friends that their love was no secret.[3] Harriet's professed solution to the matter was to have no physical relations with either her husband or Mill so she could sustain her family and keep up her friendship with Mill.[4] Consistent with that, the official line was that in their years of association prior to marriage, the friendship was not sexual. Harriet's advice to Mill when he was drafting the *Autobiography* was to describe the years of their pre-marital friendship as being full of 'strong affection, intimacy of friendship, & no impropriety'. Her view was that their story would present an 'edifying picture for those poor wretches who cannot conceive friendship but in sex – nor believe that expediency and the consideration for feelings of others can conquer sensuality'.[5]

The true state of the relationship between Mill and Harriet Taylor may be of little consequence to us today, and it is clear that biographical writings have not unearthed any special revelations.[6] A thoughtful review of the saga of Mill's relationship with Harriet prior to their marriage is by Sandra Peart, who points out that both Mill and Harriet would have been familiar with Adam Smith's *Theory of Moral Sentiments* (1759). This treatise makes a clear distinction between blame and blameworthiness. One can be blamed by others for wrongs actually done; one can be thought blameworthy for assumed wrongs. The suggestion is that Harriet and Mill lived and acted to avoid 'blameworthiness'[7], thus making plausible their profession of a friendship that did not include sexual intimacy.

Whatever the case, early in the affair, James Mill was not happy with his son's new friendship and was unconvinced by the claims of its innocence. The Scottish Presbyterian streak surfaced, and Mill was taxed by his father for having an affair with another man's wife. Mill's riposte, that he 'had no other feelings towards her than he would have towards an equally able man', put James Mill on to the defensive – but he was not convinced.[8] The wider situation gave other messages to Mill at this time when, despite his marriage, William Johnson Fox began to live openly with his lover, Eliza Flowers, a good friend of Harriet Taylor's. Then as 1836 unfolded, James Mill's health declined, and, on 23rd June, he died.[9] Once again, Mill seems to have suffered a depressive crisis. The emotional pressure this time left physical

---

[1] CW XII pp. 185-186.
[2] *Auto* p. 129.
[3] See Reeves (2007) p. 82-84.
[4] Reeves (2007) p. 84.
[5] Hayek (2020) p. 191.
[6] See for example Packe (1954) p. 315; Capaldi (2004) p. 230. Reeve (2007) pp. 152-155.
[7] Sandra J. Peart 'Editor's Introduction' to Hayek (2020) p. xxxiii.
[8] This comment appears in Bain's 1882 biography of Mill and is quoted in Himmelfarb (1974) p. 211.
[9] See *Auto* p. 115ff.

marks – increasing baldness and a series of nervous twitches that were to afflict him for the rest of his life.[1] It is as if, in 1836, at the age of thirty, Mill suddenly became middle-aged.

Through the next two decades, the pattern of Mill's personal life was to spend the week at home in Kensington with his mother and sisters and the weekends with Harriet Taylor in the country. Mr Taylor, as noted, accepted the situation unwillingly, but he did not feel constrained to make a public fuss. As Ryan notes, of the three in this triangle, John Taylor emerges with the most credit for good behaviour: '... he bore his share of the miseries with a grace and cheerfulness which neither of the others could manage'.[2]

The friends of Mill and Harriet Taylor speculated about what was going on, with the consequence that by the mid-1840s, relations with many of these friends had deteriorated to the point that few could be sustained. Then in 1849, John Taylor died after a long illness. Through this period, his wife nursed him with great devotion, and she was much reduced in her contact with Mill. She and Mill spent a further two years in protracted mourning and respectful friendship until they married, in 1851, on Easter Monday.[3]

Soon after the marriage, Mill arranged for an essay that Harriet had written – on the 'Enfranchisement of Woman' – to be published in the *Westminster Review*. He sent the piece to the magazine unsigned, and it was published without attribution.[4] Harriet's authorship was thus obscured. Later, it emerged that there was a request to reprint the article.[5] Writing to Harriet, who was away on a convalescent holiday, Mill notes that the request had been addressed to her – which means that by this time, it was known that she was the author. Mill subsequently says that he had used a daft written by Harriet to refuse permission for the reprint.[6] This was because they did not want a distraction from the ongoing thinking they were doing for the work that eventually became *The Subjection of Women*. However, to their annoyance, the article on Enfranchisement was reprinted anyway.[7]

Mill continued to suffer from difficult family relationships throughout the period of his marriage.[8] His mother and sisters had been so intimidated by the affair that they had felt obliged to keep a low profile on the matter. Mill did nothing to discourage this but then complained after his marriage because his family did not immediately welcome his new wife. Mill failed to inform his brother of the marriage and then accused him of insolence when he failed to mention it. All-round, Mr and Mrs Mill tended to have a quiet married life. They moved to 113 Blackheath Park, in South-East London, which was at that time not at the time the most fashionable part of the capital. They seldom dined out or entertained. Mill left off most of his

---

[1] See Himmelfarb (1974) p. 211.
[2] Ryan (1974) p. 49.
[3] See Capaldi (2012) p. 230. The marriage was conducted by the registrar from Melcome Regis, near Weymouth – deep in what was to become Hardy's Wessex.
[4] See Capaldi (2012) pp. 227-28.
[5] See CW XIV p. 177.
[6] See CW XIV pp. 189-90.
[7] Mill subsequently reprinted the essay, attributing it to Harriet, in one of his volumes of *Dissertations and Discussions*.
[8] Throughout the period of knowing Harriet, Mill's conduct towards his family was rife with awkward and petty exchanges which do him no credit. In no area of his life is Mill's lack of a sense of humour more in evidence.

journalism and dropped out of most of his various discussion groups. He continued to write: as noted earlier, in 1854, he drafted the material that largely contributed to *On Liberty* and *Utilitarianism*. However, he published little during the years of his marriage apart from revised editions of the *Logic* and the *Principles*.[1]

When Mill's work at India House was over, he and Harriet were consumed with fears about their health. Both suffered from versions of tuberculosis, which Mill had suffered from for some time, and it is possible that he transmitted it to Harriet, whose health deteriorated quite quickly.[2] As was common amongst those with sufficient means, they elected to travel in the hope of assisting a cure, and, as we saw, on one such trip, in November 1858, Harriet fell ill and died at Avignon. She was buried in a local churchyard.[3] In his correspondence, Mill says that her end came from an 'excessive & violent congestion of the lungs'[4]. He was devastated by her death, writing that he had lost his 'perfect friend, companion, guide, teacher, all in one'.[5] He bought a house, the Hermitage de Monloisier, at St Veran, close to the burial site, fitting it out in part with some furniture from their hotel room in town.[6] After that, Mill's stepdaughter, Helen Taylor, became his companion and kept house for him, both at Blackheath Park (and from January 1872), from the flat they moved to in Albert Mansions, Victoria Street, London, and at St Veran. Mill also encouraged Helen's career as a writer, and he resumed his friendships and renewed his publishing career. As we noted, he entered parliament for a period in the 1860s before withdrawing into less strenuous activities till his death at Avignon in 1873.

Throughout their relationship, it seems that Mill appreciated Harriet's artistic, poetic, intellectual and moral sensibilities. The qualities he discerned in her and expressed in the dedication in *On Liberty* are rather akin to the tip of an iceberg. In the *Autobiography*, Mill identifies her as 'the most admirable person'[7] he had ever known. He says of her that 'a law of her nature' was 'self-improvement' and 'progress in the highest and in all senses'. As an individual with creative and innovative capacities for self-development, Harriet exemplifies the progressive notion of human life that Mill sets out in *On Liberty*.[8] And he moves on to praise her in a passage of unstinting approbation:

'... she possessed in combination, the qualities which in all other persons whom I had known I had been only too happy to find singly. In her, complete emancipation from every kind of superstition (including that which attributes a pretended perfection to the order of nature and the universe), and an earnest protest against many things which are still part of the

---

[1] See Reeves (2007) p. 248.

[2] At this time medical science had not established that tuberculosis was a contagious viral disease. See Capaldi (2012) p. 122. Mill writes about his condition, and on an inhalation technique he had been prescribed, which expanded lung capacity and helped to counter tuberculosis – see CW XIV pp. 197-201.

[3] Mill had an inscription engraved on the monument over Harriet's grave which includes the tribute to her 'Great and Loving Heart/Her Noble Soul/Her Clear powerful and Original Comprehensive Intellect'. She was 'the Guide and Support/The Instructor in Wisdom/And the Example in Goodness'. For the full text see Capaldi (2012) pp. 247-48.

[4] CW XV p. 582.

[5] CW XV p. 581.

[6] See Reeve (2007) p. 274-275.

[7] *Auto* p. 105.

[8] See *OL* I:11 and III.

established constitution of society, resulted not from the hard intellect but from strength of noble and elevated feeling, and co-existed with a highly reverential nature'.[1]

The claims here for Harriet's many-sided and developmental capacities in this passage are high-flown and seem difficult to square with all that we know of her. Mill has more to say. Harriet's intellect is a 'perfect instrument' for reaching into the 'highest regions of speculation' and for delving into the 'smaller practical concerns of daily life'. Her mind was as 'pre-eminently practical in its judgments and perceptions of things present, as it was high and bold in its anticipations for a remote futurity'.[2] In all this, her skill and insight far exceeded his – he was, he suggests, talented in the more modest areas of methodological reflection in philosophical and political matters.[3]

Mill does not just content himself with this comparison between Harriet Taylor's ability and his. In the draft of his *Autobiography*, Mill suggests that her intellectual qualities are of the highest order. He suggests that he had never found 'any intellect in man or woman which, taken for all in all, could be compared to hers':

'All other intellects when looked at besides hers seem to be but special talents, a peculiar knack acquired by study and practice of dealing with some or one particular thing'. [4]

This estimate is not included in the published version, but he does develop a contrast between the abilities of Harriet and the poet Shelley. In spiritual and temperamental qualities, Shelley was 'but a child compared with what she ultimately became'.[5] And whereas in all other intellectual forces, Mill was obliged to sift truth from error, in her, he could find no 'mixture of error'. Even his father, who had 'no equal' among men, had 'one among women'.[6]

In the moral sphere, Mill thought that Harriet was as distinctive. Her moral character was 'at once the noblest and the best balanced'.[7] She exhibited a 'passion of justice', 'boundless generosity', and all 'excellences' that existed singly in others were united in her. Mill asserts that she could have excelled in any field had she chosen or had circumstances allowed. In fact, she had concentrated on the task of stimulating and encouraging others – notably, J. S. Mill, we may assume.

Mill wrote in these terms to Harriet Taylor for the twenty years or so of their friendship before they married, and she was involved in the revision of the first draft of the *Autobiography*: she was fully aware of the estimate that Mill had of her academic and moral worth. She did not suggest any significant revisions of Mill's text before her death, and thus one must assume that her view was that her husband had just about got it right.

The student of *On Liberty* might be curious about the nature of the external evidence for Harriet Mill's influence on the work. Mill's testimony implies that her friendship and her company throughout, and not least in the seven years of their

---

[1] *Auto* p. 106.
[2] *Auto* p. 108.
[3] See *Auto* pp. 107-108.
[4] *Auto* p. 187.
[5] *Auto* p. 106.
[6] *Auto* p. 116.
[7] *Auto* p. 106.

married life, were of great importance to his academic work. Mill's eulogy in his *Autobiography* is the main source for this view, plus the fact that Mill expresses the same sentiments in his letters to Harriet. And to this, we must add that he claims that they collaborated through their marriage to such an extent that the work from this period was essentially a 'joint production'.[1]

What Mill means by this is worth unpicking. It is useful to consider it against Mill's account of his approach to writing, which he explains in the context of relating the composition of the *Logic*.[2] Mill says, in a chapter of the *Autobiography* written after Harriet's death, that 'all' of his 'books have been composed' in the same way: Mill collected all the notes and other materials he needed from his reading and discussion and then he wrote a full draft of the work in question. Once this was complete, Mill would work over the draft, making such improvements or corrections as seemed necessary, and then the whole work was rewritten – giving a system of what he terms 'double redaction'. Mill's point is that this is what he does when writing a book. What this clearly implies is that the idea of Harriet's co-authorship has to do with the propriety of the ideas within a text that, at a stage of composition, she and Mill discussed and reviewed. What Mill always means to do is to give high tribute to the quality of input that she gave to what he was writing. He suggests that their relationship regarding the work was, as he says, a 'partnership of thought, feeling, and writing'.[3] They were two people whose 'thoughts and speculations'[4] were held 'completely in common'. They enjoyed a relationship where 'all subjects of intellectual or moral interest are discussed between them in daily life, and probed to much greater depths than are usually or conveniently sounded in writings for general readers'. In his correspondence, Mill indicates that he sometimes took into his work suggestions from Harriet in terms of phrases or sentences.[5] Given that Mill always wrote the final copy for his books prior to sending them to the publisher, the partnership of 'writing' alluded to clearly means to refer to the whole process of developing the ideas for the work in question and to the likelihood that Harriet, given that they are often apart, often wrote to Mill on her thoughts arising from what they were discussing and he was drafting. The main difficulty here is that very few of Harriet's letters survive, but those that do are helpful in shedding light on the style of the 'partnership'.

The best example concerns the correspondence, which contains most of the surviving letters of Harriet Taylor that come from the period of Mill's writing and then revising for subsequent editions, the *Principles of Political Economy*.[6] As we discovered, Mill wrote this book in a fairly speedy manner in the mid-1840s. It was published in April 1848, and Mill wanted to dedicate the book to Harriet: when she asked her husband about this, he, not unreasonably, did not think this appropriate.[7] Mill says that this was the first book he produced in which Harriet had a

---

[1] *Auto* p. 141.
[2] See *Auto* p. 125.
[3] *Auto* p. 135.
[4] *Auto* p. 135.
[5] CW XIV p. 144.
[6] See Hayek (2020) pp. 114-150. The correspondence is also reproduced as an appendix in CW III pp. 1026-1037.
[7] See *Auto* pp. 132-133 and Himmelfarb (2007) p. 111. On the dates of the editions of the *Principles* see J. Riley, 'Introduction' to Mill (1998) p. xviii. Mill had an inset printed to be pasted into gift copies of the *Principles*, bearing a lavish dedication to Harriet. See Capaldi (2012) p. 202.

'conspicuous'[1] share. Mill praises her 'accurate and clear-sighted criticism'. He thinks he contributes the 'abstract and purely scientific'[2] parts of the book, while it was 'chiefly her influence that gave to the book that general tone by which it is distinguished from all previous expositions of Political Economy'. He also suggests 'it is entirely due to her'[3] that there is a chapter in the *Principles* on 'the Probable Future of the Labouring Classes'.[4] Mill means that the first draft of the book did not have this chapter, and it was through discussion with Harriet that ideas she had on this theme were 'the cause' of him writing it, with, he says, many of the central ideas being his 'exposition of her thoughts'.[5]

The *Principles* came out in the year during which various revolutions broke out in France and various other capitals in Europe. Much publicity arose over the likely success or otherwise of the communes that for a brief period seemed to be transforming life, cheering up Karl Marx, and prompting the writing of *The Communist Manifesto*.[6] This was suddenly a time of accelerated thinking and speculation about socialism and its possible future in the political life of Britain. Harriet was emphatically keen on the ideals of socialism, seeing it as a force for positive change and improvements in equality. Mill's economic treatise reviewed socialism but with the weight of argument going towards the liberal society, the free market and self-development.

What happened over the next period is that *Principles* was selling so well that a second edition was needed in 1849. Mill and Harriet correspond in the early month of 1849, and the passages she was unhappy about are identified and discussed.[7] Harriet's comments in her letters suggest she often added marginal comments for Mill to consider and to the opportunities they have for talking things over.[8] These are the means by which she contributed to Mill's thinking on the revision of the text. The main points at stake have to de deduced from what Mill says in his letter to Harriet. A key issue was over what method of social organisation could individual self-development and enhanced individuality be best achieved.[9] Would 'individual agency or Socialism'[10] be best? Both approaches are 'imperfect' and susceptible to 'immense improvement'. The form of socialism under review did not exclude private property, and the ideal was a cooperative form of social democracy. Mill remains clear that the failure to define the liberty of action so as to include private property is a problem as socialism develops, for although Mill campaigned against 'primogeniture and entails'[11], private property was not a negotiable point and so a barrier to any full affirmation of socialism. Despite this, Mill's discussions with

---

[1] *Auto* p. 139.
[2] *Auto* p. 140.
[3] *Auto* p. 139.
[4] This is in the *Principles*, Book IV: chapter VII and the title is 'On the Probable Futurity of the Labouring Classes'. See CW III pp.758-796.
[5] *Auto* p. 140.
[6] Marx and Engels (2002).
[7] For Mill's letters on this to Harriet, see also CW XIV pp. 9-10; pp. 11-12; pp. 18-19.
[8] See Hayek (2020) pp. 124-25.
[9] See Capaldi (2012) pp. 218ff for a clear review of this matter. See also Hayek (2020). CW II p.199ff – the first chapter of Book II of the *Principles* is the chapter that deals with the issues in debate.
[10] CW XIV p. 9.
[11] *Auto* p.130. See also pp. 98f and CW XIII pp. 740-41 and CW XVII p. 1757, where his opposition to the socialist approach to private property and to socialistic nationalization is clear.

Harriet meant that ongoing edits to the text moderated the comments on socialism. By the third edition of 1852, the positive aspects of socialism are becoming more explicit. Whatever the merits of free trade, liberty, socialism or anything else, what this process of dialogues shows is that Mr and Mrs Mill review matters and adjustments are made in the light of clarified and developed understandings; but what we find in Harriet's letters is no evidence is that she forces change on Mill or that she unduly influences him to write against his better judgment.

Working Towards *On Liberty*

In the *Autobiography*, there is a passage where Mill reflects on the changes he has seen in life through to the period when he is beginning to think about composing something on the theme of liberty. He notes how, although many reforms he had pursued early in his career had come into play. Yet he observes that 'been attended with much less benefit to human well being than I should formally have anticipated'.[1] The improvement had not been sufficient for that on which 'all real amelioration in the lot of mankind depends', namely, 'their intellectual and moral state'. Too often, 'many false opinions may be exchanged for true ones' without the least alteration in 'the habits of mind of which false opinions are the result'. The upshot is that 'no great improvements in the lot of mankind are possible, until a great change takes place in the fundamental constitution of their mode of thought'. Mill wanted to effect such a change, or 'renovation', to sharpen convictions, hone intellects, and make more positive the principles for responsible life.

In 1853, Mill and Harriet were separated for a week through illness. Mill regularly wrote to her, and in the midst of his meditations on their health and their domestic arrangements, he reminded her of a scheme that they had to plan and prepare a volume of essays on a range of vital topics. Notably, he writes with the collegiate 'we':

'We must finish the best we have got to say, & not only that, but publish it while we are alive – I do not see what living depositary there is likely to be of our thoughts, or who in this weak generation that is growing up will even be capable of thoroughly mastering & assimilating your ideas, much less of reoriginating them – so we must write them & print them, & then they can wait till there are again thinkers.[2]

Mill's references to his wife's influence on his work here include that he has to assimilate her ideas to 'master' them, to reoriginate them. These insights add to our picture of how Mill characterises and acknowledges the process of how he draws from their conversations ideas that he can adapt and use in his writings. With these remarks, we have evidence of the couple's collaborative outlook, with their sense of being intellectual missionaries for the future. They convey an elevated sense of their worth for the present generation and beyond; they are amongst the few 'thinkers' of the present, and they must write out their best thoughts for the sake of some future when there will again be more 'thinkers'. Mill's writing here is also reflected in the mood and tone of *On Liberty*, and we may think there to be an echo

---

[1] *Auto* p. 134.
[2] CW XIV p. 112.

of the 'clerisy' advocated by Coleridge, but in later correspondence with Bain, Mill was not inclined to accept that the style or stance of *On Liberty* was aristocratic or elitist, or as anything akin to the notion of a clerisy. Mill writes more in an educative temper that he meant to 'convert' as many as possible.[1] He also aimed at 'keeping alive the sacred fire in a few minds when we are unable to do more':

'... but the notion of an intellectual aristocracy of *luminières* while the rest of the world remains in darkness fulfils none of my aspirations – & the effect I aim at by the book is, on the contrary, to make the many more accessible to all truth by making them more open minded'.

Mill may have intended the work in this way, and we will reconsider the criticism of its style as we study the text in more detail. There are, however, more pieces of evidence to consider from the correspondence between Mill and Harriet from the period before the work of composing *On Liberty* was started.

In the winter of 1853-54, the Mills were again in correspondence, and there was further reference to the volume of essays that was to represent their 'best thoughts', and which Mill felt they should proceed with before the threats of mortality became more severe:

'Two years, well employed, would enable us I think to get the most of it into a fit state for printing – if not in the best form for popular effect, yet in the state of concentrated thought – a sort of mental pemican, which thinkers, when there are any after us, may nourish themselves with & then dilute for other people'.[2]

Here we have more evidence of an elevated sense of intellectual mission, as well as the implied co-operative activity of reviewing the work-in-progress. As a duty to the thinkers to come, the plan is to put together an intellectually medicinal compound of their insights and wisdom to inspire and 'nourish' the thinkers to come and provide them with a resource that they may, in turn, dilute for others. The aim was to publish a volume with essays on a wide range of topics, including 'Differences of character', 'Love', 'Education of tastes', 'Socialism', and 'Liberty'.[3] When Mill wrote to Harriet, some of the essays had been written, and as we indicated earlier, by the autumn of 1854, he had completed a draft of the one on 'Liberty'.[4]

Mill then began a six-month trip on the Continent to recuperate from another bout of illness. While on this trip, he wrote so many letters to Harriet that they run for two hundred and forty-seven pages in the relevant volume of Mill's *Letters*.[5] Amidst many pages relating the travel arrangements, the scenery, the quality and cleanliness of accommodation, the cost of meals, the problem of fleas, his and Harriet's health, and his love for her, came the proposal that 'Liberty' could be issued as a single volume, rather than be a part of the 'mental pemmican'. In the *Autobiography*, Mill says that the idea for the book version of what became *On*

---

[1] CW XV p. 631.
[2] CW XIV pp. 141-142.
[3] CW XIV p. 152.
[4] As we noted earlier, Mill also drafted the material later used in *Utilitarianism* at this time. See Reeves (2007) p. 248.
[5] See CW XIV pp. 247-494.

Liberty first came to him as he was 'mounting the steps of the Capitol' in Rome.[1] There may be some imaginative fancy here, as Mill had already written of his plan to Harriet before that stage of his trip. The error in the *Autobiography* was probably deliberate – Gibbon's *Decline and Fall of the Roman Empire* (1776-1788) was conceived while Gibbon was amongst the ruins of the Capitol, and perhaps Mill thought this was an appropriate example of what he regarded as a work of the first importance.[2] From Rome, he had written as follows, referring to what he had been thinking about on the journey:

'On my way here... I came back to an idea we have talked about & thought that the best thing to write and publish at the present would be a volume on Liberty. So many things might be brought into it & nothing seems to me more needed – it is a growing need too, for opinion tends to encroach more & more on liberty, & almost all the projects of social reformers in these days are really *liberticide* – Comte, particularly so. I wish I had brought with me here the paper on Liberty that I wrote for our volume of Essays – perhaps my dearest will read it through & tell me whether it will do as the foundation of one part of the volume in question – If she thinks so I will try to write & publish it in 1856 if my health permits me as I hope it will'.[3]

At this stage, Mill thought that the best plan would be to issue a volume of existing essays, then *On Liberty*, and then the 'pemican'.[4] And here again, he gives us unwitting evidence of his methodological relationship with Harriet. Notably, Mill refers to 'the paper on Liberty that I wrote'. The suggestion is that they discuss matters: then he writes. She reads and comments; they discuss again, and he revises, and on they go. Consistent with this, he later wrote that she had been his invaluable 'prompt and guide'.[5]

At the stage of drafting ideas for *On Liberty*, Harriet's view, perhaps influenced by her declining health, seems to have been keen to keep the work for further editing. Whatever the reasons, if we looked at the dates when Mill published his work, as we noted above, it is notable that through the period of their marriage, this committed and prolific writer who had published articles, reviews and books since the 1820s, published virtually nothing apart from revised editions of his *Logic* and *Principles* and a few reviews. However, within a few months of Harriet's death, *On Liberty* and the two volumes of collected essays, *Dissertations and Discussions,* appeared, and it is clear from the speed of their appearance that most of this material had been written for some time.

Throughout 1855-57, Mill's correspondence regularly returns to the hope that *On Liberty* can soon be ready for publication.[6] In one letter to Harriet, he comments as follows:

---

[1] *Auto* p. 136.
[2] Edward Gibbon (1737-1796). Historian, critic and politician.
[3] CW XIV p. 294.
[4] In the event, the two volumes of essays became the first two volumes of *Dissertations and Discussions* (1859).
[5] CW XV p. 620.
[6] See CW XIV p. 294, p. 300, p. 320, p. 332, p. 348 and CW XV p. 519 and p. 534.

'The more I think of the plan of a volume on liberty, the more likely it seems to me that it will be read & make a sensation. The title itself with any known name to it would sell an edition. We must cram as much into it as possible of what we wish not to leave unsaid'.[1]

As regards the longer-term influence of the work, these are prescient words, but despite the urgency of tone, the work of revision continued to the end of refining and improving the form and style of the insights contained therein. It may be that this retention of the work was a part of maintaining their intimacy and seclusion from the hostile and (to them) philistine world at large. This image of Mr and Mrs Mill as the last thinkers in a savage world, as the last noble and compassionate souls of the age, is frequent in their letters.

On Liberty

In *On Liberty*, Mill defends a view of the human condition as involving a complex of people as in a society comprising a nation: some are rational, feeling, liberal individuals, but many others are inclined to favour a collective life of conformity to the whims and tastes of the majority. Mill is worried about the tension between the majority feeling and the innovative spontaneity of the individual. He fears the former will suppress the latter. Mill is keen to encourage reforms to bring about equality before the law for women as for men, to extend *laissez-faire* policies in economic matters, and improve the range and quality of education, all to secure a more innovative, just and liberal society. He conceives this project as set within the framework of utility, but as mentioned in *On Liberty,* the modified view of utility Mill has cultivated is neatly refined with the view that humans are not fixed or uniform in nature but 'progressive' (I: 11).

Mill's idea is that the development of civilization and so the interests of the greatest number, in the long run, is dependent on a minority of creative intellects for whose sake it is essential to preserve for all the liberty of thought and discussion and as almost as complete liberty of action. This is meritocratic as much as democratic and is presented as the means to the end of individuality best cultivating fresh truths for the benefit of a civilized society. Accordingly, *On Liberty* presents a negative view of conformity, conventionalism and public opinion. Creative and innovative individuality is praised, and there is concern over the consequences of democracy, in consequence of the threat within a democratic culture to individual liberty seen in the rise of the 'tyranny of the majority' (I: 5).

In contrast to the approach of Jeremy Bentham and James Mill, Mill did not believe that the economic forces of the market could alone bring about the degree or quality of progress for a possible and desirable civilisation. Due to the pressures for conformity that came from the democratic outlook, and so to avoid a drift towards stagnation, it was vital for a more radical assertion of the liberty of thought and discussion and liberty of action for individuals in and through all aspects of life, with the famous exception of acts that could be prevented due to the risk of 'harm to others'. Over such acts, according to *On Liberty*, society could rightfully constrain individual liberty.

---

[1] CW XIV p. 332.

Whatever Mill thought about aristocratic elitism, there is a sense in which he and his wife are defined into the category of intellectuals whose liberty was essential to the educative well-being of society as a whole. We may think that their personal experience over the twenty or so years before their marriage had a great deal to do with the development of the idea that society could be repressive and conformist and that individuality was best cultivated on the presupposition of reason, insight, genius and progress. Interestingly, one early review of *On Liberty* suggests that it reads as if it is written from 'the prison cell of some persecuted thinker'.[1] It was the product, or joint product, of one of the most successful and respected writers of the age, but in their own estimation, the Mills appeared to have felt under considerable pressure from sections of public opinion that they cared deeply about – the society of their friends.

It is for these reasons that, at times, the tone of *On Liberty* may strike the reader as extreme. Can the threat to the individual perceived by *On Liberty* be as real as is suggested? Is democracy really productive of a tyranny that is worse than any produced by the despots of old?[2] According to the book, individuals are of real worth and potential. Close to the end of *On Liberty,* Mill affirms that 'the worth of a State, in the long run, is the worth of the individuals composing it' (V: 23). The mass of society threatens conformity, mediocrity, suppression and anonymity. In the *Autobiography*, Mill writes a very highly pointed version of this doctrine:

'A person of high intellect should never go into unintellectual society unless he can enter it as an apostle; yet he is the only person with high objects who can safely enter it at all. Persons even of intellectual aspirations had much better, if they can, make their habitual associates of at least their equals, and as far as possible, their superiors, in knowledge, intellect, and elevation of sentiment. Moreover, if the character is formed, and the mind made up, on the few cardinal points of human opinion, agreement of conviction and feeling on these, has been felt in all times to be an essential requisite of anything worthy the name of friendship, in a really earnest mind'.[3]

Mill's reasoning here is high-minded and echoes his thought from the early 1830s of the principle of more abstract governance to guide and instruct individuals.[4] The tone of these remarks relates to how Mill presents the vision of *On Liberty*. As we saw, Mill initially saw the work as a component in a collection of essays to serve as 'a sort of mental pemican', which he suggests 'thinkers' in later generations can digest and then dilute for 'other people'.[5] In the *Autobiography,* further points add to the elevated status *On Liberty* itself has in Mill's later estimation, not least because he sees the text as something they have together produced:

'The "Liberty" was more directly and literally our joint production than anything else which bears my name, for there was not a sentence of that was not several times gone through by us together, turned over in many ways, and carefully weeded of any faults, either in thought or expression, that we detected in it. It is in consequence of this that, although it

---

[1] So wrote Richard Hutton in a review for the *National Review*, published in 1859. See Pyle (1994) p. 81.
[2] Such is Mill's claim: see *OL* I: 5.
[3] *Auto* p. 129.
[4] See Chapter 1 above and CW XII p. 84.
[5] CW XV pp. 141-142.

never underwent her final revision, it far surpasses, as a mere specimen of composition, anything which has proceeded from me either before or since. With regard to the thoughts, it is difficult to identify any particular part or element as being more hers than all the rest. The whole mode of thinking of which the book was the expression, was emphatically hers. But I was so thoroughly imbued with it that the same thoughts naturally occurred to us both. That I was thus penetrated with it, however, I owe in great degree to her'.[1]

In case we are not clear on the point, Mill adds more:

'The *Liberty* is likely to survive longer than anything else I have written…because the conjunction of her mind with mine has rendered it a kind of philosophic text-book of a single truth, which the changes progressively taking place in modern society tend to bring out into ever stronger relief: the importance, to man and society, of a large variety in types of character, and of giving full freedom to human nature to expand itself in innumerable and conflicting directions'.[2]

We have some emphatic notions in these remarks that give *On Liberty* high estimation: imbued with a distinctive 'mode of thought', the fusion of creative minds renders it a 'kind of philosophic text-book of a single truth'. That truth centres on the importance, personal and social, of varieties of character and 'of giving freedom to human nature' for expansive development. What this brings home is a degree of tension between how Mill sanctifies the creative status of the text and its actual message. If we focus on the text, one of the main apostolic teachings is that the best truths emerge where there is a free and fearless 'collision' (II: 1) of opinions. The best and most improving plans for life come as individuals pursue the 'liberty of tastes and pursuits' (I: 12). In this, there is, again, less an elitist and more a meritocratic operational ideal, and the high-minded strands in the autobiographic view contrast with the pattern of ideas in *On Liberty*.

To take an example, we can see how intellectuals with 'aspirations' would progress if they associated with their equals or betters.[3] However, to empower intellectualism and other positive qualities on a wider front, we need to be apostolic in a more general and generous sense. We need, to borrow from the faith traditions, to be less the esoteric devotee and more the embedded Franciscan: if we transpose intellectualism into high levels of potential expertise in mathematics, chess or tennis, how would it be if novices were excluded from any competition with their superiors, with those accomplished in the higher or more sophisticated modes of thought or technique?

The circumstances of Mill's life are a persuasive indication of the extent to which he was committed to a robust form of engaged but practically-orientated intellectualism. As we have remarked, it was only during his marriage that Mill, understandably, reduced his engagement with a wider intellectual life – but through that period, he does seem to have concentrated on the preparation of a theoretical statement of the approach to life that he favoured. For the rest, he moves as an activist in critical thinking and reform amongst circles of others of differing degrees of ability and potential.

---

[1] *Auto* p. 141.
[2] *Auto* p. 142.
[3] *Auto* p. 129.

With regard to *On Liberty*, in addition to the remarks we quoted earlier, in the *Autobiography,* Mill has another point about the text. He notes that after the 'irreparable loss' of Harriet:

'… one of my earliest cares was to print and publish the treatise so much of which was the work of her whom I had lost, and consecrate it to her memory. I have made no alteration or addition to it, nor shall I ever. Though it wants the last touch of her hand, no substitute for that touch shall be attempted by mine'.[1]

Mill was true to this determination: *On Liberty* went through many editions between 1859 and 1873, but Mill made no changes to the text, departing from his policy with his other writings, of revising the texts to address criticism or develop new lines of thought.

Given that Mill says of Harriet's contribution that *On Liberty* presents as the product of a 'conjunction' of their minds, this raises the question of whether Mill is right to say that the 'mode of thinking' in *On Liberty* is characteristically Harriet's rather than his. From the context of saying this, Mill is alluding to how he and Harriet worked together to discuss what he was in the process of writing. Within Mill scholarship, the case for highlighting Harriet's influence is associated with Himmelfarb, who thinks that we should consider that there are really 'two Mills' – thinking that in his writings on socio-political issues before and after his marriage – so bracketing out *On Liberty* – do not exhibit so extreme a liberty doctrine as that of *On Liberty*.[2] As a rule, Mill is said to be suspicious of and opposed to attempts to render the complexity of modern society through the lens of 'a single truth', and liberty is one amongst several principles that would render social life amenable. Himmelfarb's view is that Harriet's influence is the key factor in the accentuation that we have with the view of liberty in *On Liberty*. In this respect, her view is that Harriet was an individual whose force of personality was considerable: she considers Mill to be submissive, and her surviving 'literary efforts show evidence of a dogmatic and mediocre mind'.[3] Reeves, in contrast, thinks Harriet was a 'fiercely intelligent woman'.[4]

The questions of Harriet's intellectual prowess and of the extent to which *On Liberty* represents a deviation from the views found in Mill's work as a whole are contentious. Already we have indicated ways in which his new approach to utility aims to work harmoniously with the principles of *On Liberty*. As regards Mill's thoughts about Harriet's influence on his thinking, this remains a factor since, in the *Autobiography*, he consistently praises and esteems Harriet's quality of mind, and on this, if we take into account their correspondence and the issues they discussed related to *On Liberty*, as well as the other texts written through the time of their association, the overwhelming impression is that both Mill and Harriet both began to see greater dangers inherent in the rise of social trends towards equality and conformity. But Mill sustains a regard for the rule of law and for changes by due process to the end of achieving complete equality between men and women in and

---

[1] *Auto* p. 144.
[2] See for example Himmelfarb (1974) pp. xii-xvii. Against Himmelfarb, see Gray (1983). See also Rees (1985) pp. 109-115 – where the idea is that Mill is to be seen as a more consistent writer.
[3] Himmelfarb (1962) 'Introduction' pp. xxiv-xxv
[4] Reeves (2007) p. 221.

before the law. Against the tide of social custom and the force of majority opinions, and in and for a time he considered transitional, Mill began to think of a need to frame a clear principle to provide structure and order to the map of human relationships within and against society. In *On Liberty*, he pushes on to accentuate the principle of liberty, and as his notion of what it was to be human became more complex, the more acute the defence of liberty becomes as a corollary of the desire to have a plural variety of character and interest at work in society, where society is the sum total of human individuals seen as 'progressive' beings (I: 11).

As the comments about the composition of *On Liberty* considered earlier suggest, the work had a collaborative phase of revision. This is not to say that Harriet was the actual co-author of *On Liberty*, but it supports Mill's contention that the book also expresses her 'mode' of thought, with which he, for a long period, was 'thoroughly imbued'. And we should not doubt his claim that drafts of the book had been checked and revised by them both in the period before Harriet's death.

Part II: On Liberty: Commentary and Guide

6. Mill on Necessity and Liberty: *On Liberty* I: 'Introductory' Paragraph 1

We start our study of the text of *On Liberty* with a rather atypical focus on Mill's opening paragraph, which is neatly designed to skirt around a major issue to which Mill thinks he can allude before moving swiftly on. This might be a valid move for keen readers of all of his work in 1859 or in any period since, but for most readers coming to Mill and to the text for the first time, there is a case for a deeper elucidation.

Mill begins *On Liberty* with the following statement of guidance and intent:

'The subject of this essay is not the so-called "liberty of the will", so unfortunately opposed to the misnamed doctrine of philosophical necessity; but civil, or social liberty: the nature and limits of the power which can be legitimately exercised by society over the individual' (I: 1).

Mill immediately elaborates on some ramifications of the last clause of this opening. The issue of 'civil, or social liberty' and the matter of the 'limits' to 'the power' of 'society over the individual' gives rise, he says, to 'a question seldom stated, and hardly ever discussed in general terms, but which profoundly influences the practical controversies of the age by its latent presence, and is likely soon to make itself recognized as the vital question of the future': Mill continues:

'It is so far from being new that, in a certain sense, it has divided mankind almost from the remotest ages; but in the stage of progress into which the more civilized portions of the species have now entered, it presents itself under new conditions and requires a different and more fundamental treatment'.

As a prelude to this, Mill clarifies that his interest is in 'civil, or social liberty', as opposed to the 'liberty of the will' in relation to the doctrine of 'philosophical necessity'. What exactly Mill means by this form of liberty is one thing; another is that Mill's opening is an allusion to the issue of free will and determinism as a debate in classical and popular philosophical disputation. The point Mill wants to stress is that this area of debate is not going to be reviewed in *On Liberty*. This does not mean that Mill thinks the issue of determinism (or 'philosophical necessity') is an unimportant matter for review. He thinks it goes beyond the scope of his present discussion, and it is in no sense a spoiler alert to say that Mill proves to be as good as his opening words, for as the text of *On Liberty* unfolds, he does not return to the question of 'the liberty of the will' and the tension with 'philosophical necessity'. Attention is placed on liberty in the setting of everyday life and the right and proper conditions for individuals to think, argue, discuss and live within, but not under the compulsion or control of society. This suggests that by some means not disclosed in the text, Mill thinks that individuals have a degree and quality of liberty free from the patterns of deterministic 'philosophical necessity' and that he can proceed with his endeavour without further discussion.

The upshot is that Mill covers a large area of debate with his opening points, and if we pass on without comment on what he means, we would be leaving a substantial stone unturned. Previously, as is often said in the course of TV drama series, Mill gave a large degree of attention to the problem of philosophical necessity, or what we might call free will and determinism.[1] It is this prior review that gives the deeper reason for his reference to what he is doing and not doing in *On Liberty*. He also reached a position on the problems of necessity that he considered to have resolved certain residual difficulties, such that he could smoothly move on to the review, as in *On Liberty*, of the issue of civil or social liberty. Mill's thinking about 'philosophical necessity' is thus worth investigating to appreciate what is focused on in *On Liberty*.

Mill and the Issue of Necessity

With this topic, the issues Mill is concerned with are neatly expressed by Berlin, who, reflecting on Mill and the problem of free will and determinism, comments that Mill's thought shows how 'he was tormented by the problem of free will, and found no better solution for it than anyone else, although at times he thought he had solved it'.[2] This enigmatic comment is immediately explained: rather than focussing on the phenomenon of 'rational thought'[3] or human 'domination over nature', Mill puts forward as distinctive the human capacities of the 'freedom to choose and to experiment'. Mill, Berlin says, means to establish the human condition as involving the liberty of 'choosing both the object and manner of their worship', and this is the view that ensures Mill's 'lasting fame'. Berlin is alert to the point that the issue of tension between free will and determinism remains problematic, and it is perhaps best to think that while Mill's solution to the tensions here might not be better than any other, it might also not be that much worse.[4]

What Berlin sees, in line with other commentators on Mill, harks back to his enthusiasm for scientific thought and inductivism. Mill is steeped in a commitment to this and to a form of empiricism. This is manifest in his high degree of respect for the evidence generated from experience and for what is found through reasoned analysis. This outlook gives Mill an intellectual obligation to respect the methods that typified the natural sciences, and this, in turn, entailed seeing particular events and occurrences as outcomes of specific causal processes, explicable by reasons and laws, by relations of cause and effect. The outcome was a broadly deterministic outlook linked to the indicative inductivism that Mill develops in the *Logic*. This supports the view that, in general, what was the case was how it was out of a pattern of necessity, such that in and for that case, it could not be otherwise. Mill tended to think that the social sciences would operate in much the same way, giving the means to describe and analyse social trends.

Mill found the nub of the problem in his sense that the experience of life, and so his view of the human condition, also included the idea that human societies were composites of individuals. He makes this point explicit in *On Liberty*, as in the comment we have already noted, that 'the worth of the State... is the worth of the

---

[1] See particularly *Logic* VI: IV: 1-4.
[2] Berlin (2017) p. 250.
[3] Berlin (2017) p. 251.
[4] Mill's treatment is also not so far from Berlin's view on the matter: see Berlin (2017) pp. 322-328. For a wider review of the issue of freewill and determinism see Loxton (2021) Chapter 9.

individuals composing it' (V: 23).[1] As Mill sees them, individuals have this worth through possessing the capacity for the liberty of thought and discussion and liberty of action, and so for self-development: by these means, he thinks, insights into the best truths can be advanced, and individuality of character developed – and so society: accordingly, as *On Liberty* aims to show, these liberties matter.

To get to the insights Mill thought would work on the problems of necessity, we need to consider some of his remarks in *A System of Logic,* where he aims to set out the balance between necessity and the liberty of the will. The balance comes through what Mill sees as the conditional limitation that pertains to explanations that aim to be totalistic, and in this light, it soon emerges that in the *Logic,* Mill wants to trim the sails of philosophical necessity as it is commonly understood. He suggests that philosophical necessity may be defined 'as asserting human volitions and actions to be necessary and inevitable'.[2] He explains that this view is often imposed on the human will and the capacity for choice in a misleading way. What is lost is the true meaning, which is that 'given the motives which are present to an individual's mind, and given likewise the character and disposition of the individual, the manner in which he will act might be unerringly inferred'.[3]

'Might be' and the idea of a focus on 'an' individual are crucial here: Mill floats the idea that the issue is that if we had absolute knowledge of a person's motives, character and disposition, we would be able to predict their choices and actions accurately. This is how the doctrine of necessity is thought to work in and for explaining events through the natural sciences. Mill thinks that we often assume that causal necessity does not apply to the human will because, subjectively, we simply do not have what we cannot have, the absolute knowledge that would allow the predictive diagnosis of necessity. Then the classical idea of the freedom of the will is affirmed as an alternative complete explanation for the distinctive elements of the human condition.

While Mill sees the freedom of the will in this sense as another error, it does preserve the important insight into 'the power of the mind to co-operate in the formation of its own character'.[4] The power evoked here points up a distinctive and differentiating aspect of being human: in contrast to other natural phenomena, human actions:

'... are never (except in some cases of mania) ruled by any one motive with such absolute sway that there is no room for the influence of any other'.

Here Mill is thinking of the complexity of being human, which gives rise to the critical implication suggestive of the untenability of explaining human choice and action by single or simple causal relations. This complexity links to the human capacity for having the ability to revise through reflection and self-determination how a personal life unfolds: the person has, 'to a certain extent', Mill thinks:

---

[1] He also says in *Utilitarianism* that 'the great majority of good actions are intended, not for the benefit of the world, but for that of individuals, of which the good of the world is made up' (*Util* II: 18).
[2] *Logic* VI: II: 1.
[3] *Logic* VI: II: 2.
[4] *Logic* VI: II: 3.

'... a power to alter his character. Its being, in the ultimate resort, formed for him, is not inconsistent with its being, in part, formed *by* him'.

Mill's idea is that human individuals, like slugs, are explicable and measurable by all manner of retrospective studies. We can consider a person's background, tradition, customs, environment, individual history, disposition and character, drawing out all of these through the explanatory power of the natural and human sciences. Even so, and distinct from slugs, the human capacity for singular, distinct, innovative and creative thought and action will not be exhausted. Individual humans having these capacities renders individuality and all that it means an invaluable asset to society and the well-being of the greater number. Mill does not draw on this example, but tragically, in modern life, it is not uncommon for a family to discover that a loved one has degenerative dementia, such as Alzheimer's or Pick's Disease (or frontotemporal dementia). In such conditions, a person may lose the key quality that empowers personhood, their rational self-awareness, together with the capacity to operate with autonomy. Such a person invariably loses the capacity to take responsibility for their affairs, and someone else will have power of attorney over them. Their lives will fall into routine and patterns of necessity and lose the quintessential dimension of responsive capacities for self-determination that makes for the individuality Mill considers vital, and that liberty is integral in developing.

Mill's idea is that for all that there is a commitment to a form of scientific determinism in his thinking, there is also a sense of humans as distinct individuals, with certain capacities that only make sense through the possession of the liberty of the will in some fundamental respect. As Berlin puts it, Mill rejects 'the pseudo-scientific model'[1] that depicts all humans as possessing the same qualities, with their differences simply being a consequence of different reactions to differing circumstances. Instead, and despite believing that human thinking developed from experience and through association, Mill thought humans to be individually equipped with such freedom so they could operate, as Berlin explains, presenting:

'...the image of man as creative, incapable of self-completion, and therefore never wholly predictable: fallible, a complex combination of opposites, some reconcilable, others incapable of being resolved or harmonised; unable to cease from his search for truth, happiness, novelty, freedom, but with no guarantee, theological, logical or scientific, of being able to attain them; a free, imperfect being, capable of determining his own destiny in circumstances favourable to the development of his reason and his gifts'.[2]

In his later work, *Hamilton,* Mill defends this mode of individualism, noting the danger and limitation of coercive necessity presented by theological teaching and explanations of the natural world.[3] Mill again defends an experiential and inductive rationale for choices and actions.[4] This shows individual humans to be 'capable of moral government.'[5] What this capacity for moral autonomy requires is the opposite of what Mill found in the socialist teaching of his former partners in debate, the

---

[1] Berlin (2017) p. 250. Sir Isaiah Berlin (1909-1997). Berlin was the preeminent historian of ideas of his era – from the 1930s until his death.
[2] Berlin (2017) p. 250.
[3] CW IX p. 440 and p. 449.
[4] See CW IX p, 449-53.
[5] CW IX p. 453.

Owenites.[1] They had a version of the necessitarian teaching that says 'that volitions are effects of causes'. Thus 'human responsibility' is denied, as each person acts in consequence of his character as a social construct: so the individual is not the self-responsible 'author of his own character. It is made *for* him, not *by* him.' On this view, there is no case to justly punish the offender 'for what he cannot help'. The only valid operation for punishment is to aim 'to try to convince or persuade' the offender to 'act in a different manner'.

Mill assumes that it challenges us to the core to think that no offender bears a personal responsibility for their misdemeanours or crimes. He is sure we have something that we draw on to find a surer means by which to justly punish those who offend. He thinks the residual problem is due to a 'confusion of ideas, which makes the subjection of human volitions to the law of Causation seem inconsistent with accountability'. The problem is that if we think that an action should not be done because we will be punished, and we choose not to do it so that we avoid the punishment, such a pattern of beliefs can only be within our consciousness 'because the belief has been taught to us by our parents and tutors, or by our religion, or is generally held by those who surround us, or because we have ourselves come to the conclusion, by reasoning, or from the experience of life'.[2] To act in accordance with this acquired orientation is not to act with freedom of the will or with the sort of liberty that Mill defends.

Mill notes that the justification of protection - for the individual concerned as well as for society – is a better rational for punishment from the necessitarian perspective.[3] But he also thinks there is the possibility that we might think that 'the feeling of liability to punishment'[4] comes from 'knowing' that we would deserve it: it is one thing, and something common but misleading, to believe that we shall 'be *made* accountable'; the 'hypothesis' of 'free-will' is actually related to the truer belief that, in a given circumstance of facing punishment, 'we ought so to be' – for in such a circumstance 'we are justly accountable; that guilt deserves punishment'.

In defence of his preferred view, Mill emphasises the importance of 'moral education to educate the will'.[5] Human 'desires and aversions' must inform this process so that those 'likeliest to lead to evil' are eradicated or at least weakened. The 'desire or right conduct and the eversion of wrong' must be exalted 'to the highest pitch' as must 'all other desires and aversions of which the ordinary operation is auxiliary to right'. This 'moral education' has further tasks: the reduction of those desires and aversions that would, through any period of developed 'indulgence', lead to rendering 'them too powerful to be overcome by the moral sentiment'; the elaboration of 'a clear intellectual standard of right and wrong', and a balanced sense of the right and proper settings for the appropriate expression of the individual's desires and aversions.

In *On Liberty,* Mill is keen to support the case for a greater sense of the human capacity for self-determining action by his emphasis on the notion that individuals, as agents with considerable autonomy, are able to cultivate a plurality of interests. As Berlin's remarks suggest, what Mill has in a fashion, is a sense of individual

---

[1] See CW IX p. 453.

[2] CW IX p. 454.

[3] See CW IX p. 458.

[4] CW IX p. 454.

[5] CW IX p. 453.

humans having a capacity for creative self-development and a form of self-determining freedom. The issue with this is how to make it work with the broader mindset of empiricism and inductivism. The cumulative problem is that Mill liked to defend scientific explanations in general, but he also wanted to protect a region for individual liberty for human self-development. What needs careful resolution is the problem that if we are committed to a form of deterministic explanation for the natural and human sciences, then this will also account for the varieties of interest and the degree and range of capacity that given individuals exhibit. Each individual is how he or she is in consequence, and as the expression of the circumstances of their background and upbringing, quite apart, we would now say, from being the expression of a complex of particular but deterministic neurophysiological factors. This would mean that something more subtle than an appeal to the freedom of the will would be needed to explain the phenomena of human variability.

In his work as a whole, Mill resorts to the view – consistent with both his inductivism and his fallibilism[1] – that the problem of free will and determinism is, in the end, what is best termed an indeterminate matter. Again in his study of *Hamilton*, he remarks that the tension over this matter reflects the more basic issue of 'the final inexplicability, at which… we inevitably arrive when we reach ultimate facts'.[2]

Mill is constitutionally disinclined to follow a Kantian route to see the freedom of the will and scientific necessity as antinomies of reason, as conflicting truths of equal weight and significance, the one dealing with things as they appear to be and the other with things as they are in themselves. In the tradition of more recent thought, there is greater resonance between Kantian critical reason and modern understandings of genetics that offers a more plausible solution to the tensions Mill struggled to resolve.[3] The point is, while humans are generically all human, genetically, each human is unique, and this gives some scope for the self-determinative capacity that the defence of liberty serves. Mill does not have these ideas at his disposal; what he does have is a strong sense that something is amiss in life if human individuality is suppressed by uniformity and commonalities of outlook.

A basic point at stake in all of his writings that is pertinent to the problems Mill addresses over necessity and liberty is that if we assume, as Mill does, a naturalistic position set within the spectrum of lived and perceived experience, this entails and justifies the view that particular events are explicable by particular causes – something Mill judiciously affirms in the *Logic* – 'all inference is from particulars to particulars'.[4] This also entails that the wider generalised question of whether all particulars must conform to the laws of necessity is then practically indeterminate. This is for the extremely good reason that to answer it, we would have to sit outside the totality of the universe to see whether and how it was regulated by the laws of necessity. Since we cannot do this, we are unable, as Mill notes, to reach a definitive explicable solution to the problem of the freedom of the will and philosophical necessity.

---

[1] Mill sets out his fallibilistic view of the human condition in *OL* Chapter II – see Chapter 9 below.
[2] CW IX p. 194.
[3] For Kant's ideas on freedom and much else see his *Critique of Pure Reason* (1781/1787) – Kant (1978).
[4] *Logic* II. III. 4

Aspects of Mill's position are clarified by points made in two of his letters, where he explains what he does and does not mean by the ideas of necessary truth and necessity. This comes out first in a letter written in November 1859 to his occasional correspondent, W. G. Ward. Ward had been reading the latest edition of the *Logic* and was still puzzled by Mill's use of the idea of necessity, as in that given inferences were 'necessarily following from premises'.[1] Mill explains that in the *Logic,* he did not ever mean to use the term in a 'metaphysical' way. As in *On Liberty*, Mill is not interested in the viability of the 'misplaced doctrine of philosophical necessity' (I: 1). Instead, he means to use 'necessary' in 'its popular sense'. He means that necessity is rightly used to signal how 'the reasoning process is, to us, conclusive evidence of what it proves'. Mill means that such reason applies to what we experience and understand as in matters of fact or in accordance with the rules within grammar or mathematics, where given something, something else is said to follow of necessity.

Mill does not use the example that runs, 'If I sweep Carlyle's manuscript into the fire, it will of necessity burn', but that would illustrate the point, which puts the sense and meaning of 'necessity' into a localised and particular form. In another letter from a few years later, Mill calls himself a 'necessitarian'.[2] He explains that this has nothing to do with beliefs in invariable laws of causal necessity – as ever, Mill rejects what he considers to be metaphysical fancies. Necessity, as he understands it, is all to do with the everyday experience of 'the invariability of sequence'. For example, assuming the power is on and the bulbs are in good order, if the switch is pressed, the lights come on. Mill's point is that a form of necessitarianism is helpful as it explains our common disposition to rely on 'the possibility of predictions' between particular events that are discerned and quantifiable.

In the *Autobiography*, Mill offers a summary of the view that he takes on the proper range and limits of philosophical necessity. The summary has a measure of existential input, as Mill notes that this issue weighed heavily upon him during the later 'returns' of his 'dejection'[3] – he means the latter period of his time of crisis in 1829-30. The low points are reached in his experience as he reflects on how, if the doctrine of necessity is true in the way it is usually presented, it means that a person's life, in this case, Mill's life of misery and turmoil, is a consequence of past events. In this event, Mill's life made him 'the helpless slave of antecedent circumstances'.[4] Relief comes as Mill appreciates that there are 'misleading associations' in the doctrine of necessity relating to how matters of 'Cause and Effect' relate to 'human action'. Mill's realisation is that although a person's characteristics are shaped by circumstances, human capacities, interests and desires 'can do much to shape those circumstances'.

---

[1] CW XV p. 647. The letter to Ward is pp. 646-650. W. G. Ward (1812-1882) was a Catholic philosopher and theologian who had written a very positive review of the *Logic* in 1843 for *The British Critic*. He and Mill met in 1848, and corresponded thereafter, invariably on the higher reaches of intellectual thought.

[2] CW XVI p. 1065. The letter of 7th June, 1865, to R. G. Hazard (1801-1888). Hazard was a woollen manufacturer from Rhode Island, but he wrote some philosophy and had corresponded with Mill on matters such as freewill and necessity.

[3] *Auto* p. 96. This what Berlin means when he says that Mill was 'tormented' by these problems. See above and Berlin (2017) p. 250.

[4] *Auto* p. 97. Here Mill is consciously reporting on what he had written in the *Logic*.

All this leads to the conclusion that the 'inspiriting and enobling' influence from 'the doctrine of freewill' comes through the following 'conviction':

'That we have real power over the formation of our own character, our will, by influencing some of our circumstances, can modify our future habits or capabilities of willing. All this was entirely consistent with the doctrine of circumstances, or rather, was that doctrine itself, properly understood'.

As we mentioned, Mill's ideas here offer a version of what is now termed self-determining freedom, linked in his case to a reasoned scepticism about the extent to which causal relations can be considered significant beyond the links between particulars.[1]

Types of Liberty

The other big idea arising in the opening paragraph is that there is a reason to review the extent to which the power of society can rightly limit or control the liberty of the individual. That Mill thinks liberty is important follows from his thinking on the rightful nature of necessity. His idea is that humans live in such a complex of relations that singular causal and deterministic explanations of the sort that would be classified as philosophical necessity is not viable. He thinks that it makes much more sense to envisage humans capable of making real and justified choices, operating with what he terms 'civil, or social liberty' (I: 1).

If we are to reflect on Mill's development of his defence of this idea of liberty, it is as well to equip our thinking with the invaluable and influential considerations given by Berlin, notably in his essay, 'Two Concepts of Liberty', where he reviewed the contrasts between 'negative' and 'positive' conceptions of liberty.[2] In his detailed discussion of these types of liberty, Berlin is explicit in the view that the positive and negative modes of liberty have areas of overlap and reciprocal value for humanity.[3] This is fitting in the case of Mill, who rather obviously employs both forms as he unpacks the arguments of *On Liberty*.

The idea of liberty as we have been considering concerning Mill falls into the category of what Berlin terms 'negative' liberty, when the main emphasis is on the structural question of the areas of life 'within which the subject – a person or a group of persons – is or should be left to do or be what he is able to do or be, without interference by other persons'.[4] The point is that with this form of liberty, almost no interference by others, whether individuals, groups or the state, is seen to be legitimate. A person is possessed by liberty in the negative sense when actions can be willed and undertaken without constraint, with and through the exercise of

---

[1] For a more detailed consideration of the issues of freewill, determinism and self-determinism, see Loxton (2021), especially Chapter 9.
[2] See Berlin (2017) pp. 166-217 and also pp. 322-328, his piece called 'Final Retrospect'. Berlin originally presented 'Two Concepts of Liberty' as an inaugural lecture given in Oxford, in 1958, and was in the volume *Four Essays on Liberty*, first published in 1969. This publication has been supplanted by the volume *Liberty* (Berlin 2017), a collection of five of Berlin's essays on liberty, as well as a number of his other writings on related themes. Berlin was the preeminent historian of ideas of his era – from the 1930s until his death.
[3] See Berlin (2017) p. 169, pp. 178-179, and pp. 214-217.
[4] Berlin (2017) p. 169.

rational autonomy. It is a form of 'freedom from'.[1] When Mill argues that individuals need liberty from 'the tyranny of the majority' (I: 4), he is appealing to negative liberty.

The other category of liberty, 'positive' liberty, has, Berlin thinks, to do with the following question:

> 'What, or who, is the source of control or interference that can determine someone to do, or be, this rather than that?'[2]

With this strand of positive liberty, the key idea is that people become free only when they appreciate what and why it is that something is operating as a controlling force over them. From this process of analysis, positive liberty is acquired in the sense of 'freedom *to*'.[3] The point is that authentic positive freedom comes if we understand and critically assess what it is that shapes us, so then we become truly free to be who we are. The control in question could be subjective feelings, personal dispositions, or socio-cultural patterns of custom, history, ideology or thought, into which a person had been inculcated. The motivation for the realisation of positive liberty is, Berlin suggests, to do with human rationality and the sense that it is 'reason that distinguishes... a human being from the rest of the world'.[4] It follows from this that humans look to become rationally self-conscious 'thinking, willing, active' beings, assuming 'responsibility' for their actions and being able 'to explain them by reference' to their 'own ideas and purposes'. Mill also operates with a version of positive liberty when he reasons that individuals require the liberties of 'thought and feeling, absolute freedom of opinion' (I: 12), the liberties of 'expressing and publishing their own opinions' and of 'tastes and pursuits' so that they can frame 'the plan of... life', suiting the progressive development of their individual 'character'.

The operational difference and the relation between positive and negative liberty can be illustrated. Negative liberty seems to have a clear-cut focus: a person is at liberty if they are unconstrained and able to do as they please. A person in a developed society in the twenty-first century might think they are at liberty in this sense if they have the economic power to obtain and use when they please the latest iPhone. However, an advocate of positive liberty would say that the potential iPhone owner is not properly free until he has understood and put to one side for consideration the trends, forces or influences that lead them to feel such an unwittingly controlled commitment to have the latest iPhone. In the positive view of freedom, we are not free to be what or who we really are until we are free to live without the influences of routine, habit, oppression, enslavement, coercion, control or anything of that kind. We can then have liberty and the independence and autonomy that Mill favours

These points show the good sense in Berlin's review that the positive and negative modes of liberty are commensurable. The classification of the two aspects of liberty is helpful since, from the review we have made so far of *On Liberty*, the immediate emphasis on what is initially developed involves more of a consistent

---

[1] Berlin (2017) p. 178.
[2] Berlin (2017) p. 169.
[3] Berlin (2017) p. 326. See also p. 178.
[4] Berlin (2017). p. 178.

allegiance to 'negative' liberty. As the text unfolds, Mill's project also entails a particular form of 'positive' liberty. The distinctions here are also useful for considering issues of debate arising within modernity, where we find that liberty has taken a distinct hue, one that is explicable as a reorientation to a more prescriptive form of the 'positive' sense of liberty.[1] Here it is worth noting another important point made by Berlin, the health warning that positive liberty can become 'virtually identical' with authority.[2] This is because of the way in which, in various forms, versions of positive liberty have been conjoined with notions of freedom allied to types of rationality – as in schemes of thought for life writ large – where very particular modes of reasoning become determinative and regulatory.[3]

If we reconsider what Mill sets out with his 'one very simple principle' (I: 9), we can see this implies a clear statement of negative liberty. The individual, in respect of his (or her) 'own body and mind, is sovereign'. The attack is on the entailment of positive liberty, the issue, as Berlin puts it, of 'what or who, is the source of control or interference that can determine someone to do or be, this rather than that?'[4] Mill's answer to this sort of question is a version of personal autonomy, that what the individual should be is free to choose to do and be without anyone else 'interfering' (I: 9) to control or compel the individual. What we choose and how we develop our interests is not in the least prescribed; it is solely a matter for individuals, and only if an individual's activity risks or manifests the production 'of evil to someone else' is society warranted in constraining the individual with moral or legal penalties, so as 'to prevent harm to others'. However, Mill thinks that the 'imperative that humans beings should be free to form opinions and express them without reserve' (III: 1) links to the liberty to 'act upon their opinions – to carry these out in their lives without hindrance, either physical or moral, from their fellow men'. This shapes to give expression to his positive liberty, to the ideal of enhancing the development of humans as 'progressive' beings under the ethos of utility 'in its largest sense'(I: 11).

---

[1] See Chapters 13-15 below.
[2] Berlin (2017) p. 194.
[3] See Berlin (2017) pp.326-328. What Berlin has in mind is systems of ideology, but what he is concerned about is more than amply demonstrated by some of the trends on right thinking and such notions as we will be examining in Chapters 13-16 below.
[4] Berlin (2017) p. 169.

7. *On Liberty*: I: 'Introductory' (Paragraphs 1-16)

The first chapter of *On Liberty*, with its rather self-deprecating title, might be thought useful as the setting for Mill's definitive statement of the principle of liberty, but perhaps not for much else. It is, however, much more than that, for the chapter presents almost all of the main themes that Mill is concerned with later, and he deploys a range of the ideas and distinctions that he relies on throughout the book.[1] The chapter repays careful review to build a foundation for studying the rest of the text.

In *On Liberty*, Mill's style is clear once the reader has acclimatised, and he offers a complex range of explanations, reviews and arguments. He devotes a considerable amount of space to the generous consideration of views that oppose the line he seeks to promote. He does this to such an extent that we do not have to look far for views to oppose Mill – criticisms of his positive doctrines flow through the discussions within the text.

Mill's Key Ideas

Mill's central argument in *On Liberty* draws on and develops a tradition of liberalism in economic and social thought. Mill does not elaborate too much on this background in his text, but the main line of thought he draws on stems from John Milton, John Locke and Adam Smith, as well as a range of continental thinkers, and running through to Jeremy Bentham.[2] This suggests that economic and social development, as well as individual freedom over moral and religious opinion, requires protection from the interference of interest groups, trends of common opinion, or from authorities. Mill thus writes against paternalism by the State and public opinion in relation to the lives of individuals. Mill does not deny that there are matters of general interest related to the common good that involves the legitimate concern and involvement of the State and public opinion. Such issues as defence, welfare, and public order come into the domain of public and State interest. Underlying the range of ideas here is Mill's variable sense of how to conceive of society – something we will return to later. However, Mill holds that for all that humans are social creatures, there is a private dimension of life which is better left to the individual, better not least for the wider sense of utility, since the general interest is thereby better served.

In a proverbial nutshell, Mill's thesis is that the rest of us will benefit if all of us can freely operate with the liberties in question. He favours the idea that each of us should be at liberty to live, think, speak and do as we will, subject to defending the same entitlements for others and respecting the principle of restricting the risk of

---

[1] J. F. Stephen makes this point. See Stephen (1993) pp 5-8.
[2] John Milton (1608-1674): political activist, poet and writer: most famous for his epic poems *Paradise Lost* (1667/1674) and *Paradise Regained* (1671). His text *Areopagita* (1644) is his particular critique of tyranny, repression and censorship and defence of liberty. All of these, and his other major works can be found in Milton (2008). John Locke (1632-1704). Physician and philosopher, his *Second Treatise of Government* (1688) is the single most influential work on the development of liberal democracy as in, most notably, the USA. See Locke (2013).

harm to others – and what Mill does and does not mean by 'harm' is a key matter to keep in mind.

Mill's case rests considerably on something akin to the insight that in the history of invention and the history of creativity in all the fields of art and thought, what comes to benefit all usually derives from the insight, imagination and energy of an individual – and by an individual, Mill invariably means those who are of what we would now term the age of majority, and so capable of taking charge of their affairs. Based on this understanding, Mill thinks that liberty for all will allow that one or few to produce what will, in the long run, be advantageous to us all. To put it another way, great innovations for life do not come from masses, nations or committees. Invariably, they come from the creativity of individuals who in some way run against the mainstream and buck the trends. The benefits they bring then accrue to the advantage of all, so it is in the interests of all to have liberty for all, even if only a few will use it to great effect. The argument is that there is justification in interference with the liberty of individuals only if their actions are harmful to others: interference is not justified because the rest of us think we know best what will be for the good of other individuals: this is 'not a sufficient warrant' (I: 9).

The content of Mill's principle of liberty is distinct and yet nuanced. It affirms the 'progressive' (I: 11) character of human nature in general and the sovereignty of the individual in particular, affirming the sense of how the individual is entitled to absolute liberty except, again, over actions that cause or seem likely to cause harm to others. This implies comprehensive liberty of thought and discussion since, for Mill, 'harm' or 'injury' mainly means direct physical harm or injury and not the concerns and upsets that come from mere disagreement; harm is, in more general terms, anything that inhibits or prevents the progressive development of the individuality of the self or others – something that Mill attends to, especially in the third chapter of *On Liberty*.[1] He also defends extensive freedom of action. But despite (or because of) its radicalism, in the developed societies of modernity, in the West at least, this view of liberty became a prominent theme.[2]

Paragraph 1 Revisited

Given our review of the opening paragraph of the text in the last chapter, we know that Mill sets out a deliberate opening:

'The subject of this essay is not the so-called "liberty of the will", so unfortunately opposed to the misnamed doctrine of philosophical necessity; but civil, or social liberty' (I: 1).

Mill's thinking on the right way to see necessity, as we have seen, includes scope for individual as well as 'civil, or social liberty', and here the interface is over the dynamic between the conceptions of negative and positive liberty, again, as discussed by Berlin.[3] Mill also means to address the problem of 'the nature and limits of the power which can be legitimately exercised by society over the

[1] See Chapter 9 below.
[2] The ideas sketched here will be reviewed and discussed below.
[3] See Chapter 6 above and Berlin (2017) pp. 166-217.

individual'. This remark raises the issue of the right relation of society to its individual members – again, we see Mill's acceptance of something as close to a general truth about the human condition as it is possible to have, that humans are social beings: society, the group of humans with which each individual is associated as a component, has certain legitimate powers over the individual. Mill also thinks that 'the nature and limits' of this power are problematic: as he says, it is:

'A question seldom stated, and hardly ever discussed in general terms, but which profoundly influences the practical controversies of the age by its latent presence, and is likely soon to make itself recognized as the vital question of the future. It is so far from being new that, in a certain sense, it has divided mankind almost from the remotest ages; but in the stage of progress into which the more civilized portions of the species have now entered, it presents itself under new conditions and requires a different and more fundamental treatment' (I: 1).

In the latter part of this opening, we can underscore that for Mill, the issue of 'civil, or social liberty' is seen as a 'vital question' in relation to the 'new condition' of the 'stage of progress' of the 'more civilized portions of the species'.

Here we have the first instance of a habit Mill has, one that is far from being as 'woke' as some would now like, of making a distinction between 'civilized' societies, and those which are not, and which are seen variously as uncivilized or barbaric.[1] We also have the suggestion that there are 'new conditions' to which humans in certain states of 'progress' have come to experience, within which the problem of liberty has a new aspect. What this is all about is Mill's focus in the next portions of his text.

Tyrannies Ancient and Modern (Paragraphs 2-6)

Mill's mind is on the sense in which the problem of liberty is perennial rather than new. To explain this, he moves into the historical mode, giving an overview of the shapes and moods of liberty over time. Referencing classical and more local history, he suggests that the traditional tension 'was between subjects, or some classes of subjects, and the government' (I: 2). The meaning is that liberty was seen 'as protection against the tyranny of the political rulers'. In effect, liberty was at stake in the historic struggle of the many against the few – the people against the ruler or rulers. Historically, the right to rule was from 'inheritance or conquest', not from 'the pleasure of the governed'. The problem in such an arrangement was that the power of the ruler or rulers 'was regarded as necessary, but also as highly dangerous; as a weapon which they would attempt to use against their subjects, no less than against external enemies'.

Mill becomes zoological and mythic in his imagery:

'To prevent the weaker members of the community from being preyed upon by innumerable vultures, it was needful that there should be an animal of prey stronger than the rest, commissioned to keep them down. But as the king of the vultures would be no less bent

---

[1] 'Woke' thinking as mentioned here and on later occasions, is given more detailed treatment in Chapter 14 below.

on preying on any of the minor harpies, it was indispensable to be in a perpetual attitude of defence against his beak and claws'.

Mill's view is that 'liberty' becomes a conscious aspiration for people as, over time, they look to find means to limit the power of the rulers over the communal whole. The suggestion is that two means were developed; one was through the 'recognition of certain immunities, called political liberties or rights'. He does not mention either here, but the Magna Carta (1215/1217) and the Bill of Rights (1689) would be cases in point where the 'liberties or rights' came to expression with legal status.[1] The idea was that such immunities were, as a matter of duty, to be respected by the ruler as well as the ruled, so giving impetus to the notion of equality before the law. A failure to respect political liberties or rights would justify 'specific resistance or general rebellion'. Again, Mill does not illustrate the point, but the English Civil War would be an obvious example.[2]

The other means suggested is 'the establishment of constitutional checks'. By this, the nascent representative imperative, the consent of the many, was to be placed by a representative group before the ruler or ruling group to condition their acts. Mill's overview of history suggests that the introduction of liberties and entitlements or rights was, in general, a more successful measure than the development of representative checks and balances. He thinks that the law is more effective over time than representative governance. Nevertheless, he suggests that working to gain this latter measure 'became everywhere the principal object of the lovers of liberty' – by which Mill means that the passion grew for some form of representative government, with the democratic model developing in his own time giving a stronger basis for the law to be grounded in the interests of the people.

In the period leading up to and embracing the modernity that Mill lives through, the trend identified is increasingly strong in taking the shape of representative democracy, leading towards a dissolution of the traditional boundary between the ruler and the mass. For in modern society – and Mill means the period emerging through and after the political settlements of the 1832 Reform Act – the relation between the ruler and the mass is becoming a kind of identity: through the widening use and influence of democracy, the rulers represent the ruled and are accountable to them. The assumption in operation implies the notion associated with Abraham Lincoln that through democracy, there is the arrangement of the power of the people, by the people, for the people, as an effective way of correlating the general interest and common concern.[3] As an intellectual with a wide reputation in his life as a defender of the principle of utility, one might think that Mill would favour this move towards democracy, and indeed, there is always a sense in Mill's work of

---

[1] On Magna Carta (1215/1217) and the 1689 Bill of rights see details via the UK Parliament website – https///www.parliament.uk. After the demise of King John, the Magna Carta of 1217 was a revision of the 1215 document and is in effect the one that had influence within the political culture of England. See https://www.nationalarchives.gov.uk/education/resources/magna-carta/proclamation-magna-carta-worcester-1217/

[2] The main phase of the Civil War ran from 1642 until 1649, when Charles 1st was executed, and the Commonwealth was declared. Hostilities continued until 1651. Cromwell became Lord Protector in 1553 until his death in 1558. The restoration of Charles II was in 1660. For details see https://www.parliament.uk/about/living-heritage/evolutionofparliament/parliamentaryauthority/civilwar/key-dates/1640-1660:

[3] Lincoln's comments are made in his Gettysburg Address – see Chapter 12 below.

great support for reforming moves to give a more effective and representative democracy.[1] At the same time, Mill also sees the emerging situation as posing a new problem for liberty.

The key passage setting this out is as follows:

'What was now wanted was that the rulers should be identified with the people, that their interest and will should be the interest and will of the nation. The nation did not need to be protected against its own will. There was no fear of its tyrannizing over itself. Let the rulers be effectually responsible to it, promptly removable by it, and it could afford to trust them with power of which it could itself dictate the use to be made. Their power was but the nation's own power, concentrated and in a form convenient for exercise' (I: 3).

This sketch of the emergent democratic arrangement centres on the 'interest and will' of the people, the 'nation', being 'identified' with those who rule – they rule as representatives of the 'interest and will' of the people, and so the old problem of tyranny and liberty evaporates, and a fearless unity of will and purpose between the rulers and the ruled comes into being.

These points unfold without Mill providing any commentary, but we should note that he employs the term 'interests' to signify something distinctive in the character and commitments of both 'the people' and the 'nation'. In the historical perspective, he thinks that people had interests in gaining greater liberty from the control of the ruler, liberty for, as Mill says – stressing the most vital of his interests – the 'formation of... individuality' (I: 5), and the development of 'individual independence'. In contrast, the rulers had interests in sustaining power and control over the people. In the emergent representative form of government, there is a sense in which it is assumed that these interests fuse.

The ideas on 'interests' Mill expresses will be something else to consider further, but whatever the benefits of representative democracy, Mill thinks that this 'mode of thought' manifests another variant of the problem of tyranny: he takes care to construct a critical line of thought, probably because in attacking the implications of the democratic tendency, he is launching criticism against the ideas regularly expressed by both Jeremy Bentham and James Mill (as well as by Mill himself at times).[2] Even in 1859, regard for this tradition dictates that Mill should not specifically criticize his father or the earlier utilitarians. Nevertheless, *On Liberty* contains some clear, if indirect, criticism of the utilitarian assumption of the value of democracy and its entailments, in line with the notion that the greatest number's happiness or pleasure provides the most efficient criteria for personal and public life.

The view in *On Liberty* is that in the new era of increasing democracy, the majority will of the nation – not the political system of parliament, but the social majority of opinion on various and specific issues – stands as the ruling force and that this, in the vital domains of interpersonal and social life, can and does constitute a 'tyranny of the majority' that stands as a threat to the liberty of the individuals who collectively constitute society.

Mill sets out his view:

---

[1] Not least in his *Considerations on Representative Government* (1861). See *Util* pp. 179-405.
[2] Here see Himmelfarb's note – see *OL* p. 61 n. 1. Mill is also alluding to the problems found in James Mill's view of government in the wake of Macaulay's criticism. See Chapter 2 above.

117

'Like other tyrannies, the tyranny of the majority was at first, and still is vulgarly, held in dread, chiefly as operating through the acts of the public authorities. But reflecting persons perceived that when society is itself the tyrant – society collectively over the separate individuals who compose it – its means of tyrannizing are not restricted to the acts which it may do by the hands of its public functionaries. Society can and does execute its own mandates; and if it issues wrong mandates instead of right, or any mandates at all in things with which it ought not to meddle, it practises a social tyranny more formidable than many kinds of political oppression, since though not usually upheld by such extreme penalties, it leaves fewer means of escape, penetrating much more deeply into the details of life, and enslaving the soul itself'.

There are highly dramatic points here regarding the notion of democracy.[1] It would seem that the cruelty and oppression arising from the evocation of tyranny are not quite those that would naturally be thought to be associated with the patterns of life within the emergent democratic society, even of Mill's time. However, that is the point he wants to underscore: society can, through its democratically validated means, develop 'public authorities' that can be seen as vehicles for the majority view, but this, in turn, amounts to a 'tyranny of the majority', and so society itself can, through the generation of trends of collective opinion, 'execute its own mandates', its own regulations and stipulations.[2]

On this point, Mill is articulating a vibrant problem that in our plural modernity has transformed into an arguably greater and more complex problem: that of the trends and views flowing from this or that issue or debate, and manifesting a more general pressure for all to agree with or at the very least respect the perspective or outlook in question. What Mill is especially concerned with is how the new tyranny of social trends is as much a threat to liberty as the old-style tyranny ever was, and in a way, he sees the new form as a more severe threat to individuality. In the past, there was an overt threat manifest in the ruler. Now it is set within public authorities that are validated by the majority view, and worse, it is impersonal and omnipresent in the dominant trends of public opinion. It is, therefore, more difficult to discern and evade, and Mill fears, potentially more enslaving of more of the individual. Using the notion of tyranny to the full, Mill suggests that what is needed is a scheme to provide a specific form of protection, namely:

'Protection… against the tyranny of the prevailing opinion and feeling, against the tendency of society to impose, by other means than civil penalties, its own ideas and practices as rules of conduct on those who dissent from them; to fetter the development and, if possible, prevent the formation of any individuality not in harmony with its ways, and to compel all characters to fashion themselves upon the model of its own'.

---

[1] In the 1850's the UK was partially democratic. The 1832 Reform Act made changes to equalise constituencies, but only men who owned property to the value of at least £10 could vote. Secret ballots were introduced after 1872; in 1918 all men and some women were able to vote: women had to be 30 or older and either married to a householder, or a university graduate. The Universal Suffrage Act of 1928 enabled equality. The upshot is that the UK has one of the longest parliamentary histories but a much shorter history of democracy. All this makes clearer that what Mill was concerned about was the power of democratic or majority thinking, not political democracy *per se*.
[2] On this see:
http///www.nationalarchives.gov.uk/pathways/citizenship/struggle_democracy/getting_vote.htm and /

Mill then makes for himself a corrective agenda, suggesting that in the spectrum of activity that exists in the tension between individuals and societies, there is a key 'limit':

'There is a limit to the legitimate interference of collective opinion with individual independence; and to find that limit, and maintain it against encroachment, is as indispensable to a good condition of human affairs as protection against political despotism'.

A major project within *On Liberty* is about finding 'that limit', but in Mill's remarks, we see how it is that 'society' comes forward with pejorative connotations – 'encroachment', for example, and we have the risks of social habits, routines and customs being akin to fetters, and seen as matters of imposition, and compulsion – all of which are combined to make social tendencies the enemy of individuals. This is a large theme within the text. When society manifests a 'collective opinion' that illegitimately interferes with 'individual independence', we are confronted with a problem. Society, not in the abstract but through the dynamic of social opinion, threatens the individual, and for Mill, stands as more of a threat than class, interest groups, or government; what we need to worry about is public opinion, the prevailing convention and perhaps, the mass view.

Mill's point embraces the concession that, in general, and time out of mind, 'rules of conduct' have come about and been 'imposed' by either the law or by 'opinion' for the parts of life where the law would not ever apply. The controls are important because Mill, in an important observation again expressing his sense of humans as social, sees that 'all that makes existence valuable to anyone depends on the enforcement of restraints upon the actions of other people' (I: 6).

The problem Mill also senses is that for this matter, what the rules and controls should be is far from clear: the difficulties include differences of view as to where the rules should apply, how they are to be harmonised where they differ, and as the greatest problem, the 'all but universal illusion' of the majority view that 'rules which obtain amongst themselves appear to them to be self-evident and self-justifying' – providing evidence, Mill thinks, of 'the magical influence of custom'. Humans have many positive qualities in Mill's estimate, but they also have a weakness which lies in the ease with which the potion of custom seduces humanity into the passive acceptance of commonalities, and so to the routines of life and thought. It is to combat what Mill sees as something of a void that *On Liberty* is set: Mill thinks that for his times, the matter of 'how to make the fitting adjustment between individual independence and social control' remains 'a subject on which nearly everything remains to be done'.

With the comments considered so far, one notable feature is the tension Mill consistently plays on between individuality and society. We have seen the negative connotations he puts on social tendencies. The cumulative picture is one of society manifesting an assault on individuality, and thereby, as Mill will argue later, a somewhat suicidal attack on society itself – for society righty understood is simply the sum of 'the separate individuals who compose it' (I: 5). Against this, and as the curative means to a qualitatively greater end, the statement of the doctrine of liberty must be reaffirmed.

Mill's approach clearly places stress on the positive worth of individuality. However, arising from this, his views on the nature of individuality and society face a striking problem. We may feel in moments of high self-esteem that a society can be nothing other than the sum total of individuals who compose it. If that is the case, then the tension that Mill is concerned about may be understood as existing between some individuals and others – for as just noted, Mill's deeper point is that society is composed of 'separate individuals'. What underlies Mill's thinking is that, as we mentioned earlier, he has a malleable view of society, and in moments of emphasis, he tends to conceive 'society' in at least three significant ways.

Sometimes we have the generalised view, as in references to 'society' practising 'a social tyranny more formidable than many kinds of political oppression': in these references, 'society' is presented as exhibiting trends and tendencies that have dangerous and inhibiting threats for individuality. We also have the active and developmental form of society that is comprised of 'individuals'. Mill also sometimes refers to society in almost regulative terms as the civil society in which we all participate.

In summary, these views of how 'society' can be conceived can be listed as follows:

1. Society is viewed as a dangerous force exhibiting trends and movements of coercive opinion and the tyranny of the majority - I: 5, for example. Here social and legal measures are seen as threats to liberty and also to society.
2. Society is presented as the sum total of individuals, such individuals being the basic components of human life in a civilized society, where Mill sees scope for life as it is at its best – see again I: 5 and also V: 23, for examples. Here social and legal measures are seen as viable forms of regulating individual excesses.
3. Society is seen as civil society and as the political State – as the organised system of law and other functions of order and governance under which people lead personal and social lives with various duties and certain liberties – I: 11, for example.

The third view comes up when Mill writes of the society to which individuals rightfully owe certain debts and obligations in return for the protection that society affords. This is a conventional enough procedural view. However, the other two views present some interesting thoughts: the first – society exhibiting the tyranny of the majority – is used to reveal the most threatening features that society can reveal – those towards stifling conformity; in contrast, the second view is a portrayal of society as the organic and textured setting for the nurture and growth of varied and distinctive individuals. This view promotes an alternative ideal of a form of life for cultivated individuals, as distinct from those living under the custom of the tyranny of the majority. Society as a civilized community represents what Mill wants to highlight and is what he conceives of a society at its creative best. Mill's various sketches of historical development have a purpose in showing that civilized communities are not abstract ideals or anthropological fictions: rather, they grow and develop over time, with individuality as an emergent consequence of the prior social context of life. Individuality, not least as detailed later by Mill, is not something humans just have: they acquire it in and through a process that is nothing if not social and through engagements and tensions within the wider society into which they move.[1]

A question arising from this is that of the extent to which Mill sustains a coherent view of society, and for reference, we can tag this as the problem of the coherence of individuals and society and see how it is developed and whether it is plausibly sustained as *On Liberty* unfolds. What is also relevant to this is how Mill's thinking remains, to a degree, logged into and in dialogue with utilitarian views of society.

For the classical utilitarians, terms like the 'community' or 'society' were abstractions, denoting a 'fictitious body'.[2] This leads to the notion that Mill likes, of seeing society as the sum of the individuals that make it up. And this links to why the utilitarian approach likes to refer to individuals, singly or collectively, in discussions of morality and politics. Social goods and the public interest are conditioned by the goods and interests of individuals – and thus, the principle of utility really has a concrete reference in the greatest goods of the greatest number, within which, as we mentioned earlier, the maxim runs, 'everyone counts as one, and no one counts as more than one'.[3]

For Jeremy Bentham, the implication is that even the concept of liberty would be too abstract to serve as an axiom for social and political life. It could sustain the defence of minority interests against the interests and happiness of the greater number to an extent that would preclude the degree of elevation sought for it by Mill – bringing up again the issue of the tension between these two principles.

Mill's problem is that when he asserts that society is the sum total of individuals, it sounds as if it is hard to differ from Bentham. However, there is a qualitative difference because Mill, with the developed version of utility he has in mind, trades on the liberty-rich notion of 'sovereign' (I. 9) individuals.

Mill has an empowered notion of what individuality can become, and the worry he has is that the sovereignty of particular individuals will be conditioned and limited by the thrust of the majority perception of general goods. When Mill is referring to society in negative ways – noting the practices of 'social tyranny' (I: 5) and the 'tyranny of the majority' – for the reasons given earlier, he is not making as explicit as he might is that he is criticising the narrower and more functional mode of being human, one more associated with the classical utilitarians.

Mill avoids confronting this point head-on, and what we will see much of is that 'society' is seen as in the first sense listed above, as imposing constraining opinion that constitutes a definite threat to individuals. Mill often presents the problem of society operating through its systems and structures as an impersonal and threatening entity working contrary to the interests and concerns of actual individuals.[4] He understands that due to the trends found in consensual, majority thinking, many individuals congregate to diminish the few. In *On Liberty*, one can sense that Mill is aching to develop the idea of a socio-cultural milieu of developed and interested communal and collegiate individuals, and it is another point to tag to see the extent to which he actually makes this move.

---

[1] See *OL* Chapter III and Chapter 9 below.
[2] Bentham (1961) p. 18.
[3] *Util* V: 36.
[4] See *OL* V: 23 and Chapter 11 below, for Mill's peroration on this theme.

Social and Religious Freedoms (Paragraphs 6-8)

Widening his historical reflection, Mill next touches on issues of reform in social life concerning religious and theological traditions. He notes a general trend, that the social 'likings and dislikings' (I: 7) that shape 'the rules laid down for general observance' and regulated by 'the penalties of law or opinion' are often realised through the preferences of the most powerful and influential in society or movements, as in religious reforms.[1] As distinct from the phases of life where social morality is determined by 'an ascendant class' (I: 6), a 'grand determining principle of the rules of conduct' that emerges 'both in act and forbearance, which have been enforced by law and opinion' is empowered by 'the servility of mankind toward the supposed preferences or aversions of their temporal masters or their gods'.

Here we have Mill, within *On Liberty*, giving evidence of the rather low opinion of people in general that we found when considering the attitudes he and Harriet had when planning the book.[2] An outcome of views and attitudes developed in this way is that 'reason' has had less influence than other 'baser influences'. A further point he sees as weighty is that those with power and influence also tend to be in the vanguard of reviews of 'what things society ought to like or dislike' rather than considering whether such matters and such reviews should be 'a law to individuals'. This provides an instance of the problem we tagged, of the coherence of individuality and society – for again, if society is, as Mill likes to say sometimes, the sum of the individuals who comprise it, there is no problematic tension here for those with power and influence: the tensions are those between different individuals, between a majority who are driven by 'baser influences' and who threaten the well-being of those fewer individuals whose motivations are richer and more complex. Mill aims to make a case here that maintains his wider and more longstanding commitments to the general movement of utilitarian thought, but develops it with a more sophisticated sense of what it is to be an individual. What Mill does not weave into this is a stronger theme to explain how those with power and influence have an invariable desire to sustain that power and influence by any means possible.[3]

What Mill puts focus on is the habits of religious reformers who, eager to break 'the yoke of what called itself the Universal Church' (I: 7) – meaning the Roman Catholic Church – were then themselves 'as little willing to permit difference of religious opinion as that church itself'.

Mill sees it as an acute 'instance of the fallibility of the moral sense' that there is a consistency of theological hatred ('the *odium theologicum*') in the intense singularities and dogmatism of the protestant sects. So many diverse groups came about, without any hope of any one of them becoming dominant, that from this scenario arose 'the necessity of pleading to those they could not convert for permission to differ'.

---

[1] Mill is thinking of the social and religious changes that came through the Reformation. The Reformation is usually dated from 1517, the year in which Martin Luther (1483-1546) began his protest against aspects of Catholic belief and practice.
[2] See Chapter 5 above.
[3] Here Mill might have read more Machiavelli?

It is in this context, over the right to freedom of worship, that Mill thinks that the main emphasis came in the campaign for 'the rights of the individual against society' – here, the voyage of the Mayflower (1620) might be a relevant allusion – for in the context of arguing for 'religious liberty' comes the first flowing of the argument for something Mill strongly favours: 'freedom of conscience as an indefeasible right'. Mill finds irony in the fact that although this appeal to freedom of conscience is grounded in religious groups, in point of fact, religious sects and traditions seldom, he thinks, lead to an open and liberal tolerance. Instead, the majority views within particular groups and sects keep them going, and dissent is never tolerated to any great degree.

Reflecting on how things seem on the home front in the present age, that is, the period for which he is writing, Mill thinks that in England, 'from the peculiar circumstances of our political history, though the yoke of opinion is perhaps heavier, that of law is lighter than in most countries of Europe' (I: 8).

Mill does not labour to explain why he thinks this, but given his earlier comparative remarks about life and progress in France contrasted with what he invariably calls England, his comments seem to be cut from the same cloth. Probing more deeply, it could be that Mill's reference to the 'yoke of opinion' is an allusion to the increasing force of democratic and, indeed, utilitarian thinking that promoted the interests of the greatest number and the prolific reading that was characteristic of the period would be factors all likely to give rise to a sense of there being a participatory awareness of bodies of opinion on various topics.

There is a link here to the many reforming and campaigning groups operational in the nineteenth century, but as Mill sees it, the fusion of the democratic mood and the feelings of public sentiment come to bear to combat more overt moves to impose by law particular measures to 'control individuals'. Thus it is to be noted that Mill invokes general and social sentiments to protect individuals from the control of the law. Law and opinion, as we have seen, are the two forces for control that Mill references. Such is his concern for the dangers of the tyrannies of opinion and the majority that it is tempting to think that there can be no good whatsoever in either. In fact, when considering the measures that may be taken in a civilized society, Mill does credit social opinion as a valid force, and we will see more of this later in *On Liberty*.

What Mill thinks clearer is that there is 'no recognized principle by which the propriety or impropriety of government interference is customarily tested'. We see that government action impinging on personal life is a matter of 'interference', so not something that sounds especially attractive. Mill thinks people reference their own 'personal preferences' to determine whether or not they like a particular government proposal that would impact on personal life. The idea of 'personal preferences' conveys to Mill intimations of a reliance on intuition, and much as Mill wants to promote the individuality of response, he is never happy with individuality if it relies solely on intuition: he thinks that the implied lack of a reasoned principle means that inconsistent and erratic views are taken over governmental 'interference', so that is too often 'improperly invoked and improperly condemned'.

All these points are foothills on the route to Mill answering the problems he has raised, and we come to the most famous part of *On Liberty* with the elaboration of what is said to be the 'one very simple principle, as entitled to govern absolutely the dealings of society with the individual' (I: 9).

The 'single truth', the 'one very simple principle' (Paragraphs 9-10)

As we noted, in his *Autobiography*, Mill claimed that *On Liberty* was intended to be 'a kind of philosophic text-book of a single truth'.[1] In *On Liberty* itself, the statement of this 'single truth' is expressed in the following passage:

'The object of this essay is to assert one very simple principle, as entitled to govern absolutely the dealings of society with the individual in the way of compulsion and control, whether the means used be physical force in the form of legal penalties, or the moral coercion of public opinion. That principle is that the sole end for which mankind are warranted, individually or collectively, in interfering with the liberty of action of any of their number is self-protection. That the only purpose for which power can be rightfully exercised over any member of a civilized community, against his will, is to prevent harm to others. His own good, either physical or moral, is not a sufficient warrant. He cannot rightfully be compelled to do or forbear because it will be better for him to do so, because it will make him happier, because, in the opinion of others, to do so would be wise or even right. These are good reasons for remonstrating with him, or reasoning with him, or persuading him, or entreating him, but not for compelling him or visiting him with any evil in case he do otherwise. To justify that, the conduct from which it is desired to deter him must be calculated to produce evil to someone else. The only part of the conduct of anyone for which he is amenable to society is that which concerns others. In the part which merely concerns himself, his independence is, of right, absolute. Over himself, over his own body and mind, the individual is sovereign' (I: 9).[2]

If we reflect on this passage as a whole, it provides points that are helpful given the issues we have been considering, not least the problem identified as that of the balance between individuals and society. In the course of this passage and while setting out the active and practical parameters of the 'one very simple principle', Mill almost unwittingly throws in the concept of 'mankind' in both the individual and the collective formats that make coherent sense in relation to something else he conjoins, namely membership of a 'civilized community'. In the passage, these notions overwhelm and shape the sense that Mill refers to 'the dealings of society with the individual'.

In an apparently 'civilized community', it seems that 'individually' and 'collectively', humans can act in ways that entail 'compulsion and control' of individuals: but no such action is legitimate, save on the grounds of 'self-protection', where it can be 'calculated' that the 'conduct from which it is desired to deter him' can be judged 'to produce evil to someone else'. With the correlated remark that 'the only purpose for which power can be rightfully exercised over any member of a civilized community, against his will, is to prevent harm to others', we have Mill's view of the risk of 'harm' as the criterion of justified constraint.

It is to be stressed that in these latter remarks, Mill assumes this constraint is initially a pre-emptive deterrent action: if it can be 'calculated' that a form of

---

[1] *Auto* p. 142.
[2] Mill explains that the notion of the sovereign individual that gives this passage a strongly phrased and memorable finish, comes from a movement started by Joseph Warren (1798-1874), an American follower of Robert Owen, who at one point had tried to establish a community based on the idea of 'the Sovereignty of the Individual'. See *Auto* p. 143. In 1850 Warren established a community on Long Island, New York, and it ran for some ten years.

conduct might 'produce evil to someone else', then to 'prevent harm to others', the members of a 'civilized community' can justifiably act to constrain the individual.

Mill asserts the risk of harm to others as the conditioning factor, but he does not elaborate on his view of nature and the scope of the harm he has in mind. Instead, the passage provides a veritable litany of points that might be thought to justify force or constraint but do not: a person's 'own good, either physical or moral', that 'something would be better' to be done, that something would make a person 'happier' – here the usual criterion for the orthodox utilitarian is not considered a sufficient warrant for intervention – nor are considerations that the doing or avoiding of something would 'be wise or even right'. The implication is that an individual might think, say and do all manner of things that trouble, annoy, irritate, upset and make others deeply uneasy. All of these points justify remonstration, reasoning, persuasion and pleading – but unless the matters involve the threat of harm to others, there is no justification for compulsion or the imposition of penalties.

In the study of *On Liberty*, the meanings Mill has in mind for harm, and the ramifications for how these cohere within the spectrum of the liberty principle assume considerable importance. It is clear that Mill deploys the liberty principle in such a way that its operation is constrained by the importance of 'preventing harm to others' by calculations relating to the deterrence of actions that would 'produce evil' to others. How 'harm' and 'evil' are defined and verified are matters to review later

Mill then sets into his presentation a distinction of which he is extremely fond, and which he set out in the *Principles*, between those aspects of a person's conduct 'which concerns others', and 'the part which merely concerns himself'. This is Mill's version of the idea that individually, we have personal and private space within our fundamentally social and interpersonal lives. As he expresses it, we are individually 'amenable to society' over matters of conduct concerning others, and we face the prospect of 'power' being 'rightfully exercised' over us if we risk acting in a way that threatens 'harm to others', but in respect of matters that are self-regarding, the individual's 'independence, is of right absolute'. Then, with a deft sense of rising to a flourishing peroration, Mill's conclusion affirms individual autonomy in the memorable line that 'over himself, over his own body and mind, the individual is sovereign'.

A point to note is that in this influential passage, the last line contains the only specific reference to what can be construed as the liberty of thought as distinct from the liberty of action. We will see that Mill shortly comes back to this issue.

In the meanwhile, in the next section of his text, Mill moves on to address the matter of to whom the 'one very simple principle' of liberty applies, saying that it is to apply 'only to human beings in the maturity of their faculties' (I: 10), those who have 'attained the 'capacity of being guided to their own improvement by conviction and persuasion'. Thus liberty should not be extended to children or those without a normal relation to the capacities for responsibility – those suffering from a mental illness or disease. Liberty is, however, for all 'human beings', and Mill's generic reference embraces all women and men – a signal of Mill's radicalism and reforming spirit on these matters. Mill also thinks that liberty should not be expected or imposed in societies remote from the pace of civilization in the West – and here, Mill's comments can be seen as being rather obviously shaped by the views of his age, but he retains the sense mentioned earlier that it is through the vicissitudes of history that civilization can be won – or lost. But for any society that promotes free debate and all that it entails, the doctrine of liberty applies.

Mill's background views come in the following passage:

'Despotism is a legitimate mode of government in dealing with barbarians, provided the end be their improvement, and the means justified by actually effecting that end. Liberty, as a principle, has no application to any state of things anterior to the time when mankind have become capable of being improved by free and equal discussion. Until then, there is nothing from them but an implicit obedience to an Akbar or a Charlemagne, if they are so fortunate as to find one. But as soon as mankind have attained the capacity of being guided to their own improvement by conviction or persuasion (a period long since reached in all nations with whom we need here concern ourselves), compulsion, either in the direct form or in that of pains and penalties for non-compliance, is no longer admissible as a means to their own good, and justifiable only for the security of others'[1]

Here, as elsewhere in the text, when Mill refers to 'barbarism' – IV: 21, for example – it is more than likely that what is coming into play is Mill's early experience of learning Greek which inducted him into the original sense of the term 'barbaric' to mean any other group or culture that did not speak Greek. His use of the term suggests that he has also imbibed the more colloquial implication that the lack of a capacity for 'free and equal discussion' is the mark of an uncivilised society. That the culture of society and the quality of life as a whole is dependent on the liberty of each individual, as through 'free and equal discussion', is Mill's larger point, and this is something he moves to enhance through his brief but telling reference to utility.

Mill on Liberty, Utility and Human Interests (Paragraphs 11-12)

We need to engage in a spot of doublethink as we move into the next sections of the text. Readers of *On Liberty,* who come to the text, perhaps having studied ethics, and assuming Mill to be a utilitarian, soon begin wondering how it will work to make liberty and utility cohere. How will utility relate to liberty? Which trumps the other in Mill's scheme of thought? This area of debate forms one of the most basic issues for students of *On Liberty* – along the lines of questions such as 'To what extent is Mill's formulation of the principle of liberty consistent with utilitarianism?'

We know that Mill always considers himself a utilitarian, if not always a conventional one.[2] Against Mill's approach with liberty, the obvious problem is that were we to retain a strict adherence to Bentham's utility, this would rule out employing the 'one simple principle' used to manage all relationships between

---

[1] Akbar, or Abū al Fath, Jahāl al Dīn Muhummad Akbar (1542-1605). Mill doubtless considers Akbar an enlightened ruler: one of the Mugal (Islamic) rulers of India, (1556-1605) his success was due to his reforming attitude, his toleration of the plurality of Indian religious belief, and his promotion of culture. See https///www.britannica.com/biography/Akbar. Charlemagne (742-814) – see https///www.history.com/topics/middle-ages/charlemagne - lived and ruled much of what is now modern-day Europe (768-814). He promoted the arts and culture, the rule of law, all under the ethos of Christianity.
[2] See Chapter 4 above

individuals and society. It would be reduced to a contingent proposal that must be sacrificed to the wider interests of utility as related to the interests of the greatest happiness of the greatest number. However, we know that while Mill always held a commitment to utilitarian thought, he was a highly adaptive and far from a conventional proponent of utility.[1] We need to check how well Mill's view of utility in *On Liberty* solves this problem, and there we also recall the potentially distracting issue that in reviews of Mill in modern times, there has been a habit of trying to fit his thought into more contemporary models of utilitarian thought.[2]

For example, is Mill an 'act'-utilitarian (the greatest happiness principle applies solely to those who are engaged in or influenced by the act in question), a 'rule'-utilitarian (the greatest happiness of the greatest number will be generally enhanced if social rules and norms are usually endorsed), or an 'ideal' utilitarian (where rather than pleasure and happiness, which can be derived from many things that would not be verifiably good, the ideals of friendship and aesthetic value are seen as the greatest goods).[3] Is he simply a 'hedonistic' utilitarian concerned to maximise individual pleasures, or a 'preference' utilitarian, looking to defend the widest scope for cultivating individual preference?[4] The variant forms of utility here mostly post-date Mill, and his exposition does not fit naturally into these classifications, while in contrast, again, as Gray suggests, from Mill's own exposition, it fits much more accurately the tag of 'indirect utilitarianism'.

There is no doubt that Mill envisages harmony between utility and liberty, and we find that he wants this harmony to be through associating liberty with a revised form of utility. In a brief but significant passage, he denies that in developing his view, he will use any notion 'of abstract right as a thing independent of utility' (I: 11). He means he will not appeal to any purely theoretical notion, and certainly not to the notion of liberty as in intrinsic right. No less than Bentham, who dismissed the idea of intrinsic human rights as 'nonsense on stilts', Mill wants to ground his views on the experiential condition of being human.[5] Accordingly, he affirms that he regards utility as the 'ultimate appeal on all ethical questions', provided, he adds, that it is 'utility in the largest sense', based on the 'permanent interests of man as a progressive being'. Mill immediately adds a rider:

'Those interests, I contend, authorize the subjection of individual spontaneity to external control only in respect of those actions of each which concern the interest of other people'.

Here 'interests' is again employed in a manner intended, it seems, to extend what Mill means by the need to act to prevent 'harm to others' (I: 9). The interests now being evoked are those of 'progressive' beings (I: 11), and 'individual spontaneity' is constrainable due to the obvious interplay arising between the self and other-regarding modes of life. What Mill means is that he considers individuals to have self and other-regarding aspects of life, and it is on the individual's other-regarding obligations, duties and commitments that 'external control' might encroach on the

---

[1] Again, see Chapter 4 above
[2] See Gray (1983), especially pp. 1-18.
[3] This view is associated with G.E. Moore – See Moore (1965). On Mill's moral philosophy see Urmson (1953).
[4] Preference utility is defended by Singer (2011).
[5] See Bentham (2002) pp. 317-401.

overwise sovereign individual. Adding to the point, if an individual 'does an act hurtful to others', then there would be 'a *prima facia* case for punishing... by law, or where legal penalties are not safely applicable, by general disapprobation'. Here is a case where Mill again slips implicitly between his estimations of society: appeals to general feeling and moods to be regulative of excesses of action (as in a civilized society), even though in respect of self-regarding actions, the general or majority view can become a dangerous tyranny (when social opinion becomes over influential to the suppression of individuality).

Mill gives some examples of legitimate compulsion to which individuals should rightly be subject: giving evidence in a legal setting as and when required; contributing to the 'common defence' of 'the society of which he enjoys the protection'; acting to save a life and to protect the defenceless, such as cases 'whenever it is obviously a man's duty to do he may rightfully be made responsible to society for not doing'; Mill is firm here in the view that a person's 'inaction' – or act of omission – as much as his action 'may cause evil to others', and so either way, the individual is accountable for the 'injury'. All this gives a sense of how Mill's positive view of civilized society involves a strongly participative harmony between individuals who contribute to doing their bit.

In using 'harm' and then 'interests' in these discussions, Mill probably thought he was being clear. Commentators on his work seldom agree, finding the terms hopelessly vague and overgeneralised.[1] How the nature of harm is to be defined, and by whom, and how we work out the common and individual interests and balance them are indeed problematic matters. Mill is certainly not overly helpful in using these terms, but what he does is to make clear to the attentive reader that at stake are the individual's actions impacting others and damaging the concerns, aspirations (or interests) that arise in their self-regarding as well as in their wider sense of other-regarding life. If an individual's action threatens or brings harm to the interests of particular others or to the wider general interests shared in a civilized community, then the individual can be dealt with by either the law or by 'general disapprobation'.

Mill assumes that this is consistent with the notion of the 'harm to others' clause of the principle of liberty, his sense of the distinction between self and other-regarding action. He is protecting a more or less total liberty of thought and discussion in these remarks, and he also sees that definite actions are much more straightforward to judge than matters of inaction.

In this section of the text, Mill goes some way along the line to evoke a strong sense of the individual having extensive responsibilities for which he or she might be held to account. 'Might be' is the operative notion here because Mill also is alert to a psychologically sophisticated point, that there is another even finer line to draw on the matter of whether it is always right to call offenders to account. The argument is that a person's 'external relations' make them '*de jure* amenable to those whose interests are concerned, and, if need be, to society as their protector'.

Mill explains his view as follows:

---

[1]See Lucas (1966) p. 174. See also Gray (1983) pp. 48-52; Rees (1991) pp. 171-174, p. 176 and p. 182, and Honderich (2003) Chapter 1.

'There are often good reasons for not holding him to the responsibility; but these reasons must arise from the special expediencies of the case: either because it is the kind of case in which he is on the whole likely to act better when left to his own discretion than when controlled in any way in which society have it in their power to control him; or because the attempt to exercise control would produce other evils, greater than those which it would prevent. When such reasons as these preclude the enforcement of responsibility, the conscience of the agent himself should step into the vacant judgment seat and protect those interests of others which have no external protection; judging himself all the more rigidly, because the case does not admit of his being made accountable to the judgment of his fellow creatures'.

The emphasis here is on the human capacity for self-correction, this through an appeal to personal self-understanding and reason, rather than for any form of social control.

Mill has a point here, for anyone who has taught in, say, secondary education, for any period over a year or two will know there is a sense of value in the case Mill makes: that often it is more effective to advise and warn and not take action over the errors or lapses a student has committed, where they have failed to do their bit to help advance their own, or the more general progress of the class. Giving them a chance to use their own liberty, wit and sense to recover by means of their own self-awareness is better than consigning them to detention, reporting them to the powers that be, or setting them to write Mill's statement on the liberty doctrine some 2000 times. Mill has other points to make as to why action works less well than inaction in these cases, and we will come to them in due course.

We see from Mill's comments that his earlier ideas about the tyranny of the majority are set on one sense in which society can operate, as distinct from society operating in a civilized manner, with individuals living within relationships within and sometimes through tensions with appropriate social pressures. Mill also wants the more open approach, whereby the greater good comes through restraint and a reliance on the individual agent's capacity to resolve matters. Overall, what is suggested is that in the real world of interpersonal life, each individual owes anyone else an obligation of respect, care and protection: in effect, Mill thinks that each of us has a rightful responsibility for our own development while being the good custodian of the others with whom we interact. Individuals are the direct agents of social care, and since, in Mill's understanding, society is the sum total of such individuals, it could hardly be otherwise.

The idea of humanity being progressive and capable of development is a positive and vital aspect of Mill's emergent view, linking to the sense that humans are 'fallible' (II: 8), and embraces the thought that the interests and liberty of progressive beings permit interference only when 'individual spontaneity' concerns the interests of others.

As we have seen, Mill employs the category of 'interests' to flesh out his modified sense of utility and his understanding in *On Liberty* is that the utilitarian approach is translated into a radical species of liberalism: happiness or pleasure as in the classical forms of utility is rounded up into a more open-ended sense of well-being through progressive human development through individual spontaneity. This development is relative to that which the individual chooses to develop or explore within the constraint of looking to not causing harm to others, the prevention of such harm being a legitimate constraint of such liberty, but the cumulative benefits of what is chosen ever aimed to be conducive to 'utility in its largest sense'.

The Parameters of Liberty (Paragraphs 12-16)

Mill next wants to iron home some points on the liberty wing of his argument. He attends to the 'sphere of action' that has to do with 'that portion of a person's life and conduct which affects only himself or, if it also affects others, only with their free, voluntary, and undeceived consent and participation' (I: 12). Mill at once qualifies his sense of 'only himself' and, in so doing, aids us in revealing a core idea that is sometimes obscured in *On Liberty*.[1] Mill points up that 'only himself' applies 'directly and in the first instance': he means by this that our sovereign, self-regarding actions take place in a sphere of immediacy in those spaces of life when we are, but only temporarily, free from other duties, obligations and commitments. Mill goes on at once to state a singularly obvious point: for whatever 'affects' an individual 'may affect others through himself' – and Mill then indicates he will deal more with this point in the next chapter of the text.

The emergent point is acute and important: that self-regarding actions have a distinct but limited scope, for although Mill does not quite say it, it is clear enough that he appreciates that the human condition is predominantly social and interactive and that collaborative and communal activities are normative as the setting within which individualism also operates. Our personal or self-regarding activities are always liable to overlap with the rest of our lives.

For example, in my self-regarding sphere of action, I sit working on this book: but at any point, the phone may ring, and someone will need something doing within the wider fabric of my life – someone will call out that it is time for us to do this or that – and so like a balloon deflating, my self-regarding sphere of life shrinks, or rather like a sugar cube in a cup of coffee, it dissolves into the greater whole of the coffee. A better analogy is to borrow the Cartesian example with wax that remains wax, even though it melts into a liquid when warmed and hardens again when cooled.[2]

So it is with the self-regarding mode of life – it can reform or dissolve within and in relation to the heat and cool of the social matrix of life – but the life of the person in question is an individual's life. Mill gets this, but his imperative thought is that the weight and value of individuality in the self-regarding sphere of life are important for the wider development of humans as progressive beings.

A health warning needs to be given at this point: Mill's sense of the importance of the self-regarding sphere of life is acute, but his sense of how provisional and limited it is within the spectrum of life as a whole is much less explicit than in the portion of the text we have just examined. As a rule, he operates with the sense of there being a clear and sustainable distinction between the self and other-regarding modes of life.

Meanwhile, Mill feels empowered to come to a positive statement we earlier cited some phrases from on 'the appropriate region of human liberty':

---

[1] Rees writes well on this matter. See Rees in Gray and Smith (1991) pp. 177-178.
[2] See Descartes (2008) Meditation 2.

'It comprises, first, the inward domain of consciousness, demanding liberty of conscience in the most comprehensive sense, liberty of thought and feeling, absolute freedom of opinion and sentiment on all subjects, practical or speculative, scientific, moral or theological. The liberty of expressing and publishing opinions may seem to fall under a different principle, since it belongs to that part of the conduct of the individual which concerns other people, but, being almost of as much importance as the liberty of thought itself and resting in great part on the same reasons, is practically inseparable from it. Secondly, the principle requires liberty of tastes and pursuits, of framing the plan of our life to suit our own character, of doing as we like, subject to such consequences as may follow, without impediment from our fellow creatures, so long as what we do does not harm them, even though they should think our conduct foolish, perverse, or wrong. Thirdly, for this liberty of each individual follows the liberty, within the same limits of combination among individuals; freedom to unite for any purpose not involving harm to others; the persons combining being supposed to be of full age and not forced or deceived'.

Here Mill spells out the implications of the earlier statement of the 'one very simple' principle of liberty, giving more explicit focus to the liberty of thought and discussion. The harm to others clause is again evident, but the benefit of this positive affirmation is that it allows the expression of the three aspects to the region of liberty, giving in effect, liberty of thought and discussion, liberty of action to live and develop a life of our own choosing so as to suit our character, and the liberty to combine or unite with others.

This last provision is politically the most acute in the context of the writing of *On Liberty*. From the end of the eighteenth century, tensions ran high in Britain due to the French Revolution (1789) and the subsequent and persistent wars with France. Fears of some sort of popular revolution were doubtless accentuated, but the Combination Acts of 1799 and 1800 made uniting or combining illegal, so making illegal associations such as a trade union.[1] These acts were repealed in 1824, with another Combination Act replacing them in 1825. In the 1830s, various movements sought to increase the representation of people from all walks of life. The 1832 Reform Act, as mentioned, did something to reorganise constituencies, but it did not effectively extend the franchise. The Grand National Consolidated Trade Union of 1834 was a short-lived precursor of the Trades Union Congress – but that was not established until 1867-68. A strong influence on the movement for reform in the 1840s was the Chartist movement.[2] Writing in the later 1850s, but as one who through this period was actively engaged in promoting reform, Mill is addressing a quite turbulent political landscape and maintaining a strongly principled defence of the entitlement people have to the liberty of association. Mill is often considered a champion of liberty for the individual, but his defence of liberty is clearly wider and more socially alert, and Mill here is nothing if not a political reformer – again, the defence of negative liberty associates with aspirations for a form of positive liberty.

Moving on with the text of *On Liberty*, Mill's next points have a thumping impact on the contemporary world, not least in developed settings where 'woke' thinking is prevalent.[3] Referencing the three-fold regions of liberty as just reviewed, Mill asserts that 'no society in which these liberties are not, on the whole, respected

---

[1] On this see: https:///www.britannica.com/event/Combination-Acts.
[2] On these matters see Mathias (2015).
[3] As mentioned earlier, 'Woke' thinking is considered in Chapter 14 below.

is free, whatever may be its form of government; and no one is completely free in which they do not exist absolute and unqualified' (I: 13). There is an important point here in Mill's reference to 'whatever' the 'form of government' might be. Mill is, it seems, less concerned about the precise system of government than to affirm that if we want to defend the threefold regions of liberty, then these liberties need to be 'absolute and unqualified' in order for a society and a people to be free. One could use this point as a template to run down the nations in the contemporary world to see how many, whatever their system of government, are free. What Mill then provides is another powerful statement of his emergent view with 'freedom' subbing for 'liberty' and with a repeat of a motif used earlier in the *Principles*:

'The only freedom which deserves the name is that of pursuing our own good in our own way, so long as we do not attempt to deprive others of theirs or impede their efforts to obtain it. Each is the proper guardian of his own health, whether bodily *or* mental and spiritual. Mankind are greater gainers by suffering each other to live as seems good to themselves than by compelling each to live as seems good to the rest'.

Mill shows with this last remark, as with others earlier in the chapter, an extraordinary capacity to frame his positive ideas in striking and memorable phrases. Berlin notes a tribute of R. W. Livingstone's to *On Liberty*: Livingstone called it 'a great short book', and with phrases such as the one we have just cited, we have some evidence for the quality and power of Mill's writing.[1] The great theme Mill has that each is 'the proper guardian' of their health – mind, body and spirit – provides the point and focus for the liberty principle, as well as the impetus to the 'progressive' (I: 11) mode of human life. Once more, the deterrent sense of preventing harm is evident, in that the individual has the responsibility to avoid depriving others of achieving their sense of their own good in their own way. It also sets a clear criterion against the State as well as against the influence of social trends as potential challengers to the liberty of individuals.

In contrast with his points in praise of liberty, Mill proceeds to recapitulate the theme of social tyranny as the greatest current threat to liberty. The principle of liberty might appeal as 'a truism', implying that everyone would leap to agree with it; the reality is, Mill thinks, that 'there is no doctrine which stands more directly opposed to the general tendency of existing opinion and practice' (I: 14).

Society is, Mill suggests, putting much effort into expanding its influence so as 'to compel people to conform to its notions of personal as of social excellence'. In earlier times, the vulnerability of developing nation-states, to some extent, explains the interest in the social systems of the state in 'the whole bodily and mental discipline of every one of its citizens'. This 'mode of thinking' also justifies the attitude of control in 'small republics surrounded by powerful enemies'. However, in the larger and more stable social conditions as in modern societies, it might be thought that such controls were no longer needed and that individual self-regulation might come into its own. This is not the case, however:

'... the engines of moral repression have been wielded more strenuously against divergence from the reigning opinion in self-regarding than even in social matters; religion, the most powerful of the elements which have entered into the formation of moral feeling,

---

[1] See Berlin (2017) p. 218 and n. 3.

have always been governed either by the ambitions of a hierarchy seeking control over every department of human conduct, or by the spirit of Puritanism'.

By the 'spirit of Puritanism', Mill has in mind not just the rigid moralities of non-conformism but also the force of moralism, and near-fanatical certitude in matters of moral conduct, that he sees emergent in some of the reforming trends of the mid-nineteenth century, trends which operated with an air of certitude about the rightness of their view that brooked no alternative. He also has in mind humanistic alternatives that nevertheless replicate the 'right of spiritual domination' (I: 14).[1] Mill again has Comte in mind, thinking that the 'social system' set out in the *System de Politique Positive* gave a humanistic view of life that was over-prescriptive and antagonistic to individuality.[2]

What Mill has is a sense that the individual spontaneity he wants to defend in *On Liberty* is threatened by extreme and fanatical outcomes that flow from high levels of certitude and over-confident moralism: liberty is, and will always be threatened by these trends, and with this insight Mill offers something that plays well as an anticipation, if not quite a prophecy for later times – the twentieth century and for life up to the present.[3]

Mill builds on his criticism of social trends against the individual in his final two paragraphs. He notes the worry of the pressure for social conformity that issues from social opinion generally to embrace all in a common outlook. Mill's view is that in his contemporary world, there is an 'increasing inclination to stretch unduly the powers of society over the individual both by force of opinion and even by that of legislation' (I: 15). This is coupled with the longstanding tendency for both 'rulers' and 'fellow citizens to impose their own opinions and inclinations as a rule of conduct on others'. This power and influence are increasing such that Mill fears there is an urgent need to erect 'a strong barrier of moral conviction… against the mischief'. The strong barrier will come, as will the equipment for what was earlier characterised as proper guardianship by individuals of their own well-being, by the case that Mill wants to elaborate, for 'Liberty of Thought' (I: 16) and the 'cognate' liberties of 'speaking and of writing'.

Mill aims to focus on these matters in the next chapter, as the arguments used will provide a basis for other liberties to do with action and conduct. Mill alludes to the work done in the past to defend and develop ideas on political liberty, conceding that the problem is not new. His justification for writing more on this theme lies in his sense that in his modernity, the case for liberty is not so well known as it needs to be, not least, we may assume, because he thinks it is being swamped by the rising tide of conventionalism. In his reference to earlier considerations, and as noted earlier, he is implicitly referencing John Milton's *Areopagitica* (1644), which, as

---

[1] Mill is fond of this sort of pejorative characterisation, and returns to it in a similar form later, referencing the negative influences of 'Calvinism'. See *OL* II: 29 and III: 7.
[2] Comte's work was published in four volumes between 1851 and 1854.
[3] Berlin would be uneasy here as he does not see Mill as possessing much by way of prophetic capacity. See Berlin (2017) p.227. However, Berlin also points out that Mill's abiding relevance comes from his focus on 'saying something true and important about some of the most fundamental characteristic and aspirations of human beings'. (p. 246).

we shall see later, prefigures a number of the themes arguments of Mill's defence of the liberty of thought and discussion.[1]

Matters Arising: Ideas on Harm, Liberty and the One Simple Principle

With the considerable package of ideas introduced in his opening chapter, Mill arguably leaves a lack of clarity hanging over the nature of the 'harm' to others that he had in mind and how this links to the defence and use of the self-other distinction within the liberty principle. Mill does not elaborate much on his meaning at this stage of his exposition, which contributes evidence to a large tradition of conventional scholarly wisdom to the effect that Mill is erratic in his terminological definition and usage. We noted potential for this with how Mill referenced society – but established that he consistently reflects on each occasion one of three distinct variants on this theme.

With his self and other-regarding distinction, and the correlated references to 'harm' and, as he sometimes says, 'interests' (I: 11; V: 2), Mill employs terms that, as we noted earlier, have been variously criticised as being imprecise.[2] If we focus on what it is to cause someone else harm, we might, ordinarily, consider causing a physical injury, perpetrating an act of theft or fraud, influencing another in a manner that damages their confidence, self-esteem, and so their character. We might consider harm to be imposed if the feelings of another are unduly offended. Or we might take a tighter line and consider harm only significant if it transgresses something that, as Gray says, can be 'accorded the status of a right'.[3] Gray also notes how particular problems arise over definitions of what will register as harm, and so a person's interests because the harms flow from conflicts arising between 'different moral outlooks'. A person may feel that their concerns, values, and so their aims and interests have been challenged and so harmed by a confrontation with a different value system. Mill gives examples of this kind in his fourth chapter.[4] If we imagine that all the tensions and conflicts over differences of this sort are going to count as harm to others and see that such actions that risk this are all ruled out by Mill's harm to others restriction, this makes for a substantial limit to the scope for the liberty of action; indeed, almost all liberty of debate is likely to manifest risks of such harm as this, suggesting that Mill's fine-sounding proposals are unworkable.

In Mill's defence, it is worth noting one strikingly obvious point, which is that his references to harm of, or the risk of harm to others, are consistent in putting the emphasis on actions or deeds, whether of commission or omission. What is significant is that the liberty of thought and discussion is largely protected from constraint, and so Mill does not, for example, put any focus on the irritation, upset or ill feeling that can arise as a consequence of debate, discussion, argument or the critical review of ideas. To put it another way, Mill does not think that harms

---

[1] See Milton (2008) pp.236-273.
[2] Again see Lucas (1966) p. 174; Gray (1983) pp. 48-52; Rees (1991) pp. 171-174, p. 176 and p. 182, and Honderich (2003) Chapter 1.
[3] Gray (1983) p. 49.
[4] See *OL* IV: 13-21.

embrace giving offence.[1] By the 'harm to others' that can be prevented and which we need to avoid, he is thinking of the material or physical harm that someone else or the wider social polity might suffer due to an individual's failure to do their duty, pay their way or act with a social sense to defend the common good. The implication is also that an individual's indiscriminate and wilful acts would also be constrained and punished in the usual ways. Harm to others is then much more a matter of how the actions a person might perpetrate on others might constitute a restriction to their own liberty for self-development.[2]

Mill gives some attention to this later in the text – again, in his fourth chapter – 'Of the Limits to the Authority of Society over the Individual'., There he details various matters which might constitute 'a breach of duty to others' as warranting 'moral reprobation' (IV: 6). Mill considers that most acts that threaten or constitute harm to others are best remedied by the usual moral measures taken by the rest of us against the offender. It is only in more definite or extreme cases that the social penalties of prosecution and the imposition of penalties and punishments would apply. Accordingly, if an offender 'has infringed the rules necessary for the protection of his fellow creatures, individually or collectively' (IV: 7), then since 'the evil consequences of his acts… fall… on others', then 'society, as the protector of all its members, must retaliate on him, must inflict pain on him for the express purpose of punishment, and must take care that it be sufficiently severe' (IV: 7).

We will look again at this issue of harm and how to deal with it in considering issues arising in the later chapters of *On Liberty*. The main thing to be clear about at this stage is that Mill considers actions that risk harm to others, and so those which 'society, as the protector of all its members', must take action to prevent, or otherwise to punish, are those which are tangible acts of a failure of duty, of criminality, of fraud and all imaginable crimes against the person. Things that radiate from the liberty of thought and discussion and that offend or upset us, whether the irritations come from others we care about a lot or not, are not for Mill 'harm' – these are all matters for the processes of remonstration, reasoning, persuading and entreating, as in the statement of the 'one very simple principle'.

Another issue that impacts the reader of *On Liberty* is that Mill's statement of the principle of liberty strikes us with the heavy emphasis that comes through the stress on 'one' (very simple principle) that is 'to govern absolutely' (the dealings of society with the individual).[3] This embroidered with the 'sole end' (for which mankind are warranted, individually or collectively, in interfering with the liberty of action of any of their number….); the 'only purpose' of 'rightfully' exercising power 'over any member of a civilized community… is to prevent harm to others'; and of course, 'Over himself, over his own body and mind, the individual is sovereign' (I: 9).

With this passage, Mill is determined to convey a clear sense of a regulative principle that serves to promote the considerable scope given to individual sovereignty. In juxtaposition, 'society' is portrayed in terms of the first sense in Mill's usage noted earlier, which would not rate too highly in a test of positives:

---

[1] On this point and the ways in which Mill's emphases can be considered, the following critics are helpful: Pyle (1994) p. xvi; Morley in Pyle (1994) pp. 271-297; Wollheim (1973), and Honderich (1982) and (2003). This is a matter we will consider again as we move through the text of *On Liberty*.
[2] See Capaldi (2012) pp. 277-78.
[3] On this see Himmelfarb (1974) pp 12-17.

social action is depicted as a form of interference, and the twin features of 'compulsion and control' are presented as measures of last resort, rather than as matters for everyday deployment. The contrasting intensity of the drive to articulate the 'one very simple principle to govern absolutely' the 'dealings of society' with the ordinarily sovereign individual presents a purity of purpose and singleness of intent. If this is to do with the complex of issues that arise in the relationships between the members of a 'civilized community', a testing question is whether the problems might be too elaborate for one 'simple principle'?

This issue arises as a question of interest because Mill writes in his *Autobiography* that as his career developed from his personal crisis of the 1820s, he was not keen to work up an alternative 'system of political philosophy' to the one he 'had abandoned' – that of classical utility as in the thinking of his forebears Jeremy Bentham and James Mill. In his later reflection, Mill explains that he thought it better to have 'no system' because he took the view that 'the true system was something much more complex and many sided than I had previously any idea of'.[1] Mill employs the concept of 'many-sidedness' to signal the acceptance of diversity and complexity in his view of man that emerged as his reading extended to include a range of continental thinkers and poets, and writers in general. Antagonism to developing a system was fuelled by the ongoing work of Comte, which, as we saw, Mill studied with decreasing appreciation. In a letter of 1829, Mill says Comte is a 'clear and methodical writer, most agreeable in stile' such that one is inclined 'to mistake the perfect coherence and logical consistency of his system for truth'.[2] Mill moves on the make his criticism of Comte and others keen on precise political systems:

'They deduce politics like mathematics from a set of axioms & definitions, forgetting that in mathematics there is no danger of partial views: a proposition is either true or it is not, & if it is true, we may safely apply it to every case which the proposition comprehends in its terms: but in politics & the social science, this is so far from being the case, that error seldom arises from our assuming premises which are not true, but generally from our overlooking other truths which limit and modify the effect of the former'.[3]

In contrast, another writer he encountered and who had an abiding impact on his thinking was Wilhelm von Humboldt, whose book, *The Duties and Spheres of Government*, Mill highly valued.[4] At the start of *On Liberty*, in addition to the dedication to his wife's memory, Mill has a thematic epigraph he clearly wants to apply to his own book, taken from von Humboldt: in his text, von Humboldt's passage, which Mill slightly edits, is as follows:

'The grand, leading principle, toward which every argument hitherto unfolded in these pages directly converges, is the absolute and essential importance of human development in its richest diversity'.[5]

---

[1] *Auto* p. 92
[2] CW XII p. 35.
[3] CW XII p. 36.
[4] The book was first written in 1791, and redrafted over the next decade. It was not first published until 1852 and translation used here is of the 1854 edition. See Von Humboldt (1996). Von Humboldt (1767-1835) was an academic, administrator and diplomat.
[5] Von Humboldt (1996) p. 65. Mill's quotation omits 'hitherto'.

What Mill thinks as he constructs and completes *On Liberty* is that the potential goods for humanity of the development of diverse interests and enthusiasms inherent with individuality, are far too important to be delivered by any outlook that is reductionist. His ongoing positive aspiration is to frame a means for the progressive development of humanity, and it ties in with the redevelopments made to utilitarianism. As Mill's thinking developed through the 1850s and, as *On Liberty* takes shape, he reaffirms that over-simplistic reductionism is entailed in the classical utilitarian proposals that all that is good is whatever meets the 'greatest happiness of the greatest number'. However, in his ongoing thinking, and so in *On Liberty*, Mill does not want to cast the whole utilitarian approach into the outer darkness. He wants to overcome the error of 'insisting upon only seeing one thing when there are many, or seeing a thing only on one side, only in one point of view when there are many others equally essential to a just estimate of it'.[1] Similarly, in writings on Jeremy Bentham, we recall Mill criticises the partial and narrow approach he finds in his former mentor's work.[2] He calls it 'one-eyed'[3] and 'one-sided,'[4] giving rise to 'half of the truth'.[5]

Mill is writing against the reductive view that the complexity of being human can be rightly calibrated by a prescriptive diagnostic. It might be thought that as he means to oppose the desire of ordering society in conformity with a single principle or a particular view, he cannot be serious in defending what is proposed by *On Liberty* through the 'one very simple principle'. The critical view, stressed especially by Himmelfarb, is that Mill here appears to follow something like the 'one-sided' approach he objects to in Bentham, giving his radical liberalism an axiomatic edge as sharp and clear as that in positivism or utilitarianism.[6]

Despite appearances, it would be an error to see Mill repeating the mistakes he sees in these other thinkers. The liberty thesis of *On Liberty* is, Mill thinks, within and to the progressive utilitarian end of enhancing a wider enrichment of the many-sided and civilized community he prizes. He aims to achieve this through a modified and, he assumes, enhanced sense of a utilitarian concern with the greater good, but this in a manner that combines clarity of principle and the avoidance of one-sidedness. As Mill writes in his consideration of Bentham, 'utility, or happiness'[7] is 'much too complex and indefinite an end to be sought except through the medium of various secondary ends'. Here we have another manifestation of Mill's 'indirect' variant of utility; this is now considered, as with the larger sense of utility, to cohere with liberty as the principle to defend most effectively the complexity of progressive humanity. How this is thought to work becomes clearer, particularly as we follow Mill into his next two chapters.

---

[1] CW XII p. 36.
[2] See CW X pp. 7-9 and pp. 16-17.
[3] CW X p. 94.
[4] CW X p. 109.
[5] CW X p. 95.
[6] For Himmelfarb's view of there being 'two Mills' or of 'Mill versus Mill', see Himmelfarb (1962) 'Introduction' pp xi-xxxi and Himmelfarb (1974), especially pp. 3-139.
[7] CW X p. 110.

8. *On Liberty*: II: 'Of the Liberty of Thought and Discussion' (Paragraphs 1-44)

In the first chapter of *On Liberty,* Mill deploys the self and other-regarding distinction to note liberty of thought and liberty of discussion as separate provinces of the wider 'region of human liberty' (I: 12). His view is that the distinction is of little consequence – liberty of thought and liberty of discussion are virtually identical, and though it might be assumed that a contemporary developed society might exhibit liberal, pluralist and secular trends and currents of thought, the idea that freedom of discussion, freedom of expression and freedom of publication are unproblematic, and provinces needing no form of border control, is far from watertight.

As an example of the problems that can arise, there are the long-running debates and exchanges prompted by the British publication, in September 1988, of Salman Rushdie's novel *The Satanic Verses*. This was an event within an apparently free society – albeit in a world community of disparate values – that led to a *fatwa* – a form of a death sentence – being imposed on Rushdie. In effect, Islamic authorities in Iran pronounced that it would be a blessed deed to execute Rushdie as he had blasphemed against Islamic sensibilities concerning the prophet Muhammad.[1] A bounty of £6 million was put on Rushdie's head, and the UK government was committed to providing secret cover and security for Rushdie.[2]

In the light of the review of the first chapter *of On Liberty*, it is not hard to guess Mill's likely reaction to the state of affairs in a society where Rushdie would suffer this sort of protracted reaction to the publication of a novel, a reaction that resurfaced in the attack Rushdie suffered in August 2022, when about to give a lecture in the USA on the freedom of expression.[3] Our task is to follow his presentation of a case for the liberty of thought and discussion, and within this, we will see more clearly the reasons why extremism over the expression of opinion is to be resisted. This second and longest chapter in Mill's text reviews the role of liberty of argument to establish new truths; its role in testing and refining accepted truths, with the capacity to aid in resolving those matters where the best truths are, as yet, indefinite.

'Truths' is the important term here, because of special interest in Mill's sense that humans are 'fallible' (II: 8). Accordingly, what such humans can aspire to and, for a period, possess on the matters to hand are *truths* rather than *the* truth. Mill gives an important health warning on this as a part of the case for progressing the argument for the liberty of thought and discussion, commenting that 'everyone well

---

[1] For details in the Rushdie affair, see https:///www.indexoncensorship.org/2019/02/student-reading-list-salman-rushdie-fatwa/
[2] Since 2009 Rushdie has been more in evidence and his book *Joseph Anton* (2012) is in effect an autobiography of his years in hiding. The fatwa has never been lifted, but some Iranian governments have said that Rushdie's death is no longer an official policy.
[3] See, for example, coverage of this in *The Times* online, 13-15/08/2022. As this book goes to press Rushdie is still in hospital recovering from knife wounds sustained in the attack. Those who have publicly supported Rushdie's defence of liberty(J. K. Rowling, for example) have also received on-line threats. There are other recent controversies over the liberty of discussion and academic freedom that we examine later, in Chapters 13-15 below.

knows himself to be fallible' (II: 4), but the problem is that people consistently fail to 'take any precautions against their own fallibility'.

In snapshot form, it is Mill's view that the greatest threats to the liberties he wants to defend comes from those – whether individuals, groups, or societies – driven by the sense of infallibility. In making this focus on the phenomenon of the issue of human fallibility, Mill echoes Milton's presentation in *Areopagitica*. Writing in the highly charged period of the English Civil War, Milton, a committed parliamentarian and non-conformist, was eager to underpin the liberties the parliamentary faction had gained. He wrote against the threats of the policy of pre-publication censorship that was contained in the licensing order of 1643.[1] Using a poetic and theologically astute rather than a philosophical style of expression, Milton's worry is that we cannot know that those who are to censor can be assumed to be 'above all others in the land'[2] in being possessed of 'the grace of infallibility, and uncorruptedness'. Milton sees the free exercise of human reason as of great importance in the great scheme of things: he thinks that when 'God did enlarge the universal diet of man's body (saving ever the rules of temperance), he then also, as before, left arbitrary the diet and repasting of our minds, as wherein every mature man might have to exercise his own leading capacity'.[3]

Rather than live under ill-grounded censorship, Milton thinks a free review and reading of books is the better way. By grace, mankind is not captive 'under a perpetual childhood of prescription' but trusted to employ 'the gift of reason to be his own chooser': it is also a feature of 'the ingenuity of Truth'[4] to 'open herself faster' when given 'a free and willing hand'.

In a work that deserves to be more widely read, Milton defends liberty against those looking to impose censorship in a manner that all who are impressed with Mill would recognise:

'Liberty… is the nurse of all great wits: this is that which hath rarefied and enlightened, enlarged and lifted up our apprehensions degrees above themselves. Ye cannot make us now less capable, less knowing, less eagerly pursuing of the truth, unless ye first make yourselves, that made us so, less the lovers, less the true founders of our true liberty. We can grow ignorant again, brutish, formal and slavish, as ye found us; but you then must first become that which ye cannot be, oppressive, arbitrary and tyrannous, as they were from whom ye freed us'.[5]

Mill, no less than Milton, is eager to oppose the presumption of infallibility and the correlated error of assuming that some form of absolute truth is to be obtained and defended.

Moving on in his discussion, Mill's treatment of human fallibility and the importance of truths as distinct from the truth is not always as precautionary as it might be. His exposition sometimes sounds as if certainty and truth are ready, available and fit for use. Still, his ideas centre on the view that, given human fallibility, open debate will give us the best chance of acquiring the best-grounded

---

[1] See 'Introduction' to Milton (2008) p. xvii.
[2] Milton (2008) p. 249-50. *Areopagitica* is subtitled: 'A Speech of Mr John Milton for the Liberty of Unlicensed Printing to the Parliament of England'.
[3] Milton (2008) p. 247.
[4] Milton (2008) p. 250.
[5] Milton (2008) p. 268.

truths we can employ 'for purposes of action' (II: 6) – 'and on no other terms can a being with human faculties have any rational assurance of being right.

Here, for 'human faculties', we need to think 'fallible' human faculties, while being 'right' means being as sure as circumstances allow, and 'rational assurance' signifies a relative rather than an absolute sense of what is right, meaning that we are conscious of having done all that we can to make sure that the grounds we have for a what we consider right are the best possible.

The other point Mill reaffirms is his longstanding view that truths relate to action, with the implication that we cannot lead a good life without some reasoning and consideration as to the best, most coherent, and most persuasive ways of so doing.

Liberty of Thought & Discussion and Truth through Conflict (Paragraphs 1-9)

Mill's treatment begins by considering the traditional uses for the concept of liberty of thought and discussion. He suggests that such notions of liberty have been used in connection with the 'liberty of the press' (II: 1), as a balance and check, 'as one of the securities against corrupt or tyrannical governments'.[1] Mill wholly approves of this, but he writes in favour of the use of liberty against all forms of government – not just the manifestly corrupt and tyrannical. Moreover, as in the first chapter, he criticizes in all but name the democratic model of government that the earlier utilitarians and other radicals had envisaged as the ideal:

'Let us suppose... that the government is entirely at one with the people, and never thinks of exerting any power of coercion unless in agreement with what it conceives to be their voice. But I deny the right of the people to exercise such coercion, either by themselves or by their government. The power itself is illegitimate. The best government has no more title to it than the worst. It is as noxious, or more noxious, when exerted in accordance with public opinion than when in opposition to it'.

The point here may seem extreme; has the 'best government' really 'no more title' to exercise coercive force over the people than 'the worst'? Mill's thought is based on his sense that the tyranny of the majority, as explained earlier, can exhibit 'a social tyranny more formidable than many kinds of political oppression... penetrating much more deeply into the details of life, and enslaving the soul itself' (I: 5). The thrust of Mill's point ought to be clear: even if the government is almost totally expressive of the will of the people, it has no legitimate right, power or authority to coerce, control, or interfere with the dissenting minority's liberty of thought and discussion. Mill continues with what has become one of his most famous remarks:

'If all mankind minus one were of one opinion, mankind would be no more justified in silencing that one person than he, if he had the power, would be justified in silencing mankind' (II: 1).

---

[1] Here again Mill is doubtless thinking of Milton's defence of the freedom of the press from pre-publication censorship in his work *Areopagitica* - Milton (2008).

This is an important point. We saw how Mill clarified support for utility as the 'ultimate appeal on all ethical questions', utility grounded in humanity's 'permanent interests' (I: 11) as 'progressive' beings. With this in mind, his defence of the liberty of thought and expression is not based solely on the concept of the sovereign individual. Such individuals might have rights and authority over their own bodies and souls in self-regarding matters and over the liberty of thought and discussion, this against the threats of the tyranny of the majority and the attendant risks of conformism. No individual should be silenced by the majority of all the rest, any more than they should be silenced by the individual. But on the modified utilitarian argument related to the progressive view of the human condition, it is not for the sake of the dissenter pure and simple, but for society as a whole, as the sum total of potentially progressive individuals, that society should be denied the right to silence him.

Developing this, Mill thinks that opinions are not 'personal possessions' (II: 1), the sole property of the individual (or group) in question, deserving of absolute freedom from exposure to debate. Rather, opinions and ideas have a wider social meaning – they are a part of the currency of thought and life for everyone within society.

Thus:

'... the peculiar evil of silencing the expression of an opinion is that it is robbing the human race, posterity as well as the existing generation – those who dissent from the opinion, still more to those who hold it. If the opinion is right, they are deprived of the opportunity of exchanging error for truth; if wrong, they lose, what is almost as great a benefit, the clearer perception and livelier impression of truth provided by its collision with error' (II: 1).[1]

That opinions are social and not individual possessions, even though we need innovative individuals to generate novelties, is the first justification Mill gives for the defence of the liberty of thought and discussion. He also unpacks two other reasons for defending this mode of liberty.

Firstly, an ongoing review of the dissenting perspective may prove that it is right to a sufficient degree to replace the received outlook. Mill emphasises the power of intellectual conflict to show that if society seeks to suppress an opinion, the problem is that the opinion, even if commonly rejected as false, 'may possibly be true' (II: 3). Mill means that the opinion considered false may 'contain a portion of the truth' (II: 42) of the matter in question, so for the sake of extracting this possible portion, open discussion is needed.

Here Mill recasts another of Milton's arguments. Milton was anxious to debunk the zeal of the more extreme factions in the parliamentarian community; he noted those who fear 'schisms and sects'[2] and make into a 'calamity that any man dissents from their maxims'. But this created the problem of looking to deter those who, through dissent, might find 'dissevered pieces which are yet wanting to the body of truth'. For Milton – as for Mill – if 'truth be in the field'[3], 'falsehood' can be

---

[1] By the 'human race' Mill means humanity.
[2] Milton (2008) p. 264.
[3] Milton (2008) p. 269.

contended with, for 'who ever knew truth to be put to the worse in a free and open encounter?'

Mill, with his commitment to a broader notion of the range of possible truths that individuals can discover and develop, also wants to encourage the liberty of discussion even of matters that already seem established as erroneous. That society has the view that the idea in question is false would be unproblematic if we could assume that human societies were infallible – but neither individuals nor societies are so empowered, and so we cannot in either respect claim 'the authority to decide' (II: 3) such questions 'for all mankind and exclude every other person from the means of judging'.

Secondly, the process of critical review provides a means by which the received position, if it is the best perspective available, is grasped with 'a livelier impression' (II: 1). In other words, if an idea is challenged but through the debate is vindicated, with the challenge proving less plausible, the process of participative debate will allow a more powerful sense of the worth of the more valid ideas in question. Thus we have a basic justification – ideas are not simply individual possessions – and two other reasons for the liberty of thought and expression – humans are not infallible, and so it is unwise to assume are ideas are sacrosanct, and if ideas face a challenge and are vindicated as the best we have, for now, through the process of interrogation, we hold them with a sharper sense of why they are the best.

In the way that Mill writes, we come upon the stylistic point warned of earlier: the merging of 'opinions' with views that might be 'truth' as opposed to 'error' is potentially confusing, given what we have seen of Mill's notions of human fallibility and so the focus on 'truths'. However, the core image of 'truth' in a 'collision' with 'error', or of erroneous and true 'opinions' in conflict, gives us a central doctrine of *On Liberty*: that truths emerge best for progressive individuals and thereby for society as a whole, under the pressure of a conflict with other opinions, where those with lesser plausibility give way to those which have more of an approximation to the truth of the issue at stake. For Mill, the threshing floor or crucible of free discussion and argument is the best means to a wider and more fruitful end.

Mill plans to review the points arising in some detail, but it is worth adding that as his review unfolds, he adds other reasons in defence of the liberty of thought and discussion. The third major point he has is that on many points of debate, what is the best truth is unresolved because 'conflicting doctrines… share the truth between them' (II: 34). This is, in Mill's view, the most common state of affairs and so the most powerful evidence for the merits of the liberty of thought and discussion. He also adds to the earlier point that a dissenting view might not prove to have the better truth to overturn the received idea, but it might have 'a portion of the truth' (II: 42) that we are better off having brought into the light.

Before we follow Mill on his journey in defence of the liberty of thought and discussion, which he sees as correlated within the ethos of a liberal and progressive society, we must consider a criticism made by Berlin. He draws attention to what is presented as a powerful line of evidential counter-argument from historical analyses, 'that integrity, love of truth and fiery individualism grow at least as often in severely disciplined communities, among, for example, the puritan Calvinists of

Scotland or New England'.[1] While Berlin makes it clear that truth and progress cannot emerge 'where dogma crushes all thought', he thinks that if progress and truth are coming from societies 'under military discipline', then Mill's argument that liberty matters crucially for the cultivation of truth, and is 'a necessary condition for the growth of genius' is weakened to the point of failure.

Berlin is onto a vital point in that it is clear to any student of the twentieth century that, for example, German scientists working under the illiberal Nazi dictatorship made impressive progress with jet-powered aircraft and rockets and that Soviet scientists did well despite Stalinist tyranny and through helpful espionage, to develop atomic weapons and to take a strong lead in the space race. However, Mill is not really making quantitative appeals for liberty. It is not a matter of how often truth emerges; it is a matter of the quality of the ideas forged through the crucible of debate in and for a free and civilized society. Mill is clear that where dissention is suppressed, the expression and development of thought are constrained and that this is contrary to the human capacity for development and contrary to the aspiration of the acquisition of better truths in and for the society in question. The advances in technology and war machinery in Nazi Germany and the Soviet Union did not do a lot for the more general advance for the sum total of the quality of life for individuals in the societies in question, within which a civilized culture was defended despite, not because of, the governing tyranny.

We now have a development of the vital issue of the kinds of truth open to 'fallible' (II: 8) beings. The discussion refocuses on the issue of fallibility, something of a spin from Mill's empirical and utilitarian background. Humans are not, in his view, possessed of eternal reason or any other superlative quality to make them infallible. Developing his fallibilist notion of truth and knowledge, Mill's idea is that in no domains of knowledge does humanity ever have the whole truth: what we think individually or collectively at any point in time is simply the best that we have to hand. This is why Mill sustains the idea that to be open to better insights into the truths that matter, humanity needs maximal liberty of thought and discussion. If the scope of free debate is reduced, we also reduce the means by which we can check and know the extent of the value of a given view or theory, and critically, those who suppress debate, whether it is a government or the force of public opinion, can offer no guarantee of infallibility:

'They have no authority to decide the question for all mankind and exclude every other person from the means of judging. To refuse a hearing to an opinion because they are sure it is false is to assume that *their* certainty is the same thing as absolute certainty' (II: 3).

Here Mill could again have been more careful over defining the frame of reference for the terms he uses: 'certainty' would be a case in point. 'Certainty' in the first sense used above refers to what Mill characterises as the collective or group view, to public opinion. It is akin to the totalised version of *subjective* certainty – the view a person has as a condition or outlook when whatever is in mind is held to be 'certain'. We might be certain that our keys are in a basket on the bookcase in the living room (when they are in the pocket of a coat worn yesterday); we might be certain that Mill was born and died in London (when he was born in London and

---

[1] Berlin (2017) p. 175.

died in Avignon); we could be certain that there are no absolute certainties (but the truths within specific systems of logic have objective truth and can be said to be certain). Subjective certainty is a feature of human thinking and not an altogether helpful one, for unless we are careful, we can assume too much and make claims that slide into what Mill terms 'absolute certainty'. Mill senses that with social opinion, we can find an operational form of this element of absolutism.[1] He does not elaborate on this at this stage, but the implicit point is that conditional and improvable truths hold more generally for all truth-claims about reality as expressed in the natural and human sciences and the academic disciplines in general: they are finite, contingent, probabilistic, and so fallible, but all the more reliable as a guide for action when shared and refined through collaborative, collegiate discussion.

There is an important matter at stake here: it is obvious that the truths in science or humanities disciplines can be framed with the status of absolute truth. If we take an example: a biologist might give us the objective parameters for what is necessary for the conditions of life for particular ants – for soldier ants, for example. These parameters could be expressed as localised truths and truths that hold beyond any reasonable doubt relative to the evidence currently at hand. From this, the impression can grow that science gives facts or truths that are incontrovertible or absolute. However, in the case in question, the truths fit soldier ants, not all ants or other insects. The wider point, consistent with Mill's inductivism, is that the natural and human sciences and disciplines such as history are manifestly clear in presenting theories, explanations, models, interpretations and views that are invariably debated, disputed and modified as they enter the panoply and repertoire of ideas in the broader framework of possibilities we call knowledge.

Mill thinks that most people have a sense of the theoretical aspect of claiming that knowledge is fallible, but – here is the advice we quoted earlier – from the practical perspective, 'few seem to take any precautions against their own fallibility' (II: 4).

Mill here plays with a psychological issue, in thinking that, as a rule, people think other people are fallible but that they themselves are not. Mill likens the attitude to that of absolute rulers, who operate with no lack of confidence in their opinions.

Mill also ventures another point of psychological observation: he thinks that many people get so used to being corrected and put right on various matters that they incline more and more to affirm the ideas that cohere with the consensus in society, putting an 'implicit trust in the infallibility of "the world" in general'. Mill suggests this 'world' is what we might now term a spectrum of social plurality: it means 'the part of it' that the individual associates with – his 'party', 'sect', 'church', or 'class of society'.

Here Mill is on to a point of significant diagnostic value for the issue faced in our modernity.[2] He adds a further weighty insight in noting that the confidence people have in their current opinions (which are fallible) is not altered by their sense that the ideas of the past were perhaps 'the exact reverse' of current opinion.

Once again, what Mill might have done at this stage is to clarify that the right and proper sense for understanding what we mean by truth in respect of knowledge

---

[1] This comes out in the discussion of 'social rights' – see *OL* IV: 19 and Chapter 10 below.
[2] This will emerge with the issues considered in Chapters 14-16 below.

of the world are those truths that are relative to the best evidence and reasoning we have to date. This is what he means by knowledge: he operates with a type of epistemological scepticism: humans are fallible and capable of constant corrective understanding, using the liberty of thought and discussion to exchange weaker for stronger truths.

There is no detail or elaboration on this at this stage of the discussion because Mill instead does something else that we noted him as inclined to do: he presents a powerful objection to his own view, arguing that there is no explicit assumption of infallibility at work when governments or individuals promote the views they think right and objecting to those they think erroneous – they are simply using their 'own judgement and responsibility' (II: 5) to act on their 'conscious conviction'. This leads to the point that 'men and governments must act to the best of their ability'. People may accept that there is no such thing as 'absolute certainty' but think nevertheless that there is 'assurance sufficient' to have enough truth to provide 'guidance' for 'our own conduct; and it is assuming no more when we forbid bad men to pervert society by the propagation of opinions which we regard as false and pernicious'.

We are given a counter to this view:

'I answer, that it is assuming very much more. There is the greatest difference between presuming an opinion to be true because, with every opportunity for contesting it, it has not been refuted, and assuming its truth for the purpose of not permitting its refutation' (II: 6).

And Mill adds another of his memorable positive statements:

'Complete liberty of contradicting and disproving our opinion is the very condition which justifies us in assuming its truth for purposes of action; and on no other terms can a being with human faculties have any rational assurance of being right'.

There is helpful clarification in these remarks. We can justifiably assume the 'truth' of a view if we have kept open the means of contesting it: we err if we assume and assert it as true without allowing such means of open debate.

The emergent position is that within a culture, possessing a qualitative apprehension of the best truths possible is proportional to the degree of free thought and discussion that is encouraged within it. Mill develops and defends an adversarial or conflict theory of truth, arguing that the best insight into the truths that might be attained is reached as a result of the conflict of opinion, through the challenge of reason, the struggle and tension of debate and argument. It is thus that the danger of suppression or coercion by a government or through the force of public opinion within a society is so extreme. Suppression and coercion preclude the free discussion and rational investigation through which the best truths of which we are capable emerge to the benefit of all.

Mill explains much of his thinking on this in the following passage:

'When we consider either the history of opinion or the ordinary conduct of human life, to what is it to be ascribed that the one and the other are no worse than they are? Not certainly to the inherent force of the human understanding, for on any matter not self-evident there are ninety-nine persons totally incapable of judging of it for one who is capable; and the capacity of the hundredth person is only comparative, for the majority of the eminent men of every past generation held many opinions now known to be erroneous, and did or approved numerous things which no one will now justify. Why is it, then, that there is on the whole a preponderance among mankind of rational opinions and rational conduct? If there really is this preponderance – which there must be unless human affairs are, and have always been, in an almost desperate state – it is owing to a quality of the human mind, the source of everything respectable in man either as an intellectual or as a moral being, namely, that his errors are corrigible. He is capable of rectifying his mistakes by discussion and experience. Not by experience alone. There must be discussion to show how experience is to be interpreted. Wrong opinions and practices gradually yield to fact and argument; but facts and arguments, to produce any effect on the mind, must be brought before it. Very few facts are able to tell their own story, without comments to bring out their meaning. The whole strength and value, then, of human judgment depending on the one property, that it can be set right when it is wrong, reliance can be placed on it only when the means of setting it right are kept constantly at hand' (II: 7).

Here Mill is demonstrating how he works to develop a fuller recognition[1] of the reasoning that supports the liberty of thought and discussion, over and above earlier considerations – such as that of Milton. Mill defends a progressive, organic and clearly optimistic attitude towards human life as orientated to the cultivation of truths. There are truths, he thinks, within and for particular fields of enquiry and modes of life, rather than a truth of dogmatic certainty to which all must adhere. This links to his support for liberty as a simple principle that aims to function to the end of protecting the cultivation of truths. 'Truth' as such is almost an ideal, the open-ended goal of research and debate, so it remains dynamic and elusive.

However, Mill also believes that the development of the intellect to the extent that allows the fullest expression of human judgement requires a situation within which the individual can associate with other views in a spirit of criticism and debate. The great strength of human judgment, which encourages us to place confidence in it, is the capacity for correction and improvement. This ties in with the sense of humans as progressive and capable of development, but these capacities cannot grow *ex nihilo* – they have to be cultivated in a situation where such means of correction are 'kept constantly at hand'.

Mill continues – drawing, we may think, on his personal *modus operandi*:

'In the case of any person whose judgment is really deserving of confidence, how has it become so? Because he has kept his mind open to criticism of his opinions and conduct. Because it has been his practice to listen to all that could be said against him; to profit by as much of it as was just, and to expound to himself, and upon occasion to others, the fallacy of what was fallacious. Because he has felt that the only way in which a human being can make some approach to knowing the whole of a subject is by hearing what can be said about it by persons of every variety of opinion, and studying all modes in which it can be looked at by every character of mind. No wise man ever acquired his wisdom in any mode but this; nor is it in the nature of human intellect to become wise in any other manner. The steady habit of correcting and completing his own opinion by collating it with those of others, so far from causing doubt and hesitation in carrying it into practice, is the only stable foundation for a just reliance on it; for, being cognisant of all that can, at least obviously, be said against him, and having taken up his position against all gainsayers – knowing that he has sought for objections and difficulties instead of avoiding them, and has shut out no light which can be

---

[1] See *OL* I: 16 and Chapter 7 above.

thrown upon the subject from any quarter – he has a right to think his judgment better than that of any person, or any multitude, who have not gone through a similar process'.

The perspective outlined here emerges with a quasi-legal focus on studying the case on both sides: what is assumed is a process that is thorough, methodical, and reflective will produce the best judgments. Transposed into chess or tennis, this is like saying that the most emphatic preparation will be the ideal thing to bring the player to a peak before the match: however, in tennis, chess and in life, imagination and individual insight, ability and discernment can also play positive roles. Mill, when in more eclectic moods, discerns this, but in this passage, he does not give this side of the argument notable weight.

Moving on to illustrate his concern, Mill cites the 'Newtonian philosophy' – Newton's approach to physics – as a cherished belief, suggesting that the reason why its certainty is so generally assured is the extent to which it is open to question.[1] Mill's view is that such esteemed ideas are nevertheless to be challenged:

'The beliefs which we have most warrant for have no safeguard to rest on but a standing invitation to the whole world to prove them unfounded. If the challenge is not accepted, or is accepted and the attempt fails, we are far enough from certainty still, but we have done the best that the existing state of human reason admits of: we have neglected nothing that could give the truth a chance of reaching us; if the lists are kept open, we may hope that, if there is a better truth, it will be found when the human mind is capable of receiving it; and in the meantime we may rely on having attained such approach to truth as is possible in our own day. This is the amount of certainty attainable by a fallible being, and this is the sole way of attaining it' (II: 8).

Here Mill reaffirms a fusion of reasoning with empirical and experimental modes of thought. Human knowledge derives from experiment and through rational enquiry with reference to general experience. The truths found through this process are contingent; certainty is relative to our own limits at any given point in time, and again, the term 'truth' for Mill really denotes our best current views. Perhaps the best example of the idea that Mill has in mind is given by the history of medical developments, as in the advances in surgical techniques. With this, we see how 'the truth' would always be the best state of understanding – and that there would be a constant openness to innovation. We can add that Mill's use of Newton was wholly vindicated, as sceptical and investigative physicists in the early twentieth century found that sub-atomic physics was not explicable through Newtonian mechanics.

Mill next considers the objection that we should not push to the extremes in the process of critical inquiry, that we should apply the critical process to matters in general but hold on to 'some particular principle or doctrine' (II: 9). Here the point might be that if we deny any absolute certainties through the stress on human knowledge as the knowledge of fallible beings, we fall into cognitive relativism. Thus, if you are certain only that there are no certainties, how certain can you be that you are right, and within the flux of uncertainty over certainty, how can you discriminate to argue some views to be better and others worse?

Mill has no fear of cognitive relativism. He does not propose assessing ideas in a cognitive vacuum: he wants ideas to be reviewed within and against life and

---

[1] Sir Isaac Newton (1642-1727). Newton is best-known for his *Principia Mathematica* (1687).

against the backdrop of existing ideas that have worked well in general. He also thinks that the forms of reasoning are distinct from the specific claims to truth and understanding that arise, so he thinks that 'unless the reasons are good for an extreme case, they are not good for any case'.

Liberalism wedded to classical utility would sacrifice individual liberty to the interests that are perceived to coincide with the interests of the greater number; the utilitarians, other than Mill, take just this view, in relation to a notion of how a democratic government should function. But Mill believes that in the practical context, this view inclines toward negating the most critical mode of liberty and thence of liberty in all its manifestations. Therefore, it is not good enough just to affirm free discussion; we must also promote an open and critical attitude toward all traditions, values and customs.

The Truth and Utility of Social Opinions. (Paragraphs 10-20)

Mill next works from a quotation from the writing of Thomas Carlyle, which characterizes their age as being 'destitute of faith, but terrified of scepticism' (II: 10).[1] Mill likes this as it relates to the rise of humanistic and secular thought on the one hand and to the fear of a life without certainties on the other. People know that many traditional or customary ideas are no longer valid, but they 'should not know what to do without them'.[2]

This gives rise to an encoded passage: certain ideas must be defended 'from public attack' not because they are considered true, but because they are 'important to society', 'useful' – so much so to 'well-being' that 'it is as much the duty of governments to uphold those beliefs as to protect any other interests of society'. This means that society justifies 'restraints' on critical discussion not 'on the truth of doctrines' but on 'their usefulness'. These references to 'truth' are all conditioned by the points we considered earlier, so in Mill's estimate, these are always, at best, 'truths' of the fallibilist kind. The references to 'usefulness' could, of course, just as easily been written as 'utility', and indeed, Mill moves up a gear in his managed critique of classical utilitarian thinking by asserting that there is greater merit in seeing that 'the truth of an opinion is a part of its utility'. To impress the power of his critique, Mill notes that those who want to defend received opinions always aim to argue for both the 'truth' and the 'utility' of the ideas in question.

Mill thinks he has laid the ground for an offensive: he next wants to illustrate the 'mischief of denying a hearing to opinions because we, in our own judgement, have condemned them' (II: 11). He chooses examples, not from the area of science, along the lines of his reference to 'the Newtonian philosophy' (II: 8), but from areas of religious and moral belief:

---

[1] Mill cites an essay by Carlyle on Sir Walter Scott. In the original the 'but' is an 'and' – see *OL* p. 82 n. 7.

[2] This anticipates Nietzsche's critique of modernity in his writings, as in his book of 1882, *The Gay Science* and the parabolic passage on the death of the concept of God. See Nietzsche (1974) Section 125.

'Let the opinions impugned be the belief in a God and in a future state, or any of the commonly received doctrines of morality' (II: 11).

Mill claims that he chooses these because they are 'least favourable to him' and because there are strong arguments against freedom of opinion and liberty of discussion in relation to such matters 'both on the score of truth and on that of utility'. He means to say that there are arguments to the effect that religious and moral beliefs are held with such conviction and in the face of such a tradition of dispute that those who hold them cannot be accused of claiming infallibility in the dangerous sense and that there are further arguments with a utilitarian character that the value of the religious and moral view of life in relation to society as a whole is so positive that it would be against the interests of utility to deprive such views of the care and protection of the state within which they play this positive role.[1] Against this, Mill redeploys his argument concerning fallibility. If people are certain of their beliefs, that is one thing, but it is quite another 'to decide that question *for others*, without allowing them to hear what can be said on the contrary side'. Whatever views we hold, however strongly they may be evidenced, however beneficial they may appear in popular and general belief, if we prevent criticism and debate about those views, we assume 'infallibility'.

Mill supports his thinking with a generalised historical reference to instances when people look back with astonishment at the suffering of 'the best men' who defended 'the noblest doctrines' and where the laws in each case operated 'with deplorable success as to the men, though some of the doctrines have survived to be (as if in mockery) invoked in defence of similar conduct towards those who dissent from *them*, of from their received interpretation'.

From the general, Mill moves to the specifics and, over the next three paragraphs (II: 12-14), references Socrates, Jesus and Marcus Aurelius as historical figures who variously introduced and exemplified 'virtue' (Socrates), 'moral grandeur' (Jesus), and 'unblemished justice' (Marcus Aurelius).[2] In the long run, all are individuals acclaimed for their insights and contributions, but each in their own time fell prey to the conventions and majorities that prevailed.

Mill understands that by the laws of Athenian democracy, Socrates was condemned to death – yet he was 'the man who probably of all then born had deserved least of mankind to be put to death as a criminal' (II: 12). Jesus is crucified by the force of common opinion, by those who were not 'bad men', but simply those who were 'possessed in a full, or somewhat more than a full measure, of the religious, moral, and patriotic feelings of their time and people' (II: 13). Aurelius is given high praise for his intelligent understanding of the human condition. An honest and deep thinker, he rejected the rising impetus of Christian belief as he could not square this with his reason or experience. As Emperor, he sought to eliminate Christianity, yet in his 'moral writings' (II: 14), he was the embodiment 'of the Christian ideal,' For all this, Aurelius assumes too much of the attitude of 'infallibility' to give the Christians the benefit of the doubt, and here Mill uses the

---

[1] Mill's argument here is qualified by the more recent rise of extreme forms of religious fundamentalism.
[2] Socrates (d. 399 BCE): Jesus of Nazareth (c4 BCE – c30 CE): Marcus Aurelius (121-180).

example of Aurelius to show how even those who hold to well-reasoned values can fall prey to dangerous and inhibiting certitude that becomes a repressive tyranny.

Mill deploys these examples to bring home to his contemporaries the evidential basis of the error of intolerance and the wisdom seen in retrospect of allowing the experiment of new ideas and values on how we might best live. He dismisses what he sees as the error of thinking that 'persecution is an ordeal through which the truth ought to pass' (II: 15), for persecution 'cannot possibly… harm' the truth (II: 16). That there are truths that have, in the end, proved of value to humanity and have passed through persecution is undeniable: that they and those who promote them have an imperative need to be persecuted or be condemned as criminals is not a requirement. Those who think this, and Dr Samuel Johnson is one Mill cites who did, appear to think that 'martyrdom' is a 'splendid benefit', but such an idea is only held by those 'who think that new truths may have been desirable once, but that we have had enough of them now'.[1] Mill gives a list of religious reformers who faced persecution, but his view is that it is 'a piece of idle sentimentality that truth, merely as truth, has any inherent power denied to error of prevailing against the dungeon and the stake' (II: 17). In general, he thinks humans 'are not more zealous for truth than they often are for error'. In the right amount, legal or social penalties will 'succeed in stopping the propagation of either'. All that can be relied upon is that truths that carry real value for the human condition can be 'extinguished' many times over, but in the end, the truth will out, as there 'will generally be found persons to rediscover it', and at some point in time, circumstances will be 'favourable' to its reception.

In this section, Mill is giving focuses on matters within aspects of the history of religious and moral movements, and his point about favourable circumstances recalls his view that with these examples, he was taking cases that were, for him, the 'least favourable' (II: 11).

Himmelfarb, who has a special interest in the currents of thought in the nineteenth century, thinks he is 'so far from taking the extreme case, the hard one to prove' – he was 'taking the easy path, the path of least resistance'.[2] The point is that in the mindset of Victorian society, the criticism of religious and moral ideas was something of a commonplace and not a matter of special difficulty. As the understanding of the history and thought of other world religions grew, the historical and cultural relativism of the Christian tradition became increasingly clear, and the challenge to religious thinking from scientific thought and secular philosophy was more direct.

Mill wants to provide a case for his readers to see the vital importance of liberty of discussion, and he would make a stronger case by taking on matters that were of more comprehensive interest to the age. He could have thrown the radical doctrine of liberty into sharper relief by challenging the view that it was good to extend suffrage or against some of the social reforms that eased hours of work for children or ideas on extending education. These cases would be more obviously 'least favourable' to him. By selecting religious and moral opinions, he selects examples where the issue of fallibility is somewhat less intense than in former ages. Liberty

---

[1] Samuel Johnson (1709-1784). Student and scholar of English Literature; essayist, poet, critic, lexicographer and wit. Probably best known for his *Dictionary of the English Language* (1755).
[2] Himmelfarb (1974) p. 27.

of conscience and freedom of dissent over religion are strong if not universal principles, and Mill is thus confirming a trend with his argument, which may well reflect his personal concerns, but rather at the expense of convincing us of the application of his principle of adversarial truth over all areas of life.

Mill continues to chew over the same issues for the three long paragraphs that follow. He notes that the modern age is often thought to be more tolerant, for people are said to be no longer persecuted for their religious beliefs: Mill agrees that there is some truth here, for 'we no longer put heretics to death' (II: 18). However, people can be persecuted for their beliefs and for reasons to do with their status.

Illustrating this, Mill cites three cases from recent legal history: one is to do with a man imprisoned for saying and writing 'offensive words concerning Christianity'; a second involves people being 'rejected as jurymen' and being insulted because they had no theological belief upon which to swear an oath. A third person who had been robbed 'was denied justice against a thief' because he was a 'foreigner'. Mill does not cite these cases to show that society is engaged in an overt campaign of repressive persecution but as examples of the more insidious pressure of stigma that follows the profession of certain unconventional beliefs. The cases are presented as symptomatic of the deeper problem: an engrained conventionalism and commonality of view, an outlook and attitude that penalises difference, variety and diversity. Mill is especially unhappy at the fallacy of assuming that someone with a non-theological view is incapable of giving a sincere oath. We have what is seen as a 'relic of persecution', and the fear is that this indicates the risk of a resurgence of a limiting and oppressive level of intolerance:

'In this age the quiet surface of routine is as often ruffled by attempts to resuscitate past evils as to introduce new benefits' (II: 19).

In the light of the debates over *The Satanic Verses* as noted earlier – or in relation to the more recent debates over freedom of expression we consider later, this point of Mill's has considerable weight.[1] While Milton worried over the threats to 'philosophic freedom'[2], Mill is so moved as to come to one of his most contentious claims that due to the risks of intolerance and the oppression of disapproved views, 'this country' is 'not a place of mental freedom'.

Here we may well think that, in a highly technical phrase, Mill is laying it on with a trowel. To propose that we take seriously that Mill's life is set in a time devoid of 'mental freedom' is an extreme point to press. No study of life and thought in the nineteenth century would reach the view that it was so bleak a region for freedom of thought. Mill could have said that there were risks to the mental freedom enjoyed by people or that the country was not as secure in its mental freedom as it needed to be. As it is, his categorical judgment supports the review that we cited earlier, which suggested that *On Liberty* was written from the cell of one who was persecuted. Mill's own follow-up is to comment on the dangers of 'social stigma', which, he suggests, means that there is more pressure against the 'profession of opinions that are under the ban of society' than in other countries. He then comes

---

[1] As mentioned earlier, some of these recent debates are considered in Chapters 14-16 below.
[2] Milton (2008) p. 258.

to a high point in his writing on this theme, and the issue of the lack of 'mental freedom' is again pressed home:

'Our merely social intolerance kills no one, roots out no opinions, but induces men to disguise them or to abstain from any active effort for their diffusion. With us, heretical opinions do not perceptibly gain, or even lose, ground in each decade or generation; they never blaze out far and wide, but continue to smoulder in the narrow circles of thinking and studious persons among whom they originate, without ever lighting up the general affairs of mankind with either a true or a deceptive light. And thus is kept up a state of things very satisfactory to some minds, because, without the unpleasant process of fining or imprisoning anybody, it maintains all prevailing opinions outwardly undisturbed, while it does not absolutely interdict the exercise of reason by dissentients afflicted by the malady of thought. A convenient plan for having peace in the intellectual world, and keeping all things going on therein very much as they do already. But the price paid for this intellectual pacification is the sacrifice of the entire moral courage of the human mind'.

The use of images of combustion are in use here: we note that unconventional and, Mill thinks, perhaps new and helpful ideas 'smoulder' in the confined situation of limited ambition without getting the oxygen to illuminate 'the general affairs of mankind with either a true or a deceptive light'. Mill is after fanning these embers into a more robust fire. The mental slavery and 'intellectual pacification' that Mill has in mind is the state of keeping novelties of thought under wraps in limited and private settings rather than letting them 'blaze out' into the wider social setting. For all that we may consider the problem here something of a fiction, given the immense creativity of the nineteenth century and the many settings for argument and debate. Mill's point is that this state of affairs suits those who have an interest in continuing with existing opinions. Because the constraint is that of public or social opinion, it avoids the degree of dispute that would attach to formal campaigns of proscription. But the price of this approach is dramatic: 'the sacrifice of the entire moral courage of the human mind'. This follows from the pressure that is put on 'active and inquiring intellects' to keep silence or to fit what they have to say within the agreed assumptions of society.

Social pressure involves intimidation against the free expression of thought and thus of thought and thus causes a reduction in the pursuit of truth within the society in question. So Mill is led to an ironic turn in that he considers that the greater harm done by social constraints is to people within the social majority, 'whose whole mental development is cramped and their reason cowed by the fear of heresy' (II: 20). Against this, Mill places the case for the open development of truths for the wider benefit of all:

'No one can be a great thinker who does not recognize that as a thinker it is his first duty to follow his intellect to whatever conclusions it may lead. Truth gains more even by the errors of one who, with due study and preparation, thinks for himself than by the true opinions of those who only hold them because they do not suffer themselves to think. Not that it is solely, or chiefly, to form great thinkers that freedom is required. On the contrary, it is as much and even more indispensable to enable average human beings to attain the mental stature which they are capable of. There have been, and may again be, great individual thinkers in a general atmosphere of mental slavery. But there never has been, nor ever will be, in that atmosphere an intellectually active people'.

That Mill considers that even in a 'general atmosphere of mental slavery', there can be 'great individual thinkers' suggests that he does accommodate Berlin's criticism we discussed earlier.[1]

Mill closes this section of the chapter by giving a swift review of periods in history when, to the wider social benefit, 'the yoke of authority was broken'. He cites again the Reformation, what he calls 'the speculative movement' of the latter half of the eighteenth century – what most would call the Enlightenment – and what we would term the Romantic movement – which Mill terms 'the Goethian and Fichtean period'. In these phases, 'an old mental despotism' was overcome, and improvements followed in 'the human mind' and 'institutions'. As far as the home front is concerned, Mill considers that these creative forces 'are well now spent' and a 'fresh start' in development requires that, as individuals, 'we again assert our mental freedom'.

In Praise of Vital Truths (Paragraphs 21-33)

Mill now turns his attention to the 'second division of the argument' (II: 21), that which assumes that existing opinions are true – or at least, the best truths we have at present – and that we need to examine 'the worth of the manner in which they are likely to be held when their truth is not freely and openly canvassed'. Although Mill does not remind himself of this all that often, opinions, like those who hold them, are fallible. He thinks the degree of fallibility will become clear if they are held in a state of critical review. Within the social mix, the ideas forged by a minority of thinkers are vital to generating enhanced truths, but this depends on the conflict of freely held opinions. Mill expresses the point as follows:

'However unwillingly a person who has a strong opinion may admit the possibility that his opinion may be false, he ought to be moved by the consideration that, however true it may be, if it is not fully, frequently, and fearlessly discussed, it will be held as a dead dogma, not a living truth' (II: 21).

What we have here is a refinement of Mill's objective in promoting the conflict view of getting the best truths. The collision of views is not just the means by which better truths emerge as distinct from error; it also has the function of ensuring that truths are real, that they are 'living' truths, not 'dead dogma'. Mill is also reflecting another line of thought from Milton's *Areopagitica*, in that the contrast Mill draws between a 'living' truth and a truth held uncritically as a 'dead dogma' recalls Milton's biblically influenced image of truth as 'a streaming fountain; if her waters flow not in a perpetual progression, they sicken into a muddy pool of conformity and tradition'.[2] Milton continues:

---

[1] See above and Berlin (2017) p. 175.
[2] Milton (2008) p. 260-61.

'A man may be a heretic in the truth; and if he believe things only because his pastor says so, or the assembly so determines without knowing other reasons, though his belief be true, yet the very truth he holds becomes his heresy'.[1]

Mill perhaps appreciated Milton's image of truth flowing in a 'perpetual progression', which could be plumbed into his notion of humans as 'progressive' (I: 11) beings.

To illustrate his sense of the tensions between living and dead truths, Mill contrasts those who learn from an authority and those who learn through a dynamic of argumentation. He might well be thinking of his own education, where reasoning for himself played so vital a role.[2] He thinks those who learn from an authority assent 'to what they think true' (II: 22), but they have 'no knowledge whatever of the grounds of the opinion and could not make a tenable defence of it against the most superficial objections'. Further, if people obtain their ideas from a respected authority, they will 'naturally think that no good, and some harm, comes from its being allowed to be questioned'. Learning from a trusted authority, we will be loyal to it and unwilling to take a more experimental approach. This leads to ideas becoming formalised and, as Mill presents it, held as dogmas. This is said to be 'not the way in which truth ought to be held by a rational being'; indeed, this 'is not knowing the truth' regarding the matters in question. In contrast, those who learn through critical argument, who get into the situation where they learn 'the grounds of their opinion' (II: 23): accordingly, '... on any every subject on which difference of opinion is possible, the truth depends on a balance to be struck between two sets of conflicting reasons'. Mill considers this especially so in the subjects that fall under the humanities and social sciences, as well as over matters dealing with 'the business of life'.

Exemplifying his ability to synthesise aspects of the intellectual tradition, Mill looks back to classical Rome to take a lesson from Cicero, whose success in debate came because 'he always studied his adversary's case with as great, if not still greater, intensity than even his own'.[3] Mill derives an axiom from this: 'He who knows only his side of the case knows little of that'. To cultivate this skill, Mill thinks it is ideal if we each hear from those who believe the alternative views what it is that can be said in their favour. In effect, Mill wants authenticity in dialogues and arguments to ensure the highest impact in the collision of opinion. For a person to master ideas and clarify his own, he or she 'must be able to hear them from persons who actually believe them, who defend them in earnest and do their very utmost for them' (II: 23).

The process Mill favours provides individuals with the chance to encounter ideas 'in the most plausible and persuasive form'. They 'must feel the whole force of the difficulty which the true view of the subject has to encounter and dispose of, else he will never really possess himself of the portion of truth which meets and removes that difficulty'. Mill elaborates a strong defence of this form of educative

---

[1] By the 'assembly' Milton means the Westminster Assembly, a body of scholars, theologians, Church leaders and laity, which, form 1643 until 1652, advised the government on matters of religious conformity and settlement.
[2] See Chapter 1 above.
[3] Cicero 106 BCE – 43 BCE. Roman statesman and orator: a sceptical thinker and defender of republicanism. See www.britannica.com:biography:Cicero

argument, and considers it so important, that only if authentic representatives of the ideas in question cannot be found, then for 'moral and human subjects' it falls on some, not least teachers of philosophy, one assumes, to provide the best substitutes possible by playing a skilled role as the 'devil's advocate'.

Mill briefly expresses a counter-argument that there is no need for 'mankind in general' (II: 24) to understand all that could be said on the matter of their beliefs, that they could rely on the authority and insight of those who were properly trained for the task. What he has in mind is something like our thinking that liberal democracy is a good thing and that rampant nationalism is very dangerous. We might, in modernity, justify this with a passing reference to National Socialism in Germany: suppose we think that Hitler and his cronies are unspeakably evil; we could see that there is a mass of evidence to give good reason to shelve nationalism as an option we might consider. Mill's idea is that this is not good enough. He is keener on something like the saying that one should 'keep one's friends close, and one's enemies closer'.[1] Thus, in the case of nationalism, given its tendencies for extremism, Mill's advice transposed to the present would be that we should read and study the history and development of national socialism to really understand how such an ideology and political culture could arise and assume such influence and notoriety. Through the good offices of YouTube and other resources, we should listen to, consider, and argue the points made by the protagonists. Thereby we acquire a living sense of the power and advantage of the better truths. Mill's educative point advises us against basing our views on anything too general or second-hand. He thinks we need the widest access to sources of ideas to give the best 'rational assurance that all objections have been satisfactorily answered' (II: 25).

Mill maintains that 'the argument for free discussion' must be sustained. Thinking back to the medieval period and the dominion of Christian thought, Mill thinks that the value of knowing all sides of the case was appreciated, even if one side was that to which everything was committed, so that medieval priests were trained to argue from and for all sides of the case. In something like an aside, Mill suggests that in Protestant thinking, through and after the Reformation, this comprehensive approach was replaced by an individualistic view of how faith and knowledge were 'borne by each for himself'.[2] Living in a time of multiple publications, Mill is conscious of the power of the written word and its reach over and through society – so his view is that 'the teachers of mankind' should be aware that 'all that they ought to know... must be free to be written and published without restraint'.

Mill's fear, as in his 'dead dogma' (II: 21) versus 'living truth' contrast, is that if the best ideas we possess are held without the fire and force of criticism; they are held and transmitted without the 'worth' (II: 26) or the 'grounds' of the ideas in question being appreciated:

---

[1] This saying is well-known from *The Godfather*, but it comes from Sun Tzu's *The Art of War* – Sun Tzu (2008).
[2] Mill does not pursue the point, but he seems to be alert to the way in which sectarian protestants can assert their own view as the way as the path of righteous salvation known through faith alone: the alternative views are not wrong, they are sin.

'Instead of a vivid conception and living belief, there remains only a few phrases retained by rote; or, if any part, the shell and husk only of the meaning is retained, the finer essence being lost'.

For all the flurry of ideas within society, Mill thinks that the history of 'almost all ethical doctrines and religious creeds' (II: 27) shows how the 'meaning and vitality' of innovative ideas is a key feature that fosters allegiance. Here Mill is alluding to the history of religious movements, where the innovative and charismatic prophet or leader emerges as a reformer to recharge and redirect the tradition. As time goes on and the ideas become established, Mill's point is that it becomes harder to retain the force and energy of the ideas:

'We often hear teachers of all creeds lamenting the difficulty of keeping up in the minds of believers a lively apprehension of the truth which they nominally recognize, so that it may penetrate the feelings and acquire a real mastery over the conduct'.

In the longer term, the problem is that a notional alliance to a set of ideas pervades the majority, and what this entails is the habit of living with a strong hold to ideas that are not properly understood, as well as a clear resistance to novelty and development. This last problem is, for Mill, a further reason for promoting the liberty of thought and discussion with a focus on critical debates, for otherwise, we are led to the situation where the ideas or creeds in question are abstracted. They are:

'… outside the mind, incrusting and petrifying it against all other influences addressed to the higher parts of our nature; manifesting its power by not suffering any fresh and living convictions to get in, but itself doing nothing for the mind or heart except standing sentinel over them to keep them vacant'.

Mill deepens his illustration of how the liberty of thought and discussion can, through the free debate of ideas, generate the best of all possible truths for life by concentrating on 'the doctrines of Christianity' as held to by the majority of believers. Here Mill is a little colloquial in his language as, by 'doctrines', he does not mean the doctrines developed by the Christian Church in the Patristic Period, such as the Trinity (325) or the Person of Christ (451). He means 'the maxims and precepts contained in the New Testament'. What Mill probably has in mind is the ethical teaching of Jesus as found in the parables and in the Sermon on the Mount, and those on how to accept and live the life of the kingdom of God.[1] His point is that these teachings are held in common by all Christians. He then suggests that the 'ethical maxims' arising from these teachings are, 'on the one hand', believed by the Christian to be 'vouchsafed by infallible wisdom as rules for his government; and, on the other, a set of everyday judgements and practices which go a certain length with some of those maxims, not so great a length with others, stand in direct opposition to some, and are, on the whole, a compromise between the Christian creed and the interests and suggestions of worldly life' (II: 28). Mill thinks this creates a muddle: the follower gives 'homage' to the teachings – to loving one's

---

[1] Here one might look at Mark 2-5; Matthew 5-7 and Luke 14-16 for examples of these lines of teaching.

neighbour as oneself and the like – but 'allegiance' is really to living in the world. Consequently, in doing life, people dip into the teachings, applying some and ignoring others, and they live in a pattern of routine which means they do not live with the ideas as a part of 'that living belief that regulates conduct':

'They believe these doctrines just up to the point to which it is usual to act upon them. The doctrines in their integrity are serviceable to pelt adversaries with; and it is understood that they are to be put forward (when possible) as the reasons for whatever people do that they think laudable'.

The problem with this is that the ideas have 'no hold on ordinary believers – are not a power in their minds'. People have 'habitual respect' for the ideas, but 'no feeling which spreads from the words to the things signified and forces the mind to take *them* in and make them conform to the formula'.

For Mill, this means an acid test has been failed, for his general outlook is wedded to the notion that no reasonable person could live by whim or mere intuition, nor by a system of belief that they applied blindly with no insight or understanding. To have a 'living belief that regulates conduct' is the principle Mill endorses as the practically orientated ideal. Illustrating the point, Mill thinks that the early Church had an altogether more engaged commitment to the ideas by which the followers of Jesus lived and died, and they contested and developed them in the face of severe criticisms from those with whom they lived. Mill then reaffirms that when a tradition of ideas becomes normative and generally regulative – as when Christianity became the official religion of the Roman Empire in 312-313 – the 'teachers and learners go to sleep at their posts' because 'there is no enemy in the field' (II: 29).

Widening his focus, Mill thinks that in everyday life, the ideas and values by which we live can play a powerful role in helping us to negotiate the vicissitudes of life. It is also through this that ideas resonate within our life with their full meaning when we have relevant 'personal experience' (II: 30). However, the force of these ideas, and our capacity to use them well, will be enhanced if we have 'been accustomed' to hearing them 'argued *pro* and *con*' by those who understood them. However, Mill thinks humans have a 'fatal tendency… to leave off thinking about a thing when it is no longer doubtful'. 'Doubtful' here means in and for the humans in question, and this point offers a criticism that could be applied to many systems of belief and practice besides Christianity.

Mill then asks another question – one that typifies the sense of how he provides strong lines of criticism of his own thinking:

'Is the absence of unanimity an indispensable condition of true knowledge? Is it necessary that some part of mankind should persist in error to enable any to realize the truth?' (II: 31).

Mill, once more forgetting to emphasise his conditional view of truths, asks whether the vitality of the ideas we think as best representing the truth can only be retained if there is also a critical spectrum of doubt. Here he is again close to expressing the issue we noted earlier, as raised by Berlin, that ideas of worth and value can come from societies or mindsets closed to open and free argument.[1] An implication of this line of thought seems to be that the 'highest aim and best result of improved intelligence' are linked to uniting humanity 'in the acknowledgement of all-important truths'. This, in turn, implies that intelligence is only present for as long as these truths remain to be secured.

Mill denies that this is the right analysis: he thinks that it is a methodological principle that as time progresses in various areas of life, certain problems are solved, and questions are answered. Again, this point might have been developed through helpful illustrations from the natural and medical sciences, but he tends to sustain his discussion by referring to ethical and religious rather than scientific areas of contention. Instead, we have the generalised view that the 'well-being of mankind may almost be measured by the number and gravity of the truths which have reached the point of being uncontested' (II:32). Mill means that the approach of encouraging debate and advancing understanding will not have the consequence of keeping false and dangerous dogmas in operation. On the contrary, free discussion will have a positive, persuasive consequence and lead to a consolidation of insight over the 'uncontested points' that emerge.

However, Mill thinks that the business of moving towards this position of increased consensus carries with it the risk of complacency, and so the suggestion is that some 'contrivance' is necessary to ensure dissent and debate. So vital is the need to maintain the sharp edge of critical thought, and to sustain the sense of an 'intelligent and living apprehension of a truth', we need to supply a stream of opportunities for the explanation and review of ideas, as with the earlier suggestion of teachers playing the devil's advocate. Mill, perhaps harking back to his experiences in the debating societies of the 1820s, again thinks that teachers should construct some means of making the problems of a position or argument real for their students, 'as if they were pressed upon him by a dissident champion, eager for his conversion'.

Were people as alert to matters as Mill considers they should be, they would know that in the longer tradition of thought and intellectual life, there are means and methods that would serve the abiding need for all ideas, including those of which we are currently sure, to be given a thorough interrogation. Mill refers to 'Socratic dialectics' (II: 33) and again to the 'disputations of the Middle Ages' as examples of intellectual methods of provoking people to rethink their beliefs and to overcome 'the commonplace of received opinion', and to cultivate 'a discipline of the mind'.

We might recall that Mill considered that, in many respects, the education he received largely from his father was predicated on such methods as these, so it is no surprise they are again endorsed in the cause of defending the importance of critically reviewing the ideas we consider most compelling. In large part, these lines of thought are all about cultivating the capacity-skill of independence of thought amongst individuals, as is clear from the following:

'A person who derives all his instruction from teachers or books, even if he escapes the besetting temptation of contenting himself with cram, is under no compulsion to hear both sides; accordingly, it is a far from frequent accomplishment, even from thinkers, to know both sides... It is the fashion of the present time to disparage negative logic – that which

_____

[1] See above and Berlin (2017) p. 175.

points out weakness in theory or errors in practice without establishing positive truths' (II: 33).

Mill is sure that the 'negative logic' he praises is not adequate as an 'ultimate result': but it is a vital 'means to attaining any positive knowledge or conviction worthy of the name'.

The conclusion is that for an individual's intellectual development, an indispensable aid is to go through 'the same mental process which would have been required of him in carrying out an active controversy with opponents'.

Cases of Shared or Indefinite Truth (Paragraphs 34-36)

Mill has reviewed two aspects of the case for the liberty of thought and discussion: the case that fits situations where 'the received opinion may be false' (II:34) so that a better truth can be found, and the case that fits situations where 'the received opinion' is considered true, but 'a conflict with the opposite error' is valuable so as to generate a 'clear apprehension and deep feeling of its truth'.

Mill affirms that 'diversity of opinion' is vital for the longer term to foster the 'intellectual advancement' of humanity. However, he considers that there is a more frequent scenario where there are 'conflicting opinions' that 'share the truth between them'.

That Mill considers this the most common instance is something that needs very full emphasis. Reviews of Mill's thoughts on the liberty of discussion[1] can easily centre on the first of the cases just cited, to the neglect of the second and the complete abandonment of the third. Yet, for Mill, this is the situation that is most often faced: views are in tension, and there are truths as well as errors on both sides. We say 'both' here, as Mill frames his review as if the arguments are invariably between two contesting lines of thought, as in the actually very artificial world of debating societies. In fact, tensions might be between three or more conflicting perspectives on a problem, especially in the moral and human sciences, where Mill thinks the greatest arena for freedom of thought and discussion is found.

Mill elaborates an illustration contrasting two generalities – what he terms 'popular' and 'heretical' opinions. The popular mainstream views may contain a great deal that is plausible, but they are 'never or seldom the whole truth'. They may contain exaggeration, distortion or some form of incoherence, and so require and benefit 'from the truths by which they ought to be accompanied and limited'. Unconventional views – 'heretical opinions', as Mill terms them – possess some of these 'suppressed and neglected truths', and with a diversity of opinion and open and free arguments, partial truths can be reconciled to wider benefit.

Mill expresses his concern about the ease with which this process can be developed by noting that there is a dangerous habit in human thinking, the tendency to foster 'exclusiveness' over truth claims. Returning to ideas first cultivated in when adopting the mode of 'practical eclecticism', Mill notes that humans tend to be one-sided in their thinking and to love the security and ease of exclusive claims.[2] A minority of people, and Mill is one of them, are able to be 'many-sided' in their

---

[1] As in the essays written by I.B. students studying *On Liberty*.
[2] See Chapter 2 above.

thinking. Because the majority are not so blessed, or whatever Mill might say, the problem in developing insights is that there is what we can term an oscillation between one partial truth and another as an aspect of a wider truth is abandoned in favour of another.

As an example of this, Mill thinks that in the eighteenth century, there was a trend of thinking that the current age was in all respects superior to antiquity, and this provoked the shock encounter with the work of Rousseau, whose ideas:

'... explode like bombshells in the midst, dislocating the compact mass of one-sided opinion and forcing its elements to recombine in a better form and with additional ingredients' (II: 35).[1]

Rousseau's ideas exposed a fallacy in the assumption of inexorable human progress but left a considerable, and Mill thinks mainly positive influence of 'the superior worth of simplicity of life', as well as revealing 'the enervating and demoralizing effects of the trammels and hypocrisies of artificial society' (II: 35).

Another example comes from the political world, where Mill, whose experience of close encounters with political discussion was life-long, considers it 'almost a commonplace' (II: 36) that what is considered the welfare of the nation requires the tension between, on the one hand, 'a party of order and stability and a party of progress or reform'. Mill means the Tories and Whigs, or the Conservative and Liberal parties, as they were emerging in the middle of the nineteenth century. In such a situation, one side is defined in terms of its use, or 'utility' by 'the deficiencies of the other'. It is the balance of difference here that sustains both in staying 'within the limits of reason and sanity', which is not quite Mill's way of providing a vote of confidence in the emergent political situation.

What Mill means is that there are distinct tensions which could veer social life to one extreme or another, but the tensions and the far-from effective balance between the main two political parties are maintained because on each side there is, to a fairly strong degree, 'equal freedom' to discuss differences. Mill lists the tensions – 'democracy' and 'aristocracy', 'property' and 'equality', 'cooperation' and 'competition', 'luxury' and 'abstinence', 'sociality' and 'individuality', 'liberty' and 'discipline'. Mill sees here a complex of problems such that simple 'uniform' solutions would never be expedient, which suggests that the more recent notion, that of a mixed economy, would be more helpful in pointing up the ways in which such benefits to the common good that come from each of the aspects listed is achieved by the free debates that are a feature of political life: however, these debates do not deliver smooth pathways to solutions:

'Truth, in the great practical concerns of life, is so much a question of the reconciling and combining of opposites that very few have minds sufficiently capacious and impartial to make the adjustment with an approach to correctness, and it has to be made by the rough process of a struggle between combatants fighting under hostile banners'.

[1] J-J. Rousseau (1712-1778); Swiss/French writer, philosopher and composer. His books *Émile, or On Education* (1762) and *The Social Contract* (1762) are probably the works Mill has in mind.

Here we have a variant on the earlier sense of truths as distinct from singular and definite truth as being the more appropriate category for fallible humans to pursue.[1] In this case, Mill presses his view to maintain that in the fighting between hostile opponents, the view which at any point invariably carries the most weight to be heard and developed will always be the minority view, for that view will always express 'the neglected interests, the side of human well-being which is in danger of obtaining less than its share'.

We see that here, as earlier in the text, Mill is distinctly keen on the promotion of the minority view, even in the case of matters where the truth lies in the balance: this is because he sees the balance as set within time and space, so at any point in time, or history, he tends to think that the minority view will be the one with the greater claim for the longer-term good of the whole.

Christian Morality – An Exception? (Paragraphs 37- 39)

Mill again unpacks an argument against his position, opening up the idea that in the repertoire of views on life that operate within society, there are '*some* received principles, especially on the highest and most vital subjects', that 'are more than half-truths' (II: 37). The example is again taken from Christianity, focusing on 'Christian morality'. Mill floats the idea that such morality provides what some consider 'the whole truth on the subject' – that any variance from it will be a complete 'error'. Here, Mill operates in a manner that is characteristic of philosophers of later generations, for before proceeding further, he asks the quintessentially philosophic question of definition: so 'before pronouncing what Christian morality is or is not, it would be desirable to decide what is meant by Christian morality'. Mill suggests that if what is meant is 'the morality of the New Testament', then he thinks this is difficult to comprehend. He says it was not 'announced, or intended, as a complete doctrine of morals'. This is a wholly fair point: the main body of New Testament scholarship since 1859 would be very much in agreement with Mill, and if anyone familiar with that tradition opened the New Testament to read the moral teachings within, it would be clear that the gospel texts relate to and apply or adapt to the circumstances of composition. The scenarios and teachings presented are linked in a range of the teachings from the existing traditions that Jesus shared and to which he contributed. The teachings are figurative rather than literal; they include poetic idioms, and of course, they are not cast in the manner and style of a treatise on moral philosophy Mill's comments on this, to be fair, show little insight into the complex business of New Testament hermeneutics, but his points are nevertheless sound.

The teachings of Paul operate similarly and are equally resistant to formal or systematic expression. Mill is also right to say that Christian morality in an organised form came about later, through the ecclesiastical and theological tradition. This long tradition devised and adapted variant forms of moral teaching, drawing on various philosophical systems, and in the light of the Reformation, became a complex as expressed by the many and varied Churches and their theological traditions.

---

[1] See *OL* II: 3 and 4, as discussed above.

Mill thinks that the collective moral tradition that comes from the New Testament is something to which humanity owes 'a great debt' – and that humanity would have been worse off without it: but he considers the developed morality that emerges to be partial and 'one-sided' – a fatal matter in Mill's vocabulary. His reasons are that he thinks the one-sidedness flows from having 'an ideal that is negative rather than positive; passive rather than active; innocence rather than nobleness; abstinence from evil rather than an energetic pursuit of good'. Anticipating the Nietzschean critique of Christian morality, Mill thinks the negative 'thou shalt not' predominates over 'thou shalt'.[1]

Delving back to the early tradition, Mill thinks the root of the problem is that Christian morality 'has all the characters of a reaction; it is, in great part, a protest against paganism'. This leads to the antagonism toward 'sensuality' and the elevation of 'asceticism', leading to the high regard for 'legality'. Here, Mill seems to assume a line through monasticism and the development of the formalities of natural law theory.[2] Mill's view, that Christian morality leads to a form of passive obedience, allows the one-sided claim to have leverage, and it means he, again using his skill in the synthesis of 'practical eclecticism', can move to suggest that the corrective, in the cultivation of an 'obligation to the state' derives from 'Greek and Roman sources'. The values that matter for personal life, and so for individuals further empowered for liberty, include more themes akin to those favoured by Nietzsche: 'magnanimity, high-mindedness, personal dignity' and 'the sense of honour', also derive 'from the purely human, not the religious, part of our education'.

Given what Mill goes on to say, this list of the phenomenology of ethical values assumes some significance. He qualifies his assault on Christian morality with a much more positive appreciation of the 'doctrines and precepts' that might be found in the 'sayings of Christ' (II: 38). He seems to assume that all the sayings attributed to Jesus are equally authentic, but as mentioned earlier, he is not operating with the insights of contemporary New Testament scholarship, which would suggest a much narrower range of the sayings of Jesus as being viably authentic.[3] Mill is on the thin ice of another conventionalism in thinking Jesus 'the Founder of Christianity', a claim which, however attractive to the orthodox believer even today, begs innumerable historical problems.[4] Nevertheless, Mill's point would still apply: the teachings are not a complete moral theory – as Vermes says of Jesus' teaching, 'there was nothing systematic in his message. He was not a professional theologian who subjected the secret life of God to close scrutiny'.[5] However, the teachings contain ideas and themes which are reconcilable with what 'a comprehensive morality requires' (II: 38). Indeed, 'everything which is excellent in ethics may be brought within' these teaching – here, Mill's phenomenology reflects the synthesis

---

[1] For Nietzsche's thought on this and a few other matters, see Loxton (2021).

[2] Natural law theory in the is associated with Tomas Aquinas (1224-1274). On Christianity and its history see MacCulloch (2012).

[3] See Vermes (2004) for a helpful and lucid guide on this topic.

[4] A central problem is that Jesus was born and died a Jew, and his followers later expand into the Roman, gentile world, where they are termed 'Christians' by their critics and enemies, as they follow Jesus Christ – 'Christ' (Christus) being the Greek translation of the term from Hebrew, Messiah (anointed one). See Vermes (2004) and MacCulloch (2009).

[5] Vermes (2004) p. 398.

of what he, within the canopy of utilitarian thinking, considers of excellence in ethics as arranged within the wider project of utility in its 'largest sense' (I: 11).

Mill draws from this view a line of thought on the benefits of the breadth of learning on morality that reflects the traditions within Christian understanding and those in secular views. To argue for a pattern of instruction that is exclusive in its Christian orientation is likely, he feels, to lead to 'a low, abject, servile type of character' (II: 38). The 'moral regeneration of mankind', which appears as another strand in Mill's programme, requires what he might have termed a many-sided approach, where 'moral truths' from other than Christian sources are also used to build towards this better condition.

In charting his way over the parameters of an ethical approach for the future, Mill's concern is to reflect the fallibilism of the human condition. He fears the artificial absolutism that comes when 'a part of the truth' has an 'exclusive pretension... to be the whole'. As before, any 'one-sidedness' is seen as limited and limiting to human development and well-being.

Mill lived in an age when a great deal of philanthropic activity was motivated by evangelical and, to Mill, sectarian Christian groups. His sense of the danger of the inwardness and exclusivism associated with these movements is very real. He never wants to denigrate the good works of anyone, but he worries about the outlooks that restrain the imagination and creativity of the human spirit. In the field of 'moral teaching', Mill wants to open the lines of acceptance to include 'the most valuable and noble' ideas that come from those who 'not only... did not know, but... who knew and rejected, the Christian faith'.

Mill then hammers home that he cannot 'pretend that the most unlimited use of the freedom of enunciating all possible opinions would put an end to evils of religious or philosophical sectarianism' (II: 39). Mill is on something of a knife-edge here. His objection resonates to the present day: he is uneasy at the psychology of those who, due to 'narrow capacity', see their truth as the truth, exclusive to the point that it is 'as if no other truth existed in the world'.

What we might see as the elemental insecurity of some will guarantee their ongoing allegiance to exclusive absolutism: so free debate will not necessarily inhibit 'the tendency of all opinions to become sectarian'. Nevertheless, Mill wants that free discussion for all, and for the particular benefit of some, those of a 'calmer and more disinterested' outlook. For them, the 'collision of opinions' is needed to allow people to listen to both or all sides of an argument. Such debate offers a route to escape the sectarian habit of affirming a part of what is viable as the whole truth and suppressing the rest. Mill, as so often, manages to rise to a handy peroration for this part of his text:

'... since there are few mental attributes more rare than that of the judicial faculty which can sit in intelligent judgement between two sides of a question, of which only one is represented by an advocate before it, truth has no chance but in proportion as every side of it, every opinion which embodies any fraction of the truth, not only finds advocates, but is so advocated as to be listened to'.

Summaries of the Arguments and Comments on the Manner of Debate (Paragraphs 40-44)

Mill devotes the final paragraphs of the chapter to a summary of what he has done. In retrospect, he notes that the review has identified 'four distinct grounds' for 'freedom of opinion, and freedom of expression of opinion' as vital components in, and as the basis for 'the mental well-being of mankind' (II: 40).

These are, firstly, that free debate ensures that we keep all matters open for review and do not suppress any idea that might reveal a truth. Most importantly, it guards against our assuming 'our own infallibility' (II: 41).

Secondly, even views considered erroneous may hold 'a portion of truth' (II: 42). Since prevailing truths are fallible, they are never complete, so it is only by conflict with 'adverse opinions' that the 'remainder of the truth' can emerge.

Thirdly, even if we have the best possible truth to hand, it is better to subject it to criticism so that the view can be sustained with a sense and 'feeling of its rational grounds' (II: 43). Linked to this is the fourth point, that through ongoing critical review, ideas of what is truest avoid being held as a 'dogma', as 'a mere formal profession, inefficacious for good, but cumbering the ground and preventing the growth of any real and heartfelt conviction from reason or personal experience'. This line of thought is another with Miltonian affinity, echoing a passage from *Areopagitica* where Milton writes of the 'iron yoke of outward conformity'[1] that leaves a 'slavish print upon our necks'. To combat these limiting trends, Mill, as we discovered, wants the liberty of expression and debate for the exchange of 'error for truth' (II: 1) and for 'the clearer perception and livelier impression of truth produced by its collision with error'.

Mill then turns to a final consideration. If the freedom of discussion is to be full and committed so as to achieve all that is hoped, is it not also the case that the manner and style of all discussion must be in a fashion that is 'temperate' so that it 'does not pass the bounds of fair discussion' (II: 44). Mill immediately suggests that what these 'bounds' might be would pretty well be 'impossible' to fix; the snag is that if the test is based on 'those whose opinions are to be attacked', then the charge of intemperance is commonly raised as 'the offence is given whenever the attack is telling and powerful'. Anyone who pushes an argument to the limit can seem to be intemperate. But this is not the worst offence that can come in critical discussion. The worse problem is sophistry, when someone presents ideas but they 'suppress facts or arguments, to misstate the elements of the case, or misrepresent the opposite opinion'. This subversive style of reasoning is far worse than the problem of intemperance, which, as Mill says, is a feature of passionate argument. However, Mill thinks that those who are worried about intemperance are concerned about the use of certain devices and styles of argument: 'invective, sarcasm, personality and the like'. This objection has a problem in that, as Mill considers it, it seems always to be applied to the opponent or critic of a given view: it is never a feature of mutual agreement that both sides are guilty of pressing these 'weapons' of argument. Polemical argument is criticized as leading to the stigmatization of the opponent as 'bad and immoral'.

---

[1] Milton (2008) p. 270.

Mill urges the use of a 'studied moderation of language and the most cautious avoidance of unnecessary offence' so that new ideas can be presented against the received opinion in as well-measured a manner as possible. At the same time, the received opinion should be defended with 'unmeasured vituperation' against those who would question them. If these policies are adopted, Mill thinks ideas can collide with a certain degree of cushioning to aid their reception.

Mill is adamant that it is not the province of 'law and authority' to intervene in these matters. It is rather 'opinion' that is the right regulator of the manner of debate, and this is to be determined 'by the circumstances of the individual case':

'... condemning everyone, on whichever side of the argument... in whose mode of advocacy either want of candour, or malignity, bigotry, or intolerance of feeling manifest themselves; but not inferring these vices from the side which a person takes though it be the contrary side of the question to our own, and giving merited honour to everyone, whatever opinion he may hold, who has calmness to see and honesty to state what his opponents and their opinions really are, exaggerating nothing to their discredit, keeping nothing back which tells, or can be supposed to tell, in their favour'.

This is, Mill thinks, the form of the 'morality of public discussion' to which all who profess an interest in controversy should aspire. And so we come to the end of the second and longest chapter of *On Liberty*. Mill's idea is that what his argument reviews and establishes provides the grounds for the case for the related sphere of liberty of action, and he turns to this in his next chapter.

Issues of Style and Focus over the Liberty of Debate

Before we consider Mill's moves on the liberty of action and ahead of the review of his defence of the dimensions of liberty in the final part of this book, there are some questions arising to be reviewed.

The first has to do with Mill's level of emphasis in calling for such full and frank freedom of discussion. His sense of humans as fallible and truths always being conditional ties in with the notion that humans are 'progressive' beings (I:11). This links to the view that in the last analysis, the powers of strong, honest argument are more important than the methods and manners in debate. Nevertheless, is such a sharp formulation of liberty necessary? Do the sensitivities of others and the social bonds fundamental to life demand a more conciliatory notion of liberty – liberty linked with empathy and respect? One could have a liberal commitment yet think that there should be more conciliation than is insisted on by Mill, with more concern for a level of equality of respect and regard to be obligatory within the patterns of debate and exchange that characterise the liberty of discussion.

Against Mill, the idea is that persons of maturity and sincere endeavour could know, based on experience, what will be appropriate within the spectrum of free discussion. To affirm such a working norm affirms the social nature of life and debate – and we can reserve the right to extend beyond the bounds where situations demand – we do not have to deny such bounds, as Mill implies. From all that he says, Mill would consider this an over-schooled constraint that, in the short and longer-term, would limit the development of vital truths and progressive beings.

On another tack, Mill's attitude can be criticised for being too generalised in his review. It is Marx's contention in his *Theses on Feuerbach* that 'the philosophers have only *interpreted* the world, in various ways; the point is to *change* it'.[1] Mill's approach suggests a degree of open-mindedness and discussion that might preclude appropriate action and commitment. Mill seeks openness to correction and a determination to challenge and debate the merits of views – but his focus on the role of discussion could deter or neutralize action, implementation, and *praxis*. And given the idea that society is the sum of the total number of individuals that comprise it, Mill seems to have left undone, at least so far, how society, in this sense, has a positive and constructive role in the cultivation and development of the truths that inform human development.

Mill is keen on developing the idea of our being many-sided in our outlook and methods; he is critical of narrow, one-sided perspectives. He also points out the danger of polemics. Yet, in his portrayal of Christianity, Mill can seem one-dimensional. He stresses the aspect of seeing the Christian tradition as prone to sectarianism, as offering negative and passive modes of life and cultivating severity and subservience. As we noted, he aims to escape censure for this by distinguishing the teaching of Jesus from the theological traditions and social organization of the Christian churches. But if society is the sum total of the individuals who comprise it, so Christianity is the sum total of the individuals who comprise it, Mill might elaborate more to counter the view of the tradition as of one negative and unwholesome type.

The Christian tradition includes those who follow the teaching of Luke 10 v. 37: 'Go and do likewise', which is to say, to show mercy and care towards those found in need in life – something requiring discernment and judgment. As was noted in an early review of *On Liberty*, there is also what was termed 'a larger more ancient, more human conception of human morality' embodied in some of Paul's advice.[2] This was to live in accordance with the following:

'Whatever is true, whatever is honourable, whatever is just, whatever is pure, whatever is pleasing, whatever is commendable, if there is any excellence and if there is anything worthy of praise, think about these things'.

The ethical ideal here is a variant of themes from the wider virtue tradition, and Paul's phraseology stresses something Mill should appreciate: 'whatever is', which is not doctrinaire but open, experimental and liberal.

One of Mill's themes that resonates positively is his defence of what he terms 'negative logic' (II: 33). By this, he means using critical reason against established theory and practice without the pressure of expectation over producing positive alternative doctrines. Even if we are sure that some lines of thought are secure, Mill's point is that we should engage in criticism to keep our sense of the positive ideas fresh. Here Mill's ideas have a direct bearing on the way we live now. Operating in accordance with the ethos of a 'cancel culture', where there is more by

---

[1] Marx and Engels (1994) pp. 121-123. This comment is Theses XI.
[2] R. W. Church: *Bentley's Quarterly Review* Vol. 2, 1860 pp. 434-473, reproduced in Pyle (1994) pp. 210-254; p. 251. See also Scarre (2009) p. 57, where the same point is made without reference to Church. Paul's teaching is from Philippians 4 v. 8. Biblical quotations are from the New Revised Standard Version.

way of dismissal than discussion, would not pass muster.[1] What Mill suggests has a particular focus on political, ethical and religious areas of life, wherein there are manifold options for belief and commitment, and where the possibility of there being no error or weakness in, or no alternative to, a given theory is practically hypothetical. This implies that the creation of artificial dissent should be unnecessary. Mill's approach provides a brief for debate and argument to offer means by which the character and worth of competing theories can be established as a balance and check against extremism and intolerance.

---

[1] The term 'cancel culture' has been employed to denote the scenario whereby those whose talk or address at some event, as at a university, is 'cancelled' as a participatory event by the audience, as a whole or in part, leaving the event, or refusing to attend at the last minute because they disagree with the views of one of the speakers. For an example see: 'Professor apologises for calling students who staged Liddle walkout "pathetic"'. Article by Nicola Woolcock, *The Times* online, 06/12/2021.

9. *On Liberty*: III: 'Of Individuality, as One of the Elements of Well-Being' (Paragraphs 1-19)

The Case for Liberty of Action (Paragraph 1)

Through the consideration of liberty of thought and expression in the second chapter of *On Liberty*, Mill defends the view that liberty of thought and expression have secure utilitarian justification in relation to human nature seen in the wider sense related to its permanently progressive form. To this end, the case is presented for securing a creative collision of opinions to the end of acquiring authentic truths within society and as a means of combating narrow dogmatism and complacency. In the third chapter, Mill moves on to a correlated task of elaborating what was said earlier on the other 'appropriate region of human liberty' (I: 12), that to do with the 'liberty of tastes and pursuits, of framing the plan of our life to suit our own character, of doing as we like, subject to such consequences as may follow'. Not harming others is the limiting condition of our 'doing as we like', even if we think others 'foolish, perverse, or wrong'. The elaboration is now recast as follows: to 'examine whether the same reasons' (III: 1) as used to defend the liberty of thought and discussion 'do not require that men should be free to act upon their opinions – to carry these out in their lives without the hindrance, either physical or moral, from their fellow men, so long as it is at their own risk and peril'.

This qualification – the 'risk and peril' clause – immediately reveals a constraint pertaining to freedom of action. While Mill affirms more or less complete liberty of thought and discussion, actions should not be 'as free as opinions', and given the existing warnings of the danger of risking harm to others, a further constraint is not surprising. Mill's view is that were actions as free as opinions, there would be a great risk of the manifestation of 'a nuisance' to others, in terms of manifesting a threat to inhibit their liberty, and in consequence, that of the perpetrator of the nuisance. The 'risk and peril' constraint mentioned here by Mill intimately correlates with the common-sense reflection on general experience that 'actions speak louder than words', and Mill's qualification seems straightforward.

An illustration follows, with an implicit focus on the aspect of life that concerns others, embracing a risk of harm to others, and arising from the liberty of thought and discussion:

'No one pretends that actions should be as free as opinions. On the contrary, even opinions lose their immunity when the circumstances in which they are expressed are such as to constitute their expression a positive instigation to some mischievous act. An opinion that corn dealers are starvers of the poor, or that private property is robbery, ought to be unmolested when simply circulated through the press, but may justly incur punishment when delivered orally to an excited mob assembled before the house of a corn dealer, or when handed about among the same mob in the form of a placard'.

Here Mill is astute in using an illustration of an event where the freedom of opinion is operational – something he would generally consider inviolate – but in an interactive setting where it is clear that the expression of option constitutes an other-regarding act. In the case of speaking to a crowd outside of a corn dealer's house on the themes of commercial robbery, ideas are actively expressed to antagonise and motivate a crowd. All this makes sense: an individual's liberty of thought as such is wholly self-regarding – so thoughts may be free, and one may be at liberty to express options in many settings where active outcomes are hypothetical. But the expression of an opinion is an act that can have other-regarding implications, so the expression of opinion is not as free as the liberty of thought. This refinement shows how, when developed, the previously announced 'one simple principle' (I: 9) is more subtle and nuanced. As in the example, public discourse becomes open to censure, for example, if it incites violence or if it creates a major amount of public nuisance.[1] A regulatory theme is added, with the example from the other-regarding aspect of life making the point that there are limits to the legitimacy of liberty of expression, revealing a sense of Mill's awareness of the evocative power of language. He also puts down some clear markers for how actions may be limited by our sense of the attendant risks and perils. Assuming the values of a civilized community, harm caused to others by acts 'without justifiable cause' (III: 1) might be, and in more severe cases 'absolutely require to be, controlled by the unfavourable sentiments, and, when needful, by the active interference of mankind'.

Mill's vocabulary again needs some clarification: when he refers to 'active interference', he means the sanctions of the law – and Mill often terms legal engagement pejoratively as the manifestation of interference. The phrase 'unfavourable sentiments' means, for a given deed, and as a means of regulating future conduct, the rest of those involved are justified in making clear their disapproval of the individual. The upshot is that an individual's liberty of action is limited in the sense that 'he must not make himself a nuisance to other people'. Social pressures as within a civilized society - as contrasted with the pressures of a social tyranny – are put in the first line of control; the use of the law is something of a last resort.

Mill moves to explain this with explicit use of the distinction the individual should retain of self and other-regarding actions:

'... if he refrains from molesting others in what concerns them, and merely acts according to his own inclinations and judgement in things which concern himself, the same reasons which show that opinions should be free prove also that he should be allowed, without molestation, to carry his own opinions into practice at his own cost'.

Mill carries into this chapter his views about human fallibility, which means that we possess 'truths' that are, 'for the most part... only half-truths'. The principles that justify free debate to bring understanding to appreciate all sides of the case have the same bearing on human 'modes of action', and this brings Mill to one of his most important themes, to do with the process of improving what it is to be human: 'there should be experiments of living':

'Free scope should be given to varieties of character, short of injury to others... the worth of different modes of life should be proved practically, when anyone thinks fit to try them. It is desirable, in short, that in things which do not primarily concern others, individuality

---

[1] A verbal protest about something one disapproves of is one thing, and easy to defend with the liberty principle. Acting so as to close a motorway to make more emphatic one's protest and thereby inconveniencing countess others is another, and far harder to defend with the liberty principle.

should assert itself. Where not the person's own character but the traditions or customs of other people are the rule of conduct, there is wanting one of the principal ingredients of human happiness, and quite the chief ingredient of individual and social progress'.

Here we can note the tight manner in which Mill links the notions of 'character' and 'individuality'. Mill is clear that all humans in a mature state are 'individuals', but individuals are distinct in possessing their own 'character'. 'Character' is a term Mill uses a good deal in this chapter, and his definition is not immediately explicit. It comes a little later on in a context we will explore in a moment, but what Mill offers is the notion of human character being associated with 'a person whose desires and impulses are his own – are the expression of his own nature, as it has been developed and modified by his own culture' (III: 5). Such a person 'is said to have a character'. Mill means to highlight the capacity individuals possess to cultivate and express their own style, mood, temperament, humour, disposition and outlook. He assumes that humans are individual and capable of sustaining their individuality, but, being fallible, they are inclined to drift into the 'traditions or customs of other people', with detrimental consequences for human progression, both individual and social.

What Mill is moving to affirm is a full-blown defence of the human capacity for development, cast in terms of the exploration within the wider context of a life of the sort of character each individual has it in them to be and to try this out through experimental means of living to better ends in terms of enhanced well-being. As we mentioned in considering the arguments about the liberty of thought and discussion, Mill does not see how anyone could live by ideas they did not fully understand: he now looks at things from the other side of the proverbial fence; to understand ideas about living, we have to adopt them experimentally, and test and refine them in and through the business of life.

Accordingly, Mill's defence of the need for comprehensive liberty of action includes the view that different 'modes of life' (III: 1) and alternative 'experiments of living' should be encouraged to enable the emergence of informed and fully-conscious individuals. Just as reason develops through choice and analysis, so too individuality, the sort of person an individual can be, and the type of character that they are, derive best from choice and experimentation through various alternative modes of life; and, as Mill sees it, if individuality is enhanced, so is society.

A key objective in the chapter, and really in *On Liberty* as a whole, is the idea of 'the free development of individuality' (III: 2). This is placed before us as the end of enacting the principle of liberty of action to promote 'the person's own character' (III: 1).

Mill's concern in his own time is that people are becoming indifferent to this end and drifting into uniformity: yet the cultivation and development of the individual through experimental freedom of action is 'one of the leading essentials of well-being' (III: 2): it is 'not only a co-ordinate of all that is designated by the terms civilization, instruction, education, culture, but is itself a necessary part and condition of all those things'.

Mill feels that a major problem lies in the failure in his own times of there being sufficient appreciation by the 'common modes of thinking' for 'individual spontaneity'.

Too many people are satisfied with how they now live and are disinclined to venture into novelties of experimental living; they are antagonistic towards those who do, seeing 'troublesome and perhaps rebellious' problems from those offering reforms.

This leads Mill back to the thought of one to whom he wants to pay more allegiance, Wilhelm von Humboldt.

Wilhelm von Humboldt on Development and Originality (Paragraphs 2-4)

We noted earlier the significance von Humboldt had for Mill and that a passage from von Humboldt is presented at the start of *On Liberty*: as a reminder, the passage, as cited by Mill, runs as follows:

'The grand, leading principle, towards which every argument unfolded in these pages directly converges, is the absolute and essential importance of human development in its richest diversity'.[1]

There were several things Mill appreciated about von Humboldt's *The Sphere and Duties of Government*. As he explains in the *Autobiography*, he felt that von Humboldt encapsulated what was evident in 'a whole school of German writers'.[2] This was 'the doctrine of the rights of the individuality, and the claim of the moral nature to develope itself in its own way'.[3] Mill is focusing here on a nuanced sense of a view of rights – he has no truck with the functional and arid notion of individual rights. As we have seen, this was ever unpopular with the utilitarians. Mill articulates regard for 'the rights of individuality', alluding to the capacity or potentiality given with being human, which generates what Mill and the German writers he is alluding to want to defend – 'the theory of the right and duty of self-development'. One view of *On Liberty* puts emphasis on this theme and on the influence of von Humboldt: Bernard Semmel sees *On Liberty* as 'a tract whose major purpose was to advocate the positive freedom of self-development – and of self-control and self-dependence – of the German philosophers'.[4] Consistent with this reading, in the *Autobiography*, Mill has these ideas of self-developmental capacity in mind as he explains a core idea *On Liberty* was delivering, namely: 'the importance, to man and society, of a large variety in types of character, and of giving full freedom to human nature to expand itself in innumerable and conflicting directions'.[5]

In *On Liberty*, Mill takes the opportunity to press home the theme he finds in von Humboldt, quoting another passage from *The Duties and Spheres of Government* to stress 'the meaning of the doctrine' at stake: Mill quotes phrases from the opening of von Humboldt's second chapter:

---

[1] *OL* p. 55. The passage is from von Humboldt (1996) p. 65.
[2] *Auto* p. 143.
[3] Here we have an example of Mill's variance in spelling as noted earlier. So 'develope' for 'develop'. The spelling in English in the UK became more uniform, not least as education developed in the early to mid twentieth century.
[4] Semmel (1884) p. 14.
[5] *Auto* p. 142.

'... that "the end of man, or that which is prescribed by the external or immutable dictates of reason, and not suggested by vague and transient desires, is the highest and most harmonious development of his powers to a complete and consistent whole"; that, therefore, the object "towards which every human being must ceaselessly direct his efforts, and on which especially those who design to influence their fellow men must ever keep their eyes, is the individuality of power and development"; that for this there are two requisites, "freedom, and variety of situations"; and that from the union of these arise "individual vigour and manifold diversity", which combine themselves in "originality"' (III: 2).[1]

Mill is extremely keen on this package of ideas, stressing that however unusual the formulation of von Humboldt, no one who is capable of thought would ever want to argue that the aim of human life was simply for us to 'copy one another' (III: 3). In and through our development, the view Mill wants is for individuals to be able to 'put into their mode of life and into the conduct of their concerns' the 'impress... of their own judgement' or 'their own individual character'. Combatting the sense that this doctrine means we live in a fast-forward momentum, Mill argues that human development also has to take stock of what past experience has taught regarding various options for our 'mode of existence', providing insights into which style and forms of conduct were 'preferable'. Alluding again to education, Mill suggests that this past experience should be a part of a programme of learning, so the younger generation can come to appreciate 'the ascertained results of human experience'.

However:

'... it is the privilege and proper condition of a human being, arrived at the maturity of his faculties, to use and interpret experience in his own way. It is for him to find out what part of recorded experience is properly applicable to his own circumstances and character'.

Mill's point is that the 'traditions and customs of other people' show us what, in general, their experience has taught *them*'. To assume that there would be a direct fit for us would be akin to living on the assumption that other people's clothes or dentures would also be an exact fit. Mill's view is that there are three reasons why we cannot assume a continuity of views about the best or right modes of life.

Firstly, the experiences of other people may have been 'too narrow', or they may have misinterpreted it. Secondly, their plans for life may be right for them, but not for the wider development of individuality; looking forward, Mill has a crisp phrase to press his point:

'Customs are made for customary circumstances and customary characters; and his circumstances or his character may be uncustomary'.

A third reason not to follow the life plans of the past unquestioningly is that even if these modes of life are right for us now, 'to conform to custom merely *as* custom does not educate or develop in him any of the qualities which are the distinctive endowment of a human being'. These remarks lead to another of Mill's passages of powerful and fluent exposition:

---

[1] See von Humboldt (1996) p. 11-13.

'The human faculties of perception, judgement, discriminative feeling, mental activity, and even moral preference are exercised only in making a choice. He who does anything because it is a custom makes no choice. He gains no practice either in discerning or in desiring what is best. The mental and the moral, like the muscular, powers are improved only by being used. The faculties are called into no exercise by doing a thing merely because others do it, no more than by believing a thing only because others believe it. If the grounds of an opinion are not conclusive to the person's own reason, his reason cannot be strengthened, but is likely to be weakened, by his adopting it: and if the inducements to an act are not such as are consentaneous to his own feelings and character... it is so much done towards rendering his feelings and character inert and torpid instead of active and energetic'.

Notably, Mill here weaves together the case for the liberty of thought and discussion with the explanation of the value of an experimentalist approach to the practical side of life. He suggested earlier that the reasons for the liberty of thought and discussion were a basis for the other arguments concerning liberty, and here the point is demonstrated. An incentive for this view comes from Mill's sense that a person's life must be worked out from ideas critically reviewed and tested in action. Accordingly, we must think things through as well as try them out to evaluate them, and by doing them ourselves, we gain authentic insight. This applies to many activities: building a fire, surfing, fixing a broken fence, getting into the mindset of Taoism – all of these and plenty of other options for the things we do and how we might live are made real and fully grasped only through our doing them ourselves.

Mill maintains a vigorous style in developing the point that anyone who 'lets the world, or any portion of it, choose his own plan of life for him has no need of any other faculty than the ape-like one of imitation' (III: 4). We may feel that Mill is being a bit severe on apes: but he is perhaps on the edge of updating his view, as we know that soon after writing *On Liberty*, he revised his outlook on the natural world through reading Darwin.[1]

Mill comes closer to modernity with his next set of analogies. He suggests that what we do and how we do it makes us what we can become. Of the many 'works of man which human life is rightfully employed in perfecting and beautifying, the first of importance surely is man himself'. Mill then thinks that if we consider a range of activities – building houses, growing corn, fighting battles, testing causes, erecting and praying in churches – and imagine these might all be done 'by automatons in human form', we know that this would be inferior to what would be done by 'the men and women who at present inhabit the more civilized parts of the world'. For all their shortcomings, the process of doing and becoming through the various activities develops 'the human faculties' and humanity as such.

This brings Mill to a near-poetic point:

---

[1] Mill tells Bain in a letter of April, 1860, that he has read 'Darwin's book' – meaning *The Origin of Species* – and he says of it that 'It far surpasses my expectation. Though he cannot be said to have proved the truth of his doctrine, he does seem to have proved that it *may* be true, which I take to be as great a triumph as knowledge & ingenuity could possibly achieve on such a question'. CW XV p. 695.

'Human nature is not a machine to be built after a model, and set to do exactly the work prescribed for it, but a tree, which requires to grow and develop itself on all sides, according to the tendency of the inward forces which make it a living thing'.[1]

With the references to 'the tendency of the inward forces' and the process of making living things, we have more evidence of a teleological view within Mill's outlook. It is a commonplace to find the utilitarian ethic with its consequentialist interest in finding a means to an end of pleasure or happiness, described as teleological – as contrasted with deontological ethical theories where the emphasis is on acting in accordance with duty. With his affirmation of the tree, in contrast with a machine, Mill's teleology is generic and organic, and although he does not have the benefit of modern biogenetics, his point is nevertheless a strong one.

If we take one hundred zebra embryos and one giraffe embryo and all are, by some process of zoological IVF, bought to birth and then reared together, there will be no surprise that although the giraffe is brought up with the zebras, it will, as a result of the tendency of its 'inward forces', grow and develop as a giraffe, not a zebra. Mill's point regarding humans anticipates genetic explanations of individuality, but he senses that central to being a human being is the capacity to do, live and be in a distinctive and individual way. It is by means of this that humanity is enhanced, and the wider conditions of life are improved.

Understanding, Desires and Impulses (Paragraph 5)

Mill's next series of points start from the observation that in practice, it is probable that people will concede that individuals should use 'their understandings' (III: 5) so as to plot an 'intelligent following of custom, or even occasionally an intelligent deviation from custom'. This will be seen as better than a 'mechanical adhesion' to routine.

Mill doubts whether there is the same attitude towards human 'desires or impulses'. However, these are also aspects of what it is to be a many-sided human, developing and maturing his or her faculties. Implicitly, we get a sense that Mill assumes a view that is fearful of strong impulses or desires, but he holds that there is only a problem if strong feelings are 'not properly balanced' by 'beliefs and restraints'. By the notion of 'restraint', Mill means the sense of conscience as a moral sense within the individual, as is clear from his comment that 'it is not because men's desires are strong that they act ill; it is because their consciences are weak'. Mill's generalisation aims to make a positive point about the human condition. Aiming to build the case for considering that the mind, passions and desires are all part and parcel of what it is to be a human being, Mill points out that while there are risks and perils with those whose feelings are strong, the risks have to be taken:

'To say that one person's desires and feelings are stronger and more various than those of another is merely to say that he has more of the raw material of human nature and is

---

[1] In *The Subjectivism of Women*, Mill redeploys his tree analogy for human nature, but so as to indicate the way that women are inhibited in their development by the attitude of most men. They are like trees where 'one half' is 'kept in a vapour bath and the other half in the snow'. Mill (1988) p. 23.

therefore capable, perhaps of more evil, but certainly of more good. Strong impulses are but another name for energy. Energy may be turned to bad uses; but more good may always be made of an energetic nature than of an indolent or impassive one. Those who have most natural feeling are always those whose cultivated feelings may be made the strongest. The same strong susceptibilities which make the personal impulses vivid and powerful are also the source from whence are generated the most passionate love of virtue and the sternest self-control'.

The difficulty with this view is that it gives a scenario where all is fine so long as we have no persons with the energy and amorality of the psychotic at hand. Mill is not as alert to the risks and perils of how amoral humans can operate with intelligently calculated schemes to injure and harm others. Such individuals are some way from being perfectible humans and a serious risk to all of the others.

Innocent of these problems, Mill thinks that ideas here combine to give another useful summative point. Rightly organized, society provides the best exemplification of its duty to individuals and so to itself by encouraging the cultivation of the various qualities of passion, feeling and thought. This means we can move to an affirmation of the importance of the multi-faceted developmental capacity within individuality and so, as noted earlier, character, and with another mechanistic contrast:

'A person whose desires and impulses are his own – are the expression of his own nature, as it has been developed and modified by his own culture – is said to have a character. One whose desires and impulses are not his own has no character, no more than a steam engine has a character'.

Most of Mill's liberally-inclined readers will appreciate these sentiments. Humans should not be calibrated and assessed as if they were machines.[1] The contrast, to be developed throughout the chapter, is with all instances of uniformity, habit and custom set against the imperative of liberty, as in the liberty of choice over the mode of life for individuals. As he goes on to say:

'The only unfailing and permanent source of improvement is liberty, since by it there as many possible independent centres of improvement as there are individuals' (III: 17).

In and for the human dimension, Mill's view is that the 'strong susceptibilities' (III: 5) give a person the capacity for 'personal impulses' that are 'vivid and powerful' and provide 'the source from whence are generated the most passionate lives of virtue and the sternest self-control. Again, Mill is not shy of deploying themes that flow from the classical virtue approach, albeit under the implicit general principle of utility. However, the most emphatic theme in these paragraphs is the promotion of strong passions and feelings as vital components in the development of individual character: Mill considers that for all that he has explained why these aspects matter, his contemporary readers might well find the level of emphasis worrying, and he addresses the concerns by attacking the residual alternative outlook on life.

---

[1] The only problems are likely to arise from those who, whatever their political outlook, spend time restoring steam engines to run on one of the reopened railway lines in the UK, such as along the Severn Valley or in the Forest of Dene. For such devotees of steam engines, it would be a massive heresy to say that such engines lack character.

Conformity, Uniformity and Related Issues (Paragraphs 6-9)

Over the next four paragraphs, Mill widens a historical review of the issues he is dealing with before focusing on the problem of the prescriptive and uniform view of the human condition, which he associates with what he terms the Calvinist influence. Mill knows that promoting strong feelings, desires and impulses as core elements in developing individuality will not sit well with all thinkers and readers. It will be thought that history shows us that in the past, an excess of energy and feeling, 'of spontaneity and individuality' (III: 6), was 'too much ahead of the power which society then possessed of disciplining and controlling them'. This led, Mill thinks, to the imposition of laws – as in the mediaeval period, and one would assume, in the long legal traditions in what became the UK – that were, as Mill sees it, to control all of life as the means to control individual 'character'. Laws and the disciplines over life originally lacked the subtlety to protect against harm to the individual sphere of action, suppressing humanity under a prescriptive and inhibiting blanket of laws. Although Mill appreciates that there have subsequently been reforms, he still thinks that the upshot is that 'society has now fairly got the better of individuality'. This means that 'the danger which threatens human nature is not the excess, but the deficiency, of personal impulses and preferences'.

Giving his own age a low rating, Mill claims it is a time where 'everyone lives as under the eye of a hostile and dreaded censorship'. The 'as under' here means we are getting a rhetorical characterisation rather than a literal description. Mill is expressing under a different guise the tyranny of opinion as the regulator of behaviour. He considers this regulation excessive as it covers those matters that primarily concern individuals themselves. It gives rise to a style of life where too many are concerned to live only in such a way as conforms to what is 'customary'. The capacity to choose as an individual something of individual taste or preference has been overwhelmed by a pattern of life that is locked into the routines of custom. Mill is perhaps mindful of the rise of mass interests within mid-nineteenth century life that tend to direct and regulate conduct, such that not just 'the mind is bowed to the yoke':

'… even in what people do for pleasure, conformity is the first thing thought of; they like in crowds; they exercise choice only among things commonly done; peculiarity of taste, eccentricity of conduct are shunned equally with crimes, until by dint of not following their own nature, they have no nature to follow'.

Mill portrays the resultant state of humanity – the majority at least, as 'withered and starved' in terms of their capacity; as 'incapable of any strong wishes or native pleasures' and as 'generally without either opinions or feelings of home growth or properly their own'. To illuminate this condition, Mill turns to the tradition of reformed theology stemming from John Calvin and puts his philosophical boot into what he calls 'the Calvinistic theory' (III: 7).

Mill here builds on his earlier reservations about the 'spirit of Puritanism' (I: 14), and draws on a certain tendency of thought he considers restrictive and inhibiting and which he associates with the Calvinist tradition. [1] We are told many things about this, and all of them are negative and inhibiting in relation to the expression and development of individuality: 'whatever is not a duty is a sin' (III: 7); all 'the good of which humanity is capable is comprised in obedience'; 'Human nature being radically corrupt, there is no redemption for anyone until human nature is killed within him'. This way of life sees it as 'no evil' to eliminate 'the human faculties, capacities and susceptibilities' – meaning those which make for human individuality and development.

In the theological view of Calvinism as Mill portrays it, all that is required is the subordination of the individual to the 'will of God'. Mill concedes that the outlook being assailed is a 'theory' that is 'held in mitigated form by many who do not consider themselves Calvinists', and there is a valid point here. What Mill is touching on is really the wider problem of the human desire for finding and living by a saving truth. By 'saving', we are not moving into the soteriological domain in a theological enquiry, but meaning more colloquially that humans, faced with the finitude and uncertainty of life, have a habit of creating certainties within which to live and through which to find justification. The absolutist political ideologies of the twentieth century are examples of this on a grand scale; militant Islam since 1979 is another case in point, as are the imperative campaigns for the rights of this or that group in the most recent phase of life. Mill's examples seem somewhat less dramatic but are of the same residual disposition to find a mode of life that is secure and safe and not upset by the challenging experimentalism of progressive, developmental individuals.

Mill's view is that in his modernity, the Calvinistic outlook is 'a strong tendency' (III: 8): it promotes a 'narrow theory of life' and aims for a 'pinched and hidebound type of human character'. Mill uses favoured botanical terms for this product – humans who are 'cramped and dwarfed' – yet those who promote these limited and limiting individuals think that this is the mode of life consistent with the created order. Mill uses another arboreal example and thinks this is akin to those who think trees are all the better for being 'clipped into pollards, or cut out into figures of animals'. Mill rejects this aesthetic of fashion for a wider regard for things as 'nature made them'. [2]

Picking up more from the theological tradition, Mill thinks that if it is reasonable to envisage 'that man was made by a good Being', such a faith would be consistent in thinking that 'all human faculties were given that they might be cultivated and unfolded, not rooted out and consumed'. This is a 'type of excellence' distinct from the inhibitions and abnegations of Calvinism. Mill then repeats his earlier view that the better approach draws on the plurality of traditions, and he quotes themes from the essays of his friend Sterling – 'Pagan self-assertion' as well as 'Christian self-

---

[1] Here the root reference is the ideas associated with the French/Swiss Protestant reformer John Calvin (1509-1564), whose most famous work is probably *The Institutes of Religion* (1536). Calvin taught a doctrine of predestination, implying that few were of the elect – so guaranteed salvation, and the majority were doomed to damnation and guaranteed the opposite. A strict regime of morality was required, which owed a little at best to the New Testament. Calvinism, for all its negativity and severity, was a popular influence in the reformation churches. For a balanced view of Calvin, see MacCulloch (2009) pp. 632-633.

[2] This comment reflects Mill's long-term interest in botany and in the beauties of the natural world.

denial'[1] both contribute to the sense of 'human worth', with 'a Greek ideal of self-development' blending with 'the Platonic and Christian ideal of self-government'.[2] Here, Mill is keen to avoid extremes and build from various views. He particularly endorses the influence of Pericles, the notable figure in the early development of the city-state of Athens.[3] Pericles' qualities include high regard for the arts, more open governance through an early form of democracy, and economic reforms, such as introducing a standard system of weights and measures to make for easier and fairer trade. All round, Pericles appeals to Mill as a figure of courage, and innovative energy, with a love of variety and development. This leads him to another of his passages of affirmative summation:

'It is not by wearing down into uniformity all that is individual in themselves, but by cultivating it and calling it forth, within the limits imposed by the rights and interests of others, that human beings become a noble and beautiful object of contemplation; and as the works partake the character of those who do them, by the same processes human life also becomes rich, diversified, and animating, furnishing more abundant aliment to high thoughts and elevating feelings, and strengthening the tie which binds every individual to the race, by making the race infinitely better worth belonging to. In proportion to the development of his individuality, each person becomes more valuable to himself, and is, therefore, capable of being of more value to others' (III: 9).[4]

These ideas are developed. Mill thinks that 'the means of development which the individual loses by being prevented from gratifying his inclinations to the injury of others are chiefly obtained at the expense of the development of other people'. This implies that if a person exhibits self-control to avoid injury to others, the loss of that person's development is magnified by the loss of inspiring further development for others. This ties in with Mill's fusion of liberty with utility 'in its largest sense' (I: 11).

If we get the point of Mill's view that humans develop as 'progressive' beings, then the ideas cohere on the view that a person's value and worth are never wholly self-orientated, but linked to a wider constituency of others who, in Mill's aspirational hope, would be members of a civilized community – the model of society that Mill most emphatically endorses. Mill engages with the fine detail of the matters at stake in this. A person's social sense is greatly advanced if there is 'restraint put upon the selfish part' (III: 9). If a person is constrained by 'rigid rules of justice for the sake of others', this cultivates 'the feelings and capacities which have the good of others as their object'. The contrast is that living under the restraints of convention 'dulls and blunts the whole nature'.

Mill's point has a large bearing on the debates in modernity to be considered in the final part of this book, where various cases for restraint are seen to arise against the free expression of thought. Mill's view is that, on the basis of an implicit principle of practice, if not making perfect, at least making for improvement through

---

[1] The reference is to Sterling's *Essays and Tales*, (Edited by J. Hare), London 1848 Volume 1 p. 190 – see *OL* p. 127.
[2] Apart from his own studies, Mill also knew of Pericles from the work of his fried George Grote, who wrote a major study on the history of Greece. See Scarre pp. 67-68.
[3] Pericles (c495-429 BCE) – for details on Pericles see
https://www.nationalgeographic.com/culture/article/pericles
[4] By 'race' here, Mill means the human race.

development, that 'fair play' should be given to enable 'the nature of each' to progress: to this end 'it is essential that different persons be allowed to lead different lives', both in practice and through the defence of what is chosen through argument. These are the key themes in the liberty principle that Mill is working out – it means that the practical objective is, risks and perils notwithstanding, for the liberty of each individual to be defended consistent with the liberty of everyone else. Mill is sure that there has been a greater benefit to 'posterity' when this mode of liberty has been possible, and even the problems of political despotism are mitigated 'so long as individuality exists under it'.[1]

Mill refines his point to focus the assault: he describes as 'despotism', anything – by whatever name it may be called – that 'crushes individuality'. Custom, the habits and routines of convention, the mainstream views that become an oppressive tyranny of expectations, of conduct and opinion – all these we suppose can be modes of despotism injurious to the development of individual character and progressive humanity.

Individuality and Development:
Feelings, Reasons and Originality (Paragraphs 10-12)

Mill provides an interim summary of his thinking so far: he has shown how 'individuality is the same thing with development, and that it is only the cultivation of individuality which produces, or can produce, well-developed human beings' (III: 10). This could bring this chapter to a close, for nothing more could be said on what could help to bring 'human beings themselves nearer to the best' they could be, nor on what was the greatest 'obstruction' to that. Nevertheless, Mill thinks that nothing said so far will be enough 'to convince those who most need convincing' and that more needs to be said to persuade 'the undeveloped' of the value of becoming a 'developed human being'. Mill then comes to a potent thought – that what has to be done is to 'point out to those who do not desire liberty', those who 'would not avail themselves of it, that they may be in some intelligible manner rewarded for allowing other people to make use of it without hindrance'.

The weight of this point is that Mill is not arguing that there should be a campaign to empower everyone with liberty. As we mentioned, his point is infused with realism about the limited power of persuasion – not least in competition with human feelings, desires, impulses and wants. This is a matter Mill deals with in his essay, *The Subjection of Women*.[2] He considers the problem faced in trying to argue for 'the principle of perfect equality' in law to 'regulate the existence of social relations between the two sexes'.[3] The problem lies in the fact that the existing condition of inequality in law between women and men resides in an archaic tradition of the physically stronger sex dominating and making subordinate the

---

[1] This is a point Berlin does not seem to have taken fully into account in his countering view that evidence of progress under despotism weakens the case for liberality. See Berlin (2017) p. 175 and as discussed in Chapter 8 above.
[2] Mill (1988).
[3] Mill (1988) p. 1. See pp. 55ff for some of Mill's arguments on women's rights to vote which are developments of what is prefigured in various parts of *OL*.

weaker: force, not argument, brought this arrangement into play, and over time it became embedded in the traditions and feelings of human society. Mill thinks that 'so long as an opinion is rooted in the feelings, it gains rather than loses in stability by having a preponderating weight of argument against it'. Those whose view is based on deep feelings will consider that opposing arguments miss the point of the 'deeper ground' for those feelings'.

How Mill addresses this problem of challenging the power of feelings in *The Subjection of Women* is another story. In *On Liberty*, he considers that for the audience he is addressing, not everyone will reach the view that the degree of liberty he is defending is, in practice, a good to be reasoned and defended. He does not see a case to hope to persuade those so minded that they are wrong – the power of feelings against diversity is just too strong to take on frontally: instead, he wants to take the more strategic line of suggesting to them something else. This is that, in the long run, they will benefit from not hindering, inhibiting or suppressing those who can use liberty in the interests, as ever, of humans as 'progressive' beings – (I: 11). While this we may consider being as difficult a task in which to succeed, it is what Mill turns to explain.

The first element in the chosen task of modified persuasion is the view that whatever degree of conservatism we have, however deep our desire for the tranquil ease of a uniform life of regularity and consensus, there is, in developing the 'originality' (III: 11) of some people, something of value to all. This can be those who 'discover new truths' to replace those now seen as insufficient – as in the case developed for freedom of thought and discussion in *On Liberty's* previous chapter. It can also be what Mill has been concerned with throughout this chapter, what those who can offer who 'commence new practices and set the example of more enlightened conduct and better taste and sense in human life'. Exemplifications of better and more developed modes of living fit the template Mill works from, that humans are to be conceived as 'progressive' (I: 11) in character, this fitting within the scheme of utility in its 'largest sense'. Mill's point is that it is not at all easy for anyone to say that human life is perfected 'in all its ways and practices' (III: 11). He also says that in practice, within the spectrum of human individuality, there will be 'but few persons… whose experiments, if adopted by others, would be likely to be any improvement on established practice. But these few would become the salt of the earth; without them, human life would become a stagnant pool'.

Mill aims to strengthen his view by recalling the argument that even if we are confident that we have the best truth of the matter, it is right to retain a critical review of such truths to remain clear as to why they seem best. Similarly, the modes of living we are most confident in also need to be challenged by experimental alternatives. Humans otherwise fall into 'mechanical' ways of life and thought, more suitable, he thinks – perhaps unjustly, to cattle.[1]

Keeping the themes of liberty of thought and action in line, Mill reaffirms that 'a succession of persons of ever-recurring originality' is the means of preserving

---

[1] Amongst the links that might be made, to the mutual shock of both, between Mill and Nietzsche, is that they both have a low regard for cattle. Having grown up on a farm, I think this estimate is misplaced. I commented on this in my book on Nietzsche – see Loxton (2021) pp. 411-412 and p. 412 n. 1.

authentic insight and practices and preventing a slide into 'dead matter'. Such persons gain a high accolade:

> 'Persons of genius, it is true, are, and are always likely to be, a small minority; but in order to have them, it is necessary to preserve the soil out of which they grow. Genius can only breathe freely in an *atmosphere* of freedom. Persons of genius are, *ex vi termini*, more individual than any other people – less capable, consequently, of fitting themselves, without hurtful compression, into any of the small number of moulds which society provides in order to save its members the trouble of forming their own character'.

Such persons of character as Mill wants to promote face problems akin to those crossing a canyon on a high wire with no safety net: if they err too much on the side of 'timidity', they will not rise to shine with the qualitative improvements for life that may be in their perdue: on the other hand, if they 'are of a strong character and break their fetters', they can be pilloried for being 'wild' or 'erratic'. A geographic metaphor is employed: it would be like complaining 'of the Niagara river for not flowing smoothly between its banks like a Dutch canal'.

With the Niagara as the symbol of genius, Mill wants to promote individuals with the capacity for a surge and flood of novel energy 'to unfold itself freely both in thought and practice' (III: 12). He wrestles with the sense that on paper, or 'in theory', nobody is going to argue against genius: but he is scathing about the reality. Genius, he thinks, is considered 'a fine thing' so long as it is confined to the arts, to composing a poem or painting a picture.[1] However, in the areas of 'originality thought and action', the reactions are usually a degree of admiration, but overwhelmingly the sense is that the novelty is something better done without. Mill thinks this is 'all too natural to be wondered at':

> 'Originality is the one thing which unoriginal minds cannot feel the use of. They cannot see what it is for them: how should they? If they could see what it would for them, it would not be originality'.

If Mill is right, we seem to be heading for an impasse insofar as originality over modes of life and thought will never break into the self-consciousness of the unoriginal mind that, as Mill sees it, the majority possess. If this is so, it ties in with the fatalistic view Mill and his wife had, in thinking that the impact of *On Liberty* would have for a future when there were 'again thinkers'.[2]

Mill's sanguine point at this stage is to ask rhetorically for reflection on the plain fact that 'nothing was ever done which someone was not the first to do', which is to bring home the self-destructive futility of opposing originality in the spheres of thought and action.

---

[1] Mill mentions no names but given the time of writing he could refer to Turner's late paintings and to the poetry of Wordsworth, Shelley or Tennyson.
[2] CW XIV p. 112.

Mediocrity and the *One* or *Few* (Paragraphs 13-16)

Mill moves on to deepen his pessimistic view of his period: a time when 'the general tendency of things throughout the world is to render mediocrity the ascendant power among mankind' (III: 13). To explain this view, Mill places the responsibility on the management of society by such means as 'a democracy or a numerous aristocracy' – neither of which is capable of rising 'above mediocrity', save in those instances when they have had the rare good sense to allow 'the sovereign many' to 'be guided... by the counsels and influence of a more highly gifted and instructed *one* or *few*'. Mill eases home his view:

'The initiation of all wise or noble things comes and must come from individuals; generally at first from some one individual. The honour and glory of the average man is that he is capable of following that initiative; that he can respond internally to wise and noble things, and be led to them with his eyes open'.

The ideas Mill presents open him to another charge of elitism; his thinking disparages those – the custom-laden majority, who will always be mediocre and average, where both are pejorative terms. What will come as having the virtues of wisdom and nobility for all comes from the 'one or few' whose innovations offer opportunities for development and progression that the average person can follow, if they have sufficient 'honour and glory'. It might be that it is thought that this leads to the replication of what has been exemplified, putting Mill's project of explaining the case for the liberty of action into a quagmire. However, we should address Mill's phrase that the 'average' person's 'honour and glory' comes if they can, from the initiative that is given, 'respond internally': this does not entail mere copying of what has been shown; it is more a matter of appropriating it within and for the life of the individual concerned. The innovator is there to 'point the way': it is for others to follow as and for themselves.

Consistent with his earlier remarks on the dynamic of the individual's liberty, Mill makes it clear that the innovative individual must not seek the 'power of compelling others' – this would be 'inconsistent with the freedom and development of all the rest'. In the scenario of life where, as Mill thinks, there is an ascendancy of mediocrity, the 'counterpoise and corrective' of 'the more and more pronounced individuality of those who stand in the higher eminences of thought' comes through their determination to act 'differently from the mass'. Not only differently, but 'better':

'In this age, the mere example of non-conformity, the mere refusal to bend the knee to custom, is itself a service. Precisely because the tyranny of opinion is such as to make eccentricity a reproach, it is desirable, in order to break through that tyranny, that people should be eccentric. Eccentricity has always abounded when and where strength of character has abounded; and the amount of eccentricity in a society has generally been proportional to the amount of genius, mental vigour, and moral courage it contained. That so few now dare to be eccentric marks the chief danger of the time'.[1]

---

[1] Bending, or taking the knee, has other connotations in modernity, but Mill's point remains, that resisting customs is hard, but sometimes imperative.

What Mill remains in favour of is that individuality is a means of promoting development for the individual in question and, thereby, the greater whole of society. The virtues of courage and wisdom, the insight and reason to generate novel ideas and forms of life, all come from this signal quality of individuality that comes with personhood.

In this last passage, Mill uses the term 'eccentricity' to point up the level of individuality that is required in an age he sees as unduly conformist. The problem with Mill's terminology here is that 'eccentricity' suggests a form of waywardness and oddity, an absentmindedness or mode of abstraction from the everyday, rather than the individualism that Mill wants to encourage, of endeavour, strength of mind and will, to the end of cultivating character and originality. In his own time, his old acquaintance and sparring partner Macaulay, who died later in the year of *On Liberty's* publication, wrote in his journal that he 'did not at all like to see a man of Mill's excellent abilities recommend eccentricity as a thing almost good in itself'.[1] Macaulay's view was that the times he and Mill were living through showed an abundance of individuality and manifold instances of innovation and genius. There was a 'boldness and novelty' abounding in various disciplines and other spheres of life, with many good and plenty of errant views in debate. In the domain of literature, Macaulay thinks far too much 'odd' experimental writing is going on, and this leads him to reject Mill's portrayal of a culture steeped in mediocre uniformity – with a telling blow, he says that Mill is 'crying "Fire!" in Noah's flood'.

That Mill is exaggerating the degree of uniformity in the society of his day does not seem implausible if we consider the range of variety of ideas and innovations that were prevalent in social and political as well as in scientific and cultural life. However, under all of this, what Mill is exercised about are the conventions of manner that radiate a sense of an expectation of agreement, of consensus, of commonality of behaviour, belief and conduct – as if the debates and controversies of the age had no bearing on the business of leading better lives. For Mill, liberty always comes with the cutting edge of radicalism, to provoke and promote at least a change of perspective on, if not a change of direction in, a person's belief and conduct.

Mill moves on to engage in another burst of explanatory persuasion. Customs, he implies, may come and go over time, and so this gives a reason for there to be 'the freest scope possible to uncustomary things' (III: 14) so that over time we may discover and agree 'which of these are fit to be converted into customs'. Aiming to enlarge the scope of his argument, Mill next suggests that not only 'persons of decidedly superior mental superiority' have 'a just claim to carry on their lives in their own way. There is no reason that all human existence should be constructed on some one or some small number of patterns'. Anyone with a 'tolerable amount of common sense and experience' should be encouraged to 'his own mode of laying out his existence'.

Mill's point is not that thereby will the best way of living be found, so much as that for all individuals, self-defining acts of living out one's plan of life are 'best' – and for 'best' we might now say authentic. It is like learning to tie our own shoelaces on a larger scale.

---

[1] Quoted by Himmelfarb: 'Editor's Introduction' *OL* p. 38: Himmelfarb quotes from G. O. Trevelyan, *The Life and Letters of Lord Macaulay*, New York, 1876, Vol II, p. 385-6. See also Himmelfarb (1974) pp. 162ff.

Having contrasted humans earlier with machines, trees, steam engines, and cattle, Mill next comes to sheep. Humans 'are not like sheep, and even sheep are undistinguishably alike' – so at least a better observation here than Mill gave over cattle. His point regarding humans is that we know, even from how a person gets the clothing that fits and suits them, that humans are distinct and individualized. All this makes a life of uniformity in any sense a route to cultural and intellectual stagnation. Mill, with references to how people and indeed plants, come in all sorts and types in a rich variety, lays on his view that diversity and originality work for the greater good. He points up how what is helpful to one person to aid them in progressing to their 'higher nature' might hinder another. We might note that fishing or opera might suit some, but golf or cooking others. Mill's examples are rowing, smoking, music, athletics, chess, card games and study – some or none of which might be a vital route for self-development by progressive individuals. What is sought by whatever means helps is the case Mill has for 'diversity' in the 'modes of life' that we share within and as a part of a civilized society. However varied the range or quality of the activities through which people develop, this is the tolerant and balanced way to give equality of opportunity for individuals to 'grow up to the mental, moral, and aesthetic stature of which their nature is capable'. With the examples of activities Mill gives, it is self-evident that most are undertaken with others, and this gives another sense to the self-regarding aspect of life: a person might want to undertake a personal and self-regarding programme of improvement in music, chess or athletics – but by default, this will be through participatory activity with others in shared endeavours.

Mill is on firm ground in explaining that the problem of his modernity is that some official recognition, 'a title' or a 'badge of rank' is required to license someone to live in a manner distinct from the safe and conventional norm. He dislikes the notion of some, but not the rest, having a special sanction to be different. But this is not the only problem. Mill also gives the majority, who have been the butt of many of his criticisms, another distinct attack. Previously, majority opinion was seen as prohibitive of new insights and better and more vital truths. Now the 'general average of mankind' (III: 15) are thought 'intolerant of any marked demonstrations of individuality'. The problem is that this 'general average of mankind' is 'not only moderate in intellect', but also lacks strength in 'tastes or wishes' that might encourage the doing of 'anything unusual'.

This creates something that goes back to Mill's developed sense that argument alone cannot easily achieve much to alter outlooks: the moderate insight of the average person disables them from understanding those who will seem 'wild and intemperate' when in effect, they are really creative and distinctive in expressive novelty.

Mill moves to note reservations about 'the philanthropic spirit' that pervades the age, the movement that works to promote improvements in manners and morals.[1] This movement offers a prescriptive set of general rules for the betterment of people, but Mill observes that what is central is that people are 'to desire nothing

---

[1] There were many such movement in the nineteenth century, and in the period after the Poor Law reforms of 1834, philanthropic movements, humanistic and religious abounded. For more on this see www.bbc.co.uk › history › british

strongly', they are to be 'without any marked character': people are, by this so-called improvement, 'maimed by compression, like a Chinese lady's foot', so removing 'every part of human nature which stands out prominently and tends to make the person markedly dissimilar in outline to commonplace humanity'.

The philanthropic reforms Mill dislikes are parodied as providing half 'of what is desirable' (III: 16) by excluding the other half:

'Instead of great energies guided by vigorous reason, and strong feelings strongly controlled by a conscientious will, its result is weak feelings and weak energies, which therefore can be kept in outward conformity to rule without any strength either of will or of reason'.

Looking to a wider line of criticism, Mill suggests that the world of business is now the only arena in life where there is an 'outlet for energy'. It is easy to appreciate how the innovative economy of Britain in the middle of the nineteenth century would fit this description, but Mill thinks this is against the better frame of reference for human development.

Mill is not happy:

'The greatness of England is now all collective; individually small, we only appear to be capable of anything great by our habit of combining; and with this our moral and religious philanthropists are perfectly contented'.

From this, Mill thinks the aim should be to find people 'of another stamp' to halt the slide into mediocrity and collectivism. He elects to move into an assault against one his familiar targets for disapprobation – the despotic influence of custom.

The Despotism of Custom and the Spirit of Liberty (Paragraphs 17-19)

The particular evil that Mill identifies has a familiar ring - 'the despotism of custom' (III: 17). This is considered the main 'hindrance to human advancement' since it is opposed to the aspiration to 'aim at something better'. The 'aim' here is again teleological in character, reminding us that Mill does not envisage humans as fixed or uniform, and links with his notion of humans seen as 'progressive' (I: 11).

Mindful of his attacks on philanthropic attempts at improvement, Mill produces a deft way of showing that the spirit of improvement is fine and important if, but only if, it is inspired by liberty:

'The spirit of improvement is not always a spirit of liberty, for it may aim at forcing improvements on an unwilling people; and the spirit of liberty, in so far as it resists such attempts, may ally itself locally and temporarily with the opponents of improvement; but the only unfailing and permanent source of improvement is liberty, since by it there as many possible independent centres of improvement as there are individuals. The progressive principle, however, in either shape, whether as the love of liberty or of improvement, is antagonistic to the sway of custom, involving at least emancipation from that yoke' (III: 17).

In a bold challenge to all historians, Mill adds that the 'contest' between progression and the 'yoke' of custom 'constitutes the chief interest of the history of mankind'. Mill immediately explains that he means to say that large parts of the world have, in effect, little by way of history because 'the despotism of custom is complete'. Countries in the East – Mill is thinking mostly of India and China – were once great powers, but they have, he thinks, fallen in influence because of the deadening influence of 'conformity to custom'. A people and nations cease to develop when they 'cease to possess individuality', and Mill sees that the problem can easily arise in the society in which he lives. Turning to his own situation in life, he claims that alleged improvements in society, which one might think to provide greater scope for individual life, are actually against liberty and individuality. The improvements are portrayed as 'progress', but they oppose individuality:

'We have discarded the fixed costumes of our forefathers; everyone must still dress like other people, but the fashion may change once or twice a year. We thus take care that when there is a change, it shall be for change's sake, and not from any idea of beauty or convenience; for the same idea of beauty or convenience would not strike all the world at the same moment, and be simultaneously thrown aside by all at another moment. But we are progressive as well as changeable: we continually make new inventions in mechanical things, and keep them until they are again superseded by better; we are eager for improvement in politics, in education, even in morals, though in this last our idea of improvement chiefly consists in persuading or forcing other people to be as good as ourselves. It is not progress that we object to; on the contrary, we flatter ourselves that we are the most progressive people who ever lived. It is individuality that we war against: we should think we had done wonders if we had made ourselves all alike, forgetting that the unlikeness of one person to another is generally the first thing which draws the attention of either to the imperfection of his own type and the superiority of another, or the possibility, by combining the advantages of both, of producing something better than either'.

Mill takes as a case study China, which, mid-nineteenth century, he sees in the following terms:

'A nation of much talent, and, in some respects, even wisdom, owing to the rare good fortune of having been provided at an early period with a particularly good set of customs, the work, in some measure, of men to whom even the most enlightened European must accord, under certain limitations, the title of sages and philosophers'.[1]

In China there was, at a point in time, a discovery of 'the secret of human progressiveness', and this might have kept the country and its people 'at the head of the movement of the world'.

Mill thinks this did not happen:

'... they have become stationary – have remained so for thousands of years; and if they are ever to be farther improved, it must be by foreigners. They have succeeded beyond all hope in what English philanthropists are so industriously working at – in making a people all alike, all governing their thoughts and conduct by the same maxims and rules; and these are the fruits. The modern *régime* of public opinion is, in an unorganized form, what the Chinese educational and political systems are in an organized; and unless individuality shall be able

---

[1] Mill alludes the Confucian and Taoist traditions, and the limitations he has in mind are to do with the fusion in these traditions of religious as well as ethical and civic teachings. It would somewhat fairer to say that these traditions had a holistic perspective on the human condition.

successfully to assert itself against this yoke, Europe, notwithstanding its noble antecedents and its professed Christianity, will tend to become another China'.[1]

For all the risks Mill sees for life in the European context, he thinks that there is a two-fold resource that can play out in a redemptive manner. The first is the residual case he has been building for liberty to infuse the spirit of improvement. The other is that the setting of European culture has been enriched by a 'plurality of paths for its progressive and many-sided development' (III: 18). This insight, owing much to Mill's appreciation of von Humboldt, contributes much to what Mill sees as the great resource that aids general development and the growth of individuality.

The variety and difference between the European nations are shown by how 'individuals, classes, nations have been extremely unlike one another'; there has been a healthy and progressive 'diversity of character and culture'. Mill hopes that there is an adequate resource here to counter his fear. The worry is that the pattern of reforms, innovations and improvements in the standard of living and communication, and the extension of provision for a general education, oppose moral, cultural, spiritual and social differences. Life appears to exhibit greater similarity and uniformity. There is thus less diversity – the same goals, occupations, interests and books prevail. All this signals a levelling of society and the removal of diversity.

Against this, and in closing the chapter, Mill expresses urgent concern over the need for action against the encroachment of the majority and the assimilation of variety into uniformity. The various forces of the majority manifest 'a mass of influences hostile to individuality' (III: 19). Individuality can only hold on if 'the intelligent part of the public can be made to feel its value'. Once more, it is a matter of feeling, not reason; but the impression we have from Mill is that he thinks the time is short, and so the matter is urgent:

'If the claims of individuality are ever to be asserted, the time is now, while much is still wanting to complete the enforced assimilation. It is only in the earlier stages that any stand can be successfully made against the encroachment. The demand that all other people shall resemble ourselves grows by what it feeds on. If resistance waits till life is reduced *nearly* to one uniform type, all deviations from that type will come to be considered impious, immoral, even monstrous, and contrary to nature. Mankind speedily become unable to conceive diversity when they have been for some time unaccustomed to see it'.

On Individuality as One of the Elements of Well-Being.

Reviewing this chapter, we have seen that Mill's focus is based on his view that there are 'baneful consequences' for the 'intellectual, and through that, to the moral nature of man' (III: 1) if the liberties of thought and discussion are not both granted and extended to the sphere of active life. Regarding the latter, people should be 'free to act on their opinions'. This liberty of action, no less than the liberty of thought and discussion, links to the fallible condition of human life: just as truths are partial and improvable through ongoing open discussion, so our 'modes of action' are also

---

[1] Mill was prophetic in a sense: China was changed dramatically by the incursion of foreigners – the Japanese invasion in the 1930s – leading to civil war, as well as by the adoption and adaptation of Marxism, leading to the establishment of the Maoist People's Republic of China in 1949.

capable of improvement. The argument is for 'the worth of different modes of life' to be tried and tested by individuals in and thorough their own exploration of their 'individuality'. For this exploration, liberty of action is 'the only unfailing and permanent source of improvement' (III: 17), as this trades on the point that 'there are as many possible independent centres of improvement as there are individuals'.

That Mill is promoting individuality is never in doubt, but his point in the title of the chapter is that individuality is *one* of 'the elements of well-being', and we might therefore consider for a moment, what the other 'elements of well-being' are that matter?

We are familiar with Mill's sense that society in its pejorative mood as a system of habit and routine, is bad news, but whatever the dangers of society in its tyrannical mode coming to encroach on individuality, Mill is never able to hide from the residual view that human life and so human well-being are set in the context of social life. As we will recall, he holds to the idea of a civilized community as the preeminent mode of social existence. In such a setting, human individuality is cultivated in and through a collaborative association where reciprocal respect for the interests of individuals is the consistent order of the day. However, Mill is clear that for 'individual and social progress' – social progress in the civilized sense, the 'traditions and customs of other people' are inhibiting: what is needed for a wider development of 'human happiness' is the cultivation of individual character and originality. Given that Mill sees that society is comprised of the sum total of individuals, this is not a surprising view, but it remains something of an open question as to how Mill sees the alignment of the other 'elements of well-being'.

Mill affirms that the 'free development of individuality' (III: 2) improves not just individual well-being, but also that of humanity in the wider social sense. If we enrich the confidence, and enhance the well-being of the individual by encouraging more by way of an experimental outlook in his or her mode of life, then we make society and humanity in general better and more worthwhile:

'It is only the cultivation of individuality which produces or can produce, well-developed human beings' (III: 10).

The game plan is that if we are in a culture and context of promoting individual development, we are reducing the threat of the otherwise diminishing tendency of human life to fall into repetitive patterns of habitual life, where the human capacity for life as a distinct individual is reduced to the disadvantage of society as a whole. For all the stress in this view on the capacity of individuals for self-development, Mill also appeals to the deeper sense he sometimes obscures of respect for the view that human individuals live in a social setting with strong cultural resources. In affirming the importance of cultivating individuality, we find that Mill also sees the phenomenon of individually experimental attitudes as 'a co-ordinate' and 'a necessary condition' of 'all that is designated by the terms civilization, instruction, education, culture' (III: 2). Rightly understood, the educative process as a whole is the means through which society can enculture each generation in the active, questioning and creative mode of life that is expressive of individuality.

From the way Mill develops these ideas, we know that he draws insights from the work of von Humboldt and that the key ideas are embellished by some comparative analogies, such as between humans and cattle (III: 11), humans and machines such as steam engines (III: 5), and trees (III: 4). The points emerging from these comparisons are that if human well-being is not prospered, as through engagement with a 'plurality of paths' (III: 18), or if human life is envisaged as something mechanical and repetitive, or as something best conducted in herds of relative uniformity, well-being will be diminished. As the analogy between the human condition and trees specifically suggests to the botanically interested Mill, each species of tree grows 'according to the tendency of the inward forces which make it a living thing' (III:4), and Mill's vision is that society has the fertile resources to render each individual member an individual with the capacity to live a distinct and perhaps distinctive life.

10. *On Liberty*: IV: 'Of the Limits to the Authority of Society over the Individual'. (Paragraphs 1-21)

The Constraints of Liberty (Paragraphs 1-3)

In the preceding chapters, Mill has taken the concept of liberty to the theoretical and practical limits he thinks appropriate. He has argued for a strong degree of almost unfettered liberty of thought and discussion and a degree of liberty of action that is almost as great. In matters held to be 'self-regarding', the liberty of the sovereign individual is affirmed as being of vital worth to the end of acquiring truths and genuine individuality within and for society and its general good. Liberty is here a progressive force for development in and for society as a whole, as society is simply the body comprised of individuals.

Mill's fourth chapter flows on almost as a continuation of the previous chapter's discussion of individuality and the liberty of action, but the focus moves back to the tensions raised by the 'one very simple principle' of liberty (I: 9), which affirms that over 'the part of the conduct of anyone' that has to do with themselves, that 'person's independence, is of right, absolute'. But over conduct that concerns others, the individual is 'amenable to society'. The focus is now put on how precisely a person is 'amenable to society' and on the nature and range of the limits that apply to the authority of society over the individual: the emphasis is on the points of legitimate constraint that may be applied to liberty.

In setting this up, Mill asks himself three rhetorical questions:

'What, then, is the rightful limit to the sovereignty of the individual over himself? Where does the authority of society begin? How much of human life should be assigned to individuality, and how much to society?' (IV: 1).

Mill ventures a very straightforward response: society and individuality will be properly satisfied, receiving their 'proper share' (IV: 2) of human life if each 'has that which more properly concerns it'. Mill gives a neat proposal as the ground plan:

'To individuality should belong the part of life in which it is chiefly the individual that is interested; to society, the part which chiefly interests society'.

This proposal rests on the notion Mill has kept in mind throughout, of there being a distinction between the self and other-regarding parts of life. However, we notice that each side of the division is moderated with the vague conditional term 'chiefly', and, imprecise as it is, there is some wisdom in slotting this into play, given that, as we have indicated, it is barely credible to think that the self-other regarding distinction could be sustained as a clear divide. Human life just is not susceptible to firm compartmentalisation, and even the deceptively simple self-other regarding spheres of life seem to have obvious overlaps. A person's individual downtime to read, listen to music, drink some coffee, or garden, is seldom free for long from other-regarding responsibilities, duties and obligations. This suggests that human life operates more on an organic spectrum than along divisions. We must keep these matters in mind as we examine how Mill progresses his argument.

The next move is, in something of an aside, to dismiss the view that human society is based on a contract, meaning to refer to the tradition of social contract theory: Mill affirms that society 'is not founded on a contract', and that 'no good purpose is answered by inventing a contract in order to deduce social obligations from it…'. (IV: 3).

At a stroke, and without feeling a need to develop the point, the social contract theory[1], as employed variously by other political philosophers, is punted into the long grass. Mill has no regard whatever for such theories as may be found in the political philosophies of Hobbes, Locke and Rousseau, whereby in some way, human individuals conceived as naturally free and distinct are thought to come to some compact, contract or deal to construct the phenomenon of society.

Mill instead relies more on his third view, of society as civil society, as the organically developed operative base for individual life. Mill says that for this broader context of life, 'everyone who receives the protection of society owes a return for the benefit, and the fact of living in society renders it indispensable that each should be bound to observe a certain line of conduct towards the rest'.

Mill's view is clear: we do not have contracts: we owe obligations. He then lists the conduct by which each individual could be bound – coming to some points we considered earlier.[2] An individual's conduct must not injure any 'interests' of others. By 'interests', Mill now has a little more that is specific in mind. He means those regarded as rights through 'express legal provision' or by 'tacit understanding'. Here Mill expresses varied senses of how rights might be understood. The phrase 'express legal provision' refers to what can also be termed the 'constituted rights' of persons, meaning matters given definition and protection as entitlements through the law. These can be legally defended as positive rights: the rights to liberty are given legal defence in this sense, but given the legal provision entailed, if an individual acts in a criminal way against similar interests of others, then legal means might be enacted to roll out the procedures of justice and the individual could lose her rights to liberty. The 'tacit understanding' of rights refers to our everyday assumptions of the rights people have to be as they are and to do as they do without infringements. Scarre's example of observing the rules of taking your place in a queue in a shop or a medical surgery is a good and helpful illustration.[3] Queuing is not a matter covered by the law, so the person who barges in is not liable to legal punishment – but will face social and moral disapproval, and Mill thinks this is the appropriate response.

Other socially impregnated rules impact on individualised decisions in the setting of queues. A person might be joining a queue in a supermarket with a fairly well-loaded trolly, while another person is looking to join at the same time with just

---

[1] Mill is in similarly against social contract theory in *Utilitarianism*, describing it as a 'contrivance' and 'fiction' - see *Util* V: 28. Hobbes, Locke and Rousseau offer variant views on the human condition, positing anthropologically dubious state of nature theories involving liberty or freedom, and proffering some deal, settlement or contract by means of which society comes into being. Locke we noted earlier but Thomas Hobbes (1588-1679) is best known for his work *Leviathan* (1651), a work of devastating power on the human and political state of humanity. J-J Rousseau, as also noted earlier, was influential in the mid-eighteenth century challenging a number of the assumptions of the so-called age of reason. His *The Social Contract* (1762) had deep and disturbing influences on the French Revolution. See Hobbes (2008); Locke (2013) Rousseau (2012).

[2] See Chapter 7 above.

[3] Scarre (2007) p. 85.

a few items in a basket: the person with the trolly might well give way to the person who has to pay for just a few items. Even the legal-tacit distinction over rights can show flexibility related to individual decision-making: the distinction is important, but it is also the case that, in practice, these types of rights can fuse.[1]

The next point Mill makes is that every person should 'bear his share' of the costs of 'defending society or its members from injury or molestation'. The share of the cost should, Mill thinks, be arranged 'on some equitable principle', by which he means that the taxation used to meet the costs of defence should be raised proportionally against the relative levels of income within the membership of society. When Mill says that it is 'society or its members' that have to be defended, he is not muddled over his idea that society is simply the total of the individuals from which it is constituted: when he says 'members', he is referring to this view of society, and when he mentions 'society', he means civil society, 'society' in the third sense we identified earlier.

Consistent with this, Mill adds some further points relating to what can also be done by society. Social opinion can be used to justly punish those whose actions are 'hurtful to others or wanting in due consideration for their welfare'. This may be justified even though what has been done may not have violated their 'constituted rights'.

What this reveals is that in social life, Mill accepts that general opinion can rightly intervene with the liberty of sovereign individuals over aspects of their conduct that has a prejudicial effect on the interests of others. It remains 'open to discussion' as to whether the 'general welfare' is enhanced by the interference of society, for it is to be noted that Mill is merely saying what society 'can' or 'may' do; he is not saying that it must take this action. However, with regard to actions and matters that are self-regarding, Mill denies that there can be this sort of doubt, for, over this species of activity, there is no scope for social interference. There is 'perfect freedom, legal and social' over actions and consequences pertaining to individuals and concerning them alone.

Disinterested Benevolence and Mannerly Disputes (Paragraph 4)

Mill turns to matters that he appreciates might arise as a criticism of the view he is developing. If persons as individuals are to be encouraged into self-development and creativity, with the liberty principle guiding them so that they do this at their own risk and do not harm others, it might seem that what is being promoted is an attitude of 'selfish indifference' (IV: 4). Mill is keen to dampen down any suggestion that this is his view. Self-interest was seen as a prime motivator for human action in the thought of Jeremy Bentham and his father, and it harks back to the view of Hobbes. Mill does not want to associate his newer principles with this

---

[1] There are everyday examples of this on the roads of the USA and Zambia, where motorists encounter 4-Way Stops, junctions where the rule is that the first to come is first to go. Road rules like this are a part of legal provision, but in their operation, a great deal of traffic flow is maintained by 'tacit understanding' – for example, a motorist might be second in turn at a 4-Way Stop but lets a large truck entering the junction third to go on through to save the driver having to stop and start his large and heavy vehicle.

narrower variant of utility. By picking up on this point, he can reinforce the coherence of his sense of working with reference to 'utility in the largest sense, grounded on the permanent interests of man as a progressive being' (I: 11).

Given that 'man' is the generic term for humans, the 'interests' that are at stake in and through the project of *On Liberty* are not solely individualised. Mill offers the corrective, that it would be a 'misunderstanding' of his view to see it as one that 'pretends that human beings have no business with each other's conduct in life, and that they should not concern themselves about the well-doing or the well-being of one another, unless their own interest is involved' (IV: 4). Mill might refer here to his notion of each person being 'the proper guardian' (I: 13) of his or her own development, but stretching the idea to embrace well-being in a wider interpersonal and social sense. He does not do this explicitly, but instead, he introduces a related idea, that of disinterestedness, in terms of 'disinterested exertion' (IV: 4) and 'disinterested benevolence' as dispositions that could work to 'persuade people to their good'. Mill thinks this far better than any more draconian means and again alludes to the task of education as including the cultivation of both 'the self-regarding virtues' and 'the social'. As in education, so in life, Mill wants 'conviction and persuasion' rather than 'compulsion', and it is the former means that have the longer-term benefit in life, to propagate the 'self-regarding virtues' upon which depends human development.

Mill comes to a newly forged sense of relational human insight:

'Human beings owe to each other help to distinguish the better from the worse, and encouragement to choose the former and avoid the latter. They should be forever stimulating each other to increased exercise of their higher faculties and increased direction of their feelings and aims towards wise instead of foolish, elevating instead of degrading, objects and contemplations'.[1]

'Help' is the key term here because Mill is emphatic that in dealings between adults, those of 'ripe years', no one can tell anyone else that they cannot do what they have chosen to do for their own benefit. Each individual is the best judge or 'proper guardian' (I: 13) of their own interest and well-being, so no other person, nor society, can impose an alternative on him and can only have a possible interest in intervention if the person's conduct is orientated towards others in a harmful way. Mill has a point of inestimable significance within his outlook on liberty. Interventions by society that 'overrule' a person's 'judgement and circumstances' are likely to be 'misapplied to individual cases' because those who operate the intervention are no more likely to know the real circumstances of the case than any other outside observer. Mill means that the sovereign individual is a better self-regulator of his or her own conduct than any external agent of society. Mill develops this in a passage recalling parts of his passage on the 'one very simple principle' (I: 9):

'In the conduct of human beings towards one another it is necessary that general rules should for the most part be observed in order that people may know what they have to expect; but in each person's own concerns his individual spontaneity is entitled to free exercise. Considerations to aid his judgement, exhortations to strengthen his will, may be offered to

---

[1] Here Mill rehearses his sense of the lower and higher pleasures found in *Utilitarianism*: see *Util* II 4-8.

him, may be obtruded on him, by others; but he himself is the final judge. All errors which he is likely to commit against advice and warning are far outweighed by the evil of allowing others to constrain him to what they deem his good' (IV: 4).

As in the statement of the liberty principle, we might argue with, urge, encourage or warn someone to get them to reconsider, not their views, but their conduct – but we would not be justified in taking distinct action against them – and were we to do so we would be likely, in Mill's view, to do more harm than would otherwise accrue from the conduct in question. The advised policy has a ring of good sense if we consider how others may differ from our own view of what makes for the best way of life in general. However, Mill says 'all errors' and this covers a multitude of matters where someone might be unwittingly undertaking something highly risky or inexplicable.

We can consider the following:

1. Suppose I see someone using a chain-saw on a tree.
2. Being well-trained in using the chain-saw, I consider that the person in question is at risk because he is not wearing protective gloves or goggles.
3. Further, he appears to be cutting the tree so that it will fall onto a neighbour's house.
4. I judge that action is needed to halt the errant sawing.

Here we can rightly think that more harm will come if we simply advise and warn, that we need to intervene and halt the sawing.

On 'Self-Regarding' Faults and 'Moral Vices' (Paragraphs 5-8)

Mill does not pick up on such issues at this stage. Instead, he attends to the interpersonal dynamic and the issues concerning the self and other-regarding modes of life he has held in the frame of discussion. He considers first how a person's 'self-regarding qualities or deficiencies' (IV: 5) might influence others. Mill thinks it is inevitable that a person's qualities will bear on how others respond and react. If a person has a host of 'the qualities conducive to his own good' in the sense of being 'nearer to the ideal perfection of human nature', then such a person is 'a proper object of admiration'. If a person has the reverse of these qualities, the assumption is that he or she will become 'a subject of distaste' or 'even of contempt'. How we are in the world is influential on the others we encounter. That a person may not actually harm anyone directly by being 'a subject of distaste' (or worse) is not the point. How a person appears to be will cause others to react and, in the worst cases, act pejoratively in relation to those whose conduct is considered reprehensible.

Mill then comes to the point we made with our example of the chain saw operator: sometimes, Mill allows, we may be said to be 'doing a service' to the individual concerned if we were to give a warning to forestall a 'disagreeable consequence'. Warnings, rather than active interventions, are allowable in the battle plan of liberty as Mill sketches it, so here we get partial support to save the neighbour's house from the wayward chainsaw operative.

Mill is keen to elaborate a point of emphasis on the matter of warnings, saying that 'the common notions of politeness' are an inhibition against what would be of real 'service' to others, namely 'if one person could honestly point out to another that he thinks him at fault, without being considered unmannerly or presuming'. In like manner, a person is entitled 'to act upon our unfavourable opinion of anyone, not to the oppression of his individuality, but in the exercise of ours'. This is a typical point in *On Liberty*: we are, in the defence and development of our own individuality, right to act so as to avoid the company of someone we consider unwholesome, and we could go further:

'We have a right, and it may be our duty, to caution others against him if we think his example or his conversation likely to have a pernicious effect on those with whom he associates'.

In his mannered idiom, what Mill is dealing with is the not unfamiliar business of removing someone from our circle of associates because we consider them, in highly technical terms, a waste of space or someone whose conduct or ideas (or both) cause us unease. Given what he has written about the ideal of civilized society, and the organic nature of progressive humans, Mill sees this as a significant reduction, and he fine-tunes the manner of human association to calibrate the pattern of conduct individuals can undertake. A person might present as rash, obstinate, as full of 'self-conceit' or as incapable of living 'within moderate means; who cannot restrain himself from hurtful indulgence; who pursues animal pleasures at the expense of those of feeling and intellect'.[1] Such a person cannot be surprised to be thought less well of by others, and his associates might be justified in giving 'others a preference over him in optional good offices, except those which tend to his improvement'. In these ways, a person suffers the consequence of their own self-regarding faults. The penalties come as 'the spontaneous consequences of the faults themselves'; they are not punishments purposely inflicted.

These points all apply to how a person is in respect of their self-regarding life, and what we again notice is that the self-other relationship is highly porous. A person's self-regarding sphere of life is embedded in the social world, and so whether there are positive or negative exemplifications of what it is to be human, there are reactions and consequences. These responses are altogether more emphatic where what a person does directly impacts the other-regarding sphere of life. If we engage with life and bring about acts injurious 'to others' (IV: 6), if we encroach 'on their rights', if we inflict on them 'any loss or damage' without good reason, if we enter into 'falsehood or duplicity in our dealing with them', if we do anything by way of being 'unfair or ungenerous in our use of advantages over them', including putting self-interest over 'defending them against injury', then we might face any or all of the following: '… moral reprobation, and in grave cases, moral retribution and punishment'.

Mill is keen to point out that negative acts come from poor 'dispositions' that might be considered 'immoral and fit subjects for disapprobation which may rise to abhorrence'. A number of undesirable qualities are given – 'cruelty', 'malice and

---

[1] Here Mill again reflects the distinction between higher and lower pleasures that he makes in *Utilitarianism*. See *Util* II:4-8.

ill nature', 'envy', 'dissimulation and insincerity', 'irascibility on insufficient cause', 'resentment disproportioned to the provocation', 'the love of domineering over others', 'the desire to engross more than one's share of advantages', 'pride' from 'the abasement of others', and 'the egotism which thinks self and its concerns more important than anything else and decides all doubtful questions in its own favour'. Mill has a dozen undesirable offences here, and he elects to term them 'moral vices' that cumulatively signal 'a bad and odious character'. He explains that these offences differ from the self-regarding faults considered earlier – they are not 'immoralities' and do not constitute 'wickedness'.

Mill wants to stress the importance of the point that the 'duties to ourselves are not socially obligatory unless circumstances render them at the same time duties to others'. The circumstantial point is again the fissure that renders this whole distinction a fragile construct. Nevertheless, the point Mill wants to make unfolds with the view that the notion of duty helps emphasise that serious problems only arise for the individual when he or she commits 'a breach of duty to others'. With this sense of duty, Mill means nothing along the lines proposed in deontological ethical theories – he means duties of the social sort, the everyday personal, professional and work-related obligations that innumerable individuals in Mill's time and our own regularly encounter. In contrast, self-regarding duties, those duties we owe to ourselves – 'prudence', 'self-respect' and 'self-development' are mentioned – for these, Mill wants to say, we are not 'accountable' to others, 'because for none of them is it for the good of mankind that he be held accountable to them'. The deeper good for humanity is not developed or progressed through the censure of how other people live and care for themselves. So long as they do not directly harm others, sovereign individuality remains Mill's imperative.

Mill next wants to ensure that the distinction between the consequences of excess in our self and other-regarding forms of life is understood to be significant and 'not merely nominal' (IV: 7). In one's self-regarding actions, we might do something to lose personal dignity and then suffer a 'loss of consideration' from others. If, however, we offend 'against the rights of others', we are likely to face 'reprobation'. The differences of impact on the individual are what Mill wants to make clear, and, against an imagined offender, he says the following:

'It makes a vast difference both in our feelings and in our conduct towards him whether he displeases us in things in which we think we have a right to control him or in things in which we know we have not. If he displeases us, we may express our distaste, and we stand aloof from a person as well as from a thing that displeases us; but we shall therefore feel called upon to make his life uncomfortable'.

Mill states this with assurance, but it is a different matter to assume that this is an easy or straightforward business to transact. Judging what is and what is not a matter of feeling and conduct where we have rights of control over others is complex. What Mills rests on is the thought that it will be a matter for individuals to judge over how other people who displease us and, at our own risk and peril, take actions so that the other person faces the consequences. The idea is that having taken 'the whole penalty', the aim will be to recover his good sense and ease him back into a proper association with others. We will not tend to see such a person as an enemy of society.

It is, however, 'far otherwise' with the person who has 'infringed the rules necessary for the protection of his fellow creatures, individually or collectively'. In such cases, the outcomes, in terms of the 'evil consequences of his acts do not then fall on himself, but on others'.

At this juncture, Mill is happy to endorse the right of society, 'as the protector of all of its members' to take action against the offender. Sounding suddenly very much a retributionist on punishment, with a liberty-related sense of getting the punishment to fit the crime, Mill says society may 'inflict pain on him for the express purpose of punishment, and must take care that it be sufficiently severe'. Although we get no idea from Mill about how severe this sufficient level of severity is, he thinks it needs to be noticeable and just, yet, for all the severity, in a fashion consistent with liberty:

'...it is not our part to inflict any suffering on him, except what may incidentally follow from our using the liberty in the regulation of our own affairs which we allow to him in his'.

As Mill has established, a person develops his or own individuality at his or her own 'risk and peril' (III: 1). If in the exercise of her liberty, a person infringes the rights of others and causes harm, then society, must operate within the canons of liberty and justice to enact punishment, with the removal of the offender's liberty of action and association being a just form of punishment.

Challenging the Self and Other-Regarding Distinction (Paragraphs 8-12)

Mill next turns to the problem we have had in mind for some while, that of the ease with which the self and other-regarding distinction can be maintained. We said earlier that it seemed a rather porous distinction and that, if pressed, it was artificial to think that human life could be helpfully compartmentalised. An organic spectrum to chart the relational dynamic of human regard, flowing between the self and the others, seems a more fruitful and more plausible way to go if we want to depict the range of human relations.

Mill has affirmed with some confidence the self-regarding and other-regarding modes of life, but he now considers the problem as identified in the form of the objection that this is a distinction that 'many persons will refuse to admit' (IV: 8):

'How (it may be asked) can any part of the conduct of a member of society be a matter of indifference to the other members? No person is an entirely isolated being; it is impossible for a person to do anything seriously or permanently hurtful to himself without mischief reaching at least to his near connections, and often far beyond them. If he injures his property, he does harm to those who directly or indirectly derived support from it, and usually diminishes, by a greater or lesser amount, the general resources of the community. If he deteriorates his bodily or mental faculties, he not only brings evil upon all who depended upon him for any portion of their happiness, but disqualifies himself for rendering the services which he owes his fellow creatures generally, perhaps become a burden on their affection or benevolence; and if such conduct were very frequent hardly any offence that is committed would detract more from the general sum of good'.[1]

Even if such a person merely harms himself, he indirectly harms others by setting a bad example and 'ought to be compelled to control himself for the sake of those whom the sight or knowledge of his conduct might corrupt or mislead'. Mill adds to the force of this argument against his own position by taking an analogy from the view that society has the right to guide and take charge 'of children and persons under age' (IV: 9). If that is so, then does not society have the same right to control and manage those of 'mature years who are equally incapable of self-government?' Those who fall prey to gambling, drunkenness, idleness and uncleanliness are amongst the possible states where self-governance falls away. These states are liable to be as 'injurious to happiness and as great a hindrance to improvement' as the things prohibited by and also punishable under the law. So why not apply the same measures of legal control to these extreme self-regarding faults? Why not sanction a strong wave of opinion, in effect 'a powerful police' to combat these errors or vices, and to use penalties as severe as any we might use for other crimes against society?

In a challenge to the claim that individuality can only develop in an atmosphere of freedom is the view that there is no threat to individuality 'or impeding the trial of new experiments of living' because the activity of tighter control is simply aiming to prevent excesses in matters which 'have been tried and condemned' time out of mind. Experimental living does not need to be granted to all so that gambling or drunkenness can again be tried and found wanting; it is time, the critic might say, to move on.

Mill develops these points with his usual resolve to present the strongest views he finds to contest with those he wants to promote. However, he does not consider the criticisms of the significance of the self and other-regarding distinction to have real weight, and he moves to repel them with three main lines of discussion.

First, Mill agrees that, as in cases of gambling or drunkenness, the person committed to these activities in their self-regarding mode of life 'may seriously affect, both through their sympathy and their interests, those nearly connected with him, and to a minor degree, society at large' (IV: 10). Indeed, when cases like this lead to the violation 'of distinct and assigned obligations to any other person or persons, the case is taken out of the self-regarding class and becomes amenable to moral disapprobation in the proper sense of the term'. If, due to drink or the excesses of gambling, a person cannot pay his debts or support and educate his family, 'he is deservedly reprobated and might be justly punished'. Mill is then very precise: the criticism and the possible punishment come, not for the act of excess, but the 'breach of duty to his family or creditor'. He is clear in not wanting to castigate anyone for this or that activity, whether it is gambling, golf or writing books on philosophers – but any activity an individual might undertake in the self-regarding mode of life is problematic if it causes the individual to fail to discharge standing obligations and commitments. Again, if writing this book means that duties owed

---

[1] This passage often proves confusing to students of *On Liberty* as sometimes they miss the qualifying 'it may be said', and read the passage as one of Mill's positive statements: in fact, he is rehearsing an alternative to his preferred view.

to my family are neglected, that breach of duty will rightly bring censure, criticism and perhaps, some form of punishment.

Mill illustrates this point variously. One example is the fictional case of the character George Barnwell, who murders his uncle to get money for his mistress. Mill's observation is that had Barnwell wanted to use the money set up in business, he would still face a capital charge. Here Mill means that the act of murder is an act of extreme harm to others that circumstances cannot much mediate.

The more famous examples are of the hypothetical soldiers or policemen who are found drunk. If they are off duty, this is not a particular problem, for no one 'ought to be punished for simply being drunk'. However, if a soldier or policeman is 'drunk on duty', assuming they cannot discharge their duty, they should face punishment. This example is consistent with Mill's earlier points about the issue being the breach of duty, and he concludes that in all cases where 'there is a definite damage, or a definite risk of damage, either to an individual or to the public, the case is taken out of the province of liberty and placed in that of morality or law'. Mill did not apply his reasoning to the case of a train driver who was drunk, just as we might extend this to cover an airline pilot or a motorist. In all such cases, being on duty while under the influence of alcohol would be an offence on the premise that dutiful actions will be impaired and others endangered if the intoxicated driver or pilot undertakes his or her duty. Mill's idea that the policeman or soldier cannot rightly be drunk on duty expresses the same prohibitive, not reactive, principle for action.

The second line of defence for liberty over self-regarding actions comes in reflections on those whose excesses 'neither violates any specific duty to the public nor occasions perceptible hurt to any assignable individual except himself' (IV: 11). In other words, suppose a person's drunkenness is simply a matter of self-regarding harm. Here Mill thinks society must bear the hurt for 'the greater good of human freedom'. Mill thinks there should be no case for society to consider that, for its own sake, it has a duty of care towards adults who go astray in their self-regarding activity. It is not as if society has not had a role in inculcating the values that would give the individual the means to make wiser choices. Society has had 'absolute power over them during all the early portion of their existence; it has had the whole period of childhood and nonage in which to try whether it could make them capable of rational conduct in life'. A society has mastery of 'the training and the entire circumstances of the generation to come'. If it cannot perfect them, Mill says this is due to the imperfections of society, but he would be more consistent to see this as a consequence of the fallibility of the human condition – something he writes about clearly earlier in the text.

Developmental thinking to the fore, Mill suggests that all-round, society should aim to make each succeeding generation better than the last, but even so, perfection will never be attained. What society cannot do is to 'pretend' that as well as all the years of childhood, education and training that it has, it also needs 'the power to issue commands and enforce obedience' on those who, as individuals, should be free to act 'and to abide by the consequence'. Mill thinks if a society is so weak in managing affairs when it has charge of the young, such that they are still like children and limited in their capacity to act with the 'rational consideration of distant motives', it is the society that is to blame, not the individuals.

Elaborating his point, Mill says that there is nothing that more discredits and frustrates 'the better means of influencing conduct than a resort to the worst'. The worst forms of influence are those which are retrospectively applied by a heavy-handed society playing catch-up to make amends for its own failings in the moral and rational education of those who were in its care. Such activity is illegitimate and is more likely to inspire rebellion 'against the yoke'; it will be seen as 'a mark of spirit and courage to fly in the face of such usurped authority'. The trouble with this is that the outcome is seen as troublesome as the cause was ineffective. An example is given, drawn from history, alluding to the contrasts between the excesses of the English Restoration, which succeeded the 'fanatical moral intolerance of the Puritans'. The conclusion is that if a person fails in the self-regarding sphere of life, society is better off not intervening and, instead, seeing the example as instructional. If society tries to remedy or prevent this sort of thing, it will fail in any case, and it will blur the lesson that can be taken from errors in the self-regarding sphere of life.

Mill's third defence against those who deny the distinction between the self and other-regarding spheres of life is, he thinks, 'the strongest argument against the interference of the public with purely personal conduct' (IV: 12). The point is very stark and direct, for when the public, or society, interferes, 'the odds are that it interferes wrongly and in the wrong place'. Mill explains and defends this view with a slick sense of how 'society' should be understood. When society, in the sense of a civilized community, is dealing with matters of 'social morality, of duty to others', then in general, public opinion is more often than not right. This is because there is a correlation within the public view of matters that are of wider social concern.

Less satisfactory is the following:

'... the opinion of a similar majority, imposed as a law upon the minority, on questions of self-regarding conduct is quite as likely to be wrong as right, for in these cases public opinion means, at the best, some people's opinion of what is good or bad for other people, while very often it does not even mean that – the public, with the most perfect indifference, passing over the pleasure or convenience of those they censure and considering only their own preferences'.

Here society is viewed in the pejorative sense, and an aspect of the mechanics of the tyranny of opinion becomes clear – a popular general view abstracted into law to be applied to all, but in a way that imposes too great a constraint on the individuality of those in the minority. Mill sustains the view that there can be no benefit to assuming the continuity and so the applicability of popular opinion:

'... there is no parity between the feeling of a person for his own opinion and the feeling of another who is offended at his holding it, no more than between the desire of a thief to take a purse and the desire of the right owner to keep it. And a person's taste is as much his own particular concern as his opinion or his purse'.

What Mill appreciates here is the importance of defending a tolerance of breadth and range in how people, individually or collectively, find ways to express and develop their feeling and tastes, as well as their opinions and plans for life. That our views are seen as analogous to a purse or wallet is evocative of the value we should place on them, and we can usefully recall that humans are more akin to trees than to machines: it would thus be detrimental to the quality of life and to how humanity could develop as autonomous yet relational individuals if all tastes were subordinated to that of French Impressionism, if all legitimate feelings were those evoked by summer rain, or if all opinions were regulated by the criteria of British empiricism.

Mill's idea of the intellectual economy for life is analogous to going to a large and busy market: there is variety, range, choice, and many ways to go, with a spot of bartering to add to the max. As in the market, so in the intellectual economy, there is benefit in that not everyone is alike, the same, or uniform, and that independence of choice and personal development is given by the liberty given to each and shared by all.

Mill's promotion of variety and openness to diversity is in counterpoise with his suspicion and dislike of the elevation of public opinion into a kind of ideal that can be presented as a universal truth for all. Rather than the quest for universal truth, humanity would be wiser to reflect on 'universal experience', but Mill regrets that, generally, 'the public' manifestly does not concern themselves with that either. His view emerging is that a good step forward in defence of liberty of action if individuals abstained only from 'modes of conduct which universal experience has condemned'.

The suggestion is that the teachings of most 'religion and philosophy' as in the work of 'moralists and speculative writers' assume that particular views of what is good and right are good and right for all. From this comes a 'standard of judgement' presented as an appeal to the feeling that 'things are right because they are right'.

The sense we have is that the wider public is not going to be too inspired to seek out from this the 'modes of conduct' to avoid: instead, the suggestion is 'we' – meaning most people – build from the deep feelings 'in our own minds and hearts for laws of conduct binding on ourselves and on all others'. Thus the 'poor public' falls into this disposition of making 'their own personal feelings of good and evil... obligatory on all the world'. Mill's opposition to this habitual tendency leads to his next line of assault.

The 'Moral Police' (Paragraphs 13-21)

Mill thinks that the abstraction of some ideals and values into ideals and values expected from all, as in the waves of moral and religious opinion that are projected as social norms, comes as 'the public... improperly invests its own preferences with the character of moral laws' (IV: 13). This gives rise to what he terms a 'moral police', an overriding feeling and attitude to govern what is deemed right that is imposed so that it 'encroaches on the most legitimate liberty of the individual'. As we have seen before, anything in Mill's register of values that 'encroaches' is usually suspect.

Mill wants to show that he is not working against 'imaginary evils'; he thinks there are 'abundant instances' (IV: 13) of the problem of the 'ascendant power' (IV: 16) of majorities of social and moral opinion, and he sets out several illustrations, which, as in earlier parts of the text, are mainly taken from the religious dimension of life. He discusses the tensions caused in presumptively Christian lands by the eating of pork, which causes problems for Islamic citizens (IV: 14).[1] He looks at the dominant Catholic tradition in Spain that prohibits other forms of devotion (IV: 15); at the way that the Puritan tradition has reduced the scope for people to enjoy a wide range of entertainments and pursuits, 'especially music, dancing, public games, or other assemblages for purposes of diversion, and the theatre' (IV: 16).

Picking up on earlier reviews of democracy, Mill notes how the democratic principle in the United States leads to an outlook that resists a 'more showy or costly style of living' than that of the majority (IV: 17) – subsequent history suggests that Mill did not have to worry for long on this matter. However, he reviews the campaigns in 'one English colony, and of nearly one half of the United States' (IV: 19), where it has become illegal to produce alcohol apart from for 'medical purposes'; then the legislation that prohibits activities on the Sunday due to 'the determination not to tolerate others in doing what is permitted by their religion, because it is not permitted by the persecutor's religion' (IV: 20); he ends the chapter by looking at the criticism that has been made of the Mormons, some of whom 'sanction polygamy' (IV: 21).

Mill's point in these reviews is that they each involve in some way the reflection of the attitude of a majority or a significant group, an attitude of deep moral or religious sentiment held dear, and which leads the group to want to impose respect for its view, or even that view itself entire, on the whole of society in matters that are self as well as other-regarding. Mill sees much that is problematic in this:

'There are… gross usurpations upon the liberty of private life actually practiced, and still greater ones threatened with some expectation of success, and opinions propounded which assert an unlimited right in the public not only to prohibit by law everything which it thinks wrong, but, in order to get at what it thinks wrong, to prohibit a number of things which it admits to be innocent'. (IV: 18)

In the examples Mill gives, he thinks that in each, we see the predilections and preferences of some, even of a majority, being imposed as a general expectation on all, so that those individuals or groups of individuals who dissent and who feel, think and act differently, feel the weight of criticism that comes from the majority feeling, the force of the 'moral police' (IV: 13), and in some circumstances, the imposition of the law.

The countering view is that the situation in each case would have its frailty and fallibility exposed if we imagined the reverse of each case. For example, in switched circumstances, where Islam was ascendant, the domination of the taboo on pork would become as problematic for non-Islamic citizens as the situation for Islamic people in Mill's example. A strong view emerging is that Mill affirms that over 'the personal tastes and self-regarding concerns of individuals the public has no business to interfere' (IV: 14).

To explore this thinking in more detail, we will examine what more Mill says about the issues raised by drink and the Mormons.

---

[1] In the text of *On Liberty* Mill does not use the term Islam – he refers to 'Mohammadens' and 'Musselmen' – terms often used in nineteenth century writing. Mill worked before the development of thought in the areas of religious studies where the fusion of linguistic, historical, phenomenological, hermeneutical and philosophical skills led to rather more fruitful insights into the human experience of religion.

The Issue of Drink (Paragraph 19)

The problem of drink is an important example or case study for Mill. Alcohol created a significant social problem in what we would now call the UK, but in major cities especially. The long history of freedom over who brewed or distilled what and for whom makes for a case study of the risks and perils of the liberties of choice and action. By the mid-nineteenth century, one growing reaction was the so-called Temperance Movement, which had a major impetus from the founding of the Temperance Society in 1832.[1] Temperance involved signing a pledge to give up alcohol for life, and the temperance theme spread and was common to Chartism, the Friendly Societies, The Trade Unions, Methodism, and aristocratic philanthropy.

Reviewing this matter, Mill refers to how several states in the United States had introduced and then quickly repealed legislation prohibiting the production and distribution of alcohol. The laws were impractical and could not be imposed, and even in the state from which the legislation 'derives its name' (IV: 19) – this being an allusive reference to what was known as 'the Maine Law' since it was first passed in the state of Maine in 1851.[2] Mill then refers to 'professed philanthropists in' Britain who are keen on a law akin to the Maine Law being introduced, and in this connection, he refers to the 'Alliance', meaning The United Kingdom Alliance, founded in 1852. This was formed for the purpose of getting legislation to support the broad sweep of the Temperance Movement.[3] Mill refers to a debate between the Alliance, through its secretary, Samuel Pope, and the politician Lord Stanley, which took place through letters published in *The Times* in October 1856.

Mill supports Stanley in his criticisms of the Alliance's policies, appreciating his ability to expose the extent to which the Alliance's outlook impacts on liberty. Mill quotes Stanley as seeing the Alliance as touching on matters that are to be dealt with as 'relating to thought opinion, conscience' (IV: 19) and 'to be without the sphere of legislation'. The implication is that the key matters pertaining to drink lie principally within the self-regarding sphere of private life, not the public domain of other-regarding action. Mill wants to focus on the 'acts and habits' that are 'individual', as he thinks this has not been drawn out in the debate in *The Times*.

Mill does this with a typically neat switch of emphasis, seeing how there is a socio-economic issue in the matter that upsets the coherence of the prohibitionists:

'Selling fermented liquors... is trading, and trading is a social act. But the infringement complained of is not on the liberty of the seller, but on that of the buyer and consumer; since the State might just as well forbid him to drink wine as purposively make him impossible to obtain it'.

The Alliance's view is that the social right should be claimed – again, Mill quotes from the correspondence in *The Times* – 'to legislate whenever my social rights are invaded by the social act of another'.

---

[1] See https///spartacus-educational.com/REtemperance.htm
[2] See *OL* p. 156 n. 27.
[3] See *OL* p. 157 n. 28.

In other words, if a person's social right to a peaceful evening with friends is upset by the noise of drunken revelry, then that person has the right of recourse to the law.

As Mill presents it, the Alliance view suggests that 'the traffic in strong drink' can be said to 'invade' the 'social rights' of individuals who have 'a primary right of security by constantly creating and stimulating social disorder'. Worse, it 'invades' the 'right of equality by deriving a profit from the creation of a misery' the suffering individual is 'taxed to support'. Then it 'impedes' the individual's 'right to free moral and intellectual development' through presented unwanted 'dangers' and 'weakening and demoralizing society'. However, from this society, the harassed individual has 'a right to claim mutual aid and intercourse'.

Mill aims to draw out the worst possible implications from the Alliance's views to deliver the most severe blow to the notion at the heart of the defence of the view that society would have the right to impose a prohibitive law and policy on the activities of individuals. The notion is that of 'social rights', and Mill has things to say that flow from his earlier disregard of 'abstract right' (I: 11). All that the notion of 'social rights' signifies is, says Mill:

'That it is the absolute social right of every individual that every other individual shall act in every respect as he ought; that whosoever fails thereof in the smallest particular violates my social right and entitles me to demand from the legislature the removal of the grievance' (IV: 19).

Thus the notion of 'social rights' emerges as Mill's focus for criticism. It is, he suggests, a principle that is 'far more dangerous than any single interference with liberty':

'There is no violation of liberty which it would not justify; it acknowledges no right to any freedom whatsoever, except perhaps to that of holding opinions in secret, without ever disclosing them'.

Mill thinks the notion of 'social rights' licenses every subscriber to the rights in question to summon all the powers of opinion and law to remove anything considered 'noxious'. The idea 'ascribes to all mankind a vested interest in each other's moral, intellectual, even physical perfection, to be defined by each claimant according to his own standard'.

Mill has presented liberty as a principle where the liberty of each gives the best possible context for the development of all through the innovations of some; 'social rights', by comparison, offer the reverse. The implication of the suppression of all by any act or expression of thought that offends in any respect anyone's standards, to the end that all innovative development will be suppressed.

Mill makes a very strong case against 'social rights', and he could apply the reasoning he uses against any of the other examples of intolerance that he considers. It is something of a problem that he centres this critique in the context of his consideration of the problems associated with drink, and here there is a particular difficulty.

Mill was not quite at a period when it was properly grasped that alcohol could be addictive, that drunkenness and alcoholic dependence could be a definable medical as distinct from a behavioural condition. Mill wants to say that the process of whether or not and what to drink, in terms of an alcoholic beverage, is a matter of individual choice and discretion, so, on the face of it, a clear instance of a self-regarding act. The problem of being drunk, or the probability of being drunk while on duty, is an equally clear case of an other-regarding act. Being incapable of discharging a duty could be the consequence of a range of other maladies, and the problem would always be that such and such a condition resulted in the breach or the probability of a breach of duty.

There is nothing here to persuade Mill that the production of alcoholic drinks for consumption should be banned in the name of 'social rights'. However, it is unfortunate that he sees this as simply a matter of personal responsibility, with drunkenness as a result of poor judgement or of being weak-willed. The idea that alcoholism might be symptomatic of personal despair and anxiety and that it might come about through addiction was not all that evident in the self-help ethos to which Mill is allied. Mill suggests that the temperance movement violates liberty by improperly imposing a particular view of perfection on individuals who, in their self-regarding mode of life, should have no interference: as we have seen, in other-regarding contexts, he thinks that the penalties suffered by the offender – say the drunkard – have a beneficial rather than harmful effect on society by providing an instructive example (IV: 11).[1] If that were true, and humans were automatically self-correcting fallible beings without the slightest hint of addictive tendencies, one would think that by now, there would be no tangible problems of this sort.

A redemptive feature of Mill's conception of social rights is that it anticipates a problem arising in modernity. If we take Mill's point 'that it is the absolute social right of every individual that every other individual shall act in every respect as he ought' as well as the proposed corollary, 'that whosoever fails thereof in the smallest particular violates my social right and entitles me to demand from the legislature the removal of the grievance' (IV: 19), we have a recipe for prominent trends that have emerged. The social rights of some not to be offended by the colonial aspects of history, of others not to be upset by criticism of trans rights, or of open academic discussion by writers or composers who are male and white – all such protagonists exhibit what Mill identifies – groups who feel violated by any who deviate from actions and commitments that accord with their favoured view.[2]

All this runs counter to the ethos of *On Liberty* and to the view that the 'complete liberty of contradicting and disproving our opinion is the very condition which justifies us in assuming its truth for purposes of action; and on no other terms can a being with human faculties have any rational assurance of being right' (II: 6).

---

[1] See *OL* IV: 11 as considered above.
[2] We look at these issues in Chapters 13-15 below.

Mill and the Mormons (Paragraph 21)

The chapter ends with a relatively extended discussion of the Mormons, which was a relatively recent religious movement forged in the United States of America at the time Mill was writing. A brief sketch of the origin of Mormonism will set the scene for what Mill wants to say about it.

As a tradition, the Mormons trace their origin to a revelation claimed to have been given to a teenager, Joseph Smith.[1] His story was that in 1823, an angel – Moroni – revealed that Smith had been chosen to read and translate the 'Book of Mormon', an allegedly Fourth Century text said to be laid out on gold plates in a cave in Upper New York State. Smith's story, from his later testimony, is that he was then led to the cave to perform this task. *The Book of Mormon* was duly published in 1830, and the new, true faith was proclaimed, related to Christianity, but an upgraded version through the revelations of *The Book of Mormon*. Over the next few years, Smith established Mormon churches and communities in various states in the Midwest. However, Mormonism claimed a form of exclusivism, which encouraged separatist tendencies amongst the followers, as well as antagonism to other religious traditions. This led to criticism, and in 1844 Smith and some followers were arrested on a charge of treason.[2] A few months later, a mob in jail murdered Smith and his brother, creating martyr status for Mormonism's prophet. Another follower, Brigham Young, became the new leader, and he took the Mormon community West, aiming to move to the northern part of Mexico, an area of bleak austerity with few others in residence.[3] Hardly had they arrived when the conclusion of the war between the United States and Mexico (1846-1848) meant that the area the Mormons had settled in was in the USA – and in what became Utah, at Salt Lake City, which duly became and has remained the base for the Church of the Latter Day Saints, as the Mormons are more formally called.

Mill thinks that the 'language of downright persecution' (IV: 21) employed in press comments about the Mormons shows 'little account' of the forms of 'human liberty' that he promotes. Criticising and trying to enforce change on a group's beliefs does not sit well with Mill's defence of the liberty of thought and expression. However, we also soon discover that Mill is not impressed by Mormonism: he considers it to be 'the product of palpable imposture', but at the same time, and in the modern age of 'newspapers, railways and the electric telegraph', it has grown into a sizable body of people. He is aware that the movement has set up 'in the midst of a desert' and thinks that, but for the inconvenience of this location, there are some who would like to go and persuade 'by force' the Mormons to a more conventional position. What causes the greatest criticism of the Mormons is 'its sanction of polygamy' – and Mill, never noted for his sense of humour, sees this as ironic since polygamy is a feature of a number of other religious traditions – the problem here is that it is found in an English-speaking group who 'profess' a form of Christianity.

One might suppose that Mill will argue against the critics, that the principle of liberty and the freedom to develop a plan of life to suit one's life and character will

---

[1] Joseph Smith (1805-1844).
[2] The exclusivism of Smith's teaching ran against the American Constitution's defence of freedom of worship.
[3] Brigham Young (1801-1877).

allow, subject to risk and peril, and the harm to others clause, the freedom of people (men in this case), to have a sequence and so a number of wives, so long as the parties involved are freely consenting to this arrangement. He does not quite do this, however. He concedes that the women who enter into such arrangements may be said to be doing so 'voluntarily', but they are doing this in very particular circumstances, and Mill does not think this is in line with the principle of liberty. Accordingly, he makes his own position on polygamy clear:

> 'No One has a deeper disapprobation than I have of this Mormon institution… because, far from being in any way countenanced by the principle of liberty, it is a direct infraction of that principle, being a mere riveting of the chains of one half of the community, and an emancipation of the other from reciprocity of obligation towards them'.

Mill thinks there is no equity of liberty in polygamy. Anticipating ideas he later expressed in his *The Subjection of Women*, Mill is crystal clear in thinking that reciprocal obligation between the marital pair is the right and proper arrangement consistent with the principle of liberty. What polygamy does is offer a variant on 'teaching women to think that marriage is the one thing needful' and making it 'intelligible' that this could be 'as one of several wives', in preference to 'not being a wife at all'.

Mill thinks that as the Mormons do not look to impose their teachings on others, and as they have moved to a formally uninhabited zone in the world and 'been the first to render it habitable', it means that it is difficult 'to see on what principles but those of tyranny they can be prevented from living there under what laws they please, providing they commit no aggression to other nations and allow perfect freedom of departure to those who are dissatisfied with their ways'.[1] As we know from our past encounters with 'tyranny', there is little in Mill's pejorative vocabulary to equal the intensity of this as contrary to liberty. In the name of liberty, the Mormons could be preached against by missionaries, and alternative teachings could be presented to them. But, says Mill, no community has an obligation to attempt a '*civilizade*', a crusade to civilize another community. His idea is that the wider civilized community is better off discussing the issues – or polygamy in this case – than trying to eliminate what could be seen as a retrograde step in the development of the human condition. Mill seems to sense that any other action against the Mormons would make them martyrs for the freedom of belief.

This brings Mill to a conclusion that might be considered deeply pessimistic, redeploying his notion of barbarism as discussed earlier:

> 'If civilization has got the better of barbarism when barbarism had the world to itself, it is too much to profess to be afraid lest barbarism, after being fairly got under, should revive and conquer civilization. A civilization that can thus succumb to its vanquished enemy must first have become so degenerate that neither its appointed priests and teachers, nor anybody else, has the capacity, or will take the trouble, to stand up for it. If this be so, the sooner such a civilization receives notice to quit, the better. It can only go from bad to worse, until destroyed and regenerated (like the Western Empire) by energetic barbarians'.

---

[1] More recently, the Mormons have been more evangelical than Mill found them to be in his own time.

These remarks are wholly consistent with Mill's view that humans are, individually and so collectively, fallible. Humans are, individually and so collectively, capable of self-development, but there is no guarantee that the development will be of improvement.

Mill is, to leap toward historians of modernity, less in line with Francis Fukuyama's notion of the 'End of History' and more akin to Paul Kennedy's sense of the 'Rise and Fall of the Great Powers'.[1] Mill does not envisage an end of historical development where human life settles into a contented stasis: he calculates that the quality of life for fallible individuals and cultures can go up and down.

As to the 'energetic barbarians' and the fall of the Western Empire, Mill refers to the various tribal groups, including the Goths, Vandals and Huns, who had the skill and tactics to defeat the Roman legions and sack Rome in 410 and 455. Mill is a well-read enough historian to know that these barbaric victors did not engage in the widespread slaughter of the defeated Romans, nor did they reduce Rome to rubble. They may not have had a rich culture of literature and thought to draw on, nor a history, but they had plenty of energy, power and force, and through the ensuing period, they gradually embraced the learning and devotional culture of Christian monasticism. In due course, the successive movements of the Renaissance, the Reformation, the Enlightenment and the Romantic age gave rich evidence of cultural regeneration. Mill's point is really a health warning against the dangers of custom and mediocrity, that this fall and rise could recur.

In this chapter, Mill touches on matters that merit further consideration, not least the self and other-regarding spheres of life. His next chapter also focuses on these matters, so we will defer a review until the end of the next chapter

---

[1] Francis Fukuyama's book *The End of History and the Last Man* (1992) suggests that the liberal democratic state is the end game for human development. Paul Kennedy's *The Rise and Fall of the Great Powers* (1988) looked at the rise and fall of societies between 1500-2000, concluding that the human condition resists long-term stability. See Fukuyama (2020) and Kennedy (2017).

11. *On Liberty*: V: 'Applications' (Paragraphs 1-23)

Introduction – 'Specimens of Application' and Maxims (Paragraphs 1-2)

With the final chapter of Mill's *On Liberty,* we come to a package of material slightly different in character from that found in the last three. In those, Mill was mainly setting out, reviewing and defending aspects of the liberty principle and the limits of the authority of society over its constituent membership of individuals. In this chapter, Mill aims to clarify the doctrine of liberty by reviewing some 'specimens of applications' (V: 1). He means to take some examples of issues and concerns that should sharpen the sense and role of the concept of individual liberty he has defended as well as to the role of society concerning the individuals of which, he thinks, it is composed. In practice, he considers what we might term case studies to examine the wider practical application of his doctrine. This means that the drift of the chapter is something like the last part of the previous chapter, where Mill explored some instances of misplaced authority being deployed by society over individuals. However, to put all this in perspective, we need to give careful focus to the opening remarks of the chapter, where Mill gives his readers a great deal of food for thought:

'The principles asserted in these pages must be more generally admitted as the basis for discussion of details before a consistent application of them to all the various departments of government and morals can even be attempted with any prospect of advantage'.

The first part of this statement is, in effect, the prelude to Mill's explanation that he will be moving to consider 'specimens of application', but what is striking is the explicit ambition for the project of *On Liberty* in the second half of the sentence. Nothing less than 'all' of the 'various departments of government' as well as 'morals', by which Mill assuredly means the domain of public morality to have the 'principles asserted in these pages' applied to them.

Within his own lifetime, Mill was conscious of operating as a public intellectual: here, he considers that *On Liberty* will be an overture to a more considered 'application' of liberty to governmental activity and public attitudes and expectations concerning morality. It is unclear what Mill exactly had in mind with this 'application'. Again, it is no kind of spoiler alert to say that Mill did not ever pen a direct sequel to *On Liberty* in which the principles within the text were used to analyse the machinery of government. The *Considerations of Representative Government* (1861) gives attention to the issues and questions raised by representative democracy. To some degree, his reference to 'morals' is borne out by the publication of the articles on utilitarianism in 1861, subsequently published as *Utilitarianism* in 1863 – as well as by *The Subjection of Women* in 1869. All round, Mill seems to be indicating his assumption that *On Liberty* will itself have an impact commensurate with Mill's aspiration.

For readers with a keen sense of the progress of ideas in *On Liberty*, the reference to the 'principles asserted in these pages' will also provoke some reflection. It is natural to think back to at least the 'one very simple principle' (I: 9) and then consider that it has been developed to focus on both the freedom of thought and discussion and then the liberty of action to the end of developing individualism. But Mill lobs another provocative comment into play with the measured statement of his new hope. He has a plan:

'To bring into greater clearness the meaning and limits of the two maxims which together form the entire doctrine of this essay, and to assist the judgement in holding the balance between them in the cases where it appears doubtful which of them is applicable to the case' (V: 1).

Clearly, the 'one very simple principle' (I: 9) has undergone some form of development. What Mill has done is to finesse the 'one very simple principle' into 'two maxims' which focus on the liberty of action and cement into place his favoured but troublesome notion of self and other-regarding interests.

The 'two maxims' are as follows:

'Firstly, that the individual is not accountable to society for his actions in so far as these concern the interests of no person but himself. Advice, instruction, persuasion, and avoidance by other people, if thought necessary by them for their own good, are the only measures by which society can justifiably express its dislike or disapprobation of his conduct. Secondly, that for such actions as are prejudicial to the interests of others, the individual is accountable and may be subjected either to social or to legal punishment if society is of the opinion that the one or the other is requisite for its protection' (V: 2).

Here Mill writes with considerable economy, focusing on the domain of action and to the interests of the individual and then those actions that are 'prejudicial to the interests of others'. There is no detail or development of the nature of the 'interests' Mill has in mind, but it is not unreasonable to think that he has in mind the matters discussed earlier – those interests as 'considered as rights' (IV: 3), either by 'express legal provision or by tacit understanding'.

The first maxim restates Mill's view on the liberty of action, defending the individual's liberty of action over matters that are of no concern to any person 'but himself'. Others who disapprove may express this by offering advice, instruction and warnings. In the last resort, if they think it will be for their own good, they can avoid the person in question.

With the second maxim references such actions by the individual that become 'prejudicial to the interests of others'. Here the individual is 'accountable' to society 'and may be subjected to either social or legal punishment'. Mill layers the points on this other-regarding wing – the individual 'may be' treated to social or legal measures, but only if society – civilized society through its legitimate offices – takes the view that 'one or the other is requisite for its protection'. A line of implication seems to be lurking within this phrase: society can determine whether it needs protection from individuality; society will have to decide whether a form of social or legal punishment is better suited to the case, and in what form and degree. As in previous discussions, a strong impression emerges that Mill thinks that society – the rest of us – is seldom justified in restricting the actions of other individuals, even if they annoy and challenge us. The liberty of thought and expression is not included in these two maxims. This perhaps signals Mill's confidence that the case he made earlier in the text is sufficient, that over his own mind, the individual of mature years is sovereign.

Legitimate Competition (Paragraph 3)

Mill next points out that in life, cases arise where individuals are in situations of 'oppositions of interest' (V: 3) in terms of competing for a job in a 'crowded profession' or undertaking a series of competitive examinations. Society, through the individuals that make it up, has an obligation to ensure that all such competition for appointments or examinations is undertaken free from 'fraud or treachery, and force'. However, that is all: Mill favours what is now termed differentiation by outcome: through the examination series or the rounds of interviews, there will be winners and losers, and the interests of some will be progressed at the expense of others. In such a situation, the losers had 'no right, either legal or moral' to expect 'immunity' from suffering.

Mill thinks it is clear that it is 'better for the general interest of mankind that persons should pursue their objects undeterred by this sort of consequence', and society certainly cannot have a social or any other type of right to claim that 'disappointed competitors' should be free from the 'suffering' and distress of competition. Mill does not consider any issues along the lines of positive discrimination or of allocating a principle of sexual equality for appointments in boardrooms, professions or workplaces in general. Aside from wanting to remove all inequalities in law between women and men, it is a moot point whether Mill would consider artificial equalising policies more important than the developmental progressions that flow from a pure meritocracy.

Trade, Poison, and Preventative Measures (Paragraphs 4-6).

Turning to trade, a vital matter to Britain's economy in the nineteenth century, Mill reaffirms that trade is 'a social act' (V: 4) because the processes of production, distribution, and retail sales involve the interests of several persons. Mill is writing at a time when trade was operational at not just a national but also an international level. Mill sees trade as a clear area of legitimate concern for society. In the past, this concern has been shown in the regulation of prices by the government through the rules and controls on working conditions and rates of exchange. In more recent times, the laissez-faire or free trade approach that had come to bear through the nineteenth century and, as championed by Ricardo, James Mill and Mill himself, involved a greater reliance on the power of the market forces to freely determine the trading pattern. It also reflects the view that in trade, as in life:

'… all restraint, *qua* restraint, is an evil'.

In contrast, Mill thinks:

'Both the cheapness and the good quality of commodities are most effectually provided for by leaving the producers and sellers perfectly free, under the sole check of the buyers for supplying themselves elsewhere'.

According to Mill, the 'free-trade' doctrine 'rests on grounds different from, though equally solid with, the principle of individual liberty asserted in this essay'. Mill is eager to point up the errors of society looking to inappropriately restrain things, as such meddling fails to bring about the best outcomes. Trade should be free, but it may seem that 'public control is admissible' for a number of checks and balances. Such matters as sorting the means by which 'fraud by adulteration' is avoided, making arrangements for sanitary conditions within the workplace, and protecting the workforce in dangerous occupations are mentioned. Public control is legitimate, but Mill's view is that it is, as ever, better to 'leave people to themselves' rather than 'controlling them' overmuch. Once again, he refers again to the Maine Law and the issue of the importation of opium into China as cases where there was an issue of liberty – in these cases, what Mill is looking to defend is the liberty of the buyer, which is inhibited by the restrictions on trade.

Mill also refers to the specific matter of trade in poisons – meaning preparations used to combat vermin. He probably chose this as debates over the registration of pharmacists and attempts to legislate over the registration and sales of poison were features of public life in the 1840s and 1850s. It was in 1868, while Mill was serving as MP for Westminster, that The Pharmacy Act was passed, doing a good deal of what Mill argues about in *On Liberty*.

In the background, the Pharmaceutical Society had been founded in 1841, and various measures were introduced so that by the early 1850s, the title of Pharmacist was limited to those who were in membership of the Society. When the 1868 Act was passed, it was notable in not restricting pharmacists by sex, and many women were amongst the first to be in practice.

Writing a decade before this endgame, Mill looks at the matter of poisons as it 'opens a new question: the proper limits of what might be called the functions of police: how far may liberty be legitimately invaded for the prevention of crime, or of accident' (V: 5). On the one hand, Mill wants the buyer to be free to choose what to obtain and from the most economic source; on the other, the police, as the agents of social concern, have, like those in the medical profession, a preventative function: so what preventative duties might legitimately invade the liberty of individuals to, for example, purchase poison? When the 1868 Act was passed, such poisons as Strychnine and potassium cyanide were regulated – conditions for the sale of Arsenic had already been included in an earlier Act – but under a separate schedule of the act came Opium and its derivatives, including laudanum.

With respect to the 'preventative function', the matter of 'taking precautions', Mill thinks this 'is far more liable to be abused, to the prejudice of liberty, than the punitive function'. This is because the free activity of human life is rich in possibilities for 'delinquency', leading to an over-protectionism that inhibits the potential for development. However, circumstances alter cases in Mill's view, so if either a 'public authority' – a policeman – or a 'private person' sees someone about to commit a crime, they 'may interfere to prevent it' – we are not advised to 'look on inactive until the crime is committed'.

Mill does not illustrate this with poison as a test case. Instead, he asks us to imagine that a policeman or a private individual sees another person about to cross a bridge thought unsafe. If there were no time to warn the person, we would be justified in physically stopping him. This would not contradict that person's liberty, because 'liberty consists in doing what one desires, and he does not desire to fall into the river'. Mill adds that if we are in such a situation as this, but 'where there is not a certainty, but only a danger of mischief' – then only 'the person himself' can judge about the risk: he can be given a warning, but not 'forcibly prevented from his action'. Only if we find someone who is 'a child, or delirious' or in a condition of some abstraction might we intervene.

Mill applies a similar line of thought to the sale of poisons: he points out that if the only purpose for buying poison were to commit murder, then it would follow that we would rightly legally prohibit 'their manufacture and sale'. However, poisons are usually needed for 'innocent' and 'useful' purposes, and Mill thinks that some appropriate labelling to make clear the potency of the poison would serve well – he cannot imagine that anyone would want to buy something and not know that it has dangerous capacities. He thinks that requiring certificates from a medical practitioner would make the process too expensive and time-consuming. However, he suggests applying a variant form of a legal process, termed 'preappointed evidence'. In the case of buying poison, it would entail some formalities of making the purchase a type of contract between the buyer and seller, to record and register the 'quality and quantity sold' to make it clear to the purchaser the importance of using poison for the right purposes.

Mill has already given drink and the issues arising attention, and he returns to reconsider the problem of drunkenness to elaborate on his idea that there are occasions where society can act 'to ward off crimes against itself by antecedent precautions' (V: 6). Mill's residual view is that so long as a person causes no harm to others, drinking remains a self-regarding act. It may be that excessive drinking is a form of misconduct, but this does not justify action against the drinker. However, we know from the review in the previous chapter that drinking can become other-regarding and thus be a matter of legitimate concern and action. Thus if harm comes to others in consequence of the drinker's state, or if he fails to discharge his duties, action is appropriate.

Mill now offers a further justification for control. He considers that if a person has been convicted of a violent offence against another when drunk, then it would be appropriate to place that person under a 'special legal restriction' so that if on a subsequent occasion he or she was drunk, they 'should be liable to a penalty' – and if they reoffended with an act of violence against another, then a more severe penalty would follow. Mill does not indicate what he has in mind with any specific details, but he seems to favour a registration and licensing system for those inclined to drink, and one assumes he might think this was extendable to other modes of crime and punishment.

A slight problem with Mill's plan is that having said that drinking in the self-regarding way of life is not a matter for social action, someone who has drunk, become violent, and so rightly been punished is not, in Mill's proposed scheme, able to achieve redemptive innocence through completing the initial punishment.

Once that person is out and about and enjoying the odd drink, any hint of being slightly over the limit of sobriety and irrespective of no offence being given, a penalty is due based on a form of pre-emptive legal control against a potential act.

This is, presumably, an instance of what Mill defines as action against the risk of 'harm to others' (I: 9). It is a far from compelling example: Mill says nothing about how exactly publicans and the police are to manage this as a practical problem. That Mill abandons the principle of the presumption of innocence is a more serious problem for his view of how social controls might operate. Mill is, perhaps, working more with the idea of how what we know about a person's life as a whole ought to be taken into account when that person comes to court to face an accusation. The usual view is that the case in question is the only relevant matter and that the person's past form is covered by a blanket of secrecy under the presumption of innocence. With his treatment of those with a record of drunken violence, Mill is moving to the view that in investigating offences, the person's past usefully informs the present and so the future. This gives quite a lot of scope to social monitoring and control, and one might think, offers a high risk for the increase of the kind of interference or encroachment on life Mill is keen to reduce.

Mill does not reflect on this issue but adds a brief rider to the discussion by referring, not to those who are drunk but to those who are idle, and says that a person who, through idleness, neglects to support his children can, without 'tyranny', be forced to meet his obligations, 'by compulsory labour if no other means are available'. Again, it is unclear how exactly society will execute mandates to control this, but the comment is useful in another sense, as it touches on the relationships between parents and children, which is a matter Mill returns to later in the chapter when he considers issues concerning education. The point to see is that Mill has a strong belief that parents have obligations to children: he does not see that society has a like obligation: the child is not an agent with liberty living within society, but living under the guidance and support of the parents who, in Mill's view, chose to bring them into the world, and who therefore have the clear responsibility for them, their welfare and their education.

Public and Private Acts (Paragraphs 7-10).

Mill turns to matters that embrace 'offences against decency' (V: 7). With this definition, he skirts around the point that there are matters considered indecent by what could termed the moral majority. The argument brewing is that acts or proceedings that some disapprove of on moral grounds should not be liable to legal prohibition: Mill does not put quite so directly, but he comments that 'there are many acts which, being directly injurious only to the agents themselves, ought not to be legally interdicted' – meaning they should not be guarded against by the law. On the other hand, the same acts, 'if done publicly, are a violation of good manners and, coming within thus within the category of offences against others, may rightly be prohibited'. Mill adds that such actions violate 'good manners' and offend against 'decency', and he adds that on this, 'it is unnecessary to dwell, the rather as they are only connected indirectly with our subject'. This last comment is puzzling and obscure since it is plainly the subject of *On Liberty* to unpack the implications of both the 'one very simple principle as entitled to govern absolutely the dealings with society in the way of compulsion and control' (I: 9), and the affirmation that 'over himself, over his own body and mind, the individual is sovereign'. The upgrade given by the two maxims at the start of this chapter makes clear the self and other-regarding distinction, and we are in very much the same dynamic with Mill now using the interface between the private and public domains to point out that some things that are to be free from interference are so free as they take place in private, at, one assumes, the risk and peril of the participants, while if they took place in a public arena, there would be a series of other-regarding offences to deal with due to 'a violation of good manners' (V: 7) that constitutes a form of harm to others. This is directly, not 'indirectly', concerned with Mill's subject, and what it would be helpful to know is what sort of violations Mill envisages such that we should be worried about giving offence to public manners?

Mill gives no illustrations in this paragraph, but in the next paragraph, he refers to soliciting, to 'fornication' and gambling' – and he also returns to the problems of alcohol (V: 8).

If we consider the points made to do with private and public acts and issues of decency, the arrangements people make for conducting sexual relationships are a likely option for what Mill has in mind.[1] On Mill's liberty principle, it would seem that if two adult people arrange to meet in private for a consensual sexual encounter, at their own risk and peril, then as a private encounter, it cannot be subject to other-regarding stipulations. Suppose, however, the romantic couple meets and conducts their affair in a crowded public park or at the Epsom Racecourse on Derby Day. In that case, their actions have a high probability of violating 'good manners' (V: 7). They also offend against decency and against such actions, Mill thinks that social disapprobation and perhaps the penalties of the law are all legitimate reactions. Mill might also consider other things best kept in private, which would not be decent in a more sociable context. Two people might discuss what they really think of a third party in private: we could give much more offence if discussing that person's alleged shortcomings openly in the pub or coffee shop. Gambling might be acceptable as a private activity but not something to bring into the public domain.

These points illustrate what Mill seems to mean with his comment that there are 'many acts which, being directly injurious only to the agents themselves', are, if conducted in private, not liable to legal restrictions. How far these are wholly self-regarding matters, even when conducted privately, is another matter. For example, two people meeting for sex in private do not offend against public decency; the matter could be wholly consensual and reciprocal. However, if adultery is committed, the act may prove to be directly injurious to the adulterer, even if the adulterer does not care about this at the time. If two people are dismantling the character of a third party in private, the comments and tone of the conversation might not reflect well on either person, and this could be injurious to either or both of them in their future relations.

Mill moves on to consider an underlying matter that has a deep resonance for any defender of liberty. This comes from the type of 'cases of personal conduct supposed to be blameable, but which respect for liberty precludes society from

---

[1] Mill has some reason to consider this matter. In 1857, it was estimated by the metropolitan police that in London, some 8,600 prostitutes were at work and that here were about 2,825 brothels. See Reeves (2007) p. 281.

preventing or punishing because the evil directly resulting falls wholly on the agent' (V: 8). The question that Mill looks at is if a person – 'the agent' – is at liberty to do something – 'ought other persons be equally free to counsel or instigate?'

Mill's point resides in the nature of transactional exchanges, a great many of which are unproblematic. Suppose I choose to buy some vegetables, and I go to the market – I go there because I can find plenty of traders selling a range and variety of vegetables, and I can review, discuss and haggle over the ones I might or might not buy. Suppose I want to devote some free time to flying a kite: I go to a sports shop, and it is possible, right and legitimate for some kite salespersons to be on hand for me to consult over the type and size of the kite that would be best for me. I can discuss and review the options and decide whether or not to make a purchase. There is nothing contrary to the principles of liberty here: 'Whatever it is permitted to do, it must be permitted to advise to do'.

Consistent with this, those selling vegetables or advising on and selling kites charge for what they sell sufficient to be rewarded for their services. All this is unproblematic relative to the canons of liberty. Problems arise, perhaps, when 'the instigator' makes money from the advice and 'makes it his occupation' through something that 'society and the State consider to be an evil'. Vegetables and kites aside, suppose the advisor conducts business dealing with either fornication or gambling; here are two areas of activity of which many in society will disapprove, but Mill's point is that whatever the social evils that are feared, these advisory services 'must be tolerated'. Matters of which we disapprove are fit for debate but not for prohibition. The issue for liberty is whether 'a person' should 'be free to be a pimp, or to keep a gambling house?' On the basis of 'whatever it is permitted to do, it must be permitted to advise to do', these activities must be permitted.

Mill is looking for consistency. If it is not illegal for two people to commit fornication, then it seems intolerant to make criminal an occupation of enabling such a practice. Mill appreciates that there can be 'arguments on both sides' as to where to draw the lines of limitation on what degree of liberty to permit. Nevertheless, when Mill has a matter to hand and an issue of a limit to liberty arises, he is usually inclined to favour liberty over limitation. So it is in this case: he thinks that the liberty principle and its variant maxims suggest that 'society has no business, *as* society, to decide anything to be wrong which concerns only the individual; that it cannot go beyond dissuasion, and one person should be as free to persuade as another to dissuade'.

The alternative to this is for the social conscience – with the spectre of social rights haunting the scene – to elaborate a view that says that if something is seen as an activity that can lead to harmful outcomes for the agent, their obligations or for their dependents, then society can reasonably operate to 'exclude the influence of solicitations which are not disinterested'. Similarly, while people would be free to gamble in the privacy of their own homes or private clubs funded by subscription, 'public gambling houses should not be permitted'.

Having given two sides of the argument, Mill reflects on the problems of prohibition, focusing on how hard it is to ensure that no places are open for gambling and how easy it is for such activities to carry on in secret. Secrecy also implies problems of control and management, and so the cumulative view is that toleration and a degree of common sense should prevail, with weight being put on the view that it cannot be right to prosecute 'the accessory when the principle is allowed to go free'. In other words, it is a 'moral anomaly' to permit people to gamble, and then prosecute those who enable it.

Alcohol and related problems return for more thought, with Mill giving further reference to the Maine Law and prohibition on drink, and his view is that absolute bans are wrong on liberal grounds since those who deal in the supply of strong liquor are required to service the legitimate customer. To combat excesses, Mill – focusing on what we might think of as Off-Licenses and pubs – thinks that the State is justified 'in imposing restrictions and requiring guarantees'. Mill considers the use of higher pricing on alcohol as well as restricting the number of places for purchase to combat the social evil of drunkenness. He rejects the idea that 'stimulants' should face a higher taxation 'for the sole purpose of making them more difficult to be obtained' (V: 9) because this would differ 'only in degree from their entire prohibition'. The core problem he sees is that higher taxation increases the price so that those who cannot easily afford alcohol face prohibition.

Mill's thinking here, as before, regards drink as one among many commodities. What he says would work well for some products: Brussel Sprouts, for example: if these incorrigible components of a meal were subject to such levels of taxation as to make them unaffordable for most people, most people would find alternative vegetables. However, those with a dependency on alcohol will be forced by higher pricing on beverages to find other means of funding or obtaining the alcohol they need, at a likely cost to their other obligations.

As mentioned earlier, Mill is not alert to this side of the problem of drunkenness. He thinks consumers can and will use 'their own judgement' and continues to reflect on the inevitable move within societies to tax stimulants as a source of revenue – and in this respect, he considers that higher taxation is 'to be approved of'. He also reflects on how society is entitled to manage the premises that, as 'places of public resort' – public houses – where alcoholic drinks are bought and consumed, and where, Mill thinks, 'offences against society are especially apt to originate' (V: 10). What Mill favours became common practice: publicans should be licensed as people fit to run the establishment; there should be fixed hours for opening; establishments that appear to be a focus for problems could then be closed with ease by withdrawing the license – and so on. Mill thinks that society, through the police, can monitor public houses and keep matters in hand. He is not keen on reducing the number of 'beer and spirits houses' as this would be a hardship to the legitimate users, and he mistrusts the paternalism of those who would want to restrict and restrain the consumers, so treating them, not as free individuals, but as children.

Agreements and Engagements (Paragraph 11)

Mill next turns to the relation between the liberty of the individual in self-regarding matters and the 'corresponding liberty' (V: 11) that 'any number of individuals' share in regulating, 'by mutual agreement such things as concern them jointly'. Mill wants to move to a discussion about marriage, but he casts the opening of the review in terms more akin to the setup of some kind of business. The idea of mutuality through an association of individuals is that there is a collaborative and consensual agreement over the management and conduct of the business in question. All is well on the assumption that 'the will of all the persons implicated remains unaltered'. What Mill wants to explore is what happens if there is a change in the liberty of the will of some of the 'persons implicated'. He attends to the concerns we should have when individuals are considering or have entered 'into engagements with one another', mindful of the risk of minds changing. He is thinking of situations as in a business, where definite arrangements and formal legal protocols set out the responsibilities individuals make to each other within the association. If an individual does have a change of mind, Mill thinks that 'as a general rule, the engagements should be kept'. However, given his ideas of liberty and human fallibility, he also thinks that human agreements, including contracts for a mutual association, are not going to be free from situations where 'that will' of one or more individuals may change in a more fundamental fashion: this means that rules need exceptions:

'Not only persons are not held to engagements which violate the rights of third parties, but it is sometimes considered a sufficient reason for releasing them from an engagement that it is injurious to themselves'.

Taking a dramatic but sadly, still topical example, Mill says that in 'this and most civilized countries', no person would be able to enter into an engagement 'to be sold, as a slave' – for neither the 'law' nor 'opinion' would condone such an agreement. Society thus has a duty to limit a person's power and capacity 'of voluntarily disposing of his own lot in life'. Social action here shows 'consideration' for the 'liberty' of the individual. Mill uses the example to show a limit to self-regarding action that can remain free from any interference:

'His voluntary choice is evidence that what he so chooses is desirable, or at least endurable, to him, and that his good is on the whole best provided for by allowing him to take his own means of pursuing it. But by selling himself as a slave, he abdicates his liberty; he forgoes any future use of it beyond that single act. And he defeats, in his own case, the very purpose which is the justification of allowing him to dispose of himself. He is no longer free, but is thenceforth in a position which has no longer the presumption in its favour that would be afforded by his voluntarily remaining in it'.

Referencing the life of the individual at liberty, Mill then produces another of his crisper lines:

'The principle of freedom cannot require that he should be free not to be free'.

He adds that for the person, 'it is not freedom to be allowed to alienate his freedom'. Insofar as Mill is giving thought to the alienating act of a person who is freely selling himself into enslavement, he is generating a special kind of self-regarding act: the act of alienating one's own freedom by selling one's self into enslavement cannot be a usual type of self-regarding act, as to alienate one's own freedom in this way would curtail personal development and thereby diminish society. Society, as related to a community of civilized individuals, can therefore act to prevent people 'voluntarily disposing' of their life since it prevents a diminishing of its own number. This limitation on the freedom of action that individuals have is something Mill wants to relate back to the ways in which agreements or engagements can be binding. However, before we follow him in this, we need to pause, as the idea that a person has liberty, but not the liberty to dispose of that liberty, is something that readers of *On Liberty* find challenging.

Circumstantially, there might be occasions where a person might knowingly surrender their freedom to enter a state of enslavement to save someone else. In Hitler's Third Reich and Stalin's USSR, one can imagine this not to be an uncommon phenomenon. And one can imagine that many parents or grandparents might choose to enter a state of enslavement to protect their children or grandchildren. The notion of liberty that Mill presents could, in such circumstances as these, be enhanced by such sacrificial deeds, as instances of the exception proving the rule.

Riley suggests another defence for entering into slavery: a person could enter into enslavement willingly (for whatever reason) so long as the buyer does not use the slave to harm another person.[1]

Suppose the person selling himself lock, stock and liberty-bearing will into the ownership of another as a slave is happy with the pattern of life and activity that is promised or entailed. In that case, this is not contrary to the liberty principle, but, as Riley also suggests, things alter if the slave owner's plan for slave usage changes and our slave finds that he is caught between a rock and a hard place: he does not like the prospects ahead, but he has sold his capacity to choose to do something different. Everything hinges on the extent to which society recognises the contract. It is this matter, rather than the case of selling oneself into slavery, that Mill wants to review.

Mill's idea is that any agreements where individuals who operate with the principle of 'uncontrolled freedom of action' become 'bound to one another' should always have within them a means by which either party can be released from the engagement.[2] Mill thinks the only constraint would be arrangements that entailed a financial aspect, which would need to be sorted and settled before any other decision to end the deal. Here Mill takes a moment to distinguish his view from that of von Humboldt, who favours a set-up where even the most significant of engagements – 'marriage' – might be ended through the expression of 'the declared will of either party'.[3] Mill thinks this is too simple a solution for the complexities of human relations.

Another issue here is that in respect of slavery, Mill's focus on the extent to which a person might be bound by an agreement to enter a state of enslavement rather blurs the point that in the history of slavery down to the present, agreements have been conspicuous by their absence. The vast majority of enslaved people remain victims of crime, of abduction and enforced servitude of one sort or another. Mill would doubtless condemn this, but his concern with somewhat hypothetical considerations distracts him from such matters.

Continuing to reflect on human relations, and the condition of marriage, Mill thinks that if two people live in a reciprocal commitment, in marriage or close partnership, the situation means that each will come to envisage and plan their life on assumptions of continuity with the other, which creates a tier of 'moral

---

[1] See Riley (1998) p. 133.
[2] Mill has much the same argument again in *The Subjection of Woman*. See Mill (1988) pp. 41ff.
[3] See von Humboldt (1996) pp. 134-135.

obligations' between them. These need to be taken into account if one or the other wants to end the relationship. If the relationship is one of marriage, and if there are the interests of 'third parties' (children) to consider, more 'obligations arise', which makes the arbitrary ending of the joint commitment difficult. Mill does not argue that 'these obligations extend to requiring the fulfilment of the contract at all costs to the happiness of the reluctant party', but these obligations 'make a great difference' to 'the *moral* freedom' of the person involved.

Such a person:

'... is bound to take all these circumstances into account before resolving on a step which may affect such important interests of others; and if he does not allow proper weight to these interests, he is morally responsible for the wrong'.

Marriage is not as extreme a case as enslavement, but, in contrast with von Humboldt, as Mill sees it, marriage also provides a setting where the scope for '*moral* freedom' and liberty of action is constrained.

Family Matters and the Role of Education (Paragraphs 12-15)

Over the next three paragraphs, Mill develops the thinking he has been doing to deal with more issues of human relationships, treating some matters that deal with marriage, with children and with education.

Early in the text, Mill thought that a great deal needed to be done to determine the correct parameters of liberty. He returns to that point, noting that a persistent problem is that liberty 'is often granted where it should be withheld, as well as withheld when it should be granted' (V: 12). In 'the modern European world', he thinks the 'sentiment of liberty' is both strong and misplaced. Mill means there is a loose feeling abroad that liberty is a right and good thing – but it is not well understood, and it is misapplied.

This view allows Mill to re-state the corrective: an individual 'should be free to do as he likes in his own concerns; but he ought not to be as free to do as he likes in acting for another, under the pretext that the affairs of the others are his own affairs'. The 'pretext' is significant here, as Mill signals thereby that the human tendency to operate with inappropriate power over others is something that society or the State should maintain a 'vigilant control over'. Family life is the arena of life where things go wrong, Mill thinks, and he cites the 'almost despotic power of husbands over wives' as a singular example.

Again anticipating the ideas of *The Subjection of Women*, Mill affirms that 'nothing more is needed for the complete removal of the evil than that wives should have the same rights and should receive the protection of law in the same manner as all other persons'. This point makes a clear appeal to equality before the law and for an end to the legal anomaly of one person (the woman) becoming, in effect, a part of the property of the other (the man) at and through marriage.

Mill's writings and subsequent changes in the law show a harmonization of which he would doubtless approve – although marital and other interpersonal relations are probably destined to remain as areas of life where the personal and moral dynamics will always precede and transcend what is provided by the law.

What Mill is alert to is the scenario in his own time, which gives institutionalised legal discrimination in favour of husbands over wives. Mill sees the majority of men proud of being 'the champions of power' – power and might being, in Mill's here somewhat Hobbesian view, the basis for the control that historically held sway – a matter he details in his writing in *The Subjection of Women*.[1]

Mill brings children into the review, a matter that brings 'misapplied notions of liberty' into sharper focus, with reference to a situation that inhibits the State in one of its vital duties. Mill parodies the situation whereby one might think that 'a man's children were supposed to be literally and not metaphorically, a part of himself, so jealous is he of the smallest interference of law with his absolute and exclusive control over them'. What Mill knows well is that in the law of his day, a man's children are his responsibility until they reach the age of majority. But he also thinks that in the developing world it is, for example, an 'almost self-evident axiom that the State should require and compel the education, up to a certain standard, of every human being who is born its citizen'.

Mill is writing at a time before the establishment of state education in Britain, but there was debate growing over what forms of education might be best for children as well as over who might best provide a general education. There were private or independent schools, and many were operated by charities or out of philanthropy. The idea that the State 'should require and compel' an education for all up to a certain level is certainly an aspirational point, but it was not so pressing a matter in the political firmament of 1859.

It was not until 1870 that an Education Act established a system of elementary education, and 1902 before this was broadened to the beginning of a system of secondary education. What Mill says about education is nuanced, pertinent and radical, given the later trajectory of the State's interventions in education.

Mill affirms it to be the duty of parents to provide their children with an 'education fitting' for them to do well in life both for themselves and towards others. However, Mill notes that the reality is that there is no official obligation put on parents to provide an education. So urgent is the need to equip individuals in their youth with the capacity to develop that Mill values, that he sees it as imperative that the right style of education is encouraged.

Accordingly, he argues for substantial reforms in attitudes to education. It is 'a moral crime' to have children and not provide for their mental as much as for their physical development. Mill thinks the State is justified in seeing to it that parents make provisions for their children's education, for which the costs can be charged to the parents. However, it is important to see that Mill is not arguing for the provision of a general State education. His point is that the State has 'the duty of enforcing universal education' (V: 13). If this nettle were grasped, all the debates about whether and what 'the State should teach' would be replaced. The State should 'make up its mind to require for every child a good education'; it would then 'save itself the trouble of providing one'. It could leave parents to find and pay for their own children's education, and attend to provide aid to assist poorer families with fees, and 'defraying the entire school expenses' for those who had insufficient means. Mill does not give any space to consider what sort of administration would

---

[1] See Mill (1988) pp. 4ff.

be needed for this scheme. Instead, he reaffirms the key thought in this section of *On Liberty*:

> 'The objections which are urged with reason against State education do not apply to the enforcement of education by the State, but to the State's taking upon itself to direct that education; which is a totally different thing'.

Mill is eager to stress his opposition to a general education provided by the State, which he views as something he would 'go as far as anyone in deprecating'. He links the provision of such an education to the problems of despotism that, from the start of the text, have been his special target:

> 'All that has been said of the importance of individuality of character, and diversity of opinion and modes of conduct, involves, as of the same unspeakable importance, diversity of education. A general State education is a mere contrivance for moulding people to be exactly like one another; and as the mould in which it casts them is that which pleases the predominant power in the government – whether this be a monarch, a priesthood, an aristocracy, or the majority in the existing generation – in proportion as it is efficient and successful, it establishes a despotism over the mind, leading by natural tendency, to one over the body'.

Mill has other proposals for the State: it should set up some establishments to compete alongside other experiments in education. It could run these centres as exemplars of a good education. Only in an undeveloped nation would anything more be required by way of provision – in a developed society, just as the economy is running on the free market approach, so should education. Mill is confident there are plenty of individuals well qualified to offer the range and variety of schools that would be required.

It is a pity that Mill did not stay with this thought, and envisage a system of university and school examination boards to set out a system of public examinations grounded in the verities of the academic disciplines. Instead, and despite his examining experience from the East India Company, he thinks that the State – not to be trusted with a general education – could nevertheless set up a system of public examinations that would be age-related and start with a test to check that children could read. The trouble with this is that if the State sets the agenda for examinations, it defines what must be taught, and the curriculum becomes an instrument of control.

This has been all too evident in more recent UK educative history, in England, Wales and Northern Ireland at least, with the imposition of the National Curriculum from 1986-88, a notably top-down initiative led by the government. A feature of this process meant dispensing with the dual courses that schools used, the GCE O-level and the CSE[1] and replacing them by appropriating the newly developed Joint Examination at 16+ (the GCSE, as it became known). By adopting this examination system and encouraging the reorganisation and reduction of the examination boards, so turning them into larger, more bureaucratic organisations, the UK Government demonstrated that when the State establishes the regulative structure of examinations, it also presides over the definition of the curriculum, and it then

---

[1] Whereas GCE O levels were typically 250 minutes of traditional questions or problems, the CSE – the Certificate of Secondary Education, had been developed to test much the same material with more structured questions, and had introduced elements of centre-assessed and board moderated coursework.

regulates the curriculum's content, and so teaching and examining – so regulating and defining results. Mill's thinking here has rightly been seen as naïve.[1]

Smoothly carrying on in his reflection and locked into an other-regarding line of thought, Mill envisages a system of certified education covering a broad range of subjects. The State would set up the examination system, with Mill thinking they would not be permitted to intrude with ideas on content or lines of interpretation. Subjects would be set on 'facts and positive science', and in the humanities, the study would not be on 'the truth or falsehood of opinions' (V: 14) but on the foundations for views, the grounds for various outlooks, and so on. The aim would be for 'the rising generation' to be better instructed in the views that were available and from which their own views would be built:

> 'All attempts by the State to bias the conclusions of its citizens on disputed subjects are evil; but it may very properly offer to ascertain and certify that a person possesses the knowledge requisite to make his conclusions on any given subject worth attending to'.

Using a philosophical example, Mill thinks that a student working on modern philosophy might be expected to understand Locke and Kant and be able to give an account of either regardless of whether one or the other was a thinker with whom he or she had sympathy. All higher studies should, Mill thinks, be voluntary, and with an emphatic force, he says that it would be 'too dangerous' to give to governments the power to control entry to the professions. Governments can enable, but not exclude.

Mill is certainly aiming for an objective ideal of study free from the influences of doctrinaire or sectarian views. Getting to the bare 'facts' is probably a somewhat more complex a matter than he assumes, but there is in the reflection on education a sense of misfire: Mill has not been as thoroughgoing in his application of liberty as he could have been. His insight that the State should require but not provide a general education has liberal sense, and the implication would be a system of independent examination boards and schools with the variety and diversity that Mill alludes to, building to independent and voluntary study at the more advanced levels. Mill is right to emphasise the role of parental responsibility for their children over that of the State, but having taken power from the State, Mill gives it back in spades by suggesting that the examination system could be entrusted to the State, which guarantees that general education will be shaped, not by those with the academic expertise so to do, but by those who have political power and might.

Another area for seeing the problem of the 'misplaced notions of liberty' (V: 15) comes in the business of parenthood. Mill, like many others, thinks that 'causing the existence of a human being, is one of the most responsible actions in the range of human life'. To bring a child into the world without the means to support and nourish it, body and mind, is again, 'a crime against that being'. Mill considers the country to be in no danger of underpopulation, so it is a serious matter for children to be born if there are poor prospects for their education and future employment. To have children or not might seem to be a self-regarding matter, but given the third party of the child or the children, and their developmental potential, this becomes an other-regarding matter, where a measure of State control is appropriate. For Mill,

---

[1] See Scarre (2007) p.127.

the problem is that he is up against the convention he mentioned earlier, that people regard their children as personal possessions, as extensions of themselves. No localised policies or legislation exist for Mill to appeal to, so he refers to laws in European countries which do not allow people to marry until they can show that they have the means to support a family. This is a highly generalised reference, for it seems that only the Germanic state of Bavaria had such a scheme.[1]

Mill does not allude to his longstanding concern to promote birth control, but he thinks some kind of means test for prospective married couples is important to reduce the risks of the 'wretchedness and depravity' that befall families immersed in poverty due to the size of the family.

Mill reflects on the problem:

'When we compare the strange respect of mankind for liberty with their strange want of respect for it, we might imagine that a man had an indispensable right to do harm to others, and no right at all to please himself without giving pain to anyone'.

It is a misapplied sense of liberty for a man to think he has the liberty to marry and have children, given that unless there are prospects to provide for the family, liberty will produce harm to others as a direct consequence. At a deeper level, this reinforces the error of thinking a person can exercise liberty as a vital aspect of their development and identity regardless of the cost to others. This suggests that Mill's thinking, although it seems to propose an illiberal interference into personal life, is consistent with the sweep of his defence of liberty.[2]

The Issue of Government Interference (Paragraphs 16-22)

In the penultimate section of the paragraphs of *On Liberty*, Mill considers the question of the extent to which the state may act to interfere with the individual and social domain and where 'the reasons against interference do not turn upon the principle of liberty' (V:16). Instead, the issues are to do with the government's ability to perceive and act upon what can be seen as the general interest, to do things for the 'benefit' of individuals, rather than leaving it 'to be done by themselves'. In other words, is it right and good for the government to give benefits to individuals, rather than leaving them to achieve these benefits themselves, 'individually or in voluntary combination'. Mill clarifies at the outset that he is exploring the 'objections to government interference' in matters 'when it is not such as to involve infringement of liberty' (V:17).

Readers to this point of the text will get no prizes for guessing that Mill opposes the government acting to benefit individuals. He develops three lines of reasoning.

With regard to the first, dealing with economic matters, Mill is unequivocal and brief: 'there is no one so fit to conduct any business, or to determine how or by whom it shall be conducted, as those who are personally interested in it' (V: 18). Mill alludes to the fact that 'political economists' have dealt with this matter – and he means to include himself and his *Principles of Political Economy* – and the

---

[1] See Reeves (2007) p. 299.
[2] See Scarre (2007) p. 129 and Reeves (2007) p. 299.

226

arguments for private enterprise as distinct from a State-managed economy – what he terms the 'interferences' of 'the legislature, or the officers of government' with the processes of industry and business.

Mill then considers examples of activities where individuals may not do them well, and where government officials might do them better. He mentions jury trials as an example, where jurors come from the public and where it could be said that government law officers might better do the job. Mill disagrees. Society has a duty to the 'mental education' (V: 19) of individuals: to the 'strengthening of their active faculties, exercising their judgement, and giving them a familiar knowledge of the subjects with which they are thus left to deal'. Mill thinks officialdom should undertake this task and sees philanthropic and voluntary organisations as effective in this way, as instruments of 'development', being an aspect of a wider 'national education' to train and empower citizens, so taking them from 'the narrow circle' of their personal upbringing, 'and accustoming them to the comprehension of joint interests… habituating them to act from public or semi-public motives, and guide their conduct by aims which unite instead of isolating them from one another'. Mill is eager to stamp the themes of individuality and development to strengthen his notion of human beings as 'progressive' (I: 11).

The benefits of 'the union' of individuals in voluntary associations for business and other enterprises commends 'all the advantages which have been set forth in this essay as belonging to individuality of development and diversity of modes of action'.

The contrast is stark:

'Government operations tend to be everywhere alike. With individuals and voluntary associations, on the contrary, there are varied experiments and endless diversity of experience' (V: 19).

The government should concentrate on promoting means for discussion and the exchange of ideas, enabling 'each experimentalist to benefit by the experiments of others, instead of tolerating no experiments but its own'.

The third objection is that if the government acts to do good for individuals, so saving them the trouble of achieving those goods for themselves, government becomes accustomed to wielding greater power and causing its 'influence over hopes and fears to be more widely diffused and converts more and more, the active and ambitious part of the public into hangers-on of the government, or of some party which aims at becoming the government' (V: 20).

Mill mentions a range of endeavours within the nation – the roads, railways, banks, insurers, companies, universities, and charities – if all these were 'branches of government', the result would be a growth in administrative bureaucracy, and this would become a focus for a limited and limited ambition. Due to this risk, Mill opposes moves to bring in an examination entry for the civil service, as he thinks this will be too low an aspiration for many who would be better inspired by moving into voluntary and private sector activity where their individuality would acquire richer stimulations for development.

Using his contemporary world to illustrate the point, he considers that in Russia, the Czar is incapacitated by 'the bureaucratic body' who can enable or prevent any proposed measure by their own collective will. In other nations, the State may be held responsible for everything and overthrown when things go wrong – yet if the administrative bureaucracy does not change, things will go on as before. Mill thinks things have proceeded more effectively in France and the United States of America, as in both nations, there is a more confident ability amongst the people to 'improvise' and 'carry on' with matters irrespective of the frailties of government. However, we are left with no doubt that Mill considers administrative bureaucracies to be high on the list of the enemies of the individual – and so of society. Bureaucracies have the specific ability to manage 'an organization of the experience and practical ability of the nation into a disciplined body for the purpose of governing the rest' (V: 21). The better it becomes at this, the more the rest are put into a state of 'bondage'; this includes those in the bureaucracy too, who are 'as much the slaves of their organization' as anyone else.

The particular problem that a bureaucracy magnifies is that by drawing the 'principal ability of the country' (V: 22) into itself, it deals a severe blow 'to the mental activity and progressiveness' of the group of individuals from which it is constituted. The rules, routines and procedures by which it operates bring indolence, rigidity, and a lack of ability for innovation. Mill suggests that such a body needs as a corrective the stimulus of a further critical group of 'functionaries' to encourage and 'be willing to adopt improvements'. An interesting suggestion this, and one that Mill might have elaborated with reference to education. It would be applicable to see what he thought might work, given the emphasis he puts on the Government's role to require but not to provide a general education: he might have elaborated more on how effective and adaptive functionaries were to supplant the blanket of bureaucratic somnolence that seems likely to hamper active reforms of the type he seeks. Instead, he applies his thinking to the general business of governance.

On Liberty: The Endgame (Paragraph 23)

Mill has made clear his view that government intervention to bring benefits actually causes regressive problems. He knows that systems of administration are not exactly prone to melting like the Summer mists, and so he considers that what really matters is to make clear a method of reducing so far as possible the dangers of the machinery of government administration so that it is possible to maximise the 'well-being' (V: 23) of 'the collective application of the force of society'. The aim is to garner as far as possible 'the advantages of centralized power and intelligence... without turning into government channels too great a proportion of the general activity'. His proposal is for what today we might see as devolution: 'the greatest dissemination of power consistent with efficiency; but the greatest possible centralization of information and diffusion of it from the centre'.

Mill outlines a delegated system for local governance, modelled on the arrangements made in the New England states – where such arrangements fit well within the federal republic – and the Poor Law Board in Britain. The structure Mill favours in outline allows for representative local officers to be chosen to work alongside those 'directly interested' in their own businesses, and for each locality, there would be 'a central superintendence' to coordinate and disseminate information and knowledge. These bodies commune with the central government,

but the business and the work are done at the local level by those who are directly involved. Mill sees this as powerful and empowering, and in his final peroration, he commends it in the context of a final health warning against intrusive and inhibiting governance:

> 'A government cannot have too much of the kind of activity which does not impede, but aids and stimulates, individual exertion and development. The mischief begins when, instead of calling forth the activity and powers of individuals and bodies, it substitutes its own activity for theirs; when instead of informing, advising and upon occasion, denouncing, it makes them work in fetters, or bids them stand aside and does their work for them. The worth of a State, in the long run, is the worth of the individuals composing it; and a State which postpones the interest of *their* mental expansion and elevation to a little more of administrative skill, or of that semblance of it which practice gives in the details of business; a State which dwarfs its men, in order that they may be more docile instruments in its hands even for beneficial purposes – will find that with small men no great thing can really be accomplished; and that the perfection of machinery to which it has sacrificed everything will in the end avail it nothing, for want of the vital power which, in order that the machine might work more smoothly, it has preferred to banish'.

Alluding to machinery, Mill again evokes the alternative, the more organic view of the human condition as likened to a tree, so developing 'according to the tendency of the inward forces that make it a living thing' (III: 4). In contrast is the reality of large-scale government administration, with the phenomena of over-managed organisational structures. Mill's critical point is against all systems that assume that they can do better for people what people are better doing for themselves. That the ongoing worth and value of a community, a state, a nation, a friendship group or a family group, is the worth of the individuals that make it up is not just Mill's view; it does not require a long study of anthropology and the human and social sciences to see that this is a highly plausible insight into the human condition. It certainly appeals more than the views that suggest humans thrive best under systematic regulation, habit, custom and routines of habitual obedience.

Self and Other Regarding Life Revisited

A great deal of the discussion in Mill's last two chapters has to do with the tensi and areas of encroachment that comes between the other and self-regarding moc of life, between the wider public and the personal or private spheres of life. Mi thinking on this in *On Liberty* has been, in a key respect, consistent and, inde persistent from the start of the text. He has maintained that there is a signific distinction giving spheres of life that can be demarcated between the areas wl society can be engaged in matters and areas of activity or endeavours where soc has no case to interfere with individual self-activity. We have shown that in terms, but consistent with what Mill seems to think, the gap between what a pe does that impacts on and relates to others and what they do that is self-regar and so free from social intervention is porous, thin, slight, temporary and limi

---

[1] See *OL* I: 12 and Chapter 7 above.

For a considerable body of Mill scholarship, this estimate does not go far enough, for the way in which Mill sets out and deals with the self and other-regarding distinction is something many critics consider to be so badly conceived and weakly expressed as to be implausible.[1] Human life, the alternative view suggests, is fundamentally social and so embedded in the web of social relations to render untenable the sense in which human life can be significantly self-regarding.

In reviewing the matters at stake, there is value, as Rees suggests, in considering Mill's statements setting out the self and other-regarding distinction by looking again at the 'two maxims' set out at the start of the final chapter of *On Liberty*.[2] There, Mill says that the 'entire doctrine' (V: 1) of his essay is expressed. We are told that 'the individual is not accountable to society for his actions in so far as these concern the interests of no person but himself' and that 'for such actions as are prejudicial to the interests of others, the individual is accountable and may be subject to social or legal punishment'. In contrast, over self-regarding aspects of life, persuasive argument and ultimately our 'avoidance' of the person in question is the most we are entitled to do. With regard to these concerns, the critical point is what is in focus when Mill alludes to individuals being accountable for conduct – and so actions – 'which concern others' (I: 9) or which 'affects others' (I: 12). It is in the passage from the final chapter, that Mill impresses the point that what is at stake are the 'interests' of individuals and others, and Rees' exploration of this matter suggests that what Mill is doing in the context of his work is to use 'interests' to stress what is significant by way of a pejorative influence on the positive concerns a person might have. The point is that humans can be affected by all sorts of things - a stunning sunset, a moment or two of aesthetic delight, a drop of the finest single malt whisky, and an inspirational encounter – but by our interests, we generally mean something that 'depend for their existence on social recognition and are closely connected with prevailing standards about the sort of behaviour a man can legitimately expect from others'.[3] The point emerging is that in Mill's register of self and other-regarding matters, a good and reasoned case can be made to defend self-regarding interests and, reciprocally, the interests of other individuals and the interests that others share with us. In contrast, matters that affect us are far less likely to register as something where negative influences or reactions can really count as harm. We might be elevated by this sunset or that recital, but if none of the others around us is as positive, their reactions do not count as harms of the sort Mill considers of wider importance.

In any case, we must put against the critical view Mill's explicit sense that the 'portion of a person's life which affects only himself' (I: 12) means simply 'only himself' in the sense of 'directly and in the first instance'. This is for the starkly obvious reason that 'whatever affects himself may affect others through himself'. The understatement here is simply 'may'. As we have seen, everything a person does in the self-regarding portion of life will sooner or later have a bearing or influence on others: to illustrate this once more, an individual alone, deciding to clean the house, mow the lawn, read a book, listen to music, go shopping, or whatever, will if it is done to the delight and enjoyment of that person, but to the

---

[1] Rees highlights the tradition of criticism here – see Rees in Gray and Smith (1991) p. 172-174.

[2] Rees (1991) has an important discussion arising from this passage – pp. 171ff.

[3] Rees (1991) p. 175.

neglect of duties to others, create difficulties: cleaning the house but forgetting to collect one's child from school: mowing the lawn, but omitting to mark homework that one's students need back first thing the next morning, and so on. Mill knows that individual human life is embedded within a wider social setting. He makes this clear in the *Logic*:

'Whatever affects in an appreciable degree, any one element of the social state, affects through it all the other elements... We can never either understand in theory or command in practice the condition of a society in any one respect, without taking into consideration its condition in all other respects. There is no social phenomenon which is not more or less influenced by every other part of the condition of the same society, and therefore by every cause which is influencing any other of the contemporaneous social phenomena'.[1]

In *Utilitarianism*, Mill similarly thinks that the affirmation of 'the general happiness' is 'the strength of the utilitarian morality'.[2] This is grounded in 'the social feelings of mankind', which Mill explains as follows:

'... the desire to be in unity with our fellow creatures, which is already a powerful principle in human nature, and happily one of those which tend to become stronger, even without precise inculcation, from the influences of advancing civilization. The social state is at once so natural, so necessary, and so habitual to man, that, except in some unusual circumstances or by an effort of voluntary abstraction, he never conceives himself otherwise than as a member of a body; and this association is riveted more and more, as mankind are further removed from the state of savage independence'.

The 'effort of voluntary abstraction' alluded to here is a passing reference critical of the social contract theory that Mill consistently rejects, the 'state of savage independence' is what mankind experiences in conditions or stages of life without the elaborations of civil society that Mill always assumes to be of benefit. On the self-other regarding front, what the statements in the *Logic* and *Utilitarianism* make clear is that Mill has a residual commitment to the social aspect of life as elemental to the human condition. *On Liberty* sets out an affirmation of the importance of the spheres of liberty as key agents for human development, not against the human social condition but against some of the trends towards conformity and control that in the age for which he writes, he associates with the mood and temper of democracy.

Accordingly, for all that *On Liberty* puts a high value on what individuality of thought and action can do, the benefits in terms of better and more vital truths and more authentic patterns of life come as occasions where liberty serves the interests of 'utility in the largest sense, grounded on the permanent interests of man as a progressive being' (I: 11). Since the sum total of individuals comprises what Mill means by a civilized society, the operational scheme that he constructs means that liberty for self-regarding explorations of thought and practice for each is a means to the end of progressing the range and quality of life for all.

---

[1] *Logic* VI: IX: 2.
[2] *Util* III: 10.

Part III: *On Liberty* in Review

12. Problematic Principles and Related Matters

In this chapter, we revisit and revise some issues considered earlier and review some intermingled problems about Mill's project in *On Liberty*. These issues have a real value in framing criticisms arising from and about the text, and several issues jostle for consideration.[1]

They include, in no particular order, further consideration of the tensions between liberty and utility; the success of the harm principle to regulate liberty; the effectiveness of Mill's notions of society; the coherence of his method to enable the development of individuality; the viability of the idea of truths as distinct from the truth; the plausibility of the self and other-regarding distinction, and the effectiveness and strength of Mill's characterisation of 'the tyranny of the majority' (I: 5).

Charting a course through these, we start by reconsidering the liberty principle and the linked 'harm to others' clause. We move on to look at Mill's views on society, and we re-examine what he says about truth and truths. Then we pick up on the issue of the harmony (or otherwise) between utility and liberty through a review of one classic critique of *On Liberty*. In considering these matters, the self and other-regarding distinction will appear, and throughout, some of the presentations made in *On Liberty* will be reconsidered.

The One Not So Very Simple Principle

The statement of the 'one very simple principle' (I: 9) of liberty in the first chapter of *On Liberty* has a problem, as identified by one of Mill's earlier critics. In a piece written for *The Dublin Review*, Edward Lucas writes positively about liberty, seeing it as 'the very noblest of subjects which can occupy the human mind'.[2] Lucas then thinks that Mill has departed from the right and proper methods of philosophical writing by failing to give an adequate definition of liberty.[3] He means that from the opening of the book and the reference to 'civil or social liberty' (I: 1), we proceed for some pages until the statement of the liberty principle (I: 9). The term 'liberty is used a great deal along the way, but Mill's definitional activity is, as Lucas sees it, late, minimal, and helpful. Mill's development is further undermined by his appeal to utility as 'the ultimate appeal on all ethical questions' (I: 11).[4] Lucas thinks the defence of liberty is rootless, the more so since Mill proposes fallibilism, yet also wants to rule some ideas in as true and others out as false.

---

[1] These questions reflect topics as examined in the I.B. Philosophy paper on set texts with reference of *On Liberty*.
[2] Pyle (1994) p. 255. Edward Lucas (1822-1899) – an Irish Catholic writer and critic, who, amongst other things, sees Mill's work as English and Protestant. Lucas' review, 'Mill on Liberty' was published in 'The Dublin Review' Vol. 13 (NS) Vol 65 (OS) July 1869, pp. 62-75 and is in Pyle (1994) pp. 255-270. (NS and OS are abbreviations for 'new' and 'old' styles of dating and numbering publications).
[3] See Pyle (1994) p. 256.
[4] Pyle (1994) p. 259.

If we leave aside for a moment the issue of fallibilism, what Lucas argues is right in the sense that Mill is, as we have said before, not systematic in proceeding with total consistency through his lines of argument. Stylistically, the chapters of *On Liberty* do not always read as philosophical work carefully developed to guarantee tenure, so much as a passionate credo in staged sections on a treasured theme by a writer seized with concerns and interests. The result is, as we have seen, that Mill is sometimes loose and careless in his use of terms, and while his larger schemes are, as a rule, clearly set out, Mill's writing is occasionally imprecise as when, for example, he seems to equivocate over such matters as 'truth'.[1]

Lucas seems muddled, however, about how Mill sees liberty and utility as related and unduly pessimistic about the coherence of Mill's explanation of his 'one very simple principle' (I: 9). We know that Mill develops utility as the criterion for value, this in relation to the view taken of humans as progressive (I: 11). He then affirms liberty as a restraining strap against overzealous social trends. We will look at the tension between liberty and utility again later. Here we can reflect more on how Mill sets out the liberty principle.

To this end, a fruitful line of criticism noted by Gray is to challenge what Mill actually says: the liberty principle, as expressed, is *not* simple and *not* singular.[2] When Mill works himself up to expound the liberty principle, it is starkly obvious that no simple one-liner will do the job. We are told that the 'essay', as Mill calls *On Liberty*, has as its 'object' the assertion of 'one very simple principle, as entitled to govern absolutely the dealings of society with the individual in the way of compulsion and control, whether the means used be physical force in the form of legal penalties, or the moral coercion of public opinion': this is a rich preamble, giving, in summary, a good deal of what Mill has been arguing about in the earlier pages of the text – how society has the means, through law and opinion, to compel and control individuals: nearly all of this is now said to be a form of interference, as Mill says next:

'That principle is that the sole end for which mankind are warranted, individually or collectively, in interfering with the liberty of action of any of their number is self-protection'.

Here, as in a great deal of the statement of the liberty principle, the focus is on the liberty of action. Mill then adds eight sentences which, to be fair, do not simply assert; they unpack, and so refine our sense of the not-so-very simple principle:

'That the only purpose for which power can be rightfully exercised over any member of a civilized community, against his will, is to prevent harm to others. His own good, either physical or moral, is not a sufficient warrant. He cannot rightfully be compelled to do or forbear because it will be better for him to do so, because it will make him happier, because, in the opinion of others, to do so would be wise or even right. These are good reasons for remonstrating with him, or reasoning with him, or persuading him, or entreating him, but not for compelling him or visiting him with any evil in case he do otherwise. To justify that, the conduct from which it is desired to deter him must be calculated to produce evil to someone else. The only part of the conduct of anyone for which he is amenable to society is that which concerns others. In the part which merely concerns himself, his independence is, of right, absolute. Over himself, over his own body and mind, the individual is sovereign'.

---

[1] See *OL* II and Chapter 8 below.
[2] See Gray (1983) p. 48f.

The complex of ideas here gives the liberty principle a practical or active texture. The reference to the individuals 'independence' over his or her 'own mind' brings in the sole reference to the liberty of thought – an underplay that Mill compensates for in *On Liberty* with the extensive coverage of this topic that he gives in his second chapter. In general, the statement of the principle is mainly centred on limiting the restrictions that might impact a person's practice of life. The exposition also features two aspects of life Mill often appeals to – 'that which concerns others' and the part which ' merely concerns himself'.

Concerning the self-regarding sphere of life, where the Art of Life as Mill conceives it can be developed and individuality cultivated, society has no right to use compulsion or control to interfere with any individual against that person's will, for as we appreciate, the individual has sovereign autonomy 'over his own body and mind'. We are not permitted to intervene for that individual's own good – we can argue, entreat and persuade, and so on, but we are not to take action. This is assuming a sufficient canyon between self and other-regarding aspects of life, and concerning these latter aspects, Mill deploys the notion of the risk of 'harm to others' as the sole warrant society has for action to deter or constrain the individual – only if a person acts so that what they do may 'be calculated to produce evil to someone else' do they become 'amenable to society'.

What the reading of *On Liberty* brings home is that Mill does not leave alone the idea that the 'essay' has an 'object' that focuses on governing 'the dealings of society with the individual'. Mill moves on to deal with 'the appropriate region of human liberty' (I: 12) and sets out in some detail three zones within this region.

One is to do with 'liberty of conscience', so here Mill elaborates more on the liberty of thought and discussion and the liberty of expressing and publishing opinion; a second area is to do with the 'liberty of tastes and pursuits, of framing the plan of our life to suit our own character'. The third is the liberty of association, the freedom to meet with others for whatever purposes, again, so long as they do not involve risk of 'harm to others'.

Mill more or less makes it explicit in this passage that each of the three regions is a sub-set of 'the principle', which shows that the principle is rather like a zipped file that, once downloaded, has to be unpacked. The principle becomes more complex as the range of self-regarding concerns is detailed. The original statement of the principle is saying that society cannot interfere with or inhibit the sovereign individual's self-regarding sphere of life. The passage on the 'regions of liberty' explains what is entailed in that sphere, elevates the previously assumed but understated liberty of thought, and to that extent, the 'one very simple principle' becomes more elaborate.

As we find at the start of *On Liberty's* fifth chapter, 'the entire doctrine of this essay' suddenly became orientated to 'two maxims' (V: 1):

'Firstly, that the individual is not accountable to society for his actions in so far as these concern the interests of no person but himself. Advice, instruction, persuasion, and avoidance by other people, if thought necessary by them for their own good, are the only measures by which society can justifiably express its dislike or disapprobation of his conduct. Secondly, that for such actions as are prejudicial to the interests of others, the individual is accountable and may be subjected either to social or to legal punishment if society is of the opinion that the one or the other is requisite for its protection' (V:2).

Here the doctrine or principle as set out previously gets summarized into the duality of the modes of active life – again, the liberty of thought and discussion is subsumed, almost certainly as Mill assumes that a person's choice of a mode of life flows from prior thought and discussion. The focus is once more on the self and other-regarding forms of life, with the problem of sustaining this distinction glossed over. Mill is giving a summary at this point in the text, which given the structure of the work, is hardly bad form.

The original statement and elaboration into the positive statement on the regions of liberty come in the first chapter, and the next three explore those regions. Chapter V, which moves on to the case studies or 'applications', is given a summary reminder of the core principle. It would be a harsh conclusion to think there is inconsistency or waywardness in this aspect of Mill's exposition. Rather, he is the consistent victim of his habit of enunciating the liberty principle with a focus on the liberty of action. From the extended review Mill makes in his second chapter, we know that there he puts great weight on the role of the liberty of thought and discussion, but to a greater rather than lesser extent, he assumes this in his expositions and recapitulation of the liberty principle.

Given the time that J. S. and Harriet Mill seem to have spent revising the text, it must be assumed that they liked and wanted the extensions and elaborations that came with the developmental passages in the first and fifth chapters.[1] The emphasis is consistent with Mill's longstanding view that a person's life should have a confluence of critical reflection and experimentalism on the business of living to the end of developing character and well-being. What is sustained with a high level of consistency is Mill's emphatic distinction between the self and other-regarding aspects of life and his blanket assumption that the 'harm to others' clause is a clear and sufficient warrant for the interface with social action. This is a matter to now re-examine.

Harm to Others Revisited

According to Mill's liberty principle, the risk of harm to others is the only justification that can provide society with the right to inhibit, control or take such action as to deter the individual when that individual's actions seem likely to bring intrusions that are harmful to others.

There are many issues that might be raised over the harm to others clause. Is it sufficient for the task? What proportional relation exists between the risk of harm and the weight of action against the individual? What sort of harm is Mill considering? Is what he considers harm a sufficient understanding of the harm that is salient? Is the harm principle truly the only basis for limiting the liberty of the individual? Is harm to others sufficiently distinguished from the problem of giving others moral offence? One could go on, but the most emphatic issue with the widest implications for the application of Mill's positive teaching about the benefits of

---

[1] See *Auto* p.141.

liberty comes from getting to the heart of what he means and what he does not mean by harm.

In the first place, Mill's notion of harm has everything to do with the sphere the liberty of action: the notion of harm to others, or a clear risk of such harm, is brought into play as the sole grounds that society has to constrain the individual or to take some form of preventative action to deter the individual from the actions in question. The harm is not to the self – Mill is adamant that doing something at our own 'risk and peril' (III: 1) in the self-regarding sphere of life may justify warnings and such like, but individuals in such circumstances operate under the sovereign autonomy over mind and body that Mill's 'one very simple principle' (I: 9) defines and defends. With regard to the criterion of harm to others as that which can justify the individual being constrained by society, Mill excludes harms in terms of the offences that others may take in the domain of the liberty of thought and discussion. We recall the ideas set out at the end of his review of this topic, where he considered the idea that debate should always attend to 'the bounds of fair discussion' (II: 44) and maintain a 'temperate' manner. Mill's view is that in practical terms, it is very hard indeed to establish such boundaries for such work as this; that in strongly committed debate, people do give or take offence and can seem to each other intemperate: but this, if not ideal, is less of a problem than to 'argue sophistically' or so as to 'suppress facts or argument, to misstate the elements of the case, or misrepresent the opposite opinion'. Assuming this is the only tension possible, Mill has a point, which leads him to his sense that in arguments, the complaints against 'invective, sarcasm, personality and the like' are typically made from one side of the debate, and it is never seen as something that is found – as Mill thinks it is – on both sides.

Mill suggests that those in disputes over truths of belief, or conduct for that matter, should aim to use a 'studied moderation of language and the most cautious avoidance of unnecessary offence'. This is particularly so for those advancing ideas to contrast with or challenge 'commonly received' views. However, 'unnecessary offence' does not mean that offence will not be given or received, and here it is clear that Mill does not see such matters of offence as forms of harm.

Mill's ideas on this seem to owe a good deal to his early experiences in the debating societies he was involved in from the 1820s. He thinks that in a civilized society, the 'morality of public discussion' should be moderated by 'opinion', not by 'law and authority', which is akin to the members of the debating society who listen to the debate, voting at the end for the winner. Mill encourages frank and honourable discussion, but giving offence and causing upset is not a sufficient warrant to restrict debate or permit action against a person. He has the view that the 'common notions of politeness' (IV: 5) inhibit honest debate, which reinforces the view that upsetting someone's feelings by challenging ideas they hold dear is not something Mill thinks we should hold back from in the pursuit of clearer truths of belief and conduct. This has a distinct implication for modern disputes over the merits of discussing colonialism or such matters as to whether a person has or has not got a conscious or unconscious disposition on this or that matter.[1] Mill's imperative is that those who want to close down debates on matters they find disagreeable, wrong, or offensive should be prepared to listen to the arguments and

---

[1] These are amongst the issues examined in the next three chapters.

make their own, and not condemn those they disagree with or attempt to suppress them with public or professional condemnation.

What Mill does consider is that significant harm can arise over the active form of life concerning other-regarding matters. A powerful point he makes is to do with how the individual can be at risk. He reasons that in developing our own individuality, we are entitled 'to act upon our unfavourable opinion of anyone'. Action here is in the mode of association: a person might find a certain trader unpleasant, uncouth and ill-mannered and elect to take her business to another more courteous trader. The unwholesome trader's interests might be worsened by this, but such harm is a corollary of the liberty of action of free individuals. Mill's view is that we 'have a right', and perhaps a 'duty, to caution others against him if we think his example or his conversation likely to have a pernicious effect on those with whom he associates'. As we have seen, Mill gives plenty of instances of modes of conduct that would justify our cutting someone from our group of friends or acquaintances.

As to active life and instances of actions that are harmful or injurious 'to others' (IV: 6), Mill thinks in terms of actions such as deceit and fraud, cruelty, and all forms of crime against the person. Ill-mannered acts of self-promotion and dominance over others indicate that the person in question is 'a bad and odious character', but with these various offences, only the most serious cases, in Mill's estimate, merit punishment through the legal system within society: in general, assuming the good offices of a civilized community, he prefers opinion and social criticism to minister the disapproval that is felt to those who in these ways harm others.

It is clear from his whole approach that when Mill mentions as a form of harm 'encroachment' on the 'rights' of others, he is thinking of such crimes as theft, assault, and murder. He does not spell this out, but one can assume he would think it too obvious to detail – as would the reference to 'rights', which would not in the least be a reference to any abstract or inalienable rights – the sort that Mill and Bentham both reject – but positive rights as established and set in statute law.

The harm issue has, as discussed earlier, provoked considerable debate amongst Mill's commentators and critics.[1] Within *On Liberty*, the harm to others clause becomes a limiting factor concerning other-regarding action. No such limitation is unpacked over the liberty of thought and discussion, save in such instances as when an impassioned speech incites an excitable mob to riot, risking harm to the interests, property, security and well-being of others.[2] The self-regarding mode of life in terms of the liberty of thought and discussion and in terms of the liberties of action and association are also free from the constraint of harm, subject to the risk and peril clause. Actions that individuals might engage in that could offend others if conducted in public are considered appropriate, even if others disapprove of them, in private. The disapproval in question amounts to the others concerned becoming

---

[1] For further reflections on Mill's ideas of harm and interests, see Rees 'A Re-reading of Mill On Liberty', in Gray and Smith (1991) pp. 169-189 and Gray (1983) pp. 48ff.
[2] See *OL* III: 1. This reading of Mill is defended by Rees – in Gray and Smith (1991) as in the previous footnote.

offended, and here Wollheim suggests that, in fact, Mill has mind a more open form of protection of what has been termed 'morality-dependent harms'.[1]

Here the idea is of the harm or offence experienced when a given individual acts or is known to have acted in a manner that offends the moral views of another or others. In a developed pluralistic society, there might be a wide level of mutual respect for different religious traditions. However, the moral views of some could be seriously offended by, for example, the methods of slaughtering animals employed within some religious traditions. Here, the offence is against the morality upon which others, with the welfare of animals in mind, base their ethical outlook, and the offence registers as real, deep and in need of amelioration by the harm to others clause and by social interventions.

The problem with this reading of Mill is that it does not tally with anything said in *On Liberty*.[2] His contrary view consistently rejects the protests of those who 'consider as an injury to themselves any conduct which they have a distaste for, and resent it as an outrage to their feelings' (IV: 12). This could not be clearer: outraged they may be, but 'there is no parity between the feeling of a person for his own opinion and the feeling of another who is offended at his holding it'. What Mill terms 'the aberrations of existing moral feeling' are a great problem and far from an 'imaginary evil' (IV: 13) – it is due to this that he explores a range of issues towards the end of his fourth chapter. His point is always to show that harming the feelings of others, so offending them, does not give sufficient reason for the offending individual's views or actions to be restricted.

Mill posits an ideal situation where society leaves individuals 'undisturbed' (IV: 12) in their exercise of 'freedom and choice' over 'all uncertain matters' so long as they live free from patterns of life that 'universal experience has condemned'. However, he thinks that no society has yet existed that can be so restrained 'in its censorship' or so in tune with 'universal experience'. That being the case, the plan looking forward is to defend liberties as mentioned over self-regarding matters and in respect of thought and discussion, irrespective of the offence or distaste others are driven to express in consequence of their moral feelings.

To illuminate some of the issues here, it is worth looking at what Mill says in *Utilitarianism*. Considering that this work and *On Liberty* were both drafted in the same period, it is unsurprising that the texts usefully inform one another. In *Utilitarianism*, Mill has an extended discussion of the relationship between utility and justice.[3] He considers the 'moral rules' that commonly operate to 'forbid mankind to hurt one another'.[4] Here we have 'hurt', not 'harm', but let us assume for the moment that the meanings and entailments are not inconsistent. Mill illustrates what he has in mind: 'the wrongful interferences with each other's freedom' is an example of the sort of rule and so of hurt of which he is thinking. He uses 'freedom' here, not 'liberty', but we have no good reason to think he is here envisaging wholly distinct notions. Reciprocal respect of individual liberty would seem an obvious moral rule for Mill to affirm. He sees such 'freedom' as 'more

---

[1] See Wollheim (1973) and Honderich (2003).
[2] This is pointed out by Honderich (2003), who rightly thinks it obvious from any reading of the whole text.
[3] See *Util*: V
[4] *Util* V: 33

vital to human well-being' than other rules or maxims, and from *On Liberty*, we know that this concern with well-being relates to how liberty serves the 'progressive' development of humankind.[1]

Mill unpacks his thinking in *Utilitarianism* as follows, this time using terminology more akin to that favoured in *On Liberty* and, we can assume, thinking of how life is in the context of a civilized society:

> 'Moralities which protect every individual from being harmed by others, either directly or by being hindered in his freedom of pursuing his own good, are at once those which he has himself most at heart, and those which he has the strongest interest in publishing and enforcing by word and deed'.[2]

Mill sees the 'moralities' that relate to the freedoms here defended as the primary components in 'the obligations of justice'. At the heart of Mill's notion of justice is the conjunction of the progressive style of utility related to the development of human well-being through a reciprocal defence of liberty.

Helpfully, Mill then gives a register of instances of harm reminiscent of the points made in *On Liberty*. He mentions 'acts of wrongful aggression, or wrongful excess of power over someone', then 'wrongfully withholding' from someone 'something that was his due'. These acts can manifest harm, either through 'inflicting… a positive hurt, either in the form of direct suffering, or of the privation of some good of which he had a reasonable ground, either of a physical or a social kind, for counting upon'. If within social life, or in the pursuit of any plan of individual life or work, such harmful acts are threatened or suffered, Mill sees that if the reciprocal regard for liberty that has been put at risk or violated, this entails a retributive pattern of justice for the offenders who deserve punishment.[3] Accordingly, those who 'accept benefits, and denies a return for them when needed, inflicts a real hurt, by disappointing one of the most natural and reasonable of expectations, and one which he must at least tacitly have encouraged, otherwise the benefits would seldom have been conferred'.[4] Mill thinks 'highly immoral' such acts as 'a beach of friendship and breach of promise'. He considers these to be imperative due to how such breaches hit home as failures 'in the hour of need'.

The ideas in *Utilitarianism* and *On Liberty* are consistent in their focus, and the emergent perspective has an abiding significance when considering the issues that prevail in modernity over the liberty of discussion in public, professional and academic life. The relevance is clear given that various issues of debate have arisen where forms of insulation have been placed around people's feelings. It is now commonly found that policies are in place, backed by law, to say that in places of work and institutional life in general that no one is entitled to feel humiliated, put down, bullied, or manipulated.

In this connection, the UK law concerning harassment is a relevant example of legal insulation – as in the Protection from Harassment Act 1997.[5] A revealing

---

[1] See *OL* I: 11.
[2] *Util* V: 33
[3] See *Util* V: 34.
[4] *Util* V: 34.
[5] See https///www.legislation.gov.uk/ukpga/1997/40/section/ 1. Quotations in the text are from this source.

feature of the provision in this law is that a person 'whose course of conduct is in question ought to know' that conduct 'amounts to harassment of another if a reasonable person in possession of the same information would think the course of action amounted to harassment of the other'. The principle here is to imagine an *a priori* ideal of reasonableness for those who think that they have suffered harassment to use. The operational problem is that those who are then accused of harassment have very little room to mount any form of defence – they certainly cannot employ appeals to motive or intention, as the offence is defined by perceived consequence in terms of what seems to be the infallibility of the impressions formed by 'a reasonable person in possession of the same information'. Here, a hypothetical appeal is brought into legal consideration, moving away from the facts of the case towards an elevation of personal or subject feeling, and giving legal development a victory for a form of cruder utility over liberty and a wider definition of harm than Mill permits.

One of the main restrictions Mill suggests for liberty and the harm to others principle is that liberty applies only 'to human beings in the maturity of their faculties' (I: 10). Mill excludes children, which in the present setting means that from babies to hulking teenagers up till their eighteenth birthday, the protection and guidance of parents in particular and society, in general, has charge: liberty is, on this view, unleashed when a person becomes eighteen.

Since Mill wrote, views about the entitlements for those under-18 have progressed. With regard to those who are not yet 'in the maturity of their faculties' but who might be eight, twelve, or sixteen years old, it would now seem wholly consistent with a respect for the benefits of liberty and to the issue of harm to others to give greater and greater degrees of liberal tolerance to assist in the progressive development of such individuals. The development of character, to which Mill is greatly devoted, is something that the greater number of parents would say starts at a very early age and gives rise to the phenomenon of children developing their interests and tastes. This development gives opportunities to operate at their own risk and peril and to take responsibility for dealing with the issue of harm to others. With this, there is scope for an important corrective to Mill's formulation.

Given that Mill thinks that human beings are progressive, this pattern of development is not a surprise: a greater surprise is Mill's affirmation of this progressiveness held in combination with his view that he was living in a transitional age.[1] He meant that in so many areas of social, economic, and political life, there was a great deal of change without a consensus on how social life would settle. Mill seems to anticipate a future time of settlement. If, however, human beings are progressive, the default position will be one of persistent transition.

---

[1] See *Auto* p. 5. Mill seems to mean his life as whole is lived in a period of transition. As said in the text above, if humans are progressive, the sense of constant transition hard to avoid.

Seeing Society Aright

We now turn to Mill's outlook on society, and in so doing, some of these issues can be explored through looking at the reviews that emerged when *On Liberty* was read after its appearance in 1859. On publication, it would be fair to say that *On Liberty* had an effect doubly analogous to a nuclear weapon and a slice of toast coated in marmite.

Like a nuclear weapon, *On Liberty* made a considerable impact, albeit on just the reading public, but like a nuclear weapon, *On Liberty* has remained radiant, with an active and ongoing half-life of influence, not least in the realms of debate within political philosophy.[1] Like toast spread with marmite, *On Liberty* made a case that some people liked and some readers did not. Mill's view of the condition of and threat from society was, to several critics, unpersuasive. We noted how Macaulay was one contemporary of Mill's who did not care for *On Liberty's* critical perspective on social influences in relation to individuality, and the case made for more variety, diversity, and eccentricity.[2] Macaulay thought that the age they lived in showed far too much of that already: his impression was that Mill overstated the case for a wide tolerance of multiple freedoms. Macaulay makes it clear that he agrees with Mill that there is a grave danger in falling into a 'Byzantine' state[3] – one of indolent stagnation, but in effect, he thinks Mill's argument is too extreme: as we saw, referencing Biblical imagery, Macaulay thinks it was a case of claiming there was 'fire' as the key problem in the face of 'Noah's flood'.

In mitigation, it might be thought that Mill could defend himself by pointing to his being polemical, but while he is arguably polemical in style at times, he is also explicit in thinking that polemical debate commits 'the worst offence… to stigmatize those who hold the contrary opinion as bad and immoral men' (II: 44). In any case, in his critique of social trends, Mill is not, in his own mind, committing the sin of polemics: he thinks he is characterising the real and dangerous trend – of encroaching uniformity. If we allow that Macaulay was doing the same, the outcome is that each sees the range of lifestyle and diversity of expression in their joint age, but each views and assesses matters differently: Macaulay thinks that there is more than enough variety already, and wants a more discriminative approach to development; but Mill thinks that on key matters relating to human progression, more liberty of expression and richer varieties of individuality are vital for progressive humanity.

What Macaulay has in mind as a problem is that in the flux of activity in society, there is much energy and variety, but not, he thinks, much real quality. The point he makes resonates with the more recent trend of the proliferation of media outlets: a generation ago in the UK, for example, the public had access to four TV channels and a few more radio stations: now they have multiple platforms to stream all manner of entertainment and news. A manifestation of progressive diversity could be seen in this, but alternatively, one could argue that what is found in evidence is a dearth of quality and diffusion of talent: the current age, like the time of Mill and

---

[1] Nozick's influential *Anarchy, State and Utopia* (1974) owes a great deal to *On Liberty*. See Nozick (2003).

[2] See Chapter 9 above and *OL* 'Editor's Introduction' p. 38.

[3] Quoted in *OL* 'Editor's Introduction' p. 38. See also Himmelfarb (1974) p. 162ff.

his contemporaries, gives people increasing opportunity to enjoy what they like, but arguably too little incentive for them to explore and be challenged by ideas that are different and, perhaps, transformative. In these states, Macaulay is suggesting that more is less. In contrast, what Mill encourages would be a constant challenge to static pluralities and trends that simply confirm interests and render them fixed. The case for the liberty of thought and expression and diverse individuality through an ever more experimental approach to life is based on Mill's perception of the risks and perils to the individual arising from society. In *On Liberty*, his concern is that social life was creating a form of uniformity and mediocrity, leading to a level of stagnation damaging to individuality: this view was, however, given critical attention by other early reviewers.

One of these came in February 1859, shortly after *On Liberty* was published in *The Saturday Review*.[1] The review came in two parts, published in successive weeks. Although the reviews were published anonymously, the author was J. F. Stephen.[2]

Mill is said to have done 'an injustice to his countryman' in considering 'the causes of the want of originality' growing in society.[3] Mill underestimated the range of 'intelligence and originality' that was evident.[4] In the art, literature, politics, and theology of the age, variety and differences of view, taste and interpretation abound – so Mill's concerns are not realistic. Moreover, Stephen also thinks Mill's assault on the Calvinistic outlook is a generalised but misleading attack on Christian values as promoting passivity, so inhibiting the development of individuality and entailing and 'a want of originality.'[5] The alternative view is that Christian commitment is to a mode of discipleship that 'far from being a slavish one, is the noblest conception of life that any mortal creature can form. So far from crushing the faculties and susceptibilities, it is the best of all means of developing them to the highest pitch of excellence and glory of which they are capable'.[6]

A similar rejection of Mill's claims, and affinity with Macaulay's view, comes from the anonymous review in the *British Quarterly Review*.[7] The suggestion that 'high civilization' has the effects of making 'all men alike' and of being 'repressive' of originality is rejected: the modern age is 'distinguished by a greater *flush* of all sorts of opinions' than any previous time: 'Never has there been a period in which men have either given expression to a greater number of speculative monstrosities, or avowed them with a greater freedom or more enviable superiority to modesty or shame'. More biblical imagery is employed to expose Mill's misrepresentations: the modern age involves 'a perfect Babel of opinions'; there is 'a very Pentecost of the spirit of speculative error'. What is needed is more 'patient investigation' to

---

[1] *The Saturday Review* in Pyle (1994) pp. 6-24. There are two reviews, from the editions of the 12th and 19th of February 1859.
[2] On this see Himmelfarb (1974) pp. 163f. At this stage, Stephen was yet to work for Mill and the Jamaica Committee and it also some time until he resharpens his pen to write *Liberty, Equality, Fraternity*. J. F. Stephen's ideas in this work are considered later in this chapter.
[3] Pyle (1994) p. 20.
[4] Pyle (1994) p. 19.
[5] Pyle (1994) p. 20.
[6] Pyle (1994) p. 21.
[7] *British Quarterly Review* Vol. 31 (1860) pp. 173-195, in Pyle (1994) pp. 184-209. Quotations are from pp. 208-209.

establish the real merit of the flux of ideas being thrown into the arena of public debate.

An authored review in *Bentley's Quarterly* makes a similar but more measured criticism of Mill's assault on the tyranny of custom. The review was from R. W. Church, a distinguished Anglican priest and writer.[1]

Church appreciates Mill's thought that the influence of society 'over individual opinion and action is at present far too stringent'.[2] He sees that Mill aims to advocate liberty by demanding 'for the individual every liberty compatible with the same liberty in others, and with the preservation of that society which alone makes any real liberty possible'. However, thinking of the pattern of life that was to hand, Church thought that while there was plenty of evidence of the influence of custom, it was 'not omnipotent', and 'the current which runs through society is neither so uniform nor so irresistible' as it is in Mill's presentation.[3] As Church views it:

'... the face of society appears seamed and traversed in all directions by a vast number of currents, different in their course, strength, and tendencies, pressing on one another or violently conflicting; accelerating, diverting, retarding, with endlessly varying results from day to day; and as in the sea and the atmosphere, each strong current infallibly provoking its balancing counter-current'.

Church thinks that while there are some matters in this complex of ideas that are in various ways 'lamentable', there are plenty exhibiting 'wisdom' and other positive qualities. Mill 'underrates the degree to which individuality of any value has a fair chance to assert itself'.[4] Church also considers that Mill misrepresents the spectrum of ideas on the moral life within the Christian tradition – again, the focus on Calvinism, 'with its rugged, inflexible zeal', is criticised.[5] As we noted earlier, Mill is thought to have missed a richer and 'more human conception of Christian morality', namely, that which has to do with those things that are 'true', 'honest', 'just', 'lovely' and of 'any virtue'.

In a more recent phase of criticism, Himmelfarb, as we mentioned, makes a case for seeing Mill in binary terms.[6] She thinks there is the Mill of *On Liberty*, and then the 'Other Mill' who wrote both before and after the period of *On Liberty*.[7] As an example of what she thinks, Himmelfarb suggests that in an earlier phase of his career, Mill made criticisms akin to those of Macaulay and others about the state of intellectual life that prevailed, as in his unfinished series of essays from 1831, on 'The Spirit of the Age'.[8]

---

[1] R. W. Church (1815-1890). A theologian and writer, an ordained Anglican who in due course became Dean of St Paul's from 1871. The review, from *Bentley's Quarterly Review* Vol. 2 1860 pp. 434-473, is in Pyle (1994) pp. 210-254.

[2] Pyle (1994) p. 213

[3] Pyle (1994) p. 218.

[4] Pyle (1994) p. 243.

[5] Pyle (1994) p. 251.

[6] See Chapter 5 above.

[7] See Chapter 5 above.

[8] See Himmelfarb (1962) pp. 5-50 and CW XII p. 71: for Himmelfarb's view, see her Himmelfarb (1962) 'Introduction', and Himmelfarb (2007) p. 103ff. Himmelfarb does not rate as all that significant that Mill left off this series of essays, and that he did not reprint them in his later collections. She treats them as primary statements of the outlook of the 'other' Mill.

It is something of an issue to follow Himmelfarb's diagnosis, for the more one reads Mill's essays of this period, the less clear the binary view of Mill becomes. In these writings, Mill again sees the age as one of 'transition'[1] and one exhibiting a degree of 'intellectual anarchy'.[2] There is widespread enthusiasm for discussion and novelty. He notes the wide range of discussion prevalent in the culture of the day, but, rather, as in *On Liberty*, he thinks that the 'increase of discussion' does not mean an 'increase of wisdom'. In *On Liberty*, there is a mode reflection of what we could term the power of the social psychology of group beliefs. In 'The Spirit of the Age', Mill sees that there is a problem in the trend whereby people claim the 'right' to exercise 'private judgment'.[3] This trend leads to people assuming too readily that the knowledge they have acquired into some aspects of a subject gives definitive insight upon which to rest. In contrast, Mill wants to promote a progression of knowledge and insight through informed and dialogic review and to challenge the idea that in some solo judgement, individuals can have secure truths about matters of interest.

The ideas from this period are much more anticipations of what we find in *On Liberty* than a disconnect. In 'The Spirit of the Age', for example, Mill thinks that the transitional age gives rise to 'the *diffusion* of *superficial* knowledge'.[4] Discussion abounds, but it is too much centred on 'persons' acquiring 'knowledge adequate to the formation of sound opinions by their own lights'. This habit of the 'average' person is increasing. Mill, in this 1831 mode of thought, ponders that 'it would be carrying the notion of the march of intellect too far, to suppose that an average man of the present day is superior to the greatest men of the beginning of the eighteenth century'. But as we know, by the time of *On Liberty*, Mill did see that the problems of majority opinion manifested a dangerous influence. The ideas of 'The Spirit of the Age' on free and open discussion offer a clear prelude to what we find later in *On Liberty*:

'When all opinions are questioned, it is on time found out what those which will not bear a close examination. Ancient doctrines are then put upon their proofs; and those which were originally errors, or have become so by change of circumstances, are thrown aside. Discussion does this. It by discussion, also, that true opinions are discovered and diffused'.[5]

Mill also anticipates the fallibilism of his later notion view of truths as distinct from the truth, with the view that 'to be rationally assured that a given doctrine is *true*':

'... it is often necessary to examine and weigh an immense variety of facts. One single well-established fact clearly irreconcilable with a doctrine, is sufficient to prove that it is *false*'.[6]

---

[1] Himmelfarb (1962) p.6.
[2] Himmelfarb (1962) p. 9.
[3] Himmelfarb (1962) p. 12.
[4] Himmelfarb (1962) p. 8.
[5] Himmelfarb (1962) p. 10.
[6] Again Mill can be seen to anticipate the principle of falsification usually associated with Popper: see Popper (1981).

What Mill is arguing for is that an ongoing promotion of informed discussion – such as he later defends in *On Liberty* – is the way forward. Mill, in 'The Spirit of the Age', is not arguing for restrictions or limits to the liberty of thought and discussion.

In developing her case, Himmelfarb also draws attention to Mill's essay of 1836 on 'Civilization' where criticisms are made on the quality of reading in contemporary intellectual life: thus, 'the world reads too much and too quickly to read well'.[1] This is said to set a situation where 'the world itself with intellectual food' and opinions – not yet the tyrannical threat as in *On Liberty* – accumulate to give disproportionate weight to 'the balance of events' given 'that ideas of no value in themselves are of importance from the mere circumstance that they *are* ideas, and have a *bonâ fide* existence as such anywhere out of Bedlam'.

Mill continues:

'The world, in consequence, gorges itself with intellectual food, and in order to swallow more, *bolts* it. Nothing is now read slowly, or twice over. Books are run through with no less rapidity, and scarcely leave a more durable impression, than a newspaper article'.

The upshot is that the thirty-year-old Mill of 1836 thinks that 'few books are produced of any value', and in consequence:

'The public is in the predicament of the indolent man, who cannot bring himself to apply his mind vigorously to his own affairs, and over whom, therefore, not only he who speaks most wisely, but he who speaks most frequently, obtains the influence'.[2]

Himmelfarb thinks these ideas from the 1830s conflict with his later defence of freedom of thought and discussion in *On Liberty*. In particular, she sees a definite point of tension in the idea that the defence of liberty for all is vital for the sake of possible benefits that will come to all through the endeavours of some.[3] However, in contrast with Himmelfarb's reading, the evidence we have considered of what Mill actually says in *On Liberty* and in the essays of the 1830s illustrates the development and progress of Mill's thinking in lines far more of continuity than extremes of variation. In the 1830's he describes the proliferation of superficiality and the rise of overly subjective certitudes. In *On Liberty,* the analysis and prognosis for the defence of the liberties are deepened. In neither period of his thought is Mill departing from a defence of the freedom if even ill-informed opinion.

The continuity of Mill's progressive development is also illustrated by the examination we made of the evolution of how he understands utility.[4] For Mill, the early-mid 1830s was a period when he was reassessing his pattern of thought in the wake of his crisis as well as in the light of his new love with Harriet. He was blowing hot and cold over the Saint-Simonians and gradually moving away from their

---

[1] Himmelfarb (1962) p. 69.
[2] Himmelfarb (1962) p. 69.
[3] As mentioned earlier, Himmelfarb first raised these points on the 'two Mills' in her editorial introduction to the edition of Mill's essays published in 1962. She makes the same case in her study *Liberty and Liberalism: the case of John Stuart Mill* (1974). Her final essay on Mill, 'John Stuart Mill: The Other Mill' (2006) pulls her ideas into a compact reformulation. See Himmelfarb (2007) pp. 94-120.
[4] See Chapter 4 above.

influence.[1] He was also freeing himself from the influence of Carlyle.[2] His development is, however, not one greatly in contrast with the work that went into *On Liberty*, and continuity through development is the more persuasive way to read and assess Mill.

The main thrust of these criticisms of Mill's diagnosis brings us back to the problem of the coherence of individuals and society we identified earlier and the three-fold sense in which Mill was found referring to society. To recap briefly, these were seeing society as a dangerous force exhibiting trends and movements of coercive opinion; society taken as the sum total of individuals, such individuals being the basic components of human life in a civilized society, where Mill envisions scope for life as it is at its best; society considered as civil society and as the political state – as the organised system of law and other functions of order and governance under which people lead personal and social lives with a range of duties and obligations.

What Mill does within the text of *On Liberty* is slip between these three senses depending on the context and focus of his discussion. Society can become 'the tyrant' (I: 5) and operate by issuing 'mandates… in things with which it ought not to meddle'; here, what Mill is consistently worried about is 'the sentiment of the majority' (I: 7), which challenges and invades individuality. Society can operate as a 'civilized community' (I: 9), protecting the liberty of each individual in balance with the defence of the same liberty to all other individuals in a setting where people 'become capable of being improved by free and equal discussion' (I: 10). Society is also the context for the lives of the people who comprise it, with institutions and structures that guide and protect those in its membership, owing to it, therefore, certain obligations as 'a return for the benefit' (IV: 3). Mill's critical focus is honed on the themes he identifies early in the text, of society manifesting a danger, linked to the rise of democratic and, indeed, utilitarian thinking, that majority opinions, trends, and movements have an insatiable capacity to envelop and dominate.

Mill sees this trend under and through the hurly-burly of energetic activity that Macaulay and others see as sufficient evidence of individuality doing well enough. While Mill may well overstate his case, what is incontrovertible is that he is right to sense that dominant trends become dominant. His great concern is that a trend for mediocrity is seen as an 'enforced assimilation' (III: 19), and against this, he wants to defend the capacity for human individuals to live as the persons 'most interested' in their 'own well-being' (IV: 4).

In the *Autobiography*, Mill reflects on how *On Liberty* expressed fears over 'the inevitable growth in social equality and of the government of public opinion should impose on mankind an oppressive yoke of uniformity in opinion and practice'.[3] Mill thinks that to some – meaning it is likely, those who were critical of his portrayal of society, his presentation might well seem 'chimerical', especially he says, to 'those who look more at present facts than at tendencies'. Mill's defence is that he thinks he identifies the emergent tendencies – not simply looking at everyday life's present facts. New ideas are bubbling away in the present, but the age is, he says again, one of 'transition', and his fear remains that this will make individuals prone to

---

[1] See CW XII p. 71; p. 88; p. 106; p. 125.
[2] See CW XII p. 113; p. 126; p. 149, and p. 204.
[3] *Auto* p. 142.

influences that will diminish their creative and developmental possibilities, and so 'stunting and dwarfing human nature'.[1]

Mill's concern over how persons are vulnerable to trends, fashions, styles of life, manners, and morals resonates to the present. But whereas Mill worries about the dangers to the minority for the waves of opinion from the majority, in modernity, we might worry more about how social and cultural life has the resilience to develop into pluralistic and multi-faceted forms, where we have the coexistence of incommensurable outlooks on life, with everyone, from the perspective of their own bubble or mind-set, appealing to their right to hold to their own views and ways of life without interference, all within the framework of civil society and the bonds of law, traditions, and opportunity.

This means that instead of 'society' exercising a tyranny of opinion, where it is one particular view that is being promoted, social life generates a plenitude of options for immediate consideration, with each view getting a protective veil of legal support against anyone being harassed over their outlook. The issues arising are less to do with uniformity than diffusion, and we also face the problem of generating sustained debate over the validity of views, given that in modernity, a large trend suggests that no one is to suffer upsets for holding to their preferences. For all that Mill thinks he is dealing with deeper trends, Macaulay and the other early critics are closer to the contemporary problems of pluralism, and this sheds light on the issue of the elemental coherence in Mill's sense of the relationship between individuals and society.

If we consider the pattern of ideas in *On Liberty*, the strongest assertions and most eloquent expositions are usually affirmations of the worth of individuality and the benefits of liberty of thought and discussion for the progression of better and more vital truths. Society, in the pejorative sense, 'practices a social tyranny' (I: V), it 'compels all characters to fashion themselves upon the model of its own', set under 'the yoke of opinion' (I: 8), such that 'the despotism of custom is everywhere the standing hindrance to human advancement' (III: 17).

Given that Mill layers his view of society in at least the three ways we have noted, we know that the critique he makes is of something he sees in one variant as a clear and present danger to the well-being of individuals, the pursuit of truths, and so to civilized society. What Mill does, and largely where *On Liberty* scores well, is elaborate much that embroiders the merits of liberty for the individual, and thereby for society. The problem is that Mill does rather less by way of building up the way in which individuals owe each other patterns of reciprocal obligations in a communal life. He aims to deal with this latter issue with the sustained sense of self-regarding and other-regarding distinctions. The problem here, which Mill identifies, is that even in 'that portion of a person's life and conduct which affects only himself' (I: 12), it remains the case that 'whatever affects himself may affect others through himself'. As we said earlier, the self-regarding sphere of life turns out to be a kind of veneer over the interpersonal and social aspects of life. Like the images we used of wax or sugar, the self-orientated mode of life is set within and can merge into the mutuality of social and other-related life.

Individuality, even as Mill conceives it, turns out to be a relative and dependent element in the wider reality of social life, where the relations are not binary – either

---

[1] *Auto* p. 143.

self or other-regarding – but in varied ways, reciprocal, mutual, organic, and dynamic. Human lives are embedded in a wider socio-cultural life, which is what Mill sees when he argues that people need to live and grow in their thinking with a developed sense of what life has taught them from past 'human experience' (III: 3): it is 'the business of education' (IV: 4), he says to 'cultivate' the 'social' and 'self-regarding virtues'.

Mill, very unsurprisingly, claims he is 'the last person to undervalue the self-regarding virtues', but he says they 'are only second in importance, if even second, to the social'. This sounds like they have a mutual and reciprocal relation, of which Mill might have made more. The self-regarding virtues are, he thinks, developed in particular after the period of formal education (which, we assume, is predominantly developing the social virtues), and it works through 'conviction and persuasion'. This suggests a process of ongoing dialogue and development, progressive and organic in character, something more like a process rather than featuring divided, divisive and implausible self and other-regarding divisions.

The Problem of Truth(s)

Another critical issue for Mill arises over his concern to have more, better, and more vibrant truths through the good offices of the liberty of thought and discussion. Development here is coupled to Mill's wider notion of humans as progressive and fallible beings, so capable of self-correction and self-improvement – and on the basis of seeing that society is the sum of the individuals that make it up, Mill is working for the development of membership 'of a civilized community' (I: 9). This is an ambition that few could want to oppose, but as we noted in reviewing *On Liberty*, Mill is lax in controlling his discussion as it unfolds, and he does not keep the fallibilism he sees as tied to the residual condition of being human very much before the mind of his readers.

What Mill develops, but does not make explicit in a sustained manner, is, as mentioned earlier, a form of epistemological scepticism. This can be expressed as the view that we know with certainty only that we have no certain knowledge: we have a range and variety of 'truths' at any point in time, all of which may be revisable to the point of expendability in the light of the progression of understanding. The implication is that the best truths we have at any point in time are contingent and held as viable in a range of probability. What we hold as 'true' is held with the proverbial pinch of salt: this is the view Mill developed in *A System of Logic*, and he is committing himself to it in *On Liberty* with the development of the case for the liberty of thought and discussion, with the notion running throughout of humans as 'fallible' (II: 8).

In the work as a whole, Mill is caught in something of a dilemma. On the one hand, he does not think human individuals can transcend fallibility. On the other hand, Mill writes with some verve to argue that some views, dispositions and perspectives are distinctly superior to others.

On the side of fallibility, Mill's thinking is that although humans can be certain in the subjective sense of being in the grip of a given idea, we cannot possess certainty regarding knowledge of the world of personal or general experience. The error would be to muddle our certainty with '*absolute* certainty' (II: 3). This principle of contingency over what truths we hold applies to the natural and human sciences and the other disciplines, academic and creative.

At the same time, to promote development, Mill wants the critical debate of particular matters to flow to allow for 'the opportunity of exchanging error for truth' (II: 1); he opposes the suppression of ideas since what is suppressed 'may possibly be true' (II: 3). He ponders what to do when in the conflict between 'doctrines' (II: 34), we find that 'instead of being one true and the other false', they 'share the truth between them'.

Here, and on many other occasions, Mill uses terms like 'truth' and 'error' in an unqualified sense, blurring his more elemental insight. This, and the way Mill creates the problem we have been considering, is well expressed as 'the duty' (II: 5) that 'individuals' and 'governments' share, which is 'to form the truest opinions they can; to form them carefully, and never impose them on others unless they are quite sure of being right'. The idea that our truths are the 'truest' we can form is what Mill is committed to, but he falls into thinking that some of these 'truest' ideas assure us 'of being right'. We are then prone to thinking our current ideas are a bit more solid than is expedient.

What Mill needs, given his longstanding inductivism, is a clearer model of what he thinks about the nature of human insight and knowledge. A better analogy might have come from medicine: medical knowledge is unfailingly progressive; understanding grows through the fusion of critical reason and reflection on experimental and practical data. Ideas, methods, and techniques are constantly revised and improved, and some retain value over time while others are put aside for ones that are newer and better. This fits what Mill wants to say, but his exposition vacillates into misleading affirmations of truth and error that seem well-suited to a primary classroom but not to the wider arenas of the provinces of liberty. Due to his stylistic error in not doing this, his readers have to work harder than perhaps they should to surf his thought without being swamped by waves of inconsistency.

Regarding these matters, there is wise advice from Ryan, who reminds us 'that Mill was not a professional philosopher'.[1] Whatever benefits he gained from his education and apprenticeship, his expertise was honed through debating, journalism, and reviews rather than through the channels of academia. As a philosophical writer and thinker, Mill was, to a considerable extent, self-taught and self-developing. However, that Mill does not always write with the coherence and consistency of those who are professionals may also be contrasted with how far many of those who are, have produced work that has been of interest for as long as Mill's.[2]

---

[1] Ryan (1974) p. 96.
[2] The point is, almost all the 'great philosophers' before 1900 were not 'professional' in the modern sense. Kant and Hegel were exceptions to this.

Utility Resurgent: J.F. Stephen's Critique of On Liberty

Of all the issues raised by *On Liberty*, one of the most enigmatic is the tension over the relationship between liberty and utility. As we saw in our earlier review of this topic, Mill thinks his defence of liberty is set within and under a modified variant of utilitarianism.[1] The critical view arising from anyone disposed to appreciate utility in its crisp Benthamite style thinks Mill cannot plausibly sustain any harmonic between the two principles. This line of thought has a lineage going back to Mill himself as he revised and modified utilitarianism, and within his own era, his development was controversial.

If we revise some of the key points in *On Liberty,* Mill claims that he retains utility as the 'ultimate appeal on all ethical questions' (I: 11). As he then expresses it, all matters pertaining to liberty will be set under the notion of utility related to the 'permanent interests of man as a progressive being'.

As Mill presents it, the principle of liberty in its various modes is always guided and trumped by this form of utility that stands as the overarching end and criterion of value. In the development of ideas in *On Liberty*, the collective of society is composed of the sum of individuals, and so liberty gives the framework within which truths are improved and progressed, and individuality is enhanced through the liberty of action. Liberty thus serves the utilitarian aim of working to enhance the greatest goods for the ongoing interests of the greatest number of the progressive individuals who comprise society.

The critical retort is that if utility is the highest appeal for ethical matters, then in the interests of the greatest number, liberty can and should be constrained, which means that Mill's notion of the sovereignty of the individual, of individuals living under the canopy of liberty, finds that canopy deflated and devalued by the overarching governance of utility, and various liberties are, in some contexts to be subordinate to the wider interest of the greater number, or even to the national interest under the protection of the law.[2] If the critical view prevails, Mill always attempts to square a circle by fusing liberty and utility.[3] Those who take the critical line of thought are all inheritors of J. F. Stephen and his critique of Mill's thought, *Liberty, Equality, Fraternity* (1873).[4]

An idea in Stephen's book is that the case for liberty, rightly understood, is set under a range of constraints required because of the difficulties of being human. Mill, as we have seen, has an organic idea that humans are progressive, akin to trees that grow in accord with their inner tendencies, as well as having the capacity for self-correction and so of development. We could say this is a positive and even optimistic view of the human condition. Stephen has a fundamentally different

---

[1] See Chapters 4 and 7 above.

[2] As in time of war or under a Covid19 lockdown, for example.

[3] See Gray (1983) p. xi.

[4] Stephen (1993). As mentioned earlier, Stephen's book was worked up from a series of articles he had written in 1872-1873. As we discovered in Chapter 3 above, Stephen and Mill were well-acquainted, but not on altogether friendly terms. As we also noted above, J. F. Stephen also reviewed *On Liberty* in 1859. To ease indexing, Stephen is sometimes referred to as J. F. Stephen.

outlook, grounded in the perspective of the thinker he considered 'the greatest of English philosophers', Thomas Hobbes.[1]

The distinction between Stephen's and Mill's estimates of the human condition is, to Stephen's credit, not disguised. He is specific that Mill 'thinks otherwise than I of men and human life in general'.[2] The difference is like that between chalk and cheese: Mill thinks that humanity will progress if liberty is given freedom from pretty well all constraints. In contrast, 'the great defect' is that with this view, Mill 'has formed too favourable an estimate of human nature'.[3] J. F. Stephen, with his regard for Hobbes close to the surface, has a more pessimistic diagnosis of what it is to be human:

'I believe that many men are bad, a vast majority of men indifferent, and many good, and that the great mass of indifferent people sway this way and that according to circumstances, one of the most important of which circumstances is the predominance for the time being of the bad or the good. I further believe that between all classes of men there are and always will be real occasions of enmity and strife, and that even good men may be and often are compelled to treat each other as enemies either by conflicting interests which bring them into collision, or by their different ways of conceiving goodness'.[4]

The Hobbesian view of the human condition is clear: self-interest and the desire for security are primary factors and will motivate even good people to consider others as enemies in competition for the things that are wanted: self-interest overpowers the capacity for discrimination, hence the many being swayed towards what turns out to be the bad as well as the good; the many are vulnerable to the mood of opinion relative to situations as they arise; these primary motives compel humans, so liberty, requiring unrealistic capacities for autonomy, is never high on the list of applicable principles to serve a common good. Not only liberty but fraternity, the ideal of revolutionary France, as well as of all forms of socialism, is another inappropriate and mistaken value. Fraternity implies a form of equality, but equality is another notion untenable to J. F. Stephen: it is inappropriate to the human condition, as inequality will always emerge due to the competition that arises between self-interested individuals.

The critique emerging from *Liberty, Equality, Fraternity* merits explanation as the integration of points amounts to a heavy blow against Mill's project in his writings from *On Liberty* to *The Subjection of Women*. Regarding the role and status of morality, J. F. Stephen, bearing in mind his commitment to the legal profession, couples his regard for the rule of law with his view of human nature. As humans are driven by self-interest and thus to competition for the things in life they desire, 'all morality' operates with respect to 'either hope or fear'.[5] Stephen is sympathetic to the form of utility that Mill has for some time moved away from, that 'pleasure and pain' also feed into moral assessments so that the options for action that we face can be correctly calculated in terms of their likely consequences for the general happiness. However, given his favoured Hobbesian view of the human condition,

---

[1] Quoted in an autographical piece by Leslie Stephen, the brother of J.F. Stephen, as quoted by Warner – 'Foreword' to Stephen (1993) p. xi. See also Stephen (1993) p. 59.
[2] Stephen (1993) p. 169.
[3] Stephen (1993) p. 31.
[4] Stephen (1993) p. 169.
[5] Stephen (1993) p. 8.

Stephen thinks that morality, related to law, will relate 'to fear far more commonly and far more emphatically than to hope'. This suggests that human societies need the mantle of law to have moral parameters for an active life. The law, as Stephen knows well, has a battery of measures and controls that can be applied as and when necessary, but their deterrent function works to give scope for the proper mode of liberty.

This is not Mill's form of liberty, which Stephen characterises as the principle to 'let every man please himself without hurting his neighbour'.[1] Stephen thinks that with his attempt to present a principle of liberty, Mill asserts an abstract and ahistorical view of liberty – one that floats free from the constraints of law or opinion in the manner endorsed in Stephen's work. His view is that if liberty is properly orientated to the developed traditions of morality and law, then we can and should live in associations and relationships with others, living in a collegiate manner and managing disputes along the way, with the ever-present canopy of law to keep us on the path of righteousness. Otherwise, Stephen thinks it is as 'irrational' to ask 'whether liberty is a good or a bad thing' as it is to ask whether fire is good or bad.[2] The obvious point is that both are good in the right 'time, place and circumstance'. Moreover, Stephen doubts that 'the state of our knowledge is such as to enable us to enunciate any "one very simple principle as entitled to govern absolutely the dealings of society with the individual in the way of compulsion and control". We must proceed in a far more cautious way and confine ourselves to such remarks as experience suggests about the advantages and disadvantages of compulsion and control'.[3]

J. F. Stephen makes a point of stressing the issue of the worth of compulsion and control because in his view of the human condition, variations of compulsion and control, not least from the rule of law, are his favoured way of serving the utilitarian and other ideals that he defends. By 'other ideals', it is only fair to say that Stephen devotes a fairly considerable portion of his book to defending the role that the Christian faith has in providing a corrective to what he finds in Mill's work, commenting that 'morality depends upon religion'.[4] Since Mill would concede nothing on any such points, on the grounds that the evidences for the truth of Christianity do not pass muster, there is a sense in which he and Stephen are never for long on the same hymn-sheet. Accordingly, we will pass over these elements of Stephen's case in silence.

J. F. Stephen is not altogether convincing in his attempt to isolate Mill's analysis of liberty from history and, by implication, from the textures of real life. Mill always keeps clear that the social realities and traditions, including custom and law, have significance within human culture: the issue is that of the extent to which they should be actively and prohibitively deployed, and in Mill's view, high degrees of restraint work best in allowing the maximal scope for the engineering of fresher truths for allowing individuality to blossom and for the art of life to be pursued.

The differing perspectives of Stephen and Mill flow partly from the contrasting ways they see historical development. Mill traces the history of liberty as something

---

[1] Stephen (1993) p. 9.
[2] Stephen (1993) p. 34-35.
[3] Stephen (1993) p. 35. The quotation is from *OL* I: 9.
[4] Stephen (1993) p. 175.

shifting from the many seeking liberty from the tyrannical one to the predicament in a more democratic mindset where there is a need for liberty from the governance of the tyranny of opinion.[1] He thinks that in and through individuals engaging in debate and discussion, this associative review fosters progress and development with opinion and the law acknowledged as offering measures that might be rightly deployed to manage and correct extreme cases of individual excess.

Stephen's view of the history of liberty and progress shows that humanity accumulates benefits over time through the actions and ministrations of social and governmental action. He likens the historical pattern to a 'stream of water' that 'flows down a hill'.[2] He means, in case we are not experienced with the vagaries of streams running down a hill, that the progress of descent is irregular with some changes of pace, with various eddies and pools. Analogously, political history exhibits varied influences. Considering the period since the seventeenth century, he cites the influences of 'the Puritan, the Whig… the Radical' on the one side, and on the other, 'the Cavalier, the Tory, and the Conservative'. He thinks that all have contributed to the development of society: it is not a result of one set or group, nor is it an organised and united effort. Stephen denies the worth of any theoretical overview to interpret what he sees as a pattern of events, trends, movements, and interests that shape the emergent society. He thinks it is dangerous and distracting for theorists to abstract from one strand of this complex and then impose a template for the true solution – here, he is probably aiming a dart at Mill, the philosophical radical.

Concerning liberty, J. F. Stephen considers that 'discussions… are in truth discussions about a negation'.[3] He is thinking of what in later times is classified, as by Berlin, as negative liberty, a condition of freedom from all constraint.[4] Stephen's take on this is the view that to try to solve social and related problems through a review of liberty is 'like attempts to discover the nature of light and heat by inquiring after dark and cold'. Stephen's alternative view is that these matters are best explored through a study of 'the direction and nature of the various forces, individual and collective, which in their combinations or collision with each other, and with the outer world, make up human life'.

From this, Stephen's view is that within the range of values that form a part of what humans can use, liberty has importance as a principle involving 'not the bare absence of restraint, but the absence of injurious restraint'.[5] In this form, applications include 'the liberty of acquiring property'.[6] Stephen also thinks that 'legislation and public opinion' should protect privacy.[7] Here we may think that the region of self-regarding life is being given some credit by Stephen, but its scope is more constrained than Mill's: what is really meant is more the sphere of personal and family life and 'the relations of love and friendship', which so far as possible should be free from 'law or the coercion of public opinion'.[8] In the public sphere,

---

[1] See *OL* I: 2-5 and Chapter 4 above.
[2] Stephen (1993) p. 118.
[3] Stephen (1993) p. 119.
[4] As discussed above and with reference to Berlin (2017).
[5] Stephen (1993) p. 122.
[6] Stephen (1993) p. 120.
[7] Stephen (1993) p. 106.
[8] Stephen (1993) p 108.

however, 'the influence of public opinion is incalculably great'. This is meant in an open way – the influence may be positive or negative, for such opinion is 'multiform', ranging from local gossip to trends in reasoned opinion with much wider influence. He believes that the power of opinion is dependent on 'its nature and on the nature of the person on whom it acts'. Accordingly, anyone who is 'calm, strong, and rational… will know when to despise and when to respect it'.

Here, Stephen's appeal appears to be towards the sort of innate sense or intuition that individuals might or might not have – which is precisely what Mill thinks is not good enough as a counter to the threats of public opinion; hence the case for the liberty of thought and discussion to better prepare individuals to discern better and more vital truths. Subsequent experience suggests that the potent force of public or mass opinion, or trends, fashions, and styles, play more to the risks and perils for qualitative development we are warned against by Mill.

J. F. Stephen's thinking brings him to a neat realisation that the interrelation of liberty, equality, and fraternity means that if, as he thinks, Mill has mistaken liberty, then, like a pack of cards, equality and fraternity also fall. Equality is an ideal in democracy and certainly in Mill's thinking on marital relationships, divorce, and universal suffrage. The problem is that equality is torpedoed by the view of human nature that focuses on self-interest, as in the Hobbesian view that it is every person for himself and against all the rest. This means that however we try to manufacture a condition of equality, 'the strongest man in some form or other will always rule'.[1] If we imagine a 'pure democracy', the rulers will inevitably be the 'wirepullers and their friends'.[2] Changes such as the move to democracy, lauded as a move to greater equality, are a sham: all that happens is the changes 'alter the conditions of superiority much more than its nature'. Depending on the period and on circumstances, someone who is 'a powerful character', or one who has 'cunning', or 'the power of dispatching business', or 'eloquence', or 'having a good hold upon current commonplaces and facility in applying them to practical purposes will enable a man to climb on his neighbours' shoulders and direct them this way and that'.

J. F. Stephen sees fraternity as the expression of a fanatical outlook that rides roughshod over the rightful sense of the human condition, which is seen as being vested in the individualism of self-interest. Fraternal hopes are then articulated under the pretence that 'an indefinite number of unknown persons… may be brought into a state which the theorist calls happiness'.[3] Theorists of this kind are, it is suggested, more than ready 'to sacrifice that which living people actually do regard as constituting their happiness to his own vision of what will constitute the happiness of other generations'. Doubtless, Stephen is thinking back to the French revolution, but his comment here is prescient regarding some of the trends, ideologies, and events of the twentieth century. He has some neat lines to express the problem here that links to his liberty-rich defence of privacy:

'Nothing… is a greater nuisance, or in many cases, a greater injury, than the love of a person by whom you do not want to be loved. Every man's greatest happiness is that which makes him individually most happy, and of that that he and only he can judge'.

---

[1] Stephen (1993) p. 154.
[2] Stephen (1993) p. 155.
[3] Stephen (1993) p. 181.

Stephen's view is that social controls and government effectiveness bring about the changes that enable and mark human progress. He considers that Mill was wrong to think that liberality of thought and discussion was needed to ensure that fresh and vital truths were forged and that this theory undermined the role of established authorities in managing the transmission and development of intellectual and social or political aspects of life. Mill, in Stephen's view, had gone astray. The idea of there being a benefit in the discussion and review of varying circumstances and views on issues of truth is rejected: 'goodness is various, variety is not in itself good'.[1]

It would not ever be likely that Mill's views and Stephen's could be reconciled. The real issue is that Stephen wants to argue from and for a position in utilitarian thought from which Mill has departed by the time of *On Liberty*. Stephen seems oblivious to how Mill had been moving away from the Benthamite version from the late 1820s, what is said says about utility as a teleological end in connection with the Art of Life in the *Logic*, as well as how utility is linked to the progressive nature of human life in *On Liberty*. All this means that Mill addresses the issues of life with a set of principles that J. F. Stephen does not want or appreciate.

In his essay on Bentham, published in 1838, Mill points out that 'utility, or happiness', is 'much too complex and indefinite an end to be sought except through the medium of various secondary ends'.[2] Mill is, however, closer to Stephen in that Mill's sense of the complexity entailed in seeking the ultimate ends for life was set against his view that humans were complex, fallible, and improvable only through self-corrective development against open rather than over-prescriptive values. Mill lived before the age of flying or driving cars, but in both cases, if someone is being taught to fly or drive, instruction can only go so far. Eventually, the pilot or driver has to go solo, and how they make use of that will, all being well, make them better educated and, as individuals, capable of ongoing improvement.

Mill has high confidence in the liberality of debate and the practice of life to yield improvements: his optimism is such that, as Himmelfarb says, while he saw 'liberty as a means of achieving the higher reaches of the human spirit; he did not take seriously enough the possibility that men would also be free to explore the depths of depravity'.[3] The point is, she thinks, that Mill over-relies on the principle of the prevention of harm to others as the sole means of regulation for the active forms of liberty and individuality, and the many reservations Mill generates against preventative measures by opinion or law leaves open worrying scope for negative developments.

Mill's confidence is not, however, in liberty as a prescriptive end, so much as an enacting mode for what he sees as the operation of the Art or practice of life, with the cultivation of the range of qualities and virtues that make for a better life for individuals, and by extension, the rest of us. His ideas on education and on the range of duties that are owed to the young are some of the ways in which he thinks that the qualities that matter can be brought into play for the life that is to come.[4]

---

[1] Stephen (1993) p. 30.
[2] CW X p. 110. Mill originally published this essay in the *London and Westminster Review*. See Reeves (2007) p. 136ff.
[3] Himmelfarb (1974) p. 321.
[4] See *OL* V: 12-14.

For Mill, the strength and weakness of his view rest with his confidence in, as Ryan puts it, the human capacity for 'self-development and moral progress... the strand in his philosophy to which almost everything else is subordinate'.[1]

---

[1] Ryan (1987) p. 255.

13. Democracy, Liberty and Law

Introduction

From our review of Mill's case for liberty, a key aspect of what he favours is the understanding that people of sufficient maturity should be free, under certain conditions, to think and discuss whatever ideas appeal to them and free in their actions to do as they choose, to develop their interests and capacities, including arranging to meet with or associate with others to discuss, critique and disseminate ideas.[1]

A vital word employed here and used greatly by Mill is the term 'interests'. As we know, this term is employed regularly in *On Liberty*, where the most explicit meaning is of interests in terms of what may be considered as positive rights through 'express legal provision' (IV: 3) or those embraced under 'tacit understanding'. As a somewhat unusual liberal utilitarian, it is a feature of Mill's stance that he often prefers to use 'interest' to either happiness or pleasure. Thus, in *Utilitarianism*, there is the suggestion that 'interest' is, from the practical point of view, better than 'happiness' (which he links with pleasure) to express the 'ideal' of utilitarianism.[2]

We have seen that what that ideal turns out to be is, in his modified utility, a form of an indirect end achieved through the diverse interests, protected by liberty, that enable people to develop, explore and progress. Within the sweep of *On Liberty*, Mill is keen to advance the idea that there is a maximal benefit for all if each person, from their own distinct perspective, articulates their own ideas and views, with an equal opportunity to think, discuss and associate with those with whom they please.[3] This covers what two or more people talk about when they converse over coffee, as well as what a notable thinker says or writes to a learned audience or says in a conversation or interview. In such settings, ideas are akin to footballs, and they may be kicked around without fear or favour.

The processes held in mind here are envisaged as bringing clear benefits. Free discussion and the virtue of disagreement centre on the view that by these means, the best ideas under consideration are tested so that either they are vindicated as the most persuasive or replaced by others that offer more compelling truths; or on matters where it is unclear as to what the best perspectives are, we have through free debate and the disagreements that we work out, the opportunity to advance our understanding of the best options for life and thought.

Linked into this notion of liberty was the qualifier that the liberty of expression might only be constrained if what was thought, discussed, and disseminated through arguments in person or writing became sufficiently inflammatory to incite some to intemperate action that led to others being physically harmed or so constrained that they cannot cultivate their own individuality in the reciprocal ethos of liberty. Mill has in mind provocative teachings given to those hungering for action against some real or imagined adversary.[4] Liberty of action to the end of developing the

---

[1] See *OL* I:12 for Mill's statement of these ideas.
[2] *Util* II:17.
[3] For Mill's ideas on the history of liberty see *OL* I:1-8, and Chapter 7 above.
[4] See *OL* III: 1.

individual's character through the pattern of life best suited to them is to be similarly free from constraint, in Mill's view, conditioned by the person's action being undertaken at their own 'risk and peril' (III: 1). Again, such action would also be limited by the injunction not to risk 'harm to others' (I: 9).

In contrast, harm to the development of all is seen to rest in coercive tyrannies of the majority of opinion, and more pointedly, on particular issues with the articulation of what Mill terms 'a theory of social rights' (IV: 19), where it becomes 'the absolute social right of every individual that every other individual shall act in every respect as he ought; that whosoever fails thereof in the smallest particular violates my social right and entitles me to demand from the legislature the removal of the grievance'.

Mill sets out this warning of social rights in the context of his criticism of those who want to limit or ban the purchase and use of alcohol. He applies the notion to attitudes to forms of action but notes that the principle at stake 'is far more dangerous than any single interference with liberty' and that 'there is no violation of liberty that it would not justify'. Here Mill has a prescient point, for, in modernity, a consistent aspect of public debate focuses on how far matters of outlook and argument can be 'defined by each claimant according to his own standard' and then protected by his 'social right'. This is, in effect, a tension between the negative and positive modes of liberty as defined by Berlin. In Mill's presentation, the latter is manifest in his aspiration for progressive and diverse human development: that of the ostensibly liberal modernity is for human life to embrace a cloak of common respect for a range of outlooks held within certain currents of contemporary moral feeling.

In rehearsing some of Mill's concerns in *On Liberty*, we set the scene for the reviews in the next two chapters. We will be referencing several of Mill's lines of thought as we work through some matters of controversy where there is a consistent concern with the extent to which people are entitled to have what Mill expresses as 'a vested interest in each other's moral, intellectual, and even physical perfection', as opposed to the liberty principle's claim that, 'over himself, over his own body and mind, the individual is sovereign' (I: 9).

The unashamed implication of this tension is that there is a demonstrable case for registering the wider and truly progressive social virtue of the liberty of thought and discussion and constructive disagreement, all within the parameters of negative liberty. We test this out with the issues considered below. However, we begin by looking at how just constraints may fit the ideal of a democratic and liberal society. We then look at some issues arising from the related province of legal reform.

Democracy, Constraint and a Liberal Society

It might be thought that, in general, in developed and liberal democratic societies, the liberties of thought, discussion and action have become normative, and only in extreme times have they been constrained. In this perspective, a valid case for justified constraint would be the measures introduced in the UK in 1939, giving the government the legal power to do whatever was expedient for the defence of the realm.[1] This meant that rationing, conscription, limits on movement and travel and other challenges to the usual liberties were sanctioned and very largely accepted in the national interest and in the longer-term project of defending freedom. Related to the wider political context, a line of thought in Western democracies within which liberty is given scope was that regard for liberty was central to the defence and other responses to the fascist tyrannies of the 1930s and 1940s and the defence sustained against the communist states through the period of the cold war. A more recent and persistent example comes through the various lockdown restrictions on freedom of action and association entailed by the Covid19 Pandemic. Here, the wider concern to protect people led to a general acceptance of a range of restrictions on the liberty of action.

As we know, Mill has reservations about how democratic thinking infuses a society to give rise to a habitual reliance on conventions and majority views. However, the democratic and liberal link has strong provenance, and despite his sense of the problems which come with his criticism of the tyrannical risks of the majority, Mill is, in general, supportive of democratic progression and development.

Just before and during his time in parliament, the American Civil War was underway, with Mill emphatically supporting the cause of the Union against the Confederacy.[2] In that period, and in the wake of one of the most devastating but significant battles of the war, one major impetus was given to affirming the link between liberties in general and liberal democracy. This link, still possessing considerable heft in modernity, comes in the presentation given in President Abraham Lincoln's Gettysburg Address of 1863, as in the following extracts:

'Four score and seven years ago our fathers brought forth on this continent 'a new nation, conceived in Liberty, and dedicated to the proposition that all men are created equal.... Now we are engaged in a great civil war, testing whether that nation or any nation so conceived and so dedicated, can long endure... We are met on a great battle-field of that war. We have come to dedicate a portion of that field, as a final resting place for those who here gave their lives that that nation might live. It is altogether fitting and proper that we should do this... The world will little note, nor long remember what we say here, but it can never forget what they did here. It is for us the living, rather, to be dedicated here to the unfinished work which they who fought here have thus far so nobly advanced. It is rather for us to be here dedicated to the great task remaining before us—that from these honoured dead we take increased devotion to that cause for which they gave the last full measure of devotion—that we here highly resolve that these dead shall not have died in vain—that this nation, under God, shall have a new birth of freedom—and that government of the people, by the people, for the people, shall not perish from the earth'.[3]

In this passage, Lincoln alludes to the American Declaration and the affirmation of liberty as a given right conjoined with 'equality for all', and the passage ends with the eulogy to freedom and that ideal mode of democratic governance, 'of the people,

---

[1] Here the *Emergency Powers (Defence) Act 1939* is relevant. See the www.parliament.uk website for details: https///www.parliament.uk/about/living-heritage/transformingsociety/private-lives/yourcountry/collections/collections-second-world-war/second-world-war-legislation/emergency-powers-defence-act-c20-1940-/. It is noteworthy that this act was passed in peacetime, in August 1939.
[2] See for example CW XIV p.823 pp. 827-830; pp. 889-890, and CW XV pp 992-993
[3] https///www.britannica.com/event/Gettysburg-Address. Lincoln (1809-1865) delivered the address on November 16th, 1863. In full, the address runs to just 272 words.

by the people, for the people'. We should note how Lincoln assumes and affirms the relationship between liberty, equality and democracy.

A view over a part of the battlefield at Gettysburg, near where Abraham Lincoln delivered his Gettysburg Address.

The Statue of Liberty in New York Harbour expresses Lincoln's vision. It was not constructed until 1885-1886, after some years of difficulty with fundraising. The statue was a gift from France and designed by F. A. Bartholdi (1834-1904).

Liberty and the Law

With the liberal democratic model of life, a commonly assumed view is that personal, social and political life operates within and under the rule of law. In the UK, at least two related kinds of development have come to bear on this that relate closely to the discussions provoked by Mill.

The first can be activated by thinking back to Berlin's classification and to the strands of liberty, where we can see a range of cases for developing the liberty of thought, speech and action in the negative sense. In modernity, this has been challenged by, or on behalf of, those who seem to avow a liberal society, but in a positive sense, specifically expressive of the wish to be positively free to live a life without offence.

This trend has exercised a great deal of debate, not least within institutions of higher education, whose missions, however varied, are generally assumed to operate on the premise of free intellectual enquiry and debate. In recent times, the issue has consistently arisen over and about who can say what, even in the context of university education, where, as we mentioned earlier, what can be termed a 'cancel culture' has sometimes prevailed, whereby the contextual integrity of free debate has been eroded, and some individuals will be rebuked, criticised and ostracised for something they said or did that others dislike, disapprove of, or with which they disagree. In this, no obvious time or effort goes into a process of reasoned argument, suggesting prohibitive implications for the scope of the liberty of thought, discussion and action.[1]

Secondly, and linked to these matters, are changes in the law that show how, in an elaboration of what Mill was worried about in terms of 'social rights' (IV: 19), there is, through the accumulation in the doctrine of human rights, the development of legal sanctions to protect a wider and wider range of those who wish for equality of regard within life and so before the law. These protections and the assumed social rights work well under the ethos of positive liberty, but they provoke turbulence for those concerned with negative liberty and the positive benefits that accrue from the processes of free discussion.

To shed more light on some of the underlying problems we have identified, we turn to some of the ways that law has a bearing on the shape and condition of liberty. As we do, a point worth stressing is that it has become something of a commonplace to have the notion of liberty defended under an appeal to a sense of equality. It might, for example, be argued that as of right, people are free on matters of belief, action and association. That is to say, it is commonly assumed that, consistent with age and maturity, people are entitled at their own discretion to choose and follow whatever religious, moral and political approaches they like; that they can act in accordance with their own judgement, and that they can meet with others freely and without restriction.[2] The sense of 'their own discretion' provides a rider to all of these freedoms: if a person acts in a way that is perceived to harass, menace or injure

---

[1] A conspicuous example of this is the case of the historian Dr David Starkey, who, in July 2020, experienced emphatic 'cancellation' after a remark in an interview which led to him being accused of racism. Starkey apologised for the remark, but rejected the charge, explaining how his comments had been taken out of context and misrepresented. See 'The day I was cancelled'. Article by David Starkey, *The Critic*, September 2020: https://thecritic.co.uk/issues/september-2020/the-day-i-was-cancelled/
[2] Assuming that no Covid19 Pandemic restrictions apply.

the feelings of another, that action is seen as harmful in a way inconsistent with personal freedom. This equality-based freedom entails an obligation to be reciprocally respectful of the other, such that not only must a person's actions and words not be menacing or injurious, but they also must not cause offence or distress. Here, while menace and injury might garner wide support as undesirable for Mill's notion of liberty, terms such as 'offence' and 'distress' are extremely contentious: causing either or both offence or distress in a debate over something where ideas are under critical review is not obviously illicit, and the matter is pertinent to how we might read and react to Mill's defence of liberty, which is presented as having little regard for the risks and perils of giving offence or causing upsets in and through free debate: this Mill sees as a legitimate element in the process of developing the best truths of which we are capable.[1]

The Issue of Human Rights

If we keep the thought that the best ideas for the wider development of humanity emerge through unfettered debate, we now move on to look at the specifics that those with a concern for liberty have with a number of legal measures that might be perceived as challenging and reducing the scope of the liberty of debate and discussion.[2] The tensions which the law does something to exacerbate include a provision in the Human Rights Act 1998 (Article 10), although before we look at the detail, it is worth pointing out that the Human Rights Act (HRA) was framed in UK law when the UK was in membership of the European Community. Post-Brexit, the UK government announced in December 2020 that an independent review would be set up to report in Summer 2021 on whether and how the Act might be revised and amended in the light of the UK's change of status, not least in relation to the European Commission of Human Rights. In December 2021, reports emerged of proposals to amend the HRA through a new bill of rights that, from the details released so far, seems intended to correct some of the trends that flow from the HRA.[3]

To understand why it might be thought that the HRA needs correction, we need to look first at some of the provisions in the HRA as it stands. Within it, we have in Provision 12 a commitment to the defence of 'the right to freedom of expression' with particular reference to 'journalistic, literary or artistic material'. There is also an acknowledgement of the value of considering 'the public interest' over issues of whether or not any given material should or should not be published. One might think there is bound to be tension here, and in Article 10, the tension is explicit with the legal equivalent of two impossible things before breakfast.

On the one hand, the Act states the following:

---

[1] See *OL* Chapter II, and Chapter 5 above.
[2] See https///www.libertyhumanrights.org.uk/human-rights/free-speech-and-protest/speech-offences.
[3] The gov.uk website says the review of evidence for the report would run to the end of October 2021. In December 2021 the Justice Secretary, Dominic Raab, announced plans for a UK Bill of Rights to modify aspects of the HRA. See 'Human Rights Act plans: Criminals to be deported under new bill of rights'. Article by Jonathan Ames, *The Times* on line, 14/12/2021.

'Everyone has the right to freedom of expression. This right shall include freedom to hold opinions and to receive and impart information and ideas without interference by public authority and regardless of frontiers. This Article shall not prevent States from requiring the licensing of broadcasting, television or cinema enterprises'.[1]

Here, 'everyone' having 'the right to freedom of expression' and to 'receive and impart information and ideas without interference by public authorities' is Mill-rich in terms of affinity with *On Liberty's* defence of the liberty of thought and expression.

However, in the next clause, the Act says something by way of a qualification:

'The exercise of these freedoms, since it carries with it duties and responsibilities, may be subject to such formalities, conditions, restrictions or penalties as are prescribed by law and are necessary in a democratic society, in the interests of national security, territorial integrity or public safety, for the prevention of disorder or crime, for the protection of health or morals, for the protection of the reputation or rights of others, for preventing the disclosure of information received in confidence, or for maintaining the authority and impartiality of the judiciary'.

Here a raft of interferences in terms of 'formalities, conditions, restrictions or penalties' come into play. An implicit influence is coming, one suspects, from a view of 'the public interest' as noted in Provision 12 of the Act. The 'freedoms' to which we have a positive right by law are to be qualified in the names of duty and responsibility, where such duty and responsibility is owed to – and the list is perhaps one of those where the particular order matters – 'the interests of national security, territorial integrity or public safety'. Let us call this List A. Then, in List B, we have 'the prevention of disorder or crime, for the protection of health and morals, for the protection of the reputation or rights of others'. Finally, we have what we can call List C: 'for preventing 'the disclosure of information received in confidence, or for maintaining the authority and impartiality of the judiciary'.

The three lists derived from this second clause of Article 10 enable a convenient inspection of the many and varied restrictions presented as conditioning the liberty of 'everyone' having 'the right to freedom of expression'. The Act is alert to how, in practical terms, it will come into play in case law. Hence the modulation that the restrictions 'may be' operational – or they may not. However, the potential for constraints is clear in application to a considerable variety of matters that make up our three lists.

Suppose we are committed to freedom of expression with the implicit notion of liberty of thought. Would we be considerate of and feel a duty and responsibility to 'the public interest' such that we would self-regulate what we write or say to protect the factors grouped in List A: 'national security, territorial integrity or public safety'? A matter to reflect on is how we determine who decides what will be commensurate with 'the public interest'. As a rule, matters of national security are, for example, delegated to governments and their agencies, and if we think governments are to be wholly trusted with such matters, we will incline to self-

---

[1] On the Human Rights Act 1998 see
https:///www.legislation.gov.uk/ukpga/1998/42/schedule/1?view=plain; and for news on the Independent Review of the Act, see https:///www.gov.uk/guidance/independent-human-rights-act-review.

restraint. However, it is not hard to imagine historical and so perhaps future cases where we might think it to be in the public interest to challenge something that the government says it is in the interests of national security to keep as a matter of secrecy.[1] In the last resort, the government's interest is not identical to the national interest.

As regards 'territorial integrity', is the point that in the UK, no one should engage in discussion over the arguable case over Scottish independence – something that would definitely alter the UK's territorial integrity? Concerning public safety, the Act might be thinking of liberty not being used to incite people to endanger themselves: someone with charismatic powers preaching that all who run over Beachy Head will find eternal bliss would be worth suppressing in accordance with the harm principle as Mill conceives it. But in the interests of public safety, we might organise and speak against the interests and legal threats of others who manage licensed theme parks with exotic rides if we knew that cuts in maintenance made those rides unsafe.

Moving to List B, we have a gloss that, with the potent word 'or,' links 'disorder' and 'crime'. Suppose we allow that we have a sense of equity over justice to see a duty in general to prevent crime, even if this means that we have to suspend the exercise of freedom. However, 'disorder' would seem to be a different kettle of fish. Disorder could be a form of peaceful civil disobedience, resulting in considerable disruption, such as blocking motorways in a protest against global warming or blockading a port to protest about unlicensed fishing. However, it is in no way consistent with a worry about such disruptions to suggest that a preventative duty should inhibit the free expression of opinion and the freedom of action entailed through such civil disobedience – with the attendant risks and perils for the individuals concerned.

And what of the responsibilities to protect 'the prevention of health and morals, for the protection of the reputation or rights of others'? It is not clear that the public interest is or would ever be served if the health or well-being of individuals, their morals, reputation or rights are never subject to challenge. Problematically, the Act rolls all of these elements into the clause involving duty and responsibility in a manner that encourages a restraint of liberty, which means that the second clause in Article 10 stands in something of an implausible relation to the defence in the first clause of the right of free expression.

With this tension, the key problem is that the right to free expression is, as Lincoln thought, an axiom within a liberal democracy. A 'harm to others' restriction to inhibit inciting violence is not unreasonable. What is far less explicable and a distinct threat to the developmental possibilities of negative liberty and the principles of liberal democracy is the suggestion that the moral health of people is somehow enhanced by restrictions on the critical reviews of all of the ideas and values we might think worthwhile by others with reason to disagree. As we know, Mill's view is that it is very worthwhile to derestrict critical reviews and to see virtue in the process of disagreement.

With List C, liberty might be conditioned by the factors noted of protecting confidences and maintaining the independence – the 'impartiality' and 'authority'

---

[1] The case of R vs Ponting (1985) is worth considering in this context, or perhaps Winston Churchill's opposition to appeasement in the 1930s.

of the judiciary. This last clause has a particular weight in the UK setting, given the nature of the political settlement with the commitment to the concept and reality of the division of powers. Broadly there would be equipoise in restricting liberty to maintain the independence of an impartial and thereby authoritative judiciary that operated as such in defence of liberal democracy. But there are times and places where authoritative judiciaries have operated to serve regimes that are resolutely illiberal – and liberty might be thought a valid instrument to wage opposition in such settings. As to the protection of confidences, this is a masterly bit of vague generalisation – for everything depends on the case of what confidences are shared with whom and over what.

For all the issues of tension and concern, the overall impact of the Human Rights Act is to give force to the sense that freedoms are conditional and that the restraint of liberty is to be applied in a range of settings in the public interest. The themes resonate with a form of positive liberty that suppresses Mill's notion of the liberty of thought and discussion.

From the revisions suggested so far in the first reports about a new bill of rights, as noted above, it looks as if there is a concern to redress the practical imbalance that has grown up in practice between the HRA's defence of freedom of expression on the one hand, and of duties and responsibilities on the other. The issue is that in social life and through the practice of the law, there has been a perceived trend that promotes an oversensitivity to defend against any perceived threats to the rights and interests of those who express concerns about being offended, as opposed to defending the residual liberties of thought and expression. The proposals have, as a signal aim, the following:

'To strengthen the quintessentially UK rights, which are the cornerstone of our tradition of liberty and.. our way of life. Freedom of speech is the liberty that guards all the others. Yet, a combination of court-innovated privacy law, licensed by the HRA, and the hyper-sensitivity of some in our society to opposing views, has incrementally and surreptitiously whittled away the scope for the rambunctious debate which is essential to our democracy. That is dangerous'.[1]

To challenge the danger, Mill is drawn into the matter with his comment: 'He who knows only his side of the case knows little of that' (II: 23). Accordingly, the reforms are aiming 'to strengthen free speech from that insidious attrition, mindful of the need to preserve our ability to tackle today's online threats — from terrorist radicalisation to the grooming of the vulnerable by sexual predators'.

There are some positive signs in these proposals for a prospective improvement for the liberty of debate under the ethos of negative liberty. However, such liberty is under stress from a number of other pieces of legislation.[2]

---

[1] 'New bill of rights will be deliver a healthy dose of common sense'. Article by Domonic Raab, MP. *The Times* online, 14/12/2021. See also 'Rights and Wrongs'. Leading Article, *The Times* online, 14/12/2021.
[2] Here use is made of the www.gov.uk website and the www.libertyhumanrights sources noted earlier.

Rights and Legal Protection

The Public Order Act (1986), for example, considers it an offence if a person's behaviour, or use of threatening, abusive or insulting words either causes or is likely to cause another person harassment, alarm or distress. Here the other person is invariably the arbiter of whether harassment, alarm or distress has been experienced. This seems to place well into the middle-distance the classical notion that in the law, a major consideration is the motive or intention of the putative offender.

In the oft-used cricketing analogy, the predisposition of the Public Order Act's stipulation puts the liberty-favouring individual very much onto the back-foot, in a cautious and restrictive defensive posture: the problem is that liberty of thought and expression trades on critical review and debate, but if the criticism of ideas can be taken personally, and become alarming, distressing, harassing, and so an offence, and if no weight is given to matters of motive and intention, liberty of thought and expression is in difficulty.

Moving into the computer age of modernity, the Communications Act 2003 (Section 127) applies similar warnings and implied expressive restrictions over electronic communication, with emails and other social media platforms in mind.[1] Thus, messaging comments that are grossly offensive, menacing, indecent or obscene become offences. Again, a snag with this is that such messages or texts – notoriously one-dimensional and flat when read out of context – are to be assessed and found wanting by the person or persons offended, without due regard to the intention or motive, mood, wit or humour of the writer.

Acts that make it an offence to stir up hatred by some against others fall well within the valid restriction of the harm principle. Relevant here are the Gender Recognition Act (2004), the Racial and Religious Hatred Act (2006), and the Criminal Justice and Immigration Act (2008), which amended the Public Order Act by extending the measures to include as offences threatening behaviour or words over matters of sexual orientation.

The Terrorism Act 2006 might seem self-evidently correct in making incitement to or the celebration of terrorism an offence. However, on the principle that one person's terrorist is another person's freedom fighter, the terms of the act are such as to make it difficult to criticise oppressive or tyrannical governance through public statements.

Suppose that Country X is ruled by the military, who have ousted the democratic government, and the military rulers are using the army to prosecute and imprison all critics and suppress all opposition with violence and disregard for human life. If, for example, we live in the UK, and write that the rulers of Country X have gone to war against its own people, so the people have a just cause to fight back, we might be seen, under the 2006 Act, as inciting terrorism. That we are writing on the case

---

[1] On this, the case of Harry Miller is instructive: see 'Being offensive is part of British culture, says free speech campaigner Harry Miller'. Article by John Simpson, *The Times* online, 25/12/2021. Miller had tweeted something about transgender issues that someone found offensive. They complained and Miller received notification from the police that a 'non-crime incident' had been recorded against him, and his twitter account was suspended. He discovered the police action breached Article 10 of the Human Rights Act's defence of freedom of speech, and won the case he took to the High Court and Court of Appeal. Miller's victory is a significant defence for the liberty of thought and discussion.

for just rebellion in Country X is not the point: by writing about why and how to rebel, we might unwittingly encourage terrorism in the UK.

Gender Identity and The Gender Recognition Act

Of the Acts mentioned, the Gender Recognition Act (2004) has become a key factor in some more recent matters of controversy.[1] Before we look at some details of the Act, it is important to set the context for our later consideration of some of the disagreements over gender identity and gender self-affirmation.

Amongst those who developed the case for gender identity being more transparently a part of normative life is the American philosopher and gender theorist Judith Butler.[2] The gist of the case built through Butler's work arises from the view that people become who they are through a process of self-realisation. This means that their identity and personhood are built up through their decisions, and their power of choice and self-determination have the lead role in self-actualisation. Within this, the idea is that the individual's awareness of gender, and their sexual identity in personal, social and cultural terms, is what is significant. The ideas of male, female, woman and man are seen as linguistic terms and as social conventions, not as biological or anthropological categories. On this basis, we could say that a person is not born male or female: at birth, they are assigned a gender and given a role that they may or may not later affirm in terms of personal identity, one that might not correlate with the body that they happened to have. In this latter case, the situation is, as Helen Joyce explains it, 'transgender', or 'trans for short'.[3]

The key aspect then advocated is that it is the person's sense of 'identity', rather than 'the body, that should determine how everyone else sees and treats them'. As we will see with some of the more recent debates, the most significant word in this definition is 'determine', for the trans activist view is the self-affirmation of gender is the sufficient guarantor of the validity of the claim, and so others are thereby determined to be required to accept this as an unarguable social reality.

According to the provisions of the UK's Gender Recognition Act, a person 'of either gender' and 'who is aged at least 18' may apply for 'a gender recognition certificate' so long as they have been 'living in the other gender' or have 'changed gender under the law of a country or territory outside the United Kingdom'. In this process, the term 'acquired gender' is used to denote either 'the gender in which the person is living' or 'the gender to which the person has changed under the law of the country or territory concerned' if it is outside the United Kingdom.

Consistent with the line of thought we have traced, it is clear that the Act uses the term 'gender' rather than biological sex as the residual identifier for how persons are to be understood. The Act establishes that 'a Gender Recognition Panel' will consider applications and grant gender recognition certificates so long as certain criteria are met. These include there being clear evidence from the applicant and

---

[1] The Act can be found at Gender Recognition Act 2004 at
https://www.legislation.gov.uk/ukpga/2004/7. Quotations are from this source, from sections 1-3 of the Act. In 2018 the Act was under review, but it was not altered through this process.
[2] Judith Butler (b. 1956). Butler's *Gender Trouble*, first published in 1990, gave considerable impetus to the case for a more open approach to gender identity. See Butler (2007).
[3] Joyce (2021) p. 1.

271

from relevant medical specialists that the applicant 'has or has had gender dysphoria', has 'lived in the acquired gender throughout the period of two years ending with the date on which the application is made', and 'intends to continue to live in the acquired gender until death'.

Here the term 'gender dysphoria' is significant, and the NHS offers the following definition, saying the term:

'... describes a sense of unease that a person may have because of a mismatch between their biological sex and their gender identity. This sense of unease or dissatisfaction may be so intense it can lead to depression and anxiety and have a harmful impact on daily life'.[1]

In the cases considered by Gender Recognition Panels, the Acts says that it is also relevant to consider what has been or is being planned by the applicant in terms of 'treatment for the purpose of modifying sexual characteristics'.

Here, although the Act sets out various stipulations and procedures by means of which a person's acquired gender may be certified, it does not limit certification to those who have surgical procedures to transition. This entailment is a scenario within which, as Joyce explains, 'gender identity, rather than sex, should be centred in law'.[2] It also clarifies that self-affirmation of gender identity is, in the long run, a sufficient means to secure legal transition. This shift from sex to gender in the focus on legal status leads to what has been described pejoratively by the writer J. K. Rowling, as 'Orwellian' policies.[3]

Rowling has been much criticised for her comments challenging the trans activist view that self-affirmation of gender as distinct from biological sex signals what is right and appropriate for legal status. In this case, as a resident of Edinburgh, she is alert to revisions to Scottish law whereby it is now the case that if a trans person who has self-affirmed as female but who is and remains biologically male is to be considered legally female in cases where 'she' has committed rape using 'her' penis. Rowling's point is that this, from the perspective of common sense and with regard to the entitlements of women, requires impossible levels of doublethink.[4]

This concern may be seen as part of a reaction against a longstanding trend, for well before the time of the Gender Recognition Act, pressure was mounting for a

---

[1] https://www.nhs.uk/conditions/gender-dysphoria/
[2] Joyce (2021) p. 237-238. One could say that the Gender Recognition Act provides a procedural method to recognise gender transition, but it does not allow straightforward gender self-affirmation, any more than Abortion Acts permit abortion on demand. Like the Abortion Act, the Gender Recognition Act nevertheless enables the required outcome for those who understand how to work through the system.
[3] 'J. K. Rowling attacks "Orwellian" transgender rape policy'. Article by Mike Merritt, *The Times* online, 13/12/2021. Orwellian thinking seems well established on the Isle of Wight, where at one school, parents have been told that pupils (aged 6) will be considered transphobic if they show an 'inability to believe that a transgender person is actually a "real" female or male'. Article by Jonathan Ames, 'School said boy, six, would be transphobic if he expressed confusion over classmate'. *The Sunday Times* online, 13/02/2022. J. K. Rowling engaged in more debate on this theme in March 2022, when criticising Sir Keir Starmer's contention that under the Gender Recognition Act (2004) and the Equalities Act (2010): 'A woman is a female adult, and in addition to that trans women are women'. Article by Katie Gibbons, 'J.K. Rowling attacked over gender views'. *The Times* online, 14/03/2022. Needless to say, Rowling thought little of Starmer's view which glossed the actual legal position in an attempt at amelioration..
[4] For those unsure about the references to Orwell, see Orwell's novel of 1948, *Nineteen Eighty-Four* – Orwell (2021).

more tolerant and more liberal approach to gender self-affirmation. The pressure continued and had a bearing on the consultation undertaken in 2018 on possible reforms to the Act. The consultation focused on the means and procedures a person had to go through to transition legally, an area of the Act that trans individuals and campaigners had suggested being too cumbersome and time-consuming.[1]

As it turned out, the consultation did not alter the original measures in the Act.[2] Nevertheless, the arguments for trans recognition and gender identity as a matter for self-affirmation came into play in wider public debate. We shall come back to this debate at several points in the reviews that follow. A consistent feature in the tension between the trans activists and their critics, is that the former invariably accuse those who argue against them of being transphobic, which is in no way intended as a compliment.[3]

The tensions here mean from the gender activist's perspective, it is the person's self-affirmed gender, rather than their sex, that matters. This is increasingly controversial because, as mentioned, what can be established as matters of biology and anthropology are replaced by what can be seen as social and linguistic conventions expressive of feelings – yet it is these expressed feelings that gain legal confirmation through certification and, as said, through a process that may well not entail surgical intervention.

The difference between these outlooks is that for a long time, it has been clear that there are a very small number of cases of people who find themselves to be transexual – to be born one sex and to come to feel that they identify as and with the other sex. Notable cases are those of Einar Wegener – later Lili Elbe, and Jan (formerly James) Morris.[4] These and like cases do not generally excite great moral controversy. In more recent times, and not least due to the prominence of gender identity theory, the number of people presenting as 'trans' has greatly increased.[5] One rather dramatic reason for this is that, despite the Gender Recognition Act's stipulation that cases of gender dysphoria leading to individual's applying for a gender recognition certificate was for individuals aged at least 18, many school-age students began presenting as experiencing gender dysphoria and requiring schools to acknowledge and accommodate this, allowing trans students to dress accordingly

---

[1] See Joyce (2021) for a clear account and review of the phases of this background. See p. 236 - the first steps in the USA towards the legal recognition of gender self-identification in 1992; p. 201ff: in 2019, School District 211 in Chicago votes to give trans students 'unrestricted access to private facilities' – i.e. to toilets and changing rooms; the case in 2020 in the USA of Bostock v. Clayton County, that adapted the 1964 Civil Rights Act so that in addition to discrimination against individuals on the grounds of 'race, colour, religion, sex and national origins' , discrimination against people on the grounds of gender identity was deemed illegal. This led President Biden, on his first day in office in January, 2021, to issue an order to all federal agencies, to alter their policies in light of the Bostock ruling – see Joyce (2021) p. 221. J. K. Rowling was again engaged in trans debate over the case of an eighteen year-old sixth form student whose amicable questioning of a speaker whose views implied that critical theory had more importance that biological fact led to her being verbally abused by her peers. This led the student to be removed from normal lessons, and in December 2021, she left her school to study at home. See J K Rowling defends girl "driven out of school for questioning trans ideology"'. Article by Nicola Woolcock. *The Times* online, 18/05.22.

[2] On this see https://commonslibrary.parliament.uk/research-briefings/cbp-9079/

[3] As in the case of the six-year-olds on the Isle of Wight, as considered above.

[4] See Joyce (2021) pp. 11-17 and pp. 26-27. Lili Elbe (1882-1931); Jan Morris (1926-2020). The 2015 film *The Danish Girl* is based on the story of Lili's life.

[5] See Joyce (2021) pp. 91ff.

and to be addressed by the pronoun for the affirmed gender.[1] This led the UK's Attorney General, Suella Braverman, to the view that schools had an obligation to treat children under the terms of the Gender Recognition Act, which affirms that as 'under-18s cannot get a gender recognition certificate, under-18s cannot legally change sex'. Consequently, if in a school, a 'male child' claims to be a 'trans girl', legally, they are still 'a boy or male' and 'schools have a right to treat them as such under the law'.

The defence of statute legal and the entailments following is a vital element in fostering reasoned discussion, but amongst the problems in developing an arena for such a discussion is the alternate subjectivist view of the nature of the truths we think we can obtain. Subjectivism, whatever the problems inherent within it, has emerged as a signal force in modernity.[2] Those who are disposed to the subjectivist imperative might argue that, as all truths are expressive and relative to personal self-affirmation, gender self-affirmation is one amongst them. To deny this is then seen as a form of phobic discrimination. On the subjectivist train of thought, we ease into a form of moral and epistemological neutralism: we are saying that all truths are expressive, self-affirmed and self-validated. Some choices might not excite much serious controversy, such as the preferences we express when choosing which colour socks to wear, which ice cream to choose, or, perhaps crucially, which beer to drink.

If gender identity is simply a matter of self-affirmation, the case is made that this affirmed gender takes precedence in life over what might otherwise be thought more determinative, the person's sex. Thus, men who self-affirm as gender transitioned to women claim entitlement and access to all activities and areas reserved for females. Such matters came to the fore in UK sport in March 2022, when there was news that the trans cyclist Emily Bridges would not be able to compete in a race including Laura Kenny.[3] In a piece published the day before, the former UK swimmer and long-time commentator Sharron Davies wrote that the inclusion of trans athletes in women's sport was reminiscent of the years she spent competing in the period when East German swimmers were 'androgenised' through the use of steroids and so capable of times eclipsing those of other competitors.[4] Davies' point was that trans athletes who self-affirmed as female and who accessed women's sport would, as individuals who were biologically male, retain certain physical characteristics that would advantage them in competition with women.[5] She called for a 'reasonable discussion based on facts and science, not ideology and feelings that only one group in the debate is allowed to have', suggesting that trans

---

[1] See 'Teachers should not pander to trans pupils, says Suella Braverman'. Article by Steven Swinford, *The Times* online 27/06/2022. Quotations following are from this source.
[2] See Taylor (2010) and (2003).
[3] See 'Trans cyclist Emily Bridges blocked from Laura Kenny race'. Article by John Westerby and Craig Lord, *The Times* online 31/03/2022.
[4] 'Sharron Davies: Injustice of transgender athletes has echo of the dopers I faced'. Article by Sharron Davies, *The Times* online 30/04/2022.
[5] Davies gives the example of the 'Q-angle' that is used in cycling the measure the relationship between the width of the hips and the knees. In biological terms, men have narrower hips than women, which means with less stress, they can cycle - and run and swim – faster than women.

athletes should be given a special category for competition and not be able to go into direct competition.[1]

The residual problem with justification by self-affirmation is that by saying that the views so affirmed are in the legal sense equal, we beg the question as to how and by what we might evaluate them, which of necessity, we will need to undertake in any case of conflict or disagreement. We approach a form of moral neutralism, and the risk is that the neutralist rides roughshod over the variety of considered views suggesting that in and for certain specific perspectives on life, such as those within biology and anthropology, some truths have a grounding and validity because they are not simply a matter of subjective affirmation. Evidence, experience, reflection, and argument can make certain views significant in a more substantive sense. Being born female or male with XX or XY chromosomes would be a case in point, just as, for example, it can be argued that some ice creams and, indeed, some beers are, for clear reasons, better than others.

We will return to the issues reviewed here in the next chapter, where we consider some matters of dispute touching on the matters of gender identity and trans rights.

As it happens, in recent times, a range of issues have emerged that focus on the matters with which Mill is concerned. In these matters, arguments on the benefits of the liberty of thought and discussion and liberty of actions are deployed that assume or hint at Mill's views. All-round, in these debates, his ideas on the specific problems of limiting such liberty of discussion and lacking respect for individuality in the practice of life are assumed but not often pressed over-explicitly. Accordingly, over the next two chapters, Mill's thinking on liberty is applied to these issues of debate, both to illuminate the issues and to see what further relevance there is for Mill's views.

---

[1] In June 2022, other sports moved to ban transgender athletes from women's internationals: see 'Rugby League bans transgender athletes from women's internationals'. Article by Matt Lawson, *The Times* online, 21/06/2022.

14. Liberty and Academic Freedom

This chapter reviews instances of debate and disagreement over issues concerning the scope and desirability of open discussion. What is in focus is the case for and the problems with the liberty of debate and discussion, as well as the liberty people have to live in a fashion consistent with their outlook and choice to develop their own character. In the background, what we are testing and assessing are Mill's ideas on the viability and virtue of liberty.

Discussing Colonialism

The first case study deals with the kind of issue Mill explores in the second chapter of *On Liberty*. If humans are fallible, the sense we have of the degree of truth or error in a view cannot, in all cases, be fixed in a definite sense.[1] In some cases, we might think we can fix things more or less.

It was not an issue for Mill, but the policies and views of the Nazis could be presented as wrong, unjustified and an expression of evil. That almost everyone thinks this suggests a sound basis for thinking that we do this from a sense of value or goodness and of measurable registers of the harms perpetrated by the Nazis on innumerable innocent individuals – or else, like the moral neutralist, we would just have to say we disliked the Nazis and their doings. Mill's idea is that, in principle, we keep pretty well all ideas under review, and then the best ideas we have are held sharp and fit for use in life, but subjecting them to criticism ensures they are not held as 'a dead dogma', but as 'a living truth' (II: 21). Mill also thinks that in most cases, the best view going forward is in doubt, so ongoing discussion is again the best way to clarify and refine the options.[2] Linked into this, ideas that appear to have limitations are, if held in review, likely to aid us, either in reaffirming how and why other ways are better or giving us some grounds for reassessment.

To illustrate these matters, we can take as an initial case study something provided by an Oxford Professor of Theology who provoked a great deal of debate when thinking and writing about the social and moral aspects of colonialism.

In 2017, Nigel Biggar, the Regius Professor of Moral and Pastoral Theology at the University of Oxford, organised at the University's behest a five-year project to examine Ethics and Empire.[3] This presented as an exercise in reassessment, and to explore the issues, Biggar wrote an article for *The Times* in which he commented on some trends in modern analyses of empire and colonialism.

In contrast to the prevailing views, which saw nothing positive and much that was reprehensible in colonialism, Biggar suggested that a more balanced perspective was probably needed, one where the injustices and the benefits of

---

[1] On Mill's fallibilistic view, see *OL* (II: 3-4), and Chapter 8 above.
[2] See *OL* (II: 34), and again, Chapter 8 above.
[3] Biggar has since written a book on this theme – *Colonialism: A Moral Reckoning*. It was due for publication in November 2021, then it was said to be appearing in July 2022 – but in July 2022 the Amazon UK website said publication would be in February 2023.

colonialism were considered proportionately.[1] Ironically, Biggar began his article with a brief account of the problems faced by an American academic, Bruce Gilley of Portland State University, whose article – 'The case for Colonialism' – for the *Third World Quarterly* (*TWQ*) challenged a particular 'orthodoxy', namely, that of giving 'western colonialism… a bad name', by suggesting that western colonialism had made positive contributions: enabling 'the formation of coherent political communities, reliable social institutions and… living-spaces where individuals and their families could flourish'.

As Biggar notes, Gilley's article created a storm of protest from people who could not conceive of such unorthodoxy against the consensus which held that colonialism was a wholly negative phenomenon. Fifteen out of the thirty-four members of the *TWQ* editorial board resigned over the article. So strong were the protests, including death threats to the magazine's editor from 'Indian nationalists', that the article was withdrawn.

Biggar aimed to reconsider the points made by Gilley, and central to this was an argument taken from the Nigerian writer Chinua Achebe who argued in his last work, *There Was a Country* (2012) as follows:

'Here is a piece of heresy. The British governed their colony of Nigeria with considerable care. There was a very highly competent cadre of government officials imbued with a high level of knowledge of how to run a country . . . British colonies were, more or less, expertly run'.[2]

The case of Zimbabwe was also put into the review. The massacre of some 20,000 Ndebele in Zimbabwe in 1983-4 was not committed by the British 'but by that patriarch of African nationalism Robert Mugabe'. What Gilley wanted to clarify was 'the notion that colonialism is always and everywhere a bad thing needs to be rethought in light of the grave human toll of a century of anti-colonial regimes and policies'.

Biggar's point was that Gilley had argued that there were some distinct 'virtues of colonial rule', including 'the formation of coherent political communities, reliable state institutions and therefore living-spaces where individuals and their families could flourish'. He notes how Gilley supports this with more references to Achebe, whose ideas include a note of appreciation for the order provided by colonial rule:

'One was not consumed by fear of abduction or armed robbery… One had a great deal of confidence and faith in British institutions'.

The point Achebe wants to stress was that while British justice could be exacting, it was in principle incorruptible: 'Now all that is changed'. Reflecting on this, Biggar fuses several points into his peroration: an ordered society might not sound

---

[1] See 'Don't feel guilty about our colonial history'. Article by Nigel Biggar, *The Times* online 30/11/2017. Bruce Gilley is Director of the Graduate Programme in Public Policy in the Mark O. Hatfield School of Government at Portland State University. His thoughts on his article and his response to critics can be found at www.nas.org

[2] As quoted by Biggar in 'Don't feel guilty about our colonial history', *The Times* 30/11/2017. Chinua Achebe (1930-2013). Further quotations are from this source. See Achebe (2010) for a collection of the novels *Things Fall Apart*, *No Longer at Ease*, and *Arrow of God* – the 'African trilogy'.

exciting, but it provides the context for life to 'flourish'. A timely example is that in 'the early years of communist rule in Beijing', Hong Kong became a preferred option for millions of Chinese citizens, who sought security and the rule of law.[1] Achebe is again a source of insight. Biggar notes how, in 2012, he was interviewed by some Iranian journalists 'who were pressing him to condemn colonialism', and he replied:

'The legacy of colonialism is not a simple one but one of great complexity, with contradictions — good things as well as bad'.

Biggar turns this thinking of the need for a 'balanced reappraisal' back on the self-understanding that the British might have of their past:

'For as we British read our past, so we understand ourselves; and as we understand ourselves, so we act in the future. If we believe what strident anti-colonialists tell us — namely, that our imperial past was one long, unbroken litany of oppression, exploitation and self-deception — then our guilt will make us vulnerable to wilful manipulation, and it will confirm us in the belief that the best way we can serve the world is by leaving it well alone. If on the other hand we recognise that the history of the British Empire was morally mixed, just like that of any nation state, then pride can temper shame. Pride at the Royal Navy's century-long suppression of the Atlantic slave trade, for example, will not be entirely obscured by shame at the slaughter of innocents at Amritsar in 1919. And while we might well be moved to think with care about how to intervene abroad successfully, we won't simply abandon the world to its own devices'.

The point of profiling Gilley was to show the degree to which freedom of debate as a constructive means to revise and refine ideas was not so much in evidence as a wall of repressive and negative comment, decrying any option but the received anti-colonialist opinion. Irony is then revealed in this matter in that the fray to which Biggar alluded in his review of Gilley's article was replicated in the UK, as Biggar's article provoked a similarly hostile reaction. With this, we have what is, in effect, a case study on the problem that arises in the contingent areas of human thought, such as those concerned with social and political life, ethics and values, where absolute truth and certainty are absolutely unobtainable. Unfortunately, this fairly basic intellectual insight seems lost on many who want to sustain what they offer as the only plausible view. What Biggar and Gilley were both attempting was the reopening of the liberality of discussion on a matter against a tradition of assuming that it was a completely settled and closed affair.

A review of the debate arising from Biggar's article was written by Dominic Kennedy and published in *The Times* in December 2017. Kennedy noted that Oxford University's Africa Society had suggested that Biggar 'was a genocide denier' who attempted a form of 'colonial apologism', yearning and re-justification through the pursuit of dishonest scholarship'.[2] Further, a Cambridge University academic, Professor Priyamvada Gopal, 'accused him of being a racist, dishonest

---

[1] At the time of writing China has tightened its governance of Hong Kong, and it is unclear whether some or perhaps many Hong Kong citizens will accept the option they have to move their life and business to the UK.

[2] Dominic Kennedy: 'Academics accused of "stirring up mob" against Nigel Biggar in free speech row'. *The Times* online 28/12/2017.

apologist for the Empire'.[1] Moreover, some sixty Oxford academics – 'mostly historians' – signed an open letter, saying that Biggar's Ethics and Empire project 'asks the wrong questions' and claiming that Biggar was adopting an approach that was 'too polemical and simplistic to be taken seriously'.

Kennedy notes that Oxford University had expressed support for Biggar in his work 'to consider the historical context of the British Empire and said he was entirely suitable to lead the ethics and empire project', and Dr Alexander Morrison, a tutor in history at New College, had also written to support Biggar, disassociating himself from his colleagues' open letter, and praising Professor Biggar as a scholar of distinction and integrity whose research deserved a scholarly engagement which he found absent from the open letter:

'They are dismissing out of hand and seeking to sabotage a research project in a discipline which is not their own before it has even begun... Hostile open letters of this kind are not the way to deal with academic disagreement: they are deeply corrosive of normal academic exchange, and simply encourage more of the online mobbing, public shaming and political polarisation which have sadly characterised this debate from the outset'.

The interesting aspect of this letter is how Morrison centres on the notion of there being certain principles to employ on matters of 'academic disagreement'. What he refers to as 'normal academic exchange' is the dialogic and interactive debate that scholars should have over issues and interpretations in such finite areas of review as these to tease out and refine the lines of thought that are best validated by the weight of evidence and by the power of reason. The operational imperatives are all as defended in Mill's rationale for the liberty of thought and discussion. In this modern setting, Biggar, like Gilley, could be seen as engaging in the business of free and open debate to the end of revising existing ideas against a template of tradition, but in reality, Biggar, like Gilley, was the victim of an assault from those with an absolutist viewpoint on what was and what was not within the legitimate range of thinking, which sought to cancel out Biggar's thoughts and his project and delegitimise this area of discussion.

To put another slant on this, Biggar and Gilley, and those supporting them, could be put under the ethos of negative liberty; they are arguing for an open debate on the matters in question for the sorts of benefits we have mentioned: their critics, who hoped to be free from being confronted by the lines of thought Biggar and others were generating, hold to a variant of positive liberty, in the sense that they assume that any consideration of a balance of values in something like the colonial experience is beyond the pale, such that free debate is only viable if such matters are dispatched to the long grass of a received and settled opinion.

---

[1] Priyamvada Gopal is Professor of Postcolonial Studies in the Faculty of English at the University of Cambridge, and a Teaching Fellow at Churchill College.

Jordan Peterson and Cambridge

Over the years since 2017, a good many other issues of challenge arose over who might say what on a university campus. One of the higher-profile cases concerned the Canadian psychologist Jordan Peterson, who in 2019 was offered a visiting fellowship at Cambridge University. Shortly afterwards, the offer was withdrawn.[1]

There was some debate over whether the change in policy was due to a photograph widely circulated on the internet and through the media that showed Peterson at a book-signing event, pictured with a man wearing a shirt on which was the slogan, 'I am a proud Islamophobe'. At the time of disinviting Peterson, the university did not allude to the photo but explained that it was 'an inclusive environment and we expect all our staff and visitors to uphold our principles. There is no place here for anyone who cannot'.

Peterson was, and remains, a notable contrarian. A professor of psychology at Toronto University, he came to wider public attention in 2016, when the case for gender identity that we considered earlier came into play in Canada. Peterson questioned the value of 'a federal amendment to add gender identity and expression to the Canadian Human Rights Act. This measure would make it illegal to stop someone from getting a job or discriminate against them in the workplace based on the gender they identify with or outwardly express'.

All this came as the Canadian systems adapted to accept the notion of gender self-identity as the marker for registering individuals rather than their biological sex. Peterson argued against this development, saying that 'the law was an infringement of free speech' and that he would refuse to use any pronoun other than 'he' or 'she'. His views led to a series of protests across the campus of Toronto University. Peterson challenged the university's scheme for 'mandatory anti-bias training' and made other challenges 'against Marxism, human rights organisations, HR departments' and what he terms 'an underground apparatus of radical left political motivations' that sought to force 'gender-neutral pronouns on him', so impinging on his liberty.

All of this was in the public domain when Cambridge made Peterson the offer of a visiting fellowship. Peterson planned to visit the Divinity School at Cambridge to study the narratives in the book of Genesis and discuss ideas with staff and students.[2] He had announced the news of the offer from Cambridge on his YouTube channel, but when the offer was withdrawn, the Cambridge University Students' Union positively greeted the news:

'We are relieved to hear that Jordan Peterson's request for a visiting fellowship to Cambridge's faculty of divinity has been rescinded following further review. It is a political

---

[1] See 'Cambridge University rescinds Jordan Peterson invitation'. Article by Sarah Marsh, The Guardian online 20/03/2019. Quotations following are from this source. Peterson's book 12 Rules for Life: An Antidote to Chaos – Peterson (2018) – became an international best-seller and greatly expanded Peterson's fame. At one point the withdrawal of the offer made to Peterson was said to be due to a 'backlash' from staff and students, but this was removed (21/03/2019) as Cambridge said that is was due to a decision of the Research Committee of the Faculty of Divinity.

[2] Peterson had presented a series of lectures on YouTube on the psychology of the Genesis narratives and he was looking to discuss the narratives with the theologians at Cambridge to discover more about their literary, historical and theological significance. Peterson's lecture series can be found on YouTube.

act to associate the University with an academic's work through offers which legitimise figures such as Peterson… His work and views are not representative of the student body and as such we do not see his visit as a valuable contribution to the University, but one that works in opposition to the principles of the University'.

That the Cambridge University Student's Union identifies the 'principles of the University' with the interests of 'the student body' rather than with the ethos of intellectual enquiry is symptomatic of the problem that Peterson and others faced: defending and evolving academic study in an atmosphere of free discussion is of less importance than defending the rights claimed by various groups, who want to be free from being offended by any challenge to their ideals. Put another way, Peterson's case reveals another demonstration of the dominance of a form of positive liberty over the negative variety, and is a prominent instance of a general trend where those whose views were not of a certain consensus were finding it problematic to gain a normal participative engagement within the academic community.

Such communities, pre-eminently, one might think, the University of Cambridge, were ostensibly committed to open and free enquiry, but they were also increasingly committing to a progressive concern to a relativised neutrality over a widening range of personal and social issues. The issues emerging were, at one level showing a broad notion of equal rights, asserted in the public domain and undergirded by law. This produced a strand of thought assuming that all are (or should be) equal in not wanting to be upset and that all have an equal obligation not to say, let alone do anything, that will confound the intellectual or emotional equilibrium of anyone else.

This matter is heightened in modernity, as in the UK, where the socio-cultural form is that of a pluralistic liberal democracy. In such a setting, the ideal of an open and tolerant liberality, with freedom of expression in the negative sense being prized above all, is subordinated to the positive liberal view that no minority group should have to suffer expressions of criticism that might be found offensive, upsetting, or disagreeable: such matters being defined in practice by the members of the minority group in question. Self-defining regulation of what is permissible becomes the operational moral norm.

The Peterson saga had a second phase in 2021 when in short order, two items of news emanated from the University of Cambridge.

First of all, it was reported that the Vice-Chancellor, Stephen Toope, would stand down some two years before the end of his tenure.[1] Professor Toope had been in post during the time of Peterson's first invitation. He also had been associated with a range of other matters that touched on free speech. He had 'backed the introduction of a free speech initiative that required academics, students and visiting speakers to treat others and their opinions with "respect". The policy was overturned by a landslide vote after a campaign led by academics'. Significantly, the campaign succeeded in altering the terminology of the guidelines so that the word 'respect' was replaced by 'tolerate'. In May 2021, Toope was responsible for a method of anonymised 'reporting' that students would employ 'to accuse tutors, lecturers and

---

[1] 'Cambridge vice-chancellor Stephen Toope in free speech row steps down', article by Tom Ball, *The Times* online 20/09/2021. The quotations following are from this source.

other members of the university teaching staff' of 'racism, discrimination and micro-aggressions'. This also provoked controversy, and the ensuing debate led to the scheme's removal, with Toope saying that 'parts of it had been launched in error'.

Toope's explanation for his departure was that he had decided to return to his home in Canada to be closer to his family, as contacts during the Covid19 Pandemic had been difficult. He claimed he was proud 'of leading the university's delivery of education and research during the coronavirus pandemic'. The article also noted Toope's involvement with the Peterson affair and reported that at the time, Toope had, with reference to the photograph of Peterson and the man in the memorable shirt, said that 'Peterson's "casual endorsement" by association was believed to be "antithetical" to the work of the faculty of divinity'.

A week later, a second story emerged: *The Times* reported that Dr James Orr, University Lecturer in Philosophy of Religion at the Faculty of Divinity, had renewed the invitation for Jordan Peterson to visit.[1] Orr said that Peterson was a 'fearless advocate of academic freedom and freedom of conscience at a time when these values are widely considered to be under threat'.

Orr's view was that academics would not object to Peterson's visit and that while students had the right to protest, 'events will go ahead regardless'.

Here we might say that toleration and regard for virtue in disagreement and debate won through in a manner more consistent with Mill's values.

Freedom of Speech Under Threat

Much that is at stake here concerning the liberty of thought and discussion is further illustrated by other stories that emerged in February 2021.[2] A helpful starting point is an article by Emma Yeomans on the theme of academic staff seeking 'legal redress' for 'Free Speech'.[3] The specific issue the article was dealing with was close to the scenarios we have considered with Biggar and Peterson: it is to do with the position some academics were facing in UK universities, where they might be at risk of losing a job or of not getting one, because of some dispute over what they had said or done. That they may have exercised freedom of speech was not the issue; it was that they might have exercised this freedom in such a way as to offend others who were claiming that their freedom not to be so offended was at risk or had been broached. Again, what was at stake was a sense of positive liberty in tension with negative liberty.

In the face of this, and under considerable pressure from the liberal – negative liberal – fraternity, the then Secretary of State for Education, Gavin Williamson, announced plans to legally guarantee freedom of speech in universities. Yeomans quotes him as follows:

---

[1] 'Jordan Peterson: Academic in Islamophobia row returns to Cambridge', article by Nicola Woodcock and Ben Ellery, *The Times* on Line 27/09/21. Peterson was reported as having tweeted that 'Stephen Toope's Cambridge has become a preposterous place'

[2] See '"Free speech academics" can seek legal redress'. Article by Emma Yeomans, *The Times* online 16/02/2021. See also the follow-up in the edition of 18/02/2021.

[3] '*The Times* online 16/02/21. The quotations following are from this source.

'Free speech underpins our democratic society and our universities have a long and proud history of being places where students and academics can express themselves freely, challenge views and cultivate an open mind'.[1]

In defence of this principle of free speech as central to one form of democracy, Williamson explained that the scheme entailed the appointment of 'an academic freedom champion' to investigate possible cases where the right to free expression may have been breached. The idea was that the academic freedom champion would be appointed as a board member with the Office for Students (OfS), 'the regulator for higher education in England'. The chief executive of OfS, Nicola Dandridge, was quoted as saying that 'Free speech and academic freedom are essential to teaching and research. Universities and colleges have legal duties to protect both free speech and academic freedom, and their compliance with these responsibilities forms an important part of their conditions of registration with the OfS'.[2]

With editorial synchronicity in full flow, *The Times* also published a letter from nine prominent academics who put over points which, without mentioning him, might have flowed from the pen of J. S. Mill when drafting *On Liberty*.[3]

Concerned about the challenges to academic freedom in British universities, they (with Biggar and Peterson in mind) noted that 'too many academics have been marginalised because they hold unorthodox views on issues like gender, Brexit and the legacy of empire. Challenging speakers have been disinvited and universities often put the "emotional safety" of students before free inquiry'. The academics welcomed news of the plans to strengthen the work of the OfS and opined that the 'new powers to defend free speech and impose sanctions for breaches' gave the universities 'a duty to "actively promote" freedom of speech. This will give new protections to academics who are sidelined, reducing chilling effects for staff and students, and thereby strengthening our institutions'.

What this letter was alluding to was not so much the tangible disruption to specific events at universities as the increasing prevalence of a restrictive and inhibiting mood. The key line in the case is the situation of university teachers who are 'sidelined' because their contrarian views might not sit well with some of those who might hear them.

Pressures of a related kind came in another report neatly published in the same edition of *The Times*. It was the news that at the University of Oxford, Somerville College had decided not to proceed with a planned programme of 'unconscious bias training' for its students.[4]

---

[1] Gavin Williamson was sacked from his post as Education Secretary in the reshuffle of the UK Government in September 2021.

[2] In May 2021, legislation to implement the protection of freedom of expression was put into the agenda for the new session of the UK Parliament.

[3] The letter (published 16/02/2021) was from Professor Matthew Goodwin, Kent University; Professor Vernon Bogdanor, KCL; Professor Kathleen Stock, Sussex University; Sir Anthony Seldon, former vice-chancellor, Buckingham University; Professor Doug Stokes, Exeter University; Marie Kawthar Daouda, Oxford University; Dr Arif Ahmed, Cambridge University; Dr Paul Yowell, Oxford University; Dr Graham Gudgin, Cambridge University.

[4] See '"Free speech" group claim victory over Oxford college'. Article by Emma Yeomans, *The Times* online, 16/02/2021. The college agreed to modify the way in which the training would be used and reduced the strictures that had originally been placed on the levels of performance that were required.

The initial plan to do this had been developed to aid students to 'recognise prejudices or biases they may hold against minority groups'. An underlying hope was, we may assume, that in the positive sense of liberty, students would, by means of this process, become free to be responsive and responsible individuals when they were purged of unwarranted attitudes. However, one of Somerville's students was a member of the Free Speech Union, with, we may assume, rather more of an orientation to negative liberty. The Union intervened by writing to the College to complain that the training course was, the valid concerns of minority groups notwithstanding, 'a breach' of the 'freedom of expression' of the students.[1]

What emerged was that the training set up by Somerville involved an online assessment within which one question was as follows:

'Acknowledging your personal feelings about particular groups or individuals is a useful starting point in overcoming unconscious bias. Is this productive or unproductive in addressing your personal biases?'

The claim was that unless the student answered 'productive', it was impossible to get the 100% required for a student to pass without needing some further corrective training.

Given the culture of high academic study that Somerville invariably exhibits and endorses and that the Oxford commitment to tutorial care and collegiate values supports, it seems a mystery why such an esteemed community thought it was wise to attempt this program. There is, however, one line of explanation to dissolve the mystery of why college wisdom was seen in unconscious bias training. The College was influenced (or biased) towards such training by the cloak of concern enveloping society to challenge everyone to become alert to their unconscious prejudicial presuppositions. A factor here is that the dispositions and presuppositions a person might have are, by some others, being defined as 'unconscious biases', and as the original plan for assessments at Somerville arranged things, there was almost no scope for a candidate taking the test to escape being identifiably biased.

Underlying the thinking here was the sense that people need to be 'woke', a term helpfully defined as a state of being 'aware of and actively attentive to important facts and issues (especially issues of racial and social justice)'.[2] The term derives from African-American English and is a contraction signifying 'awakening', not in the sense of coming to consciousness after a period of sleep, but analogously, to evoke the need for white members of society to be 'woke' over the historical and social problems undergone by black communities: adaptively, it might be that men (or boys) need to be 'woke' over their outlook towards women (or girls); heterosexuals might need to be 'woke' over their assumptions about those who are in the LGBTQ+ community.

What emerges is, at one level, the sense that an 'unwoked' person is, from the rightful 'woke' perspectives, akin to a bull in a China shop – unconsciously about to commit a multitude of expensive errors. Countering this, the developed awareness of the need to be 'woke' can be conceived as a powerful moral imperative, with 'woke' promotion having a blanket effect, making 'woke attitudes

---

[1] The breach here would be of the defence of freedom of speech in the HRA as discussed in the previous chapter.
[2] See https://www.merriam-webster.com/words-at-play/woke-meaning-origin

regulative, brooking no dissent, or, more worryingly, any counter-argument. This is then in tension with another matter of imperative concern, that of individuals being at liberty to find and become who they are, in the sense of exploring their own character in the context of using the liberty of thought and discussion. However, the 'woke' imperative is sufficiently strong to be generating directives and policies that organisations and companies, and even academic communities feel that they must implement to actively embrace the merits of 'wokism'.

The pressure to be 'woke' and for institutions funded largely by public taxation to be seen to be alert to the need to be 'woke' has a great deal to do with the dilemma faced by Somerville, for as *The Times* article reported, the College puts 'freedom of speech and academic freedom' as 'central tenets of Somerville College life'. As we have already suggested, how these values are consistent with imposing a test on levels of unconscious bias is and remains a moot point. If assessments of any kind are needed, one might think they would be managed in the context of the College's academic and tutorial life.

One thing that the debate in the public arena of a national newspaper seems to have little effect on is the residual trend within the plurality of modernity, at least in those components of the plurality where the leading thought is that unconscious bias and diversity training is a good thing. In the wake of the debates we have charted, it might be thought that there would be a reaction against such measures, but later in 2021, it was reported that both the University of Kent and the University of St Andrews were introducing compulsory courses as a part of the induction of first-year students.[1]

In these cases, the universities like to say that all their courses have been 'requested by students', but they do not say how many actually consciously requested unconscious bias assessments. At Kent, the course involved questions where students had to agree that swearing and wearing second-hand clothes could signify 'white privilege', while at St Andrews, students were expected to assent to statements such as the following:

'Acknowledging your personal guilt is a useful starting point in overcoming unconscious bias'.[2]

Ticking 'disagree' here and on too many other epistemologically weak questions of this type, and the student will fail the unconscious bias assessment. The deal was that students could not begin their undergraduate course until or unless they passed the assessment, so this was a take it (and pass) or leave kind of deal. Mill would be interested in the fact that the university of which he was once Rector was engaging

---

[1] The University of Kent tried to introduce a compulsory assessment for its students, concentrating on unconscious racial bias: 'Students at University of Kent must take "white privilege" course'. Article by Sam Tobin, *The Times* online, 28/09/2021. The University of St Andrews has also imposed a bias test on diversity and consent on all first-year students, who must complete the assessment before they can begin their studies: 'St Andrews university sets bias test for entry'. Article by Nicola Woolcock, *The Times* online, 30/09/21. Quotations in the text are from these articles.

[2] 'Personal guilt'? This sounds very presbyterian, as if there is a love of the idea that the sins of the fathers will be visited up on future generations. We have no sense here of any link to concepts of repentance, forgiveness and other useful notions.

in such activity.[1] He might enjoy another of the questions set in the St Andrews' test:

'Does equality mean treating everyone the same?'

Here the answer 'Yes' is deemed wrong since 'equality may mean treating people differently and in a way that is appropriate to their needs so that they have fair outcomes and equal opportunity'. This phrase is clumsy and problematic. In explaining why the affirmative answer is wrong, the contingent 'may' is seen as weighty: but 'may' allows some variation, and the affirmative response to the question (Does equality mean treating everyone the same?) could well mean, at least to the intelligent undergraduate, 'treating everyone the same', given that each person is an individual and must be considered equally on that basis: their needs may vary – so this means treating everyone with equal consideration of their individual interests, and so not identically 'the same' therefore, but procedurally the same – but tests of this kind militate against sophisticated and thoughtful answers.[2]

Mill gives a number of warnings on the dangers of bureaucratic organisation, and one thing that he would point to in this modern trend to what has been termed a 'therapeutic' approach in education is the way that contemporary Human Resource Management teams, as well as some activists within student organisations, want to apply these self-awareness courses to combat what they perceive to be culturally damaging unconscious biases.[3] That this means that the liberal plurality of modernity becoming somewhat less liberal and less tolerant is not the obvious priority for a management bureaucracy that is seen to be playing to a very particular entitlement agenda based on a loose sense of subjectivist human rights. Perhaps the sense is less than loose, however, as a good deal of what has emerged is consistent with the body of legislation that we have considered and which has a distinct bearing on the matters we have been discussing.

If we reflect on the matters reviewed so far and ask whether and how the laws and the consequent social policies we have touched on offer help or a hindrance to liberty and the positive values Mill has in mind for honing truths and insights as

---

[1] A later report revealed that such induction courses were being deployed at the universities of Southampton, Bath, Warwick, York, and at University College London. The University of Bristol offered a course on values and consent, but this was not compulsory and not assessed. In general the courses are run online and have to be completed before students start their undergraduate course. The courses variously look to uncover unconscious dispositions or bias, and cover issues of consent, prejudice, diversity, social responsibility, inclusion, wellbeing, alcohol and drug abuse and gender. See 'Universities accused of abusing power with bias and guilt courses'. Article by Nicola Woolcock, *The Times* online, 02/10/21. To rub righteous salt into the wound, a later report explained that students at Wolfson College Cambridge would face a mandatory anti-racism course 'covering issues such as microaggressions, whiteness and privilege'. See 'Cambridge college students told to attend race workshop' Article by Tom Knowles. *The Times online*, 15/11/2021.

[2] Interestingly legal opinion has more recently suggested that the sorts of training on gender awareness being developed for some universities by Advance HE could be 'totalitarian and unlawful'. See 'University gender course offered by Advance HE is unlawful, barrister says'. Article by Jonathan Ames and Ben Ellery, *The Times* online, 06/11/2021.

[3] The idea of 'therapeutic' education is cited in *The Times* article on St Andrews, and comes from the title of the book *The Dangerous Rise Of Therapeutic Education* by K Ecclestone and D Hayes – Ecclestone and Hayes (2019). A key point in this book is the view that if education concerns itself overmuch with the emotional well-being of students, it tends to create in them a persistent sense of victimhood, and to undermine their positivity and true well-being.

well as schemes for individualised life, a short answer is that they are more seldom much of a help, and invariably something of a hindrance.

Academic Freedom and the Challenge of Ideology

More light can be shed on the issues under review by thinking back to the exchanges over freedom of speech in the February 2021 phase and touching base again with Nigel Biggar, who added to this debate through another article written for *The Times*.[1] Mindful of the government's decision to take steps to ensure that universities guaranteed freedom of speech, Biggar took up a challenge as presented by those who were suggesting that the concern about freedom of speech was 'a right-wing fabrication'.

Bigger cites some examples of writers and thinkers 'of the left': thus, Will Davies, a political economist, 'argued in the *Guardian* that the "free speech panic" had been invented by the right because its authority had been lost to anarchic social media. A year later, the journalist Nasrine Malik wrote that, far from universities succumbing to an epidemic of no-platforming, they were protecting freedom of expression'. Biggar also notes how Jo O'Grady, secretary-general of the University and Colleges Union, having obtained advanced news of the government's plans to safeguard academic freedom in universities, had accused the government 'of stoking a culture war', although, in fact, there was 'no evidence of a free speech crisis on campus'.

Biggar wrote that from his own experience, the problem was not a fabrication:

'There is empirical evidence that the free speech and academic freedom of significant minorities of university students and teachers are being inhibited. Those affected range from political and social conservatives on the right to feminist critics of transgender ideology on the left. Take Oxbridge alone. In 2018, I was organising a conference at Christ Church on Bruce Gilley's controversial article, "A Case for Colonialism". A young historian wanted to come but on two conditions: that his name not appear on any list and his face not appear in any photographs. He feared his career would suffer if senior colleagues discovered his participation. In 2019 Oxford University had to assign security guards to Professor Selina Todd, the socialist historian of the working class and feminism in Britain, after her criticism of transgenderism attracted threats of physical violence. In 2020 Todd was disinvited to a conference at Exeter College because of objections from transgender activists. Then last month Cambridge University's School of Arts and Humanities wrote to all of its departments requiring them to explain how they were addressing "the challenge" of promoting decolonisation and diversity. No space was permitted for those who doubt the inbuilt assumptions about colonialism and racism. The school marched ahead as if dissent was, literally, unthinkable'.

Biggar explains how difficult these trends are for the preservation of open debate in the university setting:

'Apart from individual cases, social scientific data indicates widespread intimidation and self-censorship. In 2017 a survey of the members of Jo O'Grady's union reported

---

[1] 'The government will offer a lifeboat to sinking free speech on campuses'. Article by Nigel Biggar, *The Times* online 17/02/2021. The quotations following are from this source.

"significantly higher levels of systematic abuse of their academic freedom than their European counterparts." In their 2019 study of academic freedom for Policy Exchange, Eric Kaufmann and Tom Simpson presented evidence of "chilling effects" on students' speech, such that "some mainstream political views cannot be discussed in the classroom"'.

Biggar alludes to Kaufmann and Simpson's follow-up report of 2020, from which the impression was that 'the chill extends to professors'. This was due to the evidence that 'more than 80 per cent of academics lean to the left'. Accordingly:

'... right-leaning professors tend to perceive their professional environment as hostile. Mindful of their careers, they censor themselves, going into inner exile and keeping their conservative thoughts to themselves'.

The emergent view is set against the backdrop of restrictive trends. In contrast, there is the positive impact expected from planned legislation and the Free Speech Champion. Biggar thinks that these 'will go a long way towards thawing the atmosphere':

'For the first time, legislation will extend the duty to secure free speech beyond universities to student unions... If a university or union is found to be delinquent, it could be fined. Not only will this give academic and student leaders pause for thought before they yield to pressure to stifle dissent. It will also encourage silent dissenters to speak up'.

Biggar takes the view that the issues at stake come from trends and moods of opinion that appeal somewhat loosely to equality, tolerance and inclusivism, but in such a way that suppresses individual freedom of expression, particularly the freedom to disagree, and the ability of liberal centres of education to be open in their capacity to develop through free and open debate citizens who have 'the virtues and art of handling controversial ideas civilly'. This a development that includes the provision of an environment within which students can 'voice and discuss diverse ideas and views with self-restraint and reason— instead of shouting or threatening — so that light might prevail rather than heat'.[1]

The line of concern Biggar articulates, which endorses government intervention to secure liberal entitlements to free debate, is not unproblematic. It is arguable, not least from Mill's perspective, that even when governments can intervene to make a corrective within society over a matter of liberty, it is generally better that they do not, for the risk is that the habit of intervention will become an illiberal addiction.[2]

---

[1]Biggar writes in similar vein on the related issue of the possible removal of a statute of Tobias Rustat (1608-1694) from the College Chapel. Rustat was a benefactor of Jesus College and the University in general. He was an investor in the slave trade in the 17th century. In March 2022, the College lost a legal case before the Consistory Court of the Diocese of Ely to remove the statue because its of the 'assumptions underlying the college's emotive petition: namely, that leaving the memorial in place would endorse slavery and its racial contempt, whereas removing it would "decolonise" the space and strike a blow against systemic racism'. Biggar's point is that feelings can be elevated by perceptions of reality, but the duty of an academic institution 'is to sift feelings and their supporting perceptions for the truth'. The Jesus College petition did not do this. See 'Cambridge slavery dispute was about feelings, not truth'. Article by Nigel Biggar. *The Times* online, 24/03/2022. For the College's view of Rustat see also
https://www.jesus.cam.ac.uk/tobias-rustat, where a link to the legal judgement of Vice-Chancellor David Hodge QC can be found.
[2] See *OL* IV:12-13, and Chapter 7 above.

Several other academics wrote to *The Times,* giving general support to the line taken by Biggar.

One to whom Biggar drew attention was Professor Selina Todd'[1] who suggested that the promotion of 'free speech in universities' would require the government to 'curb the undue influence of lobby groups such as Stonewall'. She pointed out that her 'institution, like many universities (and the Department of Education), is a "Stonewall Diversity Champion". Membership requires the adoption of policies that undermine freedom to debate'.[2] Referencing the tension we have noted between gender self-affirmation and sexual identity and taking a line that would appeal to Jordan Peterson and irk his opponents, Professor Todd also affirmed that:

'Oxford University's equalities policies, which are typical of the sector, claim "gender identity" is "assigned at birth" and define women as a "gender" rather than as a sex — which we legally are, under the Equality Act 2010. This is an ideological stance rather than evidence-based policy. It leaves those of us whose teaching and scholarship concern women, or rely on sex-disaggregated data, open to complaint and attack for our lawful view that biological sex exists'.

Suggesting another sort of champion would be welcome, Professor Todd concludes as follows:

'… universities, and the government, cannot uphold free speech while championing such policies'.

These issues involve the recent trend we have examined that suggests that a person's gender is not biologically grounded but 'assigned at birth' and manifest and so significant in and for individuals in their own right as a construct arising out of personal affirmation. This is linked to the case made by, for example, Stonewall, for individuals to have the right to affirm another gender.[3]

---

[1] *The Times* online 18/02/2021 – Letter from Selina Todd. As mentioned above in Biggar's article, Professor Todd is a specialist on the history of working-class women and feminism.

[2] Professor Todd reiterates these points in a later letter (see *The Times* online (03/11/2021) when criticising the influence and policy of Advance HE which 'advises universities to collect equality data based on respondents' gender identity but not on their sex' and suggests that inclusivity is a precondition or ongoing funding. The gender-identity issue, where gender identity comes through a person's self-affirmation, is given a detailed and robust examination in Joyce (2021). Stonewall - founded in 1989 - had campaigned for the rights of the LGBT+ community, but in more recent times it has put most emphasis on gender identity and transition. For more on the problems associated with the recent approach of Stonewall see 'Trans activism is on the retreat. Let's hope Professor Stock is these bullies' last victim'. Article by Sarah Ditum, *The Sunday Times* online 31/10/2021. See also the news that the Stonewall guidance package has been withdrawn from the NHS: 'Stonewall dropped by health department'. Article by Lucy Bannerman, *The Times* online, 03/11/2021. It also emerged that Stonewall' guidance had been accepted within the Foreign, Commonwealth and Development Office in July 20201, without the knowledge of the then Foreign Secretary, Dominic Raab. In November 20201 the Stonewall 'Diversity Champions scheme' was dropped. See 'Ministers kept in dark about Stonewall diversity scheme'. Article by Eleni Courea, *The Times* online (09/11/20201). The BBC, long considered amenable to the 'woke' agenda, announced that on the grounds of worries about impartiality, it too was dropping its use of the Stonewall scheme – 'BBC quits Stonewall diversity scheme over "impartiality concerns"'. Article by Lucy Bannerman *The Times* online (10/11/2021).

[3] As noted earlier, the organisation Stonewall became a key player in this area of debate. Originally an organisation working to oppose the ban on promoting homosexuality in schools, it gives much more focus on defending transgender rights. Details can be found on how it sees its task at Stonewall.org.uk

The idea that one's gender is something to be determined through affirmation rather than by reference to biology is a matter that we might think should be open for discussion and review, but laws and policies on equality and related matters have rapidly been altered to give protection from criticism to those, who through self-affirmation, are reassigning gender and undergoing transition. Legal rights to the entitlement to self-affirm much else, and so gender as well, are employed by trans rights activism as a protective fire blanket over matters that are not given to damaging ignition. High amongst these is the liberty of thought and discussion that underpins academic freedom. As Professor Todd sees it, illustrating something we noted earlier, those who criticise the underlying concepts, policies or laws appealed to by trans rights activists are likely to be accused of being transphobic and to be guilty in their eyes of various forms of prejudicial discrimination.

The outcome is a scenario where free discussion is inhibited, and this risks ideas being put into active use without a rational interrogation of the attendant risks and perils. Consistent with this as an emerging trend, Helen Joyce explains that in a range of developed nations, changes in law and then in official documentation, 'such as birth certificates, identification cards, passports, and drivers licences' are no longer recording sex and gender, but inviting 'gender self-identification'.[1]

The upshot is an 'abolition of sex as a concept in law'. This might seem a high point for libertarian freedom, but the harm to others issue is clear: under the ethos of self-affirmed gender re-assignment, men could self-identify as women, with consequences that are tangible in terms of risks and perils to the security, safety and well-being of others who are in the biologically real sense female.[2]

Mill's take on the dangers of closing down discussion on any such matter is unambiguous, and his ideas on how our thinking and our ways of living can be enhanced remain instructive:

'There is the greatest difference between presuming an opinion to be true because, with every opportunity for contesting it, it has not been refuted, and assuming its truth for the purpose of not permitting its refutation. Complete liberty of contradicting and disproving our opinion is the very condition which justifies us in assuming its truth for purposes of action; and on no other terms can a being with human faculties have any rational assurance of being right' (II: 6).

Returning to earlier communications to *The Times*, Professor Francis O'Gorman of Edinburgh University confirmed a sense of the widespread problem of a certain conventionalism in university life. Alluding to *The Times'* leading article of the day before, which suggested that 'universities should not be complicit in circumscribing the limits of acceptable speech on the whims of vocal minorities', O'Gorman points out that that within the universities, there is something of an issue:

'…ideological commitment to the priority of vocal minorities ensures that those claiming to be marginalised comprehensively shape the direction of much thinking, research and teaching. No one should lose their job over ideological disagreement, yet the issue becomes invidious because it concerns the willingness of academics as well as students to accept ideological certainties as unquestionable in seminars, lectures, and meetings. An occasional

---

[1] Joyce (2021) p. 238. In 2017 the European Court of Human Rights ruled that legal sex changes could be accepted without surgery. See Joyce (2021) p. 235.
[2] On this see Joyce (2021) pp. 239-243, where the recent situation in Ireland is explained.

rebel makes a splash. But the real problem is the ubiquity of conformity in the daily life of higher education'.[1]

Were Mill looking this over, he might well consider the 'ubiquity of conformity' to be another manifestation of the tyranny of custom. However, matters in this discussion were given a clear summary by Dr David Butterfield from Queen's College, Cambridge. He wrote on both a core feature of life and the right and proper purpose of a university. Thus, in life:

'We are free to say whatever we wish. In the public forum we are free to say whatever is not unlawful. Within those bounds, our universities have three core roles: to investigate what is not known, to teach what is already known, and to protect a culture in which those two functions flourish. Any university is thus unworthy of the name if its students and staff feel unable to test and challenge discordant opinions with evidence and argument in the crucible of open debate. The role of academia is no more complex, and no more simple than that'.[2]

To adapt a colloquial saying, sauce for the staff and students at a university is sauce for the wider populace of the individuals who constitute society. As within the case for negative liberty, we have the aspirational value that all need to feel and be confident of being able 'to test and challenge discordant opinions with evidence and argument in the crucible of open debate'. However, if developments in law give emphasis to positive notions of entitlement to those who can make a claim to be marginalised, then the role of law comes into direct conflict with liberty.

Butterfield is J. S. Mill-rich in defending the liberty of thought and opinion, but on the wider front, what is portrayed has the character of a tension between an open as opposed to a closed society – to borrow an idea from another thinker in the tradition of liberalism.[3]

If the recent past is one where freedom of discussion and true liberty have been overwhelmed by pressure groups who have lobbied for legal reforms to protect their position, as in the case Helen Joyce explores relating to gender self-identification, she also notes trends, not least in the UK, that are making for a resurgence of 'the Enlightenment values of open inquiry and robust debate'.[4]

This line is well-supported by Professor Dennis Hayes, who is quoted in *The Times*' article on The University of Kent's venture into unconscious bias and diversity training.[5] His point is that the approach of giving 'mandatory training on controversial topics' is misconceived, and he thinks that such ideas as are pertinent should be treated 'through discussion' – as we mentioned earlier, collegiate tutorial care beckons. Hayes worries that otherwise, universities are reduced 'to training institutions in woke ideology'.

Hayes senses that there is a predominating trend coming 'from student unions or HR departments' and this is something many academics just go along with. The problem is that it places a worrying lack of emphasis on the role of critical thinking

---

[1] *The Times* online 18/02/2021 – Letter from Francis O'Gorman.
[2] *The Times* online 18/02/2021 – Letter from David Butterfield.
[3] See Popper (2011).
[4] Joyce (2021) p. 300.
[5] See 'Students at University of Kent must take "white privilege" course'. Article by Sam Tobin, *The Times* online, 28/09/2021. Quotations are taken from this source. Professor Hayes is the co-author of the book on therapeutic education cited above: Ecclestone and Hayes (2019).

in the academy, and in life. Hayes refers to an 'exercise in which academics had to undergo unconscious bias training, adding: "It's coming out of almost all organisations, it's done with the best intentions. They say 'You must believe this' but that's not appropriate for a university': Hayes says much with his conclusion; a university 'should teach people how to think, not what to think'.

These various comments in praise of academic freedom suggest that there is considerable critical energy to hand to sustain the resurgence of rational discussion and critical debate and defend the virtue of disagreement. This was evident in June 2022, when academic values were resurgent at the University of Cambridge when the academic community rejected the guidance from Advance HE, a charitable organisation offering advice to universities that included promoting the 'collective understanding'[1] that 'gender can be chosen'. The view affirmed was that trans issues needed to remain in the arena of free debate and that the academic community needed to be fostering 'open debate' The case exists for these core elements of academic life to be urgently prosecuted for, alongside the social and political debates we have been reviewing, some have felt that the pressures that they were facing in academia were simply too great to be tolerated any longer. In our next chapter, we come to some case studies of those who have felt they have no option but to resign from academia.

---

[1] 'Cambridge academics reject trans "thought control"'. Article by Ben Ellery, *The Times* online, 18/06/1922. Quotations are taken from this source. In this article it is said that at least thirteen UK Universities have the Advance HE programme in operation.

15. Nuclear Options: Resigning from Academia

The pressures to conform to particular outlooks and agendas such as we have been considering had another consequence in some notable resignations from academia from scholars who could not square academic integrity with the perceived wave of repressive influence. Whereas it might be assumed that a university should defend above all the principles of intellectual enquiry and the liberty of academic discourse, the problem of policies or ideologies subsuming the scope for the liberty of debate is, with the cases we examine, all too real.

Professors Harper-Scott and Boghossian

Two resignations that offer complementary perspectives are those of Professor Paul Harper-Scott, from Royal Holloway, London, and Professor Peter Boghossian, from Portland State University, Oregon.[1]

In September 2021, Harper-Scott and Boghossian chose to leave successful academic careers and positions within which they had achieved much; both explained that the problems of working in their institutions had become too great to continue to combat. The problems they express reveal variations on the matters we have explored; where, so the argument runs, the principles of free, critical investigative reason have been eroded by policies, procedures and an ideological overlay that challenges and threatens the normative activity of academic research and teaching with inhibiting ideological restraints.

Music versus Ideology

Professor Harper-Scott's concerns echo those we encountered with Biggar's work on colonialism. His disillusionment with academia lies in the sense that too few people now have the courage 'to follow the truth wherever it leads'. Following a Kantian distinction, he says that he had assumed that 'universities would be *critical* places', but he found that they 'are becoming increasingly *dogmatic*'.

His case study centres on a statement that he considers to characterise the growing trend in musicology:

'Nineteenth-century musical works were the product of an imperial society. The classical musical canon must be decolonised'.

---

[1] Professor Harper-Scott's explanation of his resignation can be found online at https://jpehs.co.uk/. Professor Boghossian's resignation letter can be read in full in *The Daily Mail* online: https://www.dailymail.co.uk/news/article-9970277/Peter-Boghossians-resignation-letter-full.html. Quotations in the text are from these sources.

Harper-Scott's point is that in this statement, the second sentence is dogmatic: it 'admits of no doubt, no criticism, no challenge'. This can be contrasted with 'a critical statement' representative of 'the ideal of scholarship':

'Nineteenth-century musical works were written during the period of empire, and they carry that history within them. But as well as being part of the imperial world in which they appeared, they are also musical works. As with a protest song written at the time of the Vietnam war (which fell during the US's imperial epoch), a piece of classical music is simultaneously imbued with the history of its own time and also minimally separated from it as a partially autonomous object. As with a protest song, there therefore exists the possibility that it could offer a form of critique of existing social conditions. There is also the possibility that works of this kind will affirm the existing social conditions. What actually transpires in the music itself is therefore determinative of the question whether we can judge it to be for or against anything in particular'.

The implication of the first 'dogmatic' view would be that, for example, teaching the music of such composers as Beethoven and Wagner would be stopped 'in the (frankly insane) belief that doing so will somehow materially improve current living conditions for the economically, socially, sexually, religiously, or racially underprivileged'.

If the second view prevails, the music in question can be studied '*as music*' to inform our framework of understanding and 'offer intellectually critical insights into the social, political, economic, legal, and other structures of the world in which it was written, and later canonized, and now consumed by the musical public'.

The music, like the literature, thought, and politics of a period, offers a reading of the human condition from which we can learn. In the case of music, it 'is also, very often, an almost incomprehensibly brilliant expression of human creativity and ingenuity'.

Harper-Scott's point could be even stronger with the addition of the notion that creative works of the highest order have a transcendental quality in that what they evoke about the human condition is so elemental that it goes beyond the particularity of the time or setting of its composition. This, as an historic trend, is especially so in the art and thought of the Romantic era, which is characterised by many strands of innovative and critical independence.

Harper-Scott feared that staying in academia would mean carrying on a war of attrition to protect the canon of classical music from the antagonism of those who sought what he considered a sanitised reduction – and this he did not want to do. The alternative of a private career in music writing and criticism offered a greater allure.

A Philosopher's Dilemma

During his time at Portland State, Peter Boghossian spent a good deal of time teaching on Socrates and using the dialogic method of argument to critique ideas. He specialised in argument analysis, enjoying the business of developing expertise in sifting solid arguments from passionate expressions of opinion or feeling. Noting that a wave of policies was coming on stream, expressive of fine-sounding values, such as 'diversity, equity, and inclusion', Boghossian studied the writings of 'critical theorists' whose ideas were behind these values. He decided that 'their conclusions reflected the postulates of an ideology, not insights based on evidence'.

To expose the fallacies of the ideological approach he found, Boghossian co-authored some articles published in journals of critical theory: but the articles were fictive hoaxes, written precisely to expose the vacuity of intellectualism in critical theory.[1] Boghossian argued against the extension of suspect values translated into practical policies at Portland State, but his arguments and challenges did not have good consequences. He found clear evidences of increasing 'illiberalism' at the university, but saw too that it was 'part of an institution-wide problem'. Amongst the difficulties, he found that students were 'refusing to engage with different points of view'; that 'questions from faculty at diversity trainings that challenged approved narratives were instantly dismissed' and 'those who asked for evidence to justify new institutional policies were accused of microaggressions'. Most worryingly, if texts set for study were written by European males, the professors 'were accused of bigotry'. On this basis, it seems that Mill's *On Liberty* cannot easily be set for study at Portland State.

Boghossian's account of the issues and problems he found included a statement of his professional aim, indisputably valid within the self-understanding of philosophy, which was 'to create the conditions for rigorous thought' so that students would not be led 'to a particular conclusion' but able, with the tools of critical thought 'to hunt and furrow for their own conclusions'. Sadly, he thought that the developments at Portland State 'made this kind of intellectual exploration impossible':

'It has transformed a bastion of free inquiry into a Social Justice factory whose only inputs were race, gender, and victimhood and whose only outputs were grievance and division'.

Despite his best endeavours, students are not being taught to think. Instead 'they are being trained to mimic the moral certainty of ideologues. Faculty and administrators have abdicated the university's truth-seeking mission and instead drive intolerance of divergent beliefs and opinions. This has created a culture of offense where students are now afraid to speak openly and honestly'.

As a coda expressive of his disquiet as well as of his commitment to philosophical investigation, Boghossian offers the following:

'Every idea that has advanced human freedom has always, and without fail, been initially condemned. As individuals, we often seem incapable of remembering this lesson, but that is exactly what our institutions are for: to remind us that the freedom to question is our fundamental right. Educational institutions should remind us that that right is also our duty'.

---

[1] As Boghossian explains in his letter of resignation, the most notable hoax was the article 'The Conceptual Penis as a Social Construct'. In 2017 this peer reviewed article was published in *Cogent Social Sciences*. The hoax was revealed by the authors a month after publication. See https://pdxscholar.library.pdx.edu/phl_fac/29/

Professor Stock and Trans Rights

Professors Harper-Scott and Boghossian were not alone. Their situations were replicated in an even more publicised manner through the situation faced by Professor Kathleen Stock, a philosopher at the University of Sussex, sufficiently well-thought to have been awarded the OBE as a mark of respect for her contributions to higher education.[1] In her case, all the notions of liberty of thought and discussion and the correlated ideals and academic values affirmed in the matters discussed were in a heady mix with other, more intransigent views

Early in October 2021, student activists at the University of Sussex, notably through a group called 'Anti Terf Sussex', launched an assertive campaign against Professor Stock.[2] She was accused of being 'one of this wretched island's most prominent transphobes, espousing a bastardised variation of radical feminism'.[3] The student's reported claims included that Professor Stock was 'harmful and dangerous to trans people'; with a striking rejection of the ethos of the liberty of discussion, they also said: 'We're not up for debate. We cannot be reasoned out of existence'.

The background to this assault was that imperatives taken from laws like the Human Rights Act imply that people could hold views free from anything they consider distress, which led trans rights supporters to an antagonistic stance against Professor Stock. Her experience was that for some three years, she had argued that while trans rights needed to be respected, there were major problems with gender identity theory. This is related to the view we have encountered that adult persons were entitled to affirm their gender identity and then to have the identity they affirmed protected by law by notions of equality of regard in a manner akin to matters of sexual orientation, disability, and racial grouping or religious affiliation. As we have seen, the Gender Recognition Act (2004) made clear stipulations for how changes in gender identity could be processed, but some groups campaigned for self-affirmation of gender transition and identity to become self-sufficient.[4]

Stock's reasoning moves along the tension we have been considering.[5] A problem with gender self-affirmation was that the most expansive positive perspectives took no account of the biological facts, preferring to work on the assumption that a person's self-professed and self-assessed feelings were the right and sufficient basis for the self-affirmation of gender, and the entitlements associated with that affirmed gender. A specific worry raised was that self-affirmed gender identity where, for example, men claimed the right to transition, meant that they were claiming an entitlement to be treated as women by everyone else.

---

[1] Professor Stock was one of the co-signatories of the letter to *The Times* of 16/02/21 cited earlier in this Chapter. Professor Stock's OBE was awarded in December 2020.

[2] 'Terf': an acronym for 'trans-exclusionary radical feminist' – as used by trans lobbyists for feminists who defend sex essentialism, the view that a person's biological sex is factual. Someone who is 'Terf' will then be considered 'transphobic'. The term 'sex essentialism' glosses the biological fact of binary sexual identity as a straightforward, if to some inconvenient, view within medical and biological science.

[3] 'Sussex University students campaign to have "transphobic" professor Kathleen Stock sacked' – article by Nicola Woolcock, *The Times* online, 07/10/2021.

[4] See the previous chapter where the Gender Recognition Act was discussed. Again, for details of an organisation staunch in defending trans rights see Stonewall.org.uk

[5] Stock's views on this are close to those of Professor Selina Todd and Helen Joyce as discussed above.

Alert to the maxim that 'trans women are women', Stock's point was that nevertheless, women, meaning females, could be put at considerable risk by the entitlements given through trans rights to persons who were, and could only ever be male, gaining rights of access to activities, spaces and facilities usually reserved for females.

This led Stock to writing a book, *Material Girls*, subtitled 'Why Reality Matters for Feminism'.[1] This delivered a philosophical critique of gender identity theory, pointing out the problems this raised, particularly for women: these include difficulties in organising arrangements in many aspects of life, including healthcare and within the criminal justice system. In general, arrangements are set for the binary options of male and female, and Stock's view was that a person's biological sex was a given, and not something to be changed.[2]

At a remarkable pace, the case of Professor Stock became prominent in the daily news, with views coming in from all sides, and the pressures grew in such a way that before the end of the month, Professor Stock felt she had no option but to resign.[3]

The Stock Case in Review

The saga of the case of Professor Stock reveals much of interest to the student of *On Liberty*, as becomes clear as we trace the unfolding contours of the debate and its consequences.

In an initial media report on the situation at Sussex, it was said that posters put up on the campus at Sussex asserted: 'We're not paying £9,250 a year for transphobia — fire Kathleen Stock.'[4] And: 'Kathleen Stock makes trans students unsafe, Sussex still pays her'. Most eloquently, there was the declaration: 'It's not a debate, it's not feminism, it's not philosophy, it's just transphobia and it's not on'.

These and the affirmations of Anti Terf Sussex should prompt the keen reader of Mill's *On Liberty* to recall the restriction placed on freedom of expression when, as in the hypothetical case of arguing that corn dealers are 'starvers of the poor to an excited mob assembled before the house of a corn dealer' (III: 1), we have something that 'may justly incur punishment'. Mill is here censuring arguments that might be given in situations where argument prompts acts of aggression against persons. There is a telling contrast with the case of Professor Stock: whereas her arguments were presented with clarity and courtesy, the campaign of slogans and demonstrations by Anti Terf Sussex eschewed argument and relied on assertion

---

[1] Stock (2022). When the book was published in May 2021, Stock was interviewed for *The Guardian* and what is reported there provokes much thought given what transpired later in the year: see 'Kathleen Stock: taboo around gender identity has chilling effects on academics'. Article by Joanna Moorhead, *The Guardian* online, 22/05/2021. Stock's book was published in a paperback edition in 2022.

[2] See Stock (2022) pp.142-177. ·

[3] 'Kathleen Stock resigns from University of Sussex after trans rights row'. Article by G. Grylls, *The Times* online, 28/10/2021.

[4] 'Sussex University students campaign to have "transphobic" professor Kathleen Stock sacked' – article by N Woolcock, *The Times* online, 07/10/2021. The quotations following are from this source.

alone, with an aggressive, intolerant and disrespectful tone. Mill also notes how the most serious problems arise when through sophistry, 'facts or arguments' (II: 44) are suppressed to 'misstate' or 'misrepresent' the opposing view.

These distortions are more or less what came to expression from Anti Terf Sussex, so Professor Stock appears to suffer from these improper assaults: her opponents do not engage in argument, and they operate with little or no regard for the facts. Mill's stricture here is worth restating that the 'complete liberty of contradicting and disproving our opinion is the very condition which justifies us in assuming its truth for purposes of action; and on no other terms can a being with human faculties have any rational assurance of being right'.

Despite these shortfalls, the blitzkrieg power of the demonstrations had the desired effect of driving Professor Stock from the campus and setting off a chain of events that led to her resignation. The protesters also traded on another matter – that if action were taken against them, they would be able to claim that their rights to express their view was being suppressed. Professor Stock faced other critics at Sussex: it was also reported that 'an art historian at Sussex criticised Stock on Twitter':

'It doesn't feel right to wish a colleague should be fired but it's not been right for colleagues working in the same school to be afraid to talk about Stock for fear of litigation. This is shameful. The virulent and oppressive implications of Stock's public speaking about gender have made many people unsafe in the university and beyond. I salute these posters as an expression of resistance, intelligence and solidarity'.

It would be a shock to anyone reading Stock's book or listening to her talks or interviews, some of which are online, to find anything 'virulent' or oppressive' in her approach.[1] She is a model of calm reason: trans people have, in general, rights akin to the rights all enjoy, but her view is that gender affirmation glosses the fact the biologically, men are men and women are women, and this has a range of implications if women, and even men, are to be rightly protected.

In contrast with the critics, others offered strong support for Professor Stock, suggesting that her opponents were falling into a 'call the manager' type of entitlement and suggesting that the real problem was that Professor Stock was the victim of 'blatant harassment and bullying'.[2] Before the end of the day, Sussex issued a statement that supported all parties within the framework of reasoned debate.[3] This statement was superseded by another from the Vice-Chancellor, Adam Ticknell, who announced that an investigation was underway:

'We are investigating activity on our campus which appears to have been designed to attack Professor Kathleen Stock for exercising her academic freedoms. Disturbingly, this has included pressuring the university to terminate her employment. Everyone at the university

---

[1] See for example, her 'Unherd' interview with Julie Bindel: 'Kathleen Stock: I won't be silenced'. This is on YouTube (03/11/2012).
[2] The article refers to the writer Julie Bindel and the barrister Allison Bailey, both of whom are notable campaigners for feminism and for LGB rights.
[3] 'As a university community, we must be able to have complex discussions without bullying or harassment. We will always take swift action when this occurs. Our role as a university is to facilitate such conversations to advance shared understanding and common agreement. We insist that these are carried out respectfully and are always protective of our staff and students'.

has the right to be free from harassment and intimidation. We cannot and will not tolerate threats to cherished academic freedoms and will take any action necessary to protect the rights of our community'.

This politically alert statement emphasised that a part of the complaint against Professor Stock was that her critique of gender identity theory could be seen as a challenge to and a form of harassment to the trans (or trans-supportive) community at Sussex. Nevertheless, despite the expressions of support, concerns for Professor Stock's safety meant that she was advised to work online and to have CCTV surveillance fitted at home. What she thought about the situation was expressed in reports two days later.[1]

Through the highly contemporary medium of Twitter, Professor Stock expressed her gratitude to 'the hundreds of people who have helped or encouraged me in the last few days'. She thanked the Sussex Vice-Chancellor for 'standing up for my academic freedom' and, in lines that John Stuart Mill might have penned, she said that universities were not places 'where students should just expect to hear their own thoughts reflected back at them. Arguments should be met by arguments and evidence by evidence, not intimidation or aggression'.

Support also came through letters to *The Times*. Once more, Professor Selina Todd comes into focus, and Baroness Falkner of Margravine, head of the Equality and Human Rights Commission. Both presented clear and strong defences of academic freedom and of the academy as a place for open discussion free from intimidation.

Professor Todd wrote that 'the role of a university should be to pursue truth, via careful research and active debate'.[2] She was unimpressed with the time that Sussex took to defend Professor Stock, and felt that too much emphasis was given to 'attracting and pacifying student consumers', a point that raises wider questions about the nature of academic education in the modern age of consumerism – education becoming a commodity like socks, spaghetti and sun cream. She also noted that so far, 'the Universities and Colleges Union, and the professional associations for humanities scholars' had, to date, said nothing to defend Professor Stock, whose courage and integrity she praised.

Baroness Falkner thought 'disgraceful' both 'the attacks on Professor Kathleen Stock and the campaign to have her fired'. She thought too that Sussex was right to defend her and to launch an investigation into the matter. The Baroness set out another fluent defence of academic freedom:

'Trans rights must be protected but university is a place where we are exposed to ideas and learn to debate with each other. This involves hearing about, and challenging, opposing perspectives. It is not a place where people bully and harass professionals and berate institutions because they disagree with someone's entirely lawful expert views'.

With thought to her role with the Equality and Human Rights Commission, Baroness Falkner also noted the problems of 'the use of social media for people to

---

[1] 'Professor hits back in 'toxic' transgender row'. Article by Nicola Woolcock, *The Times* online 09/10/2021.
[2] *The Times* online 09/10/2021, Letter from Professor Selina Todd. Quotations from Baroness Falkner's letter are from the same edition.

anonymously spread hatred and harass people'. This, and the issue of how best to 'protect people's rights' would be something to consider 'through our work on the online safety bill'.

This debate expanded to include, very instructively, a group of 'transsexual people' who wrote to *The Times* to say that they were 'appalled':

'... that trans rights — our rights — are being used to excuse an unprincipled campaign of harassment and abuse. Like any other group, trans people hold a range of opinions. Attacks on the freedom of expression are not progressive and do nothing to fight against actual prejudice or win better services for trans people. If bullies manage to silence Kathleen Stock, they will not stop there'.[1]

As is sometimes the case when matters of moral weight are coming to a head, *The Times*' editorial team were moved to put aside ruminations on political and economic affairs to compose a leading article that nailed the colours of liberty well and truly to the mast:

'A university is neither a cloister nor a finishing school. It champions knowledge through the methods of critical inquiry'.[2]

It follows that:

'... it is a scandal and a disgrace that an academic at an English university must keep off campus and teach solely online because of threats to her personal safety. Yet that is the police advice given to Kathleen Stock, a philosopher at Sussex University, who has withstood a torrent of abuse for expressing conscientiously held opinions that violate the orthodoxies of radical transgender campaigners'.

Professor Stock had argued that 'a person's sex is an immutable biological fact'. While we should respect those who are transgender who may 'have a strong desire to be designated differently', this respect cannot 'be an absolute principle in all settings' since 'if facilities intended for women are automatically opened to men who self-declare female identity, then women are put at risk'. Here there is an echo of Mill's sense of human fallibility being the safeguard against the perils of 'absolute certainty' (II: 3). *The Times* concludes with thinking reminiscent of Mill's notions, that 'if all mankind minus one were of one opinion, mankind would be no more justified in silencing that one person than he, if he had the power, would be justified in silencing mankind' (II: 1): Professor Stock's views 'were hardly inflammatory':

'They are widely held and born of an acute insight into the nature of liberty. Not all desirable social goals are compatible, and a humane wish to make better the lives of transgender people may end up infringing the rights of women to safety and autonomy. But even if Professor Stock held opinions that were less obviously defensible, she would have an unqualified right to express them. She has instead been the target of hooliganism and intimidation. Protesters hiding behind masks and balaclavas have paraded on campus demanding her dismissal. A virulent campaign on social media has castigated her as "transphobic". Threats of violence have become commonplace. These are not mere criticism,

---

[1] *The Times* online. Letter from Debbie Hayton and others on transexual rights, 11/10/2021.
[2] 'Assault on the Academy'. Leading article, *The Times* online, 12/10/2021.

which a democratic society protects, but an attempt to instil fear and spread censorship. Civil society more widely should insist on certain elementary principles of academic freedom'.[1]

Matters continued to oscillate in that the next day it was reported that, as if prompted by Selina Todd, the Sussex branch of the University and College Union had issued a statement. However, they deviated from the line looked for by Professors Todd and Stock. The Union's statement supported 'trans and non-binary communities' and 'condemned the university's vice-chancellor for not having done the same'.[2] The view was that Adam Ticknell 'had not upheld the dignity and respect of trans students and staff' in his statement on Professor Stock and academic freedom. This take on the matter led Stock to conclude that the Union had effectively 'ended her career at Sussex'. The University issued another statement affirming that, in the context of diverse views on complex matters, it aimed to work 'firmly and promptly to tackle bullying and harassment, to defend the fundamental principle of academic freedom, to support our community and continue to progress our work on equality, diversity and inclusion. We care deeply about getting this balance right'.

The Union's action prompted a large group of academics, writers, lawyers, union officials and members and others from related professions to write to support Professor Stock, who was said to be 'a well-respected academic with a record of diligent care for her students', who was suffering from 'escalating bullying'.[3] In marked contrast, the Union's statement was seen as 'a betrayal of female academic staff and this treacherous act has now emboldened and empowered those who are harassing Professor Stock.' The outcome was that as the Union 'refuses to condemn the bullying and intimidation of female academic staff and instead seeks to legitimise and diminish it as "protest" then we feel that it is no longer an effective union to represent female members'.[4]

To add weight to the emerging case in support of Professor Stock, another group of academics, many with associations with the University and College Union, wrote to *The Sunday Times*.[5] They considered the issues at stake to involve matters of freedom but also to have a wider significance: the problem was not just 'an issue of freedom of expression'. It is also 'an issue of harassment and discrimination.' The universities 'are creating an intimidating and hostile environment for staff and students who recognise that sex matters'

---

[1] 'Assault on the Academy'. Leading article, *The Times* online, 12/10/2021.

[2] 'Universities union backs trans rights over threatened Sussex professor Kathleen Stock'. Article by Nicola Woolcock, *The Times* online 13/10/21.

[3] Letter on the Transgender Dispute: *The Times* online, 16/10/21.

[4] The list of signatories to this letter is too long for a footnote but can be found at the end of this chapter.

[5] 'We will not bow to trans activist bullies on campus'. Letter to *The Sunday Times* online, 17/10/2021. Signed by Michael Biggs, University of Oxford; Emma Hilton, University of Manchester; Professor Sir Partha Dasgupta, University of Cambridge; Professor Sir Michael Pepper, University College London; Professor Arif Ahmed, Cambridge; Professor Donald Nicolson, University of Essex; Professor Sophie Scott, UCL; Professor Simon Blackburn, Cambridge; Professor Mary Leng, University of York; Professor Aileen McHarg, Durham University; Professor David Curtis, UCL; Professor Jo Phoenix, the Open University; Professor Alan Sokal, UCL; Professor Judith Suissa, UCL Institute of Education; Professor Alice Sullivan, UCL; Professor Robert Wintemute, King's College London; Professor David Wootton, York; Professor Selina Todd, Oxford; Professor John Tasioulas, Oxford.

By 'sex' mattering, what was meant was the binary biological differentiation of female and male. They also wanted to allude to the organisation Sex Matters, which 'has logged 80 news reports of bullying, harassment and no-platforming at UK universities' – 'including Edinburgh, King's College London, Oxford, University College London, Essex, the Open University, Exeter, Imperial and Cambridge'.

The fear was that too many 'university leaders' lacked 'the courage or capacity to tackle the problem'. As in some previous issues of debate, the influence of Stonewall and its 'Champions scheme' was seen as a problem since it 'promulgates misleading information about the Equality Act'. Accordingly, the call was for the Equality and Human Rights Commission (EHRC) 'to undertake a review of policies and practices in UK universities that impose a radical gender orthodoxy and discriminate against those who recognise that sex matters'.

The letter crystallised the main theme of a longer article in the same edition of the paper, detailing the experiences of some of over two hundred academics who reported abuse and even death threats over issues of free speech.[1]

The cases highlighted include that of Dr Shereen Benjamin, a senior lecturer in primary education working at the University of Edinburgh. She 'has spoken about the need to protect women-only spaces such as refuges, prisons and hospital wards. Her views brought her into conflict with students and staff who saw her opinions as transphobic'. She was called 'a bigot' and 'compared to a eugenicist and a white supremacist'. According to the operating principles at Edinburgh, these complaints could be voiced, and a meeting she organised could be 'attacked by a protester', but she had no right of reply: the entitlements all lay with the persons who perceived an offence.

Dr Benjamin, like so many other academics, has been struggling to make sense of things and to combat matters locally and in a reasoned manner, but the recent debates on academic freedoms and transgender rights has troubled academics to speak out. What we discovered earlier from Nigel Biggar's writings is replicated: academics are 'trolled viciously on social media' and have been prevented from speaking and had protests and petitions against their ongoing work.

Another case is that of Professor Selina Todd herself, also a co-signatory of the letter calling for the EHRC to review UK universities, whose experiences since 2018 include facing 'harassment and intimidation' because, in her historical writings, she had argued that 'the explosion of interest in being transgender was a modern phenomenon'. This made her not a 'fit person to teach students'. As others experienced, when she was due to speak about a book she had written on the working-class playwright, Shelagh Delany, a group of academics and students sent a letter saying such a speaker should be withdrawn since she would likely be expressing 'transphobic' views.

One of the more disturbing cases concerns Professor Jo Phoenix, a long-serving criminologist at the Open University. Earlier in 2021, Professor Phoenix 'went on sick leave with PTSD... after 360 of her colleagues signed a petition trying to shut

---

[1] '200 academics tell of death threats and abuse as battle rages for free speech'. Article by Sian Griffiths, *The Sunday Times* online 17/10/2021. Quotations following are from this article.

down her research network'.[1] She explained that she was opening a test case at an employment tribunal against the university 'for allegedly failing to protect her from a "public campaign of harassment that has made my working life unbearable"'.

Significantly, Phoenix waived her right to anonymity to say 'that she was raped aged 15'. It was this experience that informed her view – the view that provoked criticism of her and her work – that transgender men should not be able to serve sentences in women's prisons'.[2] For holding this view, on the grounds that a person's biological sex cannot be altered by gender self-assignation, she was likened to a racist. Like Professor Stock, Professor Phoenix later resigned from the institution she had served.[3] She explained that she thought that the Open University had allowed things to escalate too far for her to feel able to continue. She moved to a new post at the University of Reading.

The cases here highlight a problem of what has happened over time due, on the one hand, to trends in the waves of legislation we have considered, and on the other, to changes in policies and outlooks. This gives rise to a regulative and censorial disposition in academia, in schools and in professional and workplace settings generally, leading to a controlling limitation on the liberty of thought and expression. In effect, the emphasis of support is on groups within the pluralism of modernity which, on the basis of an appeal to what Mill termed 'social rights' (IV: 19), are given protection in an absolutist manner: if they feel offended or affronted by something, then they have been wronged, and without argument or justification they can take or demand action against the offender. That the offender is an individual in an academic, educational or professional setting and that they were operating with an acceptance of liberty of thought and discussion, as in the model of a collegiate community, counts for very little.

While academic institutions articulate a commitment to a form of freedom of discussion, these aspirations are neutered by policies protecting disparate rights, which commit institutions to be protective of all in the community or organisation against anything that might harm or distress them.

If we draw on Mill's thoughts, while he is never as compelling as he hopes to be with his self and other-regarding distinction, his idea of the harm to others clause has little by way of regard for offending other people: his approach of promoting the liberty of thought is predicated on the benefits of a strong and vibrant ethos of critical debate, in contrast to the passive and one-sided notions promoting respect and harmlessness that seems prevalent in the modern settings we have considered.

Mill encourages measured and polite debate but thinks that prevailing manners and ideas of politeness should not inhibit cogent discussion, all the better to foster our grasp of the more secure and more vibrant truths and forms of life. Humans being fallible, Mill's point is that debates about matters of value should be unfettered, with the corollary being that if the debate is closed down, then absolutist perspectives on specific, partial and limited truths will invariably bring fallible beings under an insidious tyranny.

---

[1] Professor Phoenix was also a co-signatory of the letter to *The Sunday Times* of 17/10/2021 as cited above.

[2] This matter is discussed fully in Joyce (2021) – pp. 239ff.

[3] 'Jo Phoenix academic likened to racist for her trans views, resigns from Open University'. Article by Nicola Woolcock, *The Times* online, 04/12/2021.

One of the academics quoted in *The Sunday Times* was the Cambridge economist, Professor Sir Partha Dasgupta, who pointed out the essence of the problem and pointed to the kind of restoration needed:

'When I entered academic life [in the early 1970s] the thought never crossed my mind that certain topics were out of bounds. There is today in UK universities even an attempt to regulate thought, not just speech and the written word. And we criticise authoritarian regimes elsewhere for suppressing thought. Robust discourse is at the heart of academic life'.

This commitment to robust discussion, together with tutorial care and advice that ties in with the disciplines of study and the processes of debate, clearly rests on an acceptance of the liberties as articulated by Mill.

However, such defences of robust discourse notwithstanding, as mentioned earlier, at the end of October 2021, Professor Stock announced that she had resigned from her position at the University of Sussex.

The reasons for this were linked to the pressures that had arisen from the most recent campaign of protest and the strictures these placed on her of working online and not being able to come onto the campus.[1] Despite the support of the University authorities, Professor Stock felt that the lack of backing from the University and College Union had been a critical blow.

Perhaps predictably, her resignation was welcomed by the student activists.

In contrast, it was deeply regretted by the University, and a similar regret and a significant flow of support for Professor Stock came from senior government figures who shared a general concern about threats to liberty and who were looking to promote work to defend more robustly a wider regard for intellectual debate in the context of academic freedom as in the classical model of a university within a democratic society committed to liberty and equality of regard.[2]

On this theme, *The Times* mustered the energy for another leading article: 'Defence of Reason'.[3] Once more, a line of thought implicitly orientated to Mill's

---

[1] 'Kathleen Stock resigns from University of Sussex after trans rights row'. Article by G. Grylls, *The Times* online, 28/10/2021. A few days later Professor Stock was interviewed on the BBC's Women's Hour programme, giving her account of the trauma of being the target of activism. See 'Kathleen Stock "fled university hyperventilating" amid transphobia row'. Article by George Sandeman. *The Times* online 03/11/2021.

[2] On the Stock affair see also 'Sussex University inquiry after trans row'. Article by Nicola Woolcock. *The Times* online, 17/11/2021. This relates how the OfS was instructed to investigate the University of Sussex. Speaking in the House of Lords, and with reference to Professor Stock's resignation, the Education minister Baroness Barran said that 'The Office for Students has decided to open an investigation into whether the University of Sussex met its obligations on academic freedom and freedom of speech'. She said that "No academic should have to fear for their personal safety, particularly as a consequence of expressing lawful views."' The Prime Minister, Boris Johnson, was reported to be supporting Professor Stock and the work of the LGB Alliance, with government sources saying that 'the protests against Kathleen Stock' were 'corrosive to democracy and fundamentally illiberal': 'Boris Johnson backs Kathleen Stock and LGB Alliance in trans rights row'. Article by G Grylls, *The Sunday Times* online. Liz Truss, the Foreign Secretary and Equalities Minister, was reported (Article of 28/10/2021) as being, 'appalled' at how Stock had 'effectively been hounded and bullied out of a job for expressing an opinion. She thinks this sort of cancel culture is bad for our democracy and society'. Later the equalities minister Kemi Badenoch gave further support for Professor Stock: 'Trans-row professor Kathleen Stock backed by minister Kemi Badenoch'. Article by Katie Gibbons *The Times* online 01/11/2021.

[3] 'Defence of Reason'. Leading article, *The Times* online, 28/10/2021. Quotations in the text are from this source.

defence of liberty came to the fore: 'A free society protects speech. It does not protect hurt feelings'. This puts matters very crisply into Mill's fundamental view, that things rapidly go amiss if we restrict discussion with an oversensitive regard for people's feelings. Professor Stock had argued that 'transgender people are entitled to respect for their choices but biological sex is an immutable fact and the rights of women to safety and security may be breached by ignoring it'. That she was forced to resign by the pressures for arguing her case 'is a disgrace'. The conclusion was stark, but again reflects Mill's perspective on the benefits of liberty:

'Dr Stock has expressed the hope that other institutions will learn from her experience. The lessons of her case bear spelling out. In a democracy, ideas are open to challenge and refutation by the marshalling of evidence; that is how bad ideas perish. Institutions dedicated to inquiry and education have an absolute obligation to ensure that such debate takes place, and that scholars can conduct their work free of intimidation and censorship. If the forces of intolerance can get away with suppressing dissent, they will escalate that malign campaign. Dr Stock is a valiant defender of reason, whose liberty deserves defence in turn'.[1]

We see with some clarity that academics and others in this phase of the contemporary discussion are working to defend and develop a view of the liberty of thought and discussion of which Mill would approve and which is set against the trends that aim to suppress divergent and critical discussion.

As for Professor Stock, a new academic opportunity arose: in Texas, the new University of Austin, presenting as a free university – one where the liberty of thought discussion was to be unfettered – announced that Professor Stock, and amongst others, Professor Boghossian, would be joining them.[2]

As we have seen, there are grounds for concern about the ways in which universities are equivocating in their commitment to the protection of academic freedoms, the process of open research and the liberty of thought and discussion. There are plenty of eloquent reaffirmations of these values, but we have also seen multiple cases where the life and activity of academia are compromised by particular social agendas. In respect of the tension here, it is worth saying that The University of Austin, with its commitment to academic values alone, is being developed by some high-profile academic luminaries, with a range of advisers and trustees, including the eminent historian Professor Niall Ferguson and Harvard's Professor of Psychology, Steven Pinker.[3]

Interestingly, the University's first president is Dr Pano Kanelos.[4] He was previously president of St John's College in Annapolis, Maryland. This background turns out to be significant to the wider issues we are examining. St John's is the

---

[1] The following passage from *The Times* leader is relevant: 'Dr Stock's conduct throughout her ordeal has been brave and dignified, and her views accord with sound science. But even if she had been less obviously justified she would still have had an unassailable right to express her case within the academy'.

[2] See 'Kathleen Stock: Exiled academic joins free-speech college The University of Austin'. Article by Nicola Woolcock, *The Times* online (10/11/2021). Professors Stock and Boghossian were appointed Founding Faculty Fellow of The University of Austin – see https://www.uaustin.org/faculty-fellows

[3] Niall Ferguson (b. 1964); Steven Pinker (b. 1954).

[4] Kanelos' educational thinking is clear from an interview he gave when leaving St John's: see https://www.sjc.edu/news/farewell-conversation-pano-kanelos. Again, there is also useful detail on the ideas relevant to the founding of the University of Austin at https://www.thenationalherald.com/greek-american-pano-kanelos-on-starting-a-new-university-in-austin-tx/ (09/11/2021).

third oldest academic institution in the USA, dating from 1696.[1] Operating with the so-called 'Great books' ethos of academic education, St. John's cultivates an approach focussing on the study of primary texts in all fields of study, with the study and interrogation of these having precedence over the use of secondary texts. This approach was partly cultivated at the University of Virginia by the historian Stringfellow Barr and the philosopher Scott Buchanan.[2] They took it to the University of Chicago (1936-1937). From 1937 Barr (as President) and Buchanan (as Dean) were at St John's College, which they led to prominence as a liberal arts college, such that in 1964 it expanded to a second campus in Santa Fe, New Mexico.[3]

Kanelos' comments include a view of how academic staff in universities and colleges 'are being treated like thought criminals':

'Kathleen Stock resigned after mobs threatened her over her research on sex and gender... We had thought such censoriousness was possible only under oppressive regimes in distant lands. But it turns out that fear can become endemic in a free society. It can become most acute in the one place — the university — that is supposed to defend the right to think the unthinkable'.[4]

Here Kanelos' reference to 'a free society' is to a society logged into positive liberty. In contrast, the aims and values of academia in the tradition of the new University of Austin centre on a commitment to the aspiration for the positive mode of liberty of thought and discussion in an open, pluralistic, liberal collegiate setting. The aims embrace the duty in education to cultivate resilient individuals who can challenge and overcome tensions through a reasoned argument against those who want to restrict discussion and intimidate those they oppose. It will be an ongoing task to examine and assess the success of this venture, but given the increasingly perilous situation for intellectual freedom in the UK university sector, it is to be hoped that it is contagiously successful.

---

[1] On this see https://www.sjc.edu/about/history Harvard (1636) is the oldest college cum university in the USA.
[2] Stringfellow Barr (1897-1982); Scott Buchanan (1895-1968).
[3] On Barr, see the entry at https://encyclopediavirginia.org/entries/barr-stringfellow-1897-1982/ Barr was at The University of Virginia from 1924 to 1937, and was President of St John's (Annapolis) 1937 to 1947. On Buchanan, see https://education.stateuniversity.com/pages/1803/Buchanan-Scott-1895-1968.html
[4] 'Kathleen Stock: Exiled academic joins free-speech college The University of Austin'. Article by Nicola Woolcock, *The Times* online (10/11/2021).

Addendum

List of signatories to the letter in *The Times* of 16/10/2021 on Professor Stock and tansgender rights cited above.

The signatories were: Julie Bindel, journalist and author; Lucy Masoud, Barrister and trade unionist; Jean Hatchet, feminist activist; Dr Shonagh Dillon; Dame Jenni Murray; Rosie Duffield, MP; Joanna Cherry, QC, MP; Joan Smith, author and Journalist; James Dreyfus, actor; Julia Hartley-Brewer, talkRADIO presenter; David Bridle, founder, Lesbian and Gay News; Karen Ingala Smith; Paul Embery, trade unionist and writer; Belinda de Lucy, former MEP for South East; Cllr Nina Killen, Sefton MBC; Beatrix Campbell, author; Baroness Nicholson of Winterbourne, chairwoman, Parliamentary Campaign Group childrenandwomenfirst.org; Dr Emma Hilton, research biologist and member of UCU, University of Manchester; Catherine Costello, associate lecturer, Open University; Stephanie Davies-Arai, founder and director, Transgender Trend; Dr Jane Clare Jones, DIrector, Centre of Feminist Thought; Kristina Harrison, trans political campaigner; Nicole Jones, MA student at University of Edinburgh; Prof James Treadwell, Professor of Criminology, Staffordshire University; Professor Michele Moore, Head of Centre for Social Justice and Global Responsibility London South Bank University and UCU member; Judith Rowbotham, Visiting Professor, University of Plymouth, member of UCU; Neil Oliver, broadcaster and author; Jae D Quinn, MSW, MPH and transexual man; Bev Jackson, former lecturer and trade unionist; Ruth Serwotka, co-founder WPUK, member of Unite; Dennis Kavanagh, non-practising barrister and legal commentator at Lesbian and Gay News; Susie Hawkes, principal lecturer, University of Wolverhampton and member of UCU; Helen Saxby, writer and women's rights campaigner; Jess De Wahls, artist; Allison Bailey, barrister; Dr Peter Williams, Tyndale House, Cambridge; Sian Griffiths, retired fire officer and FBU member; Helen Steel, former union shop steward and McLibel defendant; Dr Eleanor Scott, retired academic, Universities of Newcastle, Leicester, Reading, Winchester and the Open University; Dr Natalya Vince, Reader in North African and French Studies, University of Portsmouth, member of UCU; Ruth Tweedale, Senior Lecturer, University of Greenwich; Dr Kerry Ashton Shaw, Consultant Child & Adolescent Clinical Psychologist; Prof Jo Phoenix, Chair in Criminology and Cofounder of The Gender Critical Research Network, The Open University; Laura Briggs, Lancashire teacher and member of NEU; Pilgrim Tucker, PhD researcher, Open University; Kevin Ovenden, Labour movement journalist; Cllr Sue Lent (Cardiff); Sall Grover, founder & CEO of Giggle, The Female App; Rachel Horman-Brown, Solicitor; Kate Harris, Trustee LGB Alliance; Rhona Hotchkiss, Management Team LGB Alliance; Malcom Clark, Trustee LGB Alliance; Conrad Roeber, Trustee LGB Alliance; Dermot Kehoe, Trustee LGB Alliance; Eileen Gallagher, Chair of Trustees LGB Alliance; Alice Bondi, Retired psychotherapist and LGB Alliance; Dr Hannah Quirk, Reader in Criminal Law; Robert Wintemute, Professor of Human Rights Law, King's College London; Rebecca Durand, ESOL Lecturer, New City College, UCU member; Anna Melamed, UCU and RCM member. Midwife and Master's student; Iseult White, Psychotherapist and author; Lisa Mackenzie, independent researcher; Ruth Swirsky, former lecturer at the University of Westminster; Irena Fick, York University, the Institute of Education member of the National Education Union; Fionne Orlander, Campaigner; Cathy Devine, Independent Researcher and member of UCU, former Senior Lecturer, University of Cumbria; Dr Lesley Semmens, Senior Lecturer (retired), Leeds Beckett University, Honorary Life Member of NATFHE (predecessor union to UCU); Dave Ward, Councillor; Laura Marcus, Journalist; Lucy Porteous, Teaching Fellow at the University of Portsmouth; M L Quinn, Unison; Dr Helen Rogers, Research Fellow, Liverpool John Moore's University, ex-member UCU; Fiona Macdonald, Trade Union Activist; Jane Harris, Writer; Ian Acheson, Visiting Professor University of Staffordshire; Claire Heuchan, Author; Andrea Shemwell, University administrator & ex-Labour Party member.

16. Conclusion

Through the last three chapters, we explored a range of legal developments and some contemporary expressions of concern around the perennial core issue of whether the liberality of debate is needed on matters of sensitivity that some people want to protect. This built on our review of Mill's case for liberty and on the view we have promoted that there is virtue in disagreement and, in sharp contrast, dire risks of intolerance and illiberalism if the range of debate is over-protected, whether by over-zealous laws or bubbles of social opinion demanding general acceptance and respect.

Once, the protective tendency was related to appeals to received traditions of religious values that the majority were unwilling to challenge; now, it is done by varied appeals to the accumulating range of human rights, where those rights are, or are required to be, under the protection of the law as well as by the certitudes of some social groups. The rule of law and opinion emerges, in a manner that might trouble others besides Mill. A growing trend has been in evidence, one with the character of a form of positive liberty. On a range of matters, such as sexual identity, gender self-affirmation and colonialism, specific interest groups within the plural modernity assume propriety over what can and cannot be discussed, so as to protect their view of the truth of the matter, their interests, and to avoid some forms of distress.

The near-incommensurability of some of the diverse claims for rights protected equally under the law makes difficulties of a deeply illiberal kind for those who look to review and develop revisionary thinking in the interests of refining the best truths for life and for action for ever-fallible humans in general. In modernity, the trend is not to encourage critical review and debate on the somewhat infallibilist assumption that a full and rightful explanation has been established on specific matters. Thus people can be free to move on into a less troubled future of equality and consensus. There is a form of a liberal society in mind with all of this, positive in character and shaped by a prescriptive framework

In contrast, we have some emphatic views supporting greater openness of discussion along the lines that the tradition of negative liberty endorses, and not less a passion for collegiate and communal life to be positive and collaborative. As the last cases indicate, the tensions are so acute that there is perhaps a limit we are reaching for the continuation of the academy, which is nothing if it is not a collegiate community of learning, scholarship and free enquiry. Where these elements are in place in the ethos of a more open form of positive liberty, what Mill is defending is more fruitfully cultivated: the development of sovereign individuality to the end of enriching the wider culture of a civilized community.

Not just academia faces strain. The legal profession is also engaged with the tension. In November 2021, the Middle Temple, one of the historic Inns of Court in London, planned to organise a debate through its LGBTQ forum. The debate then came into question due, first of all, to protests coming in from 'several members of

Middle Temple'[1] as the focus for the debate was from speakers – including Nancy Kelley, the Chief Executive of Stonewall – all of whom were sympathetic to trans rights. There were 'no gender-critical commentators… to give balance to the debate': The report continues:

'Kelley was scheduled to be joined by Kieran Aldred, Stonewall's head of policy, and Robin Allen, QC, who was on a working party that lobbied for the proposed ban on conversion therapy to be included in the Queen's Speech…. Stonewall campaigns for a wide definition of conversion therapy that would make it a criminal offence for therapists to try to help patients with gender dysphoria to feel comfortable in their birth sex. Critics claim that the organisation's position would result in outlawing the "watch and wait" approach taken by others supporting young people who think that they may be transgender'.

The organisers took the criticism on board and arranged to have another person join the debate – Naomi Cunningham – who was 'a prominent gender-critical barrister', and they modified the focus of the debate to 'Banning Conversion Practices: The Path to Good Law'.

This step was immediately criticised by another group of barristers and law students who wrote anonymously to the organisers to say 'that the decision to include Cunningham' changed the event from one that was 'meant to be a celebration of inclusion into a debate between those who support and oppose trans rights'. This was seen to send 'a damaging message to trans members and prospective members of the Inn that their inclusion is not something they can take for granted but is up for debate'.

Here we have an echo of the Anti Terf Sussex approach against Professor Kathleen Stock, with a scenario where no critical discussion was acceptable to the defenders of the received views and assumptions of self-affirmed gender identity and trans rights. Encouragingly, the Middle Temple organisers decided to hold to a more balanced panel, supporting the view that 'the Bar should be a place to encourage respectful debate'. A spokeswoman for Middle Temple explained that the Inn was 'not in favour of de-platforming people because they have different views'.

As we have seen, this and the earlier controversies we considered centre on the combative differences in perspective between those inclined to think that on certain issues, there is no scope for debate, as the interests of inclusion, or some group's sense of what Mill would term their social rights, articulates that the rights and interests of some must be accepted and respected by all. This is challenged by the outlook of Mill and a host of contemporary academics and writers who avow the

---

[1] 'Barristers rebel against 'anti-trans' speaker at LGBTQ event'. Article by Catherine Baksi and Jonathan Ames. *The Times* online, 16/11/2021. Quotations are from this source. 'LGBTQ' (or QUA+) covers 'lesbian, gay, bi+, trans, queer, undefined (for those who are questioning or who choose not to define their sexual orientation, in the latter case some individuals may also use the word queer), asexual/aromantic'. See 'Warwick University "captured" by Stonewall equality drive'. Article by Nicola Woolcock, *The Times* online 19/11/2021.

benefit of the liberty of thought and discussion as a qualitative catalyst in and for the development of all by the progression of each.

In the face of this, a point to lay out is that the study of *On Liberty* sheds penetrating light on the issues and tensions that now arise on matters of the liberty of discussion. Mill articulates a sense of the vibrant issue of the dangers of conformity and intolerance that in our modernity has transformed into an arguably greater and more complex problem: that of the trends and views that can flow from this or that issue or debate and manifest a more general pressure for all to agree with the perspective or outlook in question. The cases all entail that the views of some become the supported views of all. What Mill is especially concerned with remains a clear and present danger, that what he would see as the new tyranny of social trends is as much a threat to liberty as any old-style tyranny, and like Mill, we may see the forms as a more severe threat to individuality.

Mill's background view is worth revising. He sees that the issue of liberty was classically a concern of the many against an overt threat manifest in the ruler. The issue changes so that governance is now set within public authorities validated by the majority view, and worse, it is impersonal and omnipresent in the dominant trends of public opinion. It is, therefore, more difficult to discern and evade, and Mill fears, potentially more enslaving of more of the individual. The emergent suggestion is that what is needed is a scheme to provide a specific form of protection, namely:

'Protection... against the tyranny of the prevailing opinion and feeling, against the tendency of society to impose, by other means than civil penalties, its own ideas and practices as rules of conduct on those who dissent from them; to fetter the development and, if possible, prevent the formation of any individuality not in harmony with its ways, and to compel all characters to fashion themselves upon the model of its own' (I: 5).

Mill wants to build a corrective agenda. He suggests that in the spectrum of activity that exists in the tension between individuals and societies:

'There is a limit to the legitimate interference of collective opinion with individual independence, and to find that limit, and maintain it against encroachment, is as indispensable to a good condition of human affairs as protection against political despotism'.

As we appreciate, *On Liberty* is about finding 'that limit', and one instructive indication of the limits to the 'legitimate interference of collective opinion with individual independence' comes in phases of action in professional and then legal circles between 2019 and 2021 over the case of the tax specialist, Maya Forstater.[1]

Maya Forstater worked in the London office of the Center for Global Development, which has its head office in Washington D.C.[2] In addition to work, Forstater had other interests. From about 2012, she was involved with the Mumsnet feminism chat board. She was also engaged with a campaign she co-founded, Let Toys Be Toys, which looked to oppose the stereotypical packaging of toys for boys and girls. Through these activities, Forstater became aware of gender self-identification and the issue of trans rights. She gradually realised the problem of

---

[1] See Joyce (2021) pp. 261-264.
[2] See the CGD's website for more information: https://www.cgdev.org/

how the biological facts were being lost under the case being made for gender self-identity and saw that this 'would harm women'.[1]

Forstater began tweeting about this to raise awareness of the problem, but she found that colleagues, especially in the American office, were very hostile to her concerns, which they brought to the attention of the HR department at the Center for Global Development, who decided that no new contracts should be awarded to extend Maya Forstater's career with the organisation. As Helen Joyce puts it:

'Because she had stated publicly why she thought laws banning sex discrimination and protecting single-sex spaces should remain anchored in material reality, she found herself out of a job'.[2]

Forstater moved to take her former employer to an employment tribunal. This was in 2019, and in the case against her, Forstater was said to have deployed language that was 'offensive and exclusionary' on 'social media'.[3] She had tweeted such remarks as 'woman means adult human female' and was said to be 'fear-mongering'. Against this, she argued that her views were a 'protected belief' according to the Equality Act (2010).[4] Despite making a case that was seen by the judge as meeting a number of the criteria required, through 'being sincere, cogent, serious and important', he ruled against her on the grounds that her views were 'not worthy of respect in a democratic society'.

The import of this ruling was that Forstater was being legally constrained in what Mill would consider her just opinions, with the rationale being that whatever else, her views were not consonant with social opinion, and her employers were thus vindicated in their policy of ending her contract because they disliked and disapproved of her views.

Forstater's case went to appeal, which was heard in April 2021. When the ruling came – in June 2021 – it was in her favour. One outcome of this was a leading article in *The Times* – 'Right to Think' – that sparkles with insights resonating with themes from *On Liberty*.[5]

Alluding first to Mill's view that within 'a liberal society... the law does not exist to force us into conformity, but to protect us from actual harm', the article's argument was that this principle had been the theme of the appeal court decision, where the panel of judges affirmed 'that holding a view that biological sex never changes regardless of a person's gender identification is a protected philosophical belief under equality law'. That 'this basic tenet of a free and open democracy has needed reaffirmation is a troubling sign of the times', but the appeal judges' ruling had weight because it clarified that in law, 'the beliefs of Ms Forstater were not, as the initial tribunal ruled, antithetical to the human rights of others and hence unworthy of respect'. Although she was 'critical of gender reassignment', her

---

[1] Joyce (2021) p. 262.
[2] Joyce (2021) p. 264.
[3] As quoted in *The Times* leading article 'Right to Think', *The Times* online 11/06/2021. Other quotations following are from this source.
[4] Joyce (2021) p. 262.
[5] As cited above: 'Right to Think'. Leading article, *The Times* online 11/06/2021. Again, quotations in the text are taken from this source.

remarks, in the opinion of the reporting judge, Mr Justice Choudhury, 'did not seek to destroy the rights of trans persons'.[1]

So far as the limits are concerned over where society and the individual have legitimacy for liberty, this case offers spectacular clarity. If the employment tribunal rule had prevailed, it would give to as many as wanted it, the means to suppress any view they disagreed with by which they could say they were offended. Mill would not be alone in seeing this as a form of the tyranny of social rights. The appeal ruling reaffirms the importance of the liberty of thought and discussion and, with reference to the matters we have considered, works to contribute to the revision of the Human Rights Act (1998), where both the right to freedom of expression and a protective constraint of freedom in respect of a range of national and public interests, are held in a discordant tension. *The Times*' view was that the appeal court ruling did something to redress the balance to give legal support to the liberty of thought and discussion, and make clear that 'a person should not lose their livelihood for expressing a belief'.

Another of Mill's ideas is invoked with the following point:

'The judgment rightly delineates the essential difference between holding an opinion and how one expresses it. Importantly it does not give a licence for people to act on their beliefs in a way that would be harmful to others'.

Forstater had never been directly offensive to any specific person, so she had done no one any harm simply by saying things with which others disagreed. Then, with implicit reliance on Mill's defence of both liberty and individuality, 'Right to Think' concludes:

'In a democratic society people have to tolerate each other and that includes tolerating others' beliefs. What's more, plurality of opinion is the necessary condition for social progress, and a society that stops talking to itself is one that atrophies. It is imperative that courts continue to protect this fundamental principle'.

There was a substantial coda to the case raised by Forstater.

In December 2021, the Law Commission produced a set of recommendations that built on the Court of Appeal ruling. These included the point that those making criticism of transgender reform 'should have greater legal protection to ensure their freedom of expression'.[2]

The Law Commission has the role of considering issues arising from society and from the practice of the Law to frame lines of recommendation for law reform to be considered by ministers. Their report, in this case, considered hate crimes and suggested 'that expanding offences around "stirring up" — verbally encouraging

---

[1] The ruling can be found at https://www.gov.uk/employment-appeal-tribunal-decisions/maya-forstater-v-cgd-europe-and-others-ukeat-slash-0105-slash-20-slash-joj -Employment Appeal Tribunal judgment of Mr Justice Choudhury, Mr C Edwards and Mrs MV McArthur on 10 June 2021.

[2] 'Critics of trans reforms need "greater protection."'. Article by Jonathan Ames, *The Times* online, 07/12/2021. Quotations in the text are from this source. See also www.lawcom.gov.uk for details of the report 'Reforms to protect disabled and LGBT+ victims, criminalise extremist misogynist "incel" hate material, and safeguard free speech', 7th December 2021.

hatred of specific groups — had to be balanced with concerns over freedom of expression'. There was also a call for:

'An "explicit protection for so-called gender critical views, criticism of foreign governments, and discussion of cultural practices, and immigration, asylum and citizenship policy". It also said that there should be specific protection for "neutral reporting" of inflammatory hate speech by third parties'.

One of the Law Commissioners, Professor Penny Lewis, said that 'hate crime has a terrible impact on victims and it's unacceptable that the current levels of protection are so inconsistent'. She added that the emergent recommendations 'would improve protections for victims while also ensuring that the right of freedom of expression is safeguarded'.

The report was welcomed by Forstater, who noted the recommendation for 'a specific protection against stirring up hatred offences for gender critical views' – she also appreciated the recognition that the 'use of language, including pronouns can not be covered by blanket rules'. Forstater added that 'everyone should be protected from unlawful harassment, including transgender people — but as some of the submissions to the Law Commission's consultation showed some activists want to go further than this and constrain free speech'.

These matters translate back into Mill's thinking, and his ideas and suggestions have powerful resonance for the current scenario. In his own time, Mill feared that legal penalties unduly related to defending traditional religious views made the country 'not a place of mental freedom' (II: 19). His concerns would apply to the penalties risked now by those who challenge different orthodoxies with the rightful concern to 'strengthen and enlarge' human understanding with 'free and daring speculation on the highest subjects'.

Mill's advice remains salutary: 'if the lists are kept open, we may hope that, if there is a better truth, it will be found' (II: 8). By the same token, if certitudes and ideological commitments prevail, as in the sense of the social rights various factions might claim, and there is a lack of the scrutiny of free debate, then in the context of the life of 'fallible' beings, we have fallen short of improving the truths by which we might best orientate our beliefs, values and life. We need that degree of liberty to be free to live to develop and test 'different experiments if living' (III: 1) to enhance both 'individual and social progress'.

We see that in the current modernity, 'the lists', as Mill would say, are open, in the sense that the debates we have been considering are current and some issues are ongoing, with no sense emerging as to whether a progressive liberal outlook will prevail over the more, and perhaps over-protective alternative.

To the litany of cases to which we have referred, there is another that illuminates the predicament. This concerns Professor James Treadwell, a specialist in criminology at the University of Stafford.[1] His work and position came under investigation because some of his 'tweets on gender'[2] resulted in 'formal and official' complaints being made to his employer.

---

[1] Professor Treadwell one of the many signatories to the letter in *The Times* of 16/10/2021 on Professor Stock and transgender rights cited in Chapter 15 above.

[2] 'James Treadwell: Professor fears for his job after tweets on gender': Article by Charlie Parker, *The Times* online: 14/01/2022. Further quotations are from this source.

As in so many cases, Professor Treadwell had no idea who had complained about his tweets, although he understood it to be a complaint alleging transphobia. In the five years that he had worked at the University of Stafford, he had used social media to comment on various issues, 'including Black Lives Matter and racism in football'. He defended the view that there should be protected spaces for women and, with reference to the issue of prison populations, said that 'criminologists are finding the voice to say men should not be put in women's prisons'. This point was made after a case came to light of 'a transgender prisoner…who had been convicted of sex offences and went on to sexually assault two inmates at a women's jail' and was then 'given a life sentence'.

Treadwell commented:

'It is a shame it took more victims to get that, but I'm sure the previous reluctance to speak was a result of how allegations of bigotry can be used to silence'.

Here Treadwell anticipates the scenario that emerges and which he then faces of what is often termed the 'cancel culture', where debate is non-existent, and someone's being morally offended is sufficient to activate measures against the perpetrator of the offence. This confronts the pattern of the liberty of thought and discussion as defended by Mill. Treadwell confessed that he could be 'brusque, opinionated and stubborn,' but consistent with academic values, he respects 'anyone's right to disagree and hold a different view'. Reflecting on his expressions of opinion, he said he has 'tried to be balanced and reasonable and promote fair debate'. He emphasised that 'trans people like all people deserve dignity and respect. Academics giving their personal views do too'.

Treadwell noted the absence of anyone wanting to debate his views, but given the mood in modernity, of supporting the entitlements claimed through what Mill thought over-inflated social rights, Professor Treadwell should not be surprised.

The University of Stafford issued a statement on the case saying, with all efforts at moral and legal equipoise, that a review was underway 'in accordance with the university's procedures':

'As a university we are committed to equality, diversity, and inclusion to ensure we promote a positive culture where everyone is able to be themselves. We are equally committed to academic freedom and lawful freedom of speech'.

The case of Professor Treadwell is ongoing, but he will doubtless take heart from the case of Harry Miller, noted earlier, which arose similarly, where the criticisms were defeated under Section 10 of the Human Rights Act.[1] As far as the issue as to whether, as a feature of the liberty of thought and discussion, giving or receiving offence should be taken seriously as a crime, there is, at the time of writing, a new

---

[1] Harry Miller's case is referred to in Chapter 13 above. Another pertinent case concerns the journalist Hadley Freeman, who contributes regularly to *The Guardian*. She has written that the paper refused to let her write on the issue of trans ideology for fear of the social media storm it would provoke – in other words, *The Guardian* did not support the liberty of thought and expression on this matter, and is presented as operating in fear of antagonising trans activism: 'Guardian columnist Hadley Freeman says left-wing media bows down to trans bullies'. Article by Jake Kanter, *The Times* online, 21/02/2022.

line of guidance within the UK from The College of Policing.[1] The clear advice is that the police 'should no longer investigate legitimate debate or treat trivial online spats at hate incidents'. This advice had a pragmatic aspect, in that over the past five years, some 120,000 individuals had been 'recorded by police even though their behaviour did not meet the criminal threshold'. The advice makes clear that evidence of hostile intent must be in evidence for an incident to be recorded. The new guidance is provisional, and it will, in due course, be superseded by a new code of practice to be issued by the Home Office.

This gives evidence of a trend that sits more in line with the ethos of *On Liberty*, and as for Mill's advice, we may be reminded of the encouragement that, as invariably fallible beings, each of us is the 'proper guardian' (I:13) of our health and welfare – each of us in the social whole of the sum total of individuals. If we are to cultivate and sustain a civilized society and one within which there are balanced safeguards against repression, we need the corollary of the liberties, not least the liberty of thought and discussion, operating in the interpersonal and collegiate sphere combatting inhibiting tyrannies of opinion, ideologies, and narrow group interests.

For the academy and the future of positive intellectual and social development, Mill's aims link well with the important findings of the Kalven Report, delivered to the University of Chicago in 1967.[2] The report rivals Lincoln's Gettysburg Address for brevity and impact, affirming that the nature and purpose of a university are 'defined by the distinctive mission' and by 'the distinctive characteristics of the university as a community', which points centre on the 'defence of academic freedom'. Accordingly:

'The mission of the university is the discovery, improvement, and dissemination of knowledge. Its domain of inquiry and scrutiny includes all aspects and all values of society. A university faithful to its mission will provide enduring challenges to social values, policies, practices, and institutions. By design and by effect, it is the institution which creates discontent with the existing social arrangements and proposes new ones. In brief, a good university, like Socrates, will be upsetting'.

Crucially, the Kalven Report insists that agents for academic development through 'dissent and criticism' must be 'the individual faculty member or the individual student':

The university is the home and sponsor of critics; it is not itself the critic. It is, to go back once again to the classic phrase, a community of scholars. To perform its mission in the society, a university must sustain an extraordinary environment of freedom of inquiry and maintain independence from political fashions, passions, and pressures. A university, if it is to be true to its faith in intellectual inquiry, must embrace, be hospitable to, and encourage the widest diversity of views within its own community. It is a community but only for the

---

[1] 'Causing offence isn't a crime, police told'. Article by Fiona Hamilton, *The Times* online, 22/07/2022. Quotations in the text are from this source.

[2] The Kalven Report into the University's Role in Political and Social Action was undertaken by a committee under the chairmanship of Harry Kalven (1914-1974. Kalven was a Professor of Law at the University of Chicago. The Kalven Report is available as a pdf at https://www.thefire.org/first-amendment-library/special-collections/university-of-chicago-kalven-report/. Quotations are from this source.

limited, albeit great, purposes of teaching and research. It is not a club, it is not a trade association, it is not a lobby'.

As a community of scholarship, it is for the individual members of the university to engage in free inquiry, review and debate. The institution must maintain neutrality and eschew ideological commitment. In consequence, and as a counter to a number of the trends we have seen emerging in academic as well as in social life, a university community 'cannot take collective action on the issues of the day without endangering the conditions for its existence and effectiveness':

> 'There is no mechanism by which it can reach a collective position without inhibiting that full freedom of dissent on which it thrives. It cannot insist that all of its members favor a given view of social policy; if it takes collective action, therefore, it does so at the price of censuring any minority who do not agree with the view adopted. In brief, it is a community which cannot resort to majority vote to reach positions on public issues'.

Upsetting others is, on this basis, as in Mill's rationale, a risk and peril we must accept as part and parcel of deriving benefits from disagreements and developing the interests of which we are individually the proper guardians. The scenario that we face is, perhaps as ever, one where, as Mill perceived, actually fallible humans have the escapist habit of looking to develop from very particular perspectives 'laws of conduct' (IV: 12) that are 'right because they are right', so they apply to themselves and 'all others'. Activism of the type commonly found in modernity makes 'their own personal feelings of good and evil... obligatory on all the world'.

If, as Mill prefers, we embrace our fallibility and cultivate more modest prescriptions, we can build a renewed socio-cultural tradition embracing the energy and progressive vitality of open debate. Through expanding endeavours fuelled by liberty, individuals can address and counter the troubling risks and perils of passivity, loose relativism, and ideological commitment.

Bibliography[1]

Achebe, Chinua, (2010) *The African Trilogy*. New York. London and Toronto: Everman's Library/Alfred A. Knopf.

Aristotle (1989) *Prior Analytics*. (Translated et al by R. Smith). Indianapolis: Hackett.

Aristotle (2004a) *Metaphysics*. (Translated and introduced H. Lawson-Tancred). London: Penguin.

Aristotle (2008) *Physics*. (Translated by R. Waterfield. Introduction and notes by D. Bostock). Oxford: Oxford World Classics.

Aristotle (2004b) *Nicomachean Ethics*. (Translated by J. A. K Thomson; Revised et al by Hugh Tredennick; Introduction and Further reading by J. Barnes. London: Penguin.

Austen, Jane (2019) *Sense and Sensibility* (Edited by J. Mullan) Oxford: Oxford World Classics.

Ayer, A.J. (1970) *Language Truth and Logic*. London: Gollancz.

Bate, J. (2021) *Radical Wordsworth*. London: William Collins.

Bentham, J. (1961) *An Introduction to the Principles of Morals and Legislation*. New York: Dolphin.

Bentham, J. (2002) *Rights, Representation and Reform: Nonsense upon Stilts and Other Writings on the French Revolution*. (Edited by P. Schofield, C. Pease-Watkin and C. Blamires). Oxford: Oxford University Press.

Berlin, Sir Isaiah. (1989) *Four Essays On Liberty*. Oxford: Oxford University Press.

Berlin, Sir Isaiah. (2017) *Liberty*. (Edited by Henry Hardy) Oxford: Oxford University Press.

Brogan, Hugh. (2006) *Alexis de Tocqueville: Prophet of Democracy and the Age of Revolution*. London: Profile.

Butler, Judith. (2007) *Gender Trouble: Feminism and the Subversion of Identity*. New York and London: Routledge.

Byatt, A. S. (1997) *Unruly Times. Wordsworth and Coleridge in their Time*. London: Vintage

Capaldi, Nicolas. (2004) *John Stuart Mill: A Biography*. Cambridge: Cambridge University Press.

Coleridge, Samuel Taylor. *The Major Works*. (Edited with an Introduction and Notes by H. J. Jackson. Oxford: Oxford University Press.

---

[1] Mill's works are listed in the Introduction above, and online sources are cited in the footnotes.

Descartes, R. (2008) *Meditations on First Philosophy with Selections from the Objections and Replies*. (Translated and Introduced by M. Moriarty). Oxford: Oxford World Classics.

Ecclestone, K. and Hayes, D. (2019) *The Dangerous Rise of Therapeutic Education*. London & New York: Routledge Education Classic Education Services.

Foot, Philippa (Editor) (1967) *Theories of Ethics*. Oxford: Oxford University Press.

Fukuyama, F. (2020) *The End of History and the Last Man*. London: Penguin.

Gray, J. (1983) *Mill on Liberty: A Defence*. London: Routledge.

Gray, J. and Smith, G. W. (*Editors*) (1991) *J. S. Mill On Liberty in focus.* London & New York: Routledge.

Haac, O. A. (2018) *The Correspondence of John Stuart Mill and Auguste Comte*. (Translated and edited with a foreword by O. A. Haac. Introduction by A. Kremer-Marietti). London & New York; Routledge.

Hayek, F. (2020) *Hayek on Mill: The Mill-Taylor Friendship and Related Writings. The Collected Works of F. A. Hayek* Volume 16. (Edited & Introduced by Sandra. J. Peart). London: Routledge.

Himmelfarb, G. (1962) *Essays on Politics and Culture by John Stuart Mill*. (Edited and Introduced by G. Himmelfarb). New York, Doubleday.

Himmelfarb, G. (1974) *On Liberty and Liberalism: The Case of John Stuart Mill*. New York: Knopf.

Himmelfarb, G. (2007) *The Moral Imagination*. London: The Souvenir Press.

Hobbes, Thomas. (2008) *Leviathan*. (Edited, with Introduction and Notes, by J. C. A. Gaskin). Oxford: Oxford World Classics.

Holmes, Richard. (2005) *Coleridge: Early Visions*. London & New York: Harper Perennial.

Holmes, Richard. (1999) *Coleridge: Darker Reflections*. London & New York: Harper Perennial.

Honderich, Ted. (1982) Article: '"On Liberty" and Morality Dependent Harms'. *Political Studies* 30: pp. 504-514.

Honderich, Ted. (2003) *On Political Means and Social Ends*. Edinburgh: Edinburgh University Press.

Honderich, Ted. (2003b) Article: 'John Stuart Mill's On Liberty, and a Question about Liberalism'. Accessed from https://www.ucl.ac.uk/~uctytho/MillAndLiberalism.html - the article is also Chapter 1 of Honderich (2003).

Humboldt, W. von (1996) *The Duties and Spheres of Government*. (Translated by J Couthard). Bristol: Thoemmes Press.

Joyce, Helen. (2021) *TRANS: When Ideology Meets Reality*. London: Oneworld.

Kant, I. (1978) *Critique of Pure Reason*. (Translated by N. Kemp Smith). London: Macmillan.

Kant, I. (1983) *Perpetual Peace and Other Essays*. (Translated by E. Humphrey). Indianapolis and Cambridge: Hackett.

Kennedy, Paul. (2017) *The Rise and Fall of the Great Powers*. London: William Collins.

Locke, John. (2013) *Two Treatises of Government*. (Edited by P. Laslett). Cambridge: Cambridge University Press,

Loxton, S. D. (2020) *Words and Deeds: An Introduction to the Thought of Ludwig Wittgenstein*. (Revised Second Edition). London: New Generation Publishing.

Loxton, S. D. (2021) *Nietzsche and the Old Flame*: an *Introduction to Nietzsche and On the Genealogy of Morals*. London: New Generation Publishing.

Loxton, S. D. (2022) *Dialogic Life*: *Charles Taylor's The Ethics of Authenticity: An Introduction and Guide*. London: New Generation Publishing.

Lyons, David (Editor) (1997) *Mill's Utilitarianism: Critical Essays*. Oxford and New York: Rowman and Littlefield.

Marx, K and Engels (1994) *The German Ideology* (Students Edition; Second Edition; edited and introduced by C. J Arthur). London: Lawrence & Wishart.

Marx, K and Engels, F. (2002) *The Communist Manifesto*. (Introduced by G. Stedman-Jones; translated by S. Moore) London: Penguin Classics.

Mathias, P. (2015) *The First Industrial Nation: The Economic History of Britain 1700-1914*. London & New York: Routledge.

Moore, G. E. (1965) *Principia Ethica*, Cambridge: Cambridge University Press.

MacCulloch, D (2009) *A History of Christianity: The First Three Thousand Years*. London: Viking.

Milton, John. (2008) *The Major Works*. (Edited, with Introduction and Notes by S. Orgel and J. Goldberg). Oxford: Oxford World Classics.

Nietzsche, F (1974) *The Gay Science*. (Translated with commentary by W. Kaufmann). New York: Vintage.

Nozick, R (2003) *Anarchy, State and Utopia*. Oxford: Blackwell.

Orwell, George. (2021) *Nineteen Eighty-Four*. London: Collins Classics.

Packe, Michael St. John (1954) *The Life of John Stuart Mill.* London: Macmillan.

Peterson, J (2018) *12 Rules for Life: An Antidote to Chaos*. London: Allen Lane.

Pope, Alexander (2008) *The Major Works*. (Edited by Pat Rogers). Oxford: Oxford World Classics.

Popper, Sir Karl (1981) *Conjectures and Refutations*. London: Routledge.

Popper, Sir Karl (2011) *The Open Society and its Enemies*. London: Routledge.

Pyle, A. (Editor). (1994) *Liberty: Contemporary Responses to John Stuart Mill*. Bristol: Thoemmes Press.

Quinton, Anthony. (1989) *Utilitarian Ethics*. London: Duckworth.

Rees, J. C. (1985) *John Stuart Mill's On Liberty*. Oxford: Clarendon Press.

Rees, J. C. (1991) Article: 'A Re-Reading of Mill On Liberty', in Gray and Smith (1991) pp. 169-189.

Reeves, Richard. (2007) *John Stuart Mill: Victorian Firebrand*. London: Atlantic Books.

Riley, J. (1998) *Mill on Liberty*. London & New York: Routledge.

Rousseau, J-J. (2012) *On The Social Contract and Other Political Writings*. (Edited by C. Bertram and translated by Q. Hoare). London: Penguin Classics.

Ryan, A. (1974) *J. S. Mill*. London: Routledge & Kegan Paul.

Ryan, A. (1987) *The Philosophy of John Stuart Mill*. London: Macmillan.

Ryan, A. (Editor) (2004) *John Stuart Mill and Jeremy Bentham: Utilitarianism and Other Essays*. London: Penguin.

Scarre, G. (2007) *Mill's On Liberty: A Reader's Guide*. London: Continuum.

Semmel, B. (1984) *John Stuart Mill and the Pursuit of Virtue*. New Haven, CT: Yale University Press.

Singer, Peter. (2011) *Practical Ethics* (3rd edition). Cambridge: Cambridge University Press.

Stephen, J. F. (1993) *Liberty, Equality, Fraternity*. (Edited by S. D. Warner). Indianapolis: Liberty Fund.

Stock, K. (2022) *Material Girls: Why Reality Matters for Feminism*. London: Fleet.

Taylor, C. (2003) *The Ethics of Authenticity*. Cambridge MA: Harvard University Press.

Taylor, C. (2010) *Sources of the Self*. Cambridge MA: Harvard University Press.

Ten, C. L. (1980) *Mill on Liberty*. Oxford: The Clarendon Press.

Ten, C. L. (1991) Article: 'Mill's Defence of Liberty', in Gray and Smith (1991) pp. 212-138.

Tzu, Sun (2008) *The Art of War*. (Translated by J. Minford). London: Penguin.

Urmson, J. O. (1953) Article: 'The Interpretation of the Moral Philosophy of J. S. Mill'. *Philosophical Quarterly* 3/10, January 1953: pp. 33-39. This article has been anthologised, as in Foot (1967) Chapter IX and Lyons (1997) pp. 1-18.

Wittgenstein, L. (2009) *Philosophical Investigations*. (Revised 4th Edition. Translated by G.E.M. Anscombe, P.S.M. Hacker and J. Shulte). Oxford: Wiley-Blackwell.

Wolff, Jonathan. (1998) Article: 'Mill, Indecency and the Liberty Principle'. Utilis 10/1: pp. 1-16.

Wollheim, Richard. (1973) Article: 'John Stuart Mill and the Limits of State Action'. *Social Research* 40: pp. 1-30.

Wollheim, Richard. (1991) Article: 'John Stuart Mill and Isaiah Berlin: The ends of life and the preliminaries of morality'. In Gray and Smith (1991) pp. 260-277.

Acknowledgements

The work for this book was undertaken in Zambia in 2020 and 2021. For some weeks in July and August 2021, I was in the UK visiting a new granddaughter and other members of the family. Between visits, I worked on the book while staying at a number of establishments, including Dover Lodge and The Royal Shalom Lodge in Avondale, Lusaka, the Novotel near Stansted, the Premier Inn at Petersfinger, Salisbury, Gray Manor Hotel, Cholderton, and the Victoria Lodge in Salisbury. I thank the staff of all these hotels for their support and tolerance of having a writer in residence. I did more work on the book back in Zambia but finished it on my return to the UK in 2022.

In Lusaka, I am grateful to Diangs Graphics and Printing for their rapid work in producing a draft to facilitate proofreading. In Weston, I thank Rebecca and Clive of C&S Printers for more speedy work in printing late drafts to aid the checking of references. As ever, thanks to the team at New Generation for their help and care in producing the book.

With particular appreciation, this book is dedicated to Abigail Mumbi: she knows the reasons why.

Stephen Loxton
Weston Village
Weston-super-Mare
North Somerset
2022

Index

A

Achebe, Chinua, 278, 279
Allston, Washington, 35
Ames, Jonathan, 266, 287, 312, 315
Anti Terf Sussex, 298, 299
Aquinas, St Thomas, 163
Aristotle, vi, 47, 48, 70, 76, 321
Art of Life, Mill's theory of the, 71, 74, 75, 76, 77, 79, 82, 237, 258
Austen, Jane, 77, 321
Austin, Charles, 20
Austin, John, 20
Austin, The University of, 307, 308
Autobiography, Of John Stuart Mill, The, 3, 5, 14, 15, 19, 21, 22, 27, 29, 30, 38, 43, 61, 70, 71, 74, 75, 86, 87, 89, 90, 91, 94, 95, 97, 99, 124, 136, 172, 249
Avignon, 41, 58, 89, 145
Ayer, A. J, 77, 321

B

Badenoch, Kemi, 306
Bailey, Allison, 300, 309
Bain, Alexander, 57, 87, 94, 174
Baksi, Catherine, 312
Bannerman, Lucy, 290
barbarism, Mill on, 126, 208
Barr, Stringfellow, 308
Bate, J, 31, 321
Benjamin, Shereen, 304
Bentham, J, 15, 17, 19, 24, 30, 62, 65, 121, 127, 137, 258, 321
Bentham, Sir Samuel, 19
Bentham's work, Mill's work on, 32, 61
Benthamite thinking, 24, 61, 63, 74, 81, 136, 253, 258
Berlin, Sir Isaiah, 6, 8, 104, 106, 107, 109, 110, 111, 112, 114, 132, 133, 143, 144, 158, 159, 180, 265, 321
Biggar, Nigel, 277, 278, 279, 280, 283, 284, 288, 289, 290, 295
Bill of Rights, The, 116

Bindel, Julie, 300, 309
Boehm, Edgar, 42
Boghossian, Professor Peter, 295, 296, 297
Braverman, Suella, 274
Brogan, Hugh, 43, 321
Buchanan, Scott, 308
Butler, Judith, 271, 321
Butterfield, Dr David, 292
Byatt, A. S, 321
Byron, George Gordon, Lord, 31, 38

C

Calvinism, 178
Calvinistic theory, Mill on the, 177
Cambridge, University of, 20, 279, 281, 282, 284, 288, 321, 323, 324
Capaldi, Nicholas, 7, 14, 15, 16, 17, 18, 19, 20, 21, 22, 23, 24, 32, 33, 34, 36, 43, 45, 51, 87, 88, 89, 92, 135, 321
Carlyle, Thomas, 17, 41, 42, 43, 55, 63, 64, 65, 109, 149, 249
Center for Global Development, The, 313, 314
Chadwick, Sir Edwin, 24
Choudhury, Mr Justice, 315
Christianity, 126, 150, 152, 157, 158, 163, 167, 188, 207, 255, 323
Church, R W, 167, 246
Civil War, American, 263
Civil War, English, 116
coherence of individuals and society, the problem of the, 121, 249
Coleridge, Samuel Taylor, 33, 34, 35, 36, 37, 40, 41, 53, 67, 69, 94, 321, 322
Collins, Wilkie, 8, 321
Communications Act 2003, the, 270
Comte, Auguste, 38, 52
Courea, Eleni, 290
Criminal Justice and Immigration Act (2008), the, 270
custom, the despotism of , Mill on, 186

D

d'Eichthal, Gustave, 38, 63
Dandridge, Nicola, 284
Darwin, Charles, 8, 174
Dasgupta, Sir Partha, 303, 306
Davies, Will, 288
Descartes, R, 130, 322
determinism, the problem of, 2, 103, 104, 106, 108, 110
Dickens, Charles, 8
drink, Mill on, 191, 199, 203, 204, 205, 206, 215, 216, 219

E

East India Company, The British, 17, 45, 224
eccentricity, Mill on, 86, 177, 183, 184, 244
Ecclestone, K, 322
Edinburgh, The University of, 14, 322
Eliot, George, 8
elitism, Mill and, 97, 98, 183
Ellery, Ben, 283, 287, 293
Empiricism, 48, 58, 76, 104, 108, 202
Engels, F, 1, 92, 167, 323
Eyre, E J, 54, 55

F

Falkner, Baroness, 301
fallibility, Mill on, 122, 140, 144, 145, 150, 151, 200, 203, 220, 251
Ferguson, Professor Niall, 307
Foot, Philippa, 322, 325
Forstater, Maya, 313, 314, 315, 316
Fox, William Johnson, 41, 85, 86, 87
free will, the problem of, 103, 104, 108
Freeman, Hadley, 317
French Revolution, The, 42, 131, 321
Fukuyama, F, 209, 322

G

general education, Mill on the idea of a, 188, 223, 224, 225
Gibbons, Kate, 272, 306
Gilley, Bruce, 278, 279, 280, 288

Gladstone, W E, 18, 58
Goethe, J W von, 69
Gopal, P, 279
Gray, J, 51, 69, 77, 83, 99, 127, 128, 130, 134, 230, 236, 240, 253, 322, 324, 325, 327
Griffiths, Sian, 304, 309
Grote, George, 22, 57
Grylls, G, 299, 306

H

Haac, O. A, 38, 322
Hamilton, Fiona, 3, 4, 52, 53, 57, 106, 108, 318
Harper-Scott, Professor Paul, 295, 296
Hayek, F, 42, 86, 87
Hayek, F. A, 9, 87, 91, 92, 322
Hayes, D, 322
Hayes, Professor Dennis, 287, 292, 293
Hayton, Debbie, 302
Hazard, R. G, 109
Himmelfarb, Gertrude, 4, 8, 9, 27, 29, 51, 86, 87, 91, 99, 117, 137, 151, 184, 246, 248, 258, 322
Hobbes, Thomas, 192, 254, 322
Holmes, Richard, 34, 35, 41, 322
Honderich, Ted, 128, 134, 135, 241, 322
human development, Mill on, 40, 129, 136, 164, 167, 172, 173, 186, 194, 209, 231
Human Rights Act 1998, the, 266, 267
Humboldt, Wilhelm von, 129, 136, 172, 173, 188, 189, 221, 322
Hutton, Richard, 97

I

Inductivism, 104, 108, 252

J

Jesus of Nazareth, 18, 150, 158, 162, 163, 167
Johnson, Boris, 306
Johnson, Dr Samuel, 151
Joyce, H, 291, 292, 298, 305, 323

Newton, Sir Isaac, 148
Nietzsche, F, vi, 2, 149, 163, 181, 323
Nozick, R, 244, 323

O

O'Gorman, Professor Francis, 291, 292
O'Grady, J, 288
Okin, Susan M, 5
one very simple principle of liberty, the,
    3, 112, 123, 124, 125, 135, 136, 137,
    191, 194, 211, 212, 216, 235, 236,
    237, 239, 255
onesidedness, of outlook, 65
originality, Mill on, 173, 181, 182, 184,
    185, 245
Orr, Professor James, 283
Orwell, George, 272, 323
Other-regarding actions or sphere of life,
    127, 130, 139, 170, 191, 195, 196,
    197, 198, 201, 203, 204, 206, 212,
    215, 217, 225, 235, 237, 238, 240,
    250, 251
Owen, Robert, 32, 124
Oxford, The University of, 279, 280,
    284, 288, 290, 321, 322

P

Packe, Michael St. John, 323
Paris, 20, 39, 61, 86
Parker, Charlie, 316
permanent interests of man as a
    progressive being, Mill on the, 79,
    127, 194, 231, 253
Peterson, Professor Jordan, 281, 282,
    283, 284, 290, 323
philosophic radicalism, Mill and, 23
philosophical radicalism, Mill and, 28,
    40
Philosophy of Religion, the, vi
Phoenix, Jo, 303, 304, 305, 309
Pinker, Steven, 307
Plato, vi, 16
Political Economy Club, The, 17, 18, 55
Pope, Alexander, 31, 204, 324
Popper, Sir Karl, 292, 324
Portland State, University of, 278, 295,
    296, 297

practical eclecticism, Mill's, 33, 34, 37,
    69
Principles of Political Economy, 3, 17,
    37, 45, 48, 56, 226
private and public acts, Mill on, 217
Public Order Act (1986), the, 270
Puritanism, 133
Pyle, A, 97, 167, 235, 245, 246, 324

Q

Quinton, Anthony, 78, 324

R

Raab, Dominic, 266, 290
Racial and Religious Hatred Act (2006),
    the, 270
Rees, J. C, 99, 324
Reeves, Richard, 13, 20, 22, 23, 58, 81,
    86, 89, 94, 226, 324
Reformation, the, 156
Ricardo, David, 14, 15
Riley, J, 91, 221, 324
risk and peril clause, the, 169, 170, 198,
    208, 217, 239, 243, 262
Robinson, John, 4
Robson, John, 3, 4
Roebuck, J A, 22
Romantic movement, the, 34, 154
Romanticism, 64
Rome, 95, 155, 209
Rousseau, J-J, 15, 161, 192, 324
Rowling, J K, 272
Rushdie, Salman, 139
Ryan, Alan, 45, 48, 81, 88, 252, 259,
    324

S

Saint-Simon, Claude-Henri, 20
Saint-Simonians, Mill and the, 38, 40,
    248
Sandeman, George, 306
Scarre, G, 167, 192, 225, 226, 324
Self-regarding actions or sphere of life,
    125, 128, 130, 132, 191, 193, 194,
    195, 196, 197, 198, 199, 200, 201,
    204, 206, 215, 217, 219, 220, 225,

Lightning Source UK Ltd.
Milton Keynes UK
UKHW052045270223
417740UK00007B/194/J

9 781803 695228